THE SUPERVISORY EXPERIENCE

THE SUPERVISORY EXPERIENCE

Robert Langs, M.D.

NEW YORK • JASON ARONSON • LONDON

ISBN: 0-87668-342-1

Library of Congress Catalog Number: 79-51514

Manufactured in the United States of America

in devoted supervision,
to Charles

CLASSICAL PSYCHOANALYSIS AND ITS APPLICATIONS

A Series of Books
Edited by Robert Langs, M.D.

William A. Console, M.D., Richard D. Simons, M.D., and Mark Rubinstein, M.D.	**THE FIRST ENCOUNTER: THE BEGINNINGS IN PSYCHOTHERAPY**
Peter L. Giovvachini, M.D.	**PSYCHOANALYSIS OF CHARACTER DISORDERS**
Peter L. Giovacchini, M.D.	**TREATMENT OF PRIMITIVE MENTAL STATES**
edited by Simon Grolnick, M.D., and Leonard Barkin, M.D., with Werner Muensterberger, Ph.D.	**BETWEEN REALITY AND FANTASY: TRANSITIONAL OBJECTS AND PHENOMENA**
Mardi J. Horowitz, M.D.	**STRESS RESPONSE SYNDROMES**
edited by Mardi J. Horowitz, M.D.	**HYSTERICAL PERSONALITY**
Otto Kernberg, M.D.	**BORDERLINE CONDITIONS AND PATHOLOGICAL NARCISSISM**
Otto Kernberg, M.D.	**OBJECT-RELATIONS THEORY AND CLINICAL PSYCHOANALYSIS**
Judith Kestenberg, M.D.	**CHILDREN AND PARENTS: PSYCHOANALYTIC STUDIES IN DEVELOPMENT**
Robert Langs, M.D.	**THE TECHNIQUE OF PSYCHOANALYTIC PSYCHOTHERAPY VOLS. I AND II**
Robert Langs, M.D.	**THE THERAPEUTIC INTERACTION 2 VOLS.**
Robert Langs, M.D.	**THE BIPERSONAL FIELD**
Robert Langs, M.D.	**THE THERAPEUTIC INTERACTION: A SYNTHESIS**
Robert Langs, M.D.	**THE LISTENING PROCESS**
Robert Langs, M.D.	**TECHNIQUE IN TRANSITION**
Robert Langs, M.D.	**THE SUPERVISORY EXPERIENCE**
Heinz Lichtenstein, M.D.	**THE DILEMMA OF HUMAN IDENTITY**
W.W. Meissner, S.J., M.D.	**THE PARANOID PROCESS**
Humberto Nagera, M.D.	**FEMALE SEXUALITY AND THE OEDIPUS COMPLEX**
Humberto Nagera, M.D.	**OBSESSIONAL NEUROSES: DEVELOPMENTAL PSYCHOPATHOLOGY**
Victor Rosen, M.D.	**STYLE, CHARACTER AND LANGUAGE**
Charles Sarnoff, M.D.	**LATENCY**
Melitta Sperling, M.D.	**THE MAJOR NEUROSES AND BEHAVIOR DISORDERS IN CHILDREN**
Melitta Sperling, M.D.	**PSYCHOSOMATIC DISORDERS IN CHILDHOOD**

Contents

Preface

A group of natural and developed gifts and proclivities, acquired knowledge, personal therapy or psychoanalysis, and supervision—these are the cornerstones upon which a therapist is built. Nonetheless, supervisory practices are generally known to be relatively unsystematic and even arbitrary, while the literature remains in want of clear definition. In fact, the one-day supervisory seminar which stands as the first part of this book was the result of the honest and forthright realization, by a dedicated committee of a department of psychiatry at a teaching hospital and medical center, that the supervisory practices of their full-time and visiting faculty were not meeting the needs of their students and residents. In an effort to initiate a more systematic investigation and delineation of the supervisory situation, this committee invited me to chair a seminar on this topic for their supervising faculty; I accepted, with the sole condition that the conference unfold on the basis of two separate, sequential presentations of actual supervisory transactions. It is the edited transcript of this meeting (done mainly to disguise the material from the patient) that constitutes the bulk of this book.

The conference stimulated my personal thinking on supervision, a subject of great interest to me, and led me over the ensuing months to consider systematically a number of dimensions of this complex topic. This resulted in the development of three papers, two of which are published here for the first time. They cover specific issues in the supervisory situation, a definitive format for supervising, and the much neglected topic of self-supervision. These papers constitute the second part of this book.

In substance, then, this volume is an attempt to investigate and define the supervisory bipersonal field, its ground rules and boundaries, and the nature of its conscious and unconscious transactions, and to extend these insights into the daily practice of self-supervision. It endeavors to specifically define a predictive supervisory methodology capable of yielding validation, and to deal with a number of issues of supervision previously unresolved in the literature. It is designed with three main goals in mind: (1) to offer supervisors extensive insight into the nature, challenges, and special gratifications of their work; (2) to provide supervisees a relatively sound means of better utilizing and evaluating their own supervisory experience; and (3) to develop a basic model of self-supervision for the daily practitioner of psychoanalysis and psychotherapy.

The first part of this volume follows, in modified form, the format established by two earlier works, *The Bipersonal Field* (Langs 1976a) and *The Listening Process* (Langs 1978d)—books which reflect selected aspects of my own interpretation and application of the supervisory concepts and principles established here. The supervisees discussed in this seminar were at the time both Senior Residents in Psychiatry, while the supervisors are graduates of classical psychoanalytic institutes. For reasons of anonymity and confidentiality, and with considerable regret, I will not identify the center at which this conference took place, although I do with to express my gratitude to the two supervisees, and especially to the two supervisors who had the courage to present their own supervisory work at a conference of their peers and colleagues. While certainly a burdensome experience, I very much believe that the opportunity to study in detail these two supervisory interactions more than justified the exposure involved. In this context, I wish also to express my appreciation to the committee that selected me to chair this conference and for their calling to my attention the need for careful clinical clarification of the supervisory experience.

Within these pages we deal with many issues, beginning with a delineation of the framework of the supervisory situation and its implications for the nature, potential, and limitations of the transactions that occur within its confines. We study too the communicative properties of the supervisory bipersonal field, and are soon embroiled in a consideration of the *supervisor's* countertransferences, their manifestations and the means through which they may be detected and modified—a much-neglected subject. The perplexing problem of how to deal with the *supervisee's* countertransferences in the supervisory situation also comes under extensive scrutiny, and a special solution is offered based primarily on the patient's own unconscious supervisory efforts. The material presented to us touches on many additional issues, such as the nature and fate of supervisory introjects, the overall methodology of supervision, and a variety of special problems, including supervisory and therapeutic crises.

Virtually all of these topics are considered in a more formal way in chapter 5, in which my paper "A Model of Supervision: The Patient as Unconscious Supervisor" is reprinted from *Technique in Transition* (Langs 1978h) under a shortened title. The systematic and broad consideration of supervisory models and issues developed in that presentation is then supplemented, clarified, and further refined in chapter 6. There I also offer a basic strategy for supervision—one that has evolved from my latest insights into the therapeutic interaction. It is a format useful both for self-supervision and for supervising others.

In the final chapter, I turn directly to the topic of self-supervision. It is no coincidence that this particular exploration occupies the final pages of this volume. It is a remarkably neglected subject, considering its great importance; it takes a great deal to clear the way for a detailed study of its domain. This effort, written as the book itself went to press, has proven quite illuminating for me personally, and I trust it will be both informative and evocative for the reader as well.

One final offering completes this volume: a glossary of terms, many of them coined by myself or subjected to special use in my writings. It is designed as a means of facilitating the understanding of the book.

Returning now to Part I—the conference—much of the first presentation was devoted to a detailed study of the framework of the supervisory situation and to a delineation of my adaptational-interactional conception of both psychotherapy and supervision itself. While this delayed the presentation of much of the specific clinical material that we eventually began to investigate in some detail, it provided a framework for the discussions and formulations related to supervision developed later, and should serve the reader in similar fashion. In addition, the first presentation brought forth a wide range of supervisory problems, many of them unanticipated; much of the discussion focuses on these concerns. Some definitive issues arose in respect to the model of supervision utilized by the presenting supervisor as compared to my own, and this provided additional impetus for definition and clarification.

However, the tone changed dramatically with the second supervisory presenation. Here, extensive discussion was stimulated in regard to the supervisor's countertransference communications to the supervisee, who in turn conveyed them to his patient, who then responded unconsciously, both exploitatively and curatively, an influence that the supervisee then brought back to the supervisor. Much of this process is considered in terms of the supervisory introject and its vicissitudes. This particular presentation was a most compelling and humbling experience, and it served as a vivid reminder of how much we can learn about psychotherapy and psychoanalysis when matters go awry.

My gratitude is extended once again to others who also helped make this book a reality: Jason Aronson for his untiring support and constructive suggestions; Michael Farrin for his excellent editorial work and for his assistance with the production of this book; and Sheila Gardner and Norma Tankenbaum for their untiring efforts at typing and retyping the manuscript.

Therapeutic and supervisory work and models go hand in hand. One dimension of the history of psychoanalytic understanding has been the slow and incomplete resolution of shared countertransference-based blind spots, many of which, ironically enough, involve the therapist's or analyst's countertransferences themselves. Through this conference, I realized that as much as we have begun to modify our sometimes blatant and all too often subtle and concealed overidealization of ourselves as therapists and analysts, and have begrudgingly acknowledged that countertransference is ever present and expressed in some measure, however small, in our every transaction with a patient, we have yet to come to terms with the need for a comparable soul-searching and acknowledgment of the truth about ourselves as supervisors. Supervision has been, in this sense, among the last bastions of unanalyzed countertransference-based expressions, thereby providing opportunities to turn away from the enormous burden of continuous self-scrutiny, self-analysis, and self-supervision that we must maintain as therapists or analysts. An atmosphere which lacks these elements is unhealthy, and quietly but persistently undermines a supervisor's efforts.

I therefore especially dedicate this volume to the insightful understanding of both supervisee and supervisor. So long as they both wish to discover the truth about each other (within the limits of the nature and purposes of supervision, and its inevitable stress on discovering the truth about the supervisee), about their interactions, and, most important, about what has transpired between the supervisee and his patient, and so long as this quest is founded on a search for self-awareness and self-knowledge for both supervisor and supervisee, even the most inappropriate and disruptive inputs can eventually be turned to the personal growth of both participants to this very human and unique dialogue.

Robert Langs, M.D.
New York, N.Y.
January 1979

Part I

Chapter 1

The Framework of Supervision and Therapy

Moderator: I want to welcome you here as a representative of the Department of Psychiatry, and as a member of our local Psychiatric District Branch. This Workshop on Supervision has been developed by a liaison committee in the Department of Psychiatry consisting of members of the voluntary and full-time faculty. We have spent the last eighteen months looking at the experiences that our residents and other trainees have had in the supervision of individual psychotherapy, and have felt the need to develop an open forum within which to discuss problems and issues related to supervision. We decided to initiate these efforts with some type of experience for the current supervisor of residents and we feel fortunate in having Dr. Langs accept the responsibility for the Workshop today.

We will have two extended sessions. In the first, Dr. A will present to Dr. Langs his process notes on the supervision of a resident doing individual psychotherapy, and Dr. B will offer a similar presentation for the second half of our program. This is material all of us, including Dr. Langs, will be hearing for the first time, and we will be able to observe the kind of material that the resident in the supervisory process has presented to these supervisors, and, in turn, their comments and reactions as conveyed to the resident during supervision. Dr. Langs has promised to develop a series of concepts of general applicability based on these presentations, and we trust that this will provide us with much to debate and discuss, not only today but in future meetings. Perhaps Dr. Langs would like to orient us.

Langs: In terms of introductory comments, I will try to be brief. I think that this conference is an indication of the long-standing interest of therapists and analysts in the supervisory process and experience, and part of a growing trend to more openly discuss and debate the many complex problems and issues related to supervision. As we all know, along with personal analysis or therapy, the supervisory experience is a major means through which therapists learn and develop. It seems inconceivable to me that one could become a sensitive therapist—and my comments today will be confined to the supervision of psychotherapy, though the principles I am developing are, I believe, equally applicable to the supervision of psychoanalysis—without extensive and constructive supervisory experiences. And yet, while there is a rather extensive literature on this subject (see the bibliographies in Ekstein and Wallerstein 1958 and Schuster, Sandt, and Thaler 1972), my impression, based on the supervision I received, my experiences as a supervisor, and on a selected review of the literature, is that we are far from having established this literature as truly definitive.

It may be well for me to indicate some of my goals in this workshop. While I will not have anticipated many of the issues we will eventually consider, I do think that I can say something about the framework of my efforts today. First, I have found that in order to work meaningfully with any issue related to psychotherapy, we must have an interaction in front of us—a means of organizing observations, generating hypotheses, validating concepts, revising heretofore tentative formulations, and the like. For this reason I have asked Drs. A and B to present material to us which we will then use as a takeoff point or guide for our discussion. In this way we will have something more than just your unsubstantiated concept of supervision, or mine, and I will have an opportunity to outline in some detail an approach to supervision—and to therapy, as well—that I have developed and validated in recent years. I will offer it to you as a model, open to debate and revision, but hopefully clearly defined and supported by both clinical observations and theoretical justification.

Arlow, in a paper on supervision (1963), suggested that one could generate separate studies of the technique of supervision, the function of supervision, the theory of supervision, and measures of progress in supervision. It is the first of these—supervisory technique—that I will focus on here, and with the aid of clinical observations I hope to develop some ideas on the theory of supervision as well.

In this connection, I must say that my experiences as a supervisor of psychotherapy and, most recently, as a psychoanalytic writer on technique to whom various therapists have presented material in the context of meetings and lectureships, I have found that it is neither superfluous nor demeaning to spend a good deal of time with the fundamentals—the ground rules, the basic structure of the situation, the mode of presentation and interaction, techniques of validation, and the like. In fact, as I hope to demonstrate quite soon, it is precisely this careful attention to details previously disregarded that actually generates the most original and useful concepts.

I always look forward to presentations of this kind with a most pleasurable form of anticipatory excitement. I come to you prepared by a brief review of the literature and hours of reflection on my own supervisory work. And frankly, I do believe that I will have some relatively novel and I hope stimulating ideas to offer you. Furthermore, I am quite certain that this particular multipersonal field—the interaction between myself, Drs. A and B, and you the audience—will generate a creativity of its own. I will take it as my responsibility, with your assistance, to harness and organize our shared output and to use it as a basis for stating and clarifying the fundamentals of the supervisory experience.

Well, I think that's enough of an introduction. What will emerge here will be a clinically and empirically derived conception of supervision, rather than one that might arise through a careful study of the literature. I make no claim for originality; I have invariably discovered in the literature remarkable antecedents for what seemed my most original ideas. But I have reason to believe that, given one or two lively supervisory experiences to observe sequentially and in detail, a group such as ours will be able to derive all the basic principles of supervision we need—and more. This said, let's now turn to the clinical material.

Supervisor A: The chairman of today's workshop contacted me about two months ago, asking me to present material from a supervision of a resident doing psychotherapy. At that time I didn't have a resident in supervision, and arrangements had to be made to get someone who had an appropriate case, and so forth. This was done, and the material that I have for this workshop relates to some five or six supervisory sessions that were held with this resident over the past month and a half.

Langs: Before you get into the material, tell us how the arrangements were made. If we wish to look at every aspect of this process, we find that it really begins with how the supervisor and the supervisee get together. Of course, we could broaden our investigation to consider how the supervisee becomes a resident or other type of trainee in the first place, but here we will limit our inquiry to factors more immediate to the supervisory experience. So, addressing ourselves to the conditions under which supervisor and supervisee meet, we rather quickly become engaged in an effort to define the special bipersonal field within which supervision takes place. Thus delineation of the conditions under which supervision is initiated very soon merges with an examination of the specific contract or ground rules—concepts that by now must have a familiar ring to all of you, and an area that I have studied in particular detail (Langs 1973, 1976a,b). As a group, these elements constitute the *framework* of the *bipersonal field*, and it will be our job to define the specific necessary framework of the *supervisory* bipersonal field; we will also take time to compare the framework of the supervisory field with that of psychotherapeutic situation itself and to discuss how the management of the ground rules in these two distinctive though related bipersonal fields both overlap and differ.

Would you tell us, then, what arrangements were made between yourself and the supervisee?

Supervisor A: This resident had contacted me toward the beginning of the summer of this past year and had asked if I would supervise him on a case sometime during the year. I had agreed but hadn't heard any more from him since then. Apparently he was waiting for an appropriate case and also for the initiation of the academic year in the fall. At the point at which I was contacted regarding this workshop, I hadn't yet heard from him and did not have a case in supervision. When I mentioned this to the chairman for the workshop, he contacted the resident, who then got in touch with me. He told me about his caseload over the phone, saying that he didn't have an ongoing case that was being seen a couple of times a week in truly analytic psychotherapy; he had had such a case, but she had interrupted treatment several months earlier. I told him that we would go ahead anyway and make arrangements to meet and discuss the cases he had in therapy to try to pick a case that would be suitable. So arrangements were made for him to see me in my office, and that was just six weeks ago.

Now, he was late for the . . . (laughter) . . .

Langs: So this is how we begin . . .

Supervisor A: . . . for the first appointment. He had gotten lost getting to my office . . .

Langs: So, this is our initial bit of data. Now I could rather quickly get into the question of how the supervisor should deal with the supervisee's lateness, but that would take us far too prematurely into issues related to how the supervisor handles indications of countertransference in the supervisee as expressed both in his work with his patients and, at times, more directly in his relationship with the supervisor himself. In the latter case I am using the term *countertransference* in a broad sense that extends its application beyond its usual definition, which, as you know, restricts it to the therapeutic relationship. To avoid possible confusion in this area, Ekstein and Wallerstein (1958) termed this *problems with learning*. On the other hand, I prefer to use the same term for all expressions of the therapist's pathology as they emerge in any situation related to his therapeutic work. Actually, it is my belief that expressions of the supervisee's emotional problems, which I will rather loosely term his countertransferences, must be handled somewhat differently when they appear in his therapeutic work with his patient, than when they emerge directly in his relationship with the supervisor. In the case at hand, then, I would certainly not comment immediately, though I would make a mental note that there was some sign of anxiety and enactment, and would wait for information with which to appraise the underlying factors.

But as I said, we can hardly discuss the techniques of supervision until we have established a set of conditions for the supervisory field. For that reason I would like to offer a few comments on the question of finding a suitable case for supervision. It immediately occurs to me in this context that much of what we do in the course of supervision depends on our own model of therapy, as well as on our conception of supervision itself. I point this out because it will prove necessary to develop a model of therapy as a basis for building a model of supervision.

To my way of thinking, there is really no case that isn't suitable for supervisory work. Every patient-therapist interaction lends itself to learning in supervision, because though I have unfortunately observed many bad therapists, I have never once discovered a bad patient. I am prepared to supervise the therapy of any patient, just as I am prepared to take into therapy or analysis any patient who comes to me for a consultation.

However, I know that this sort of issue does come up in selecting patients for supervision. There are certain patients seen in a center like this for whom some therapists or supervisors will recommend drug treatment or the use of other nonpsychoanalytic treatment modalities. I would myself, however, prefer some form of insight-oriented psychotherapy for every patient, even if just once a week; this entails therapeutic utilization of a secure relationship and interpretive efforts directed toward insight and inner change. Quite rarely, perhaps with a psychotically depressed patient or with a disorganized schizophrenic, it might be necessary to use medication, but I firmly believe that one goal of supervision is to enable young therapists to develop their skills to the point where they can effectively help all patients with the same basic techniques, varying them in keeping with the special needs of each patient while avoiding modifications and deviations in technique which alter to the patient's detriment the basic framework and ground rules.

So personally I would have no need to discuss with a supervisee the issue of suitability. I would want him to have supervision with a wide range of patients, including those that he happens to feel would benefit from analytically oriented therapy, as well as those with whom he would take a different approach. Certainly he will be more cooperative in presenting the former type of patient, but, on the other hand, he will probably learn a great deal more about the treatment process and himself if he presents the second type.

In any case, it is important to recognize that such a discussion is best undertaken in the framework of an actual case presentation, by which I do not mean a vague or general presentation of a case as pieced together by the supervisee but, rather, the specific unfolding of process notes related to the initial hour with the patient in question—whether that session is thought of as a consultation, an evaluation, a screening, or the first therapy hour. While inevitably there will be exceptions, I strongly recommend that all supervisory work be undertaken in the context of the specific presentation in sequence of process notes related to the sessions held by the resident with his patient. Without such data, the supervisory situation is open to deterioration, undocumented debate, unvalidatable hypotheses, and general chaos.

One other point: if you do have ideas as to what constitutes a suitable case, you must recognize that such recommendations will convey your own attitudes about the treatability of patients and about the kind of patients you feel capable of working with in psychotherapy. You should realize that there may well be strong personal biases in this respect, especially if you feel that certain patients are not suitable for insight therapy at all. This is another supervisory issue that quickly touches upon your model of psychotherapy and your concept of its applicability. It would take us too far afield to debate the issue of whether certain types of patients are better treated with some form of therapy other than the insight-oriented modality, but I have already indicated my position on the question.

Two additional areas for discussion present themselves: first, the differences in the supervisory field that arise when a supervisor is assigned to the supervisee, rather than being selected by him; and second, the issue of what similarities obtain between psychoanalysis and psychotherapy as treatment modalities. In regard to the first point, we are all aware that the conditions under which a supervisor is selected or assigned will influence the supervisory experience. For example, if the supervisee is assigned by the chief of the residency program to a particular supervisor, there will be an expectation that the teacher will not only educate this student, but also judge his level of competence—an aspect of the supervisory field I prefer to either eliminate or minimize. When such an assignment is made, the supervisee may anticipate a positive learning experience or a more negative one, depending on his own propensities and on the reputation and known orientation of the supervisor. There are evident risks of antagonism or anxiety-provoking interactions under such conditions, and these are somewhat lessened when the supervisee has selected the supervisor and wishes to work with him. Under the latter circumstances, the supervisee usually has an initial positive image of the supervisor and a strong investment in the learning experience. This can have both positive and negative effects on the supervisor, at times playing into undue narcissistic needs and blind spots, while at other times promoting the development of a secure *supervisory alliance* that enables him to be more candid and direct—though always tactful—in his work with the resident. Under these circumstances there will as a rule be fewer *supervisory crises*, a problem that I will discuss later on.

As to the similarities between analysis and therapy, it is my opinion, based on extensive clinical observations (Langs 1976a, b), that the same basic rules and qualities of interaction apply, although this by no means implies the absence of important differences. However, I do not make—as I was taught to do—a very sharp distinction between analysis and psychotherapy, nor do I make a sharp differentiation in regard to the indications for each treatment form.

Now I certainly do believe that analysis is the preferred mode of therapy for many patients—in fact, for a wider group of patients than many would suggest. I also am aware that for certain types of borderline and ambulatory schizophrenic patients, psychotherapy is to be preferred, but, since I do not want to go too far into the issue of the range of indications for the two modalities, I will leave the matter at that for the moment. I have brought the subject up largely because I think that if you have a basic feeling for insight psychotherapy as a treatment modality, if you have a certain kind of belief and trust in it and a creative capacity to carry it out, then the issue of picking a suitable case, whether it's a once or twice or three times a week patient, the issue of picking a so-called suitable case kind of fades into the background.

This reminds me that I realized as I went over the literature on supervision that—how to put it?—a lot of problems that are debated in the literature aren't issues at all as far as I'm concerned. Now that's kind of brash because, after all, analysts and therapists are arguing them, but, as I hope to show you, among the rewards of the model of psychotherapy that I will propose is the discovery that certain repetitive and seemingly irresolvable difficulties usually found in the supervisory experience are rather easily resolved, at least in principle. For example, the problem I mentioned earlier: the handling of expressions of countertransference difficulties in the supervisee's work with his patient. I am not suggesting that my model will handle every issue of supervision, but it will dispose of a number of them, including this one, as you shall see later on. So the whole question of selecting a suitable case loses much of its meaning and I will not address it further.

Now I must add that personally I have preferred that supervision be undertaken in connection with a twice-a-week patient. But this is because I find that two sessions a week seem to offer a sense of continuity and an optimal opportunity in supervision to develop hypotheses and to validate them—for example, by offering a formulation in the first hour that can be tested out in the second. In fact, I must tell you this: having worked with presentations of analytic cases, I find that a psychotherapy presentation of a patient seen less frequently is often far more serviceable for general teaching purposes. Certainly the supervision of analytic patients offers a unique opportunity for in-depth understanding of unconscious processes, the genetic dimension, and the therapeutic interaction, but it is remarkable to me that one can find quite meaningful data in each of these areas in psychotherapy supervision as well, sometimes sacrificing depth for a less cluttered view of the therapeutic situation. Many of my own formulations were derived from psychotherapy supervision and only later confirmed in my analytic work—a fact that underscores the distinctive and creative opportunities available to the supervisor in his work, a point I will discuss later on.

Returning now to the more immediate problems of this workshop, the only information that I had in advance about the two supervisory experiences that we will hear today is that they both involve a once-a-week patient. And I am sure that we will find that this provides us a quite workable and meaningful teaching situation. However, I would stress that my own experience suggests that the supervision of a twice-a-week patient approximates the ideal supervisory situation. I have found that in the fifty to sixty minutes of the typical supervisory session the supervisee has ample time to present process notes on both sessions, and the supervisor has sufficient time to develop formulations, predictions, and other types of discussion. In addition, it is quite helpful to have the second hour on hand, so that the ideas suggested by the supervisor based on the material from the first hour can be validated within the same supervisory session through a study of the second hour rather than having to wait for the following week, as one must with a once-a-week patient, or being confined to validating responses within a single session. Such an experience suffers to some extent from the memory decay that takes place during that weekly interval or from the limitations inherent in the material from a single hour.

It occurs to me as I make these remarks that a number of basic principles and concepts are beginning to emerge and are in need of definition. In my experience, much of what each individual supervisor does is carried out with few principles in mind, and with little specific consideration. As a rule, a supervisor will unconsciously use a model of supervision based on his own poorly defined model of therapy and on his supervisory experiences. He will practice forms of the supervision that he felt were especially helpful in his own training, and forms fulfilling his own particular needs as a supervisor, needs that, despite their importance, are seldom consciously identified to any large extent. In addition, as he gains experience the supervisor learns what seems to work for him, as well as what creates difficulty for him and the supervisee. A particular supervisory experience may prove so impressive as to modify his style a bit, but on the whole the manner in which the supervisor creates the teaching setting and intervenes seldom receives the extensive consideration it deserves. Every supervisor has his hands full with a lot of other concerns—his own work, the rest of his life—and so supervision seems to be set aside.

Now since this is a one-day conference, I will spend a great deal of time identifying basic issues and commenting upon them briefly. It will give you a great deal to think about and I doubt that we will be able to effect any sense of closure. But I do believe that it will offer a basic framework not only for future studies of the supervisory experience, but also for a personal reconsideration of the supervisory work that each of us carries out individually. Along the way I am going to concentrate on issues that I feel are important or especially interesting—or troublesome or relatively neglected—and I expect that the clinical material will soon point us in just these directions. And it is natural that we begin by defining the conditions under which the supervisee and supervisor get together and by making note of some of the possible variations and their ramifications.

Just so we can't be accused of neglecting the literature entirely, I would like to make further mention of two basic readings that I found helpful, both in defining certain issues related to supervision and in providing a compendium of the literature on the subject. The first is Ekstein and Wallerstein's *The Teaching and Learning of Psychotherapy* (1958). Written in the 1950s, it was the first really extensive discussion of the supervisory process. A more recent book, *The Clinical Supervision of the Psychiatric Resident*, by Dan Schuster, John Sandt, and Otto Thaler (1972), who are at Rochester, offers an extensive review and discussion of the literature. The focus of the Rochester group was on the use of a supervisory conference: a group of supervisors getting together and sharing experiences, something they strongly advocate. But if you look at the Ekstein and Wallerstein book, written at the Menninger Clinic, they describe a basic supervisory field that takes the form of a rhombus. I have thought of calling the supervisory situation a *tripersonal field*, but they suggest a quadrapersonal field, and here today we've got a multipersonal field, and so on and on. They point out that there is an administrator, a supervisor, a supervisee, and a patient, and that to achieve a full understanding of the supervisory process you have to look at the interaction between all concerned.

Well, it is certainly important to recognize that in any setting, inpatient or outpatient, the influence of this four-party interaction may appear not only in the supervision itself, but in the material from the patient. However, unless it comes up in the material that we will be hearing, I will not particularly stress the extensive influence on supervision of administrators, chairmen, or the like. Suffice it to say that they effect—in both gross and subtle ways—the very structuring and ambience of the supervisory relationship, the nature of the psychotherapy, and the supervisory process. Since my focus today will be on the supervision of the material presented from the treatment situation—on the supervisory work itself—I want at least to acknowledge the importance of these factors at the outset. At times they may be significantly facilitating; at others, they may create important problems.

I will refer to issues of this kind when I discuss what I term *crisis situations*—some of which make it necessary for the supervisor to deal with matters beyond the clinical interaction between the supervisee and his patient. But much of what I will have to say in this area will relate to how the setting of treatment—the clinic, administrators, personnel, and the rest—influences the direct therapeutic interaction. In general, one hopes that these factors, which are more peripheral to supervision, will be silently helpful, unobtrusive, and quiet contributors to the supervisory alliance; in the real world, however, this is not often the case. So while it certainly seems to me that the central focus of supervision must derive from the presentation of the process notes of the therapeutic experience under scrutiny, the supervisor must be prepared to deal with intrusions from other sources when they disturb either the therapeutic alliance between the supervisee and his patient, or the supervisory alliance itself.

Now, preparing for this workshop I conceptualized the supervisory experience as taking place within a *tripersonal* field involving patient, supervisee, and supervisor, and already I've had to recognize the possibility of additional participants to the total field. But now as I talk it becomes apparent that there is actually a series of essentially bipersonal subfields. The two main fields, of course, are those between the supervisor and the supervisee, and between the patient and the supervisee. There may be supplementary fields, such as those between the supervisee and administrators or members of his department. As I talk, it seems more and more evident that the concept of the tripersonal field does not work; it would be impossible to define the framework of such a field without getting into a great deal of confusion, and it will be much simpler and clearer to define the important bipersonal fields—the participants, the boundaries, the ground rules or framework, and the nature of the communications within each—and to view them as fields that interact intensely and extensively.

So this is how we will attempt to develop our discussion: by first defining the nature of the supervisory setting—the ground rules, the framework, and the types of communications within the field. And we will do this for each bipersonal field that we will study—especially that between the supervisor and the supervisee, and between the supervisee and his patient. This will enable us to take into account the influence of the setting—the training situation, the hierarchy of the personnel, and the like—as they influence both the supervisory and the treatment situations.

In this context I want to stress again that the central focus in supervision as I conceive it is on the supervisee-patient interaction, and that I tend to see all other factors as peripheral, both as determinants of the supervisory interaction and as areas within which the supervisor will intervene. To be a bit more specific, this implies that the main responsibility of the supervisee is to present detailed process notes of each session with his patient—notes that preferably have been written in careful sequence just after the session—and that are presented in the sequence in which they occurred, without comments that would break such a sequence, such as a reference to how an hour ended as an introduction to the presentation. I am quite strict about this policy: first, because I spend much of my supervisory time attempting to identify with the patient and what he is experiencing both within himself and from the therapist; second, because I also wish to experience the therapeutic interaction as it unfolded for the supervisee; and third, because this approach enables me to make formulations and predictions that can be validated with subsequent material within the same session, as well as the following hour—this is not feasible when sessions are presented in a disorganized manner, with a disregard for the time sequence.

I think that it is evident that the manner in which the supervisory situation is structured significantly influences the supervisory technique and the supervisory experience for both participants—a point I will elaborate later on. However, having indicated the nature of the main communications from the supervisee (and there certainly will be peripheral comments from him that must be understood by the supervisor, who could then decide whether he will respond directly to them or allow them to pass), I want to characterize the supervisor's main communications as entailing responses to the presentation of the therapeutic interaction under supervision. These would take the form primarily of formulations of its nature for both supervisee and patient, and of extended comments related to general principles of treatment, the clinical and other theories of psychotherapy and psychoanalysis, the relevant psychotherapeutic and psychoanalytic literature, and the like.

With this as an initial basic model, you can understand why I tend to minimize such supervisory functions as evaluating the supervisee, or dealing with such issues as clinic policy or problems created by administrators and others. Now I am not suggesting that these dimensions be set aside entirely—that is, I think that the supervisor does have a responsibility to detect major problems in the supervisee and, if they are at a significant level, to discuss them in some manner with the trainee, preferably in a context related to his clinical presentation. The supervisor has in addition the obligation to report his assessment to those responsible for the training program and to confront any major issue in clinic policy that appears detrimental to the treatment situation he is supervising. But important as these are, they remain secondary considerations for the supervisory situation.

What I try to create is a supervisory situation with an alliance strong enough to help the supervisee endure discussions of his countertransferences and his problems as a therapist—issues I bring up in a way I will describe once we have more material. But I do not make a fuss about assessing the student therapist; I stress the supervisory experience as a unique and crucial opportunity for learning and try not to worry about the rest. It is, of course, there and should not be denied or split off. If it becomes an issue, it must be recognized and handled.

To return now more directly to this supervisory situation: here is a student therapist who contacts the supervisor. We are not talking about supervision in a private setting; there the bipersonal field would display in certain respects a different configuration, though its essential properties would be comparable to those we will formulate today. So here we have a therapist who contacts his supervisor, who would like to work with him, and yet he comes late and gets lost, reminding us that we must discuss the nature of the anxieties in the supervisee and even in the supervisor. This I will do in a moment.

So here the supervisee makes the contact and, in this situation, has not been assigned to the supervisor, as is usually the case in the training situation. So we might expect that this aspect of the framework will have a positive influence on this supervisory interaction. In all, then, we must consider the role of the administration, the manner of assignment to supervision, the supervisee's relationship with the administration, and finally his relationship with the supervisor if we are to fully comprehend the supervisory interaction.

Now I recognize that I have been making rather extended comments based on a minimum of material, but I think it important to develop a basic orientation, a framework within which we can discuss the issues that will soon arise. Much of my present discussion involves the basic attitudes of the supervisor and the fundamental structure of the supervisory situation. So it occurs to me that another fundamental question is that of who the supervisor is responsible to. Is his primary responsibility to the clinic and training program or to the supervisee? And, more importantly, to patient or to the therapist?

As to the first question, I would opt for the supervisor's basic commitment to the supervisee. As for the second question, the answer may seem obvious to some, while to others the question may seem meaningless; the welfare of therapist and patient, they might argue, are so interdependent as to admit of no distinction. And yet at times the supervisor is faced with a real choice: if his main commitment is to the patient, he may be forced to confront the therapist with problems (countertransference difficulties in particular) whose discussion he might otherwise postpone.

So just in case I have left any doubt as to my position, let me say straight out: A supervisor's first responsibility is to the patient. Any time a supervisor has an influence on a treatment situation, the patient and his needs must come first. I would in fact consider the patient whose therapy is under supervision a secondary patient, a patient once removed, and would therefore consider the supervisor bound by a physicianly commitment to that patient. Of course, the treatment of the patient is primarily the responsibility of the supervisee, but that is a different consideration. I am stressing only that the supervisor must have as his first concern that the patient receive the therapy he needs. This commitment is expressed through the supervisee, and the supervisor's obligations to the student therapist therefore entail not only a responsibility to assist him in learning how to do psychotherapy, but a basic commitment to the patient as well.

Now, I will soon say more about the manner in which a supervisor should structure the supervisory situation, but I do not want to leave you with the impression that I am suggesting that there is a need to be as stringent in the supervisory relationship as in the therapeutic. As I will indicate, the supervisor can be a bit more relaxed, more overtly flexible. He should develop a cordial and friendly relationship and may occasionally allow himself to be diverted into peripheral issues, even of a personal note. But I do want to stress the main responsibilities of the supervisor because many supervisory experiences degenerate into casual conversation in which the focus is on side issues and vague generalities. Thus are created what I would call *bastions* or *misalliances* of the supervisory bipersonal field, whereby the crucial and necessary work of supervision is set aside through mutual collusion between supervisor and supervisee.

Discussant: I would like to know whether you believe that the supervisor should ask the supervisee about his personal life, his professional background, and especially whether or not he is in therapy or analysis.

Langs: That's a very interesting question. To respond briefly in anticipation of some relevant material, I tend to structure the supervisory situation in keeping with its main functions, in recognition of the range and form of communication that should exist within the supervisory field, with due consideration of the scope and limitations of the material available for study. As a result, I do not ask personal questions of the supervisee. I accept him as he presents himself, and work with him in terms of his efforts with his patient, allowing his presentation to speak for itself. I respond to him almost entirely in terms of his therapeutic endeavors, as they are revealed in his presentation of process notes from sessions, and structure the supervisory field so that he is required only to present these notes in strict sequence, indicating the patient's associations and his interventions—both verbal and in regard to managing the framework. Since I find it sufficient and effective to teach under these conditions, trying to whatever extent feasible to empathize with what the patient has experienced, I also do not especially require that the supervisee reveal his subjective experiences and fantasies to me, since these are not communicated to the patient. I will, however, take them into consideration if the student therapist has a need to reveal them to me. Also, I will not, by and large, modify my supervisory technique or interventions based on such considerations as whether or not the therapist is in treatment.

Discussant: It seems to me that the overall setting within which the supervision takes place may often exert considerable influence on both the treatment and the supervision, and perhaps supervisors should be more adequately informed of clinic policies and similar matters.

Langs: Yes, that is quite true, and in my own personal experience as a supervisor, I find this to be a much neglected area. In general, I have found that I discover such issues only when they come up between the presenting therapist and the patient. Quite often, the supervisor will strongly disagree with aspects of clinic policy. Here we could discuss the issue of communication between supervisors and administration, another area that tends to be set aside at most training centers, so far as I know. And yet such contacts could be extremely productive.

As you may know, there is a tendency toward all kinds of information leakages in clinics. Those of you who are familiar with my work know that I have a very strong, empirically founded commitment to the maintenance of the framework and boundaries of the therapeutic relationship. I believe that the frame should be as secure as possible if one is to do effective psychotherapy, and if one is to have a stable relationship, an open communicative field, and a full opportunity to analyze the patient's inner pathology.

And when you learn to listen to the unconscious communications from patients—the indirect material—you find that they are extremely sensitive to the many violations of confidentiality and privacy that are all too common in clinics: the notes that are written and read by others, the secretarial clerks to whom the patient must pay his fee, the public calling out of names, therapists discussing sessions in the halls or in the clinic waiting area—these are a few of the many infractions that are destructive both to the patient and to the therapist.

So at times there are aspects of the clinic situation that the supervisor truly believes are detrimental to the patient and the therapy—conditions that he will directly criticize, though he should establish and support his position with material from the patient. This material should be the ultimate source of every intervention made, whether in supervision or therapy. And not infrequently the supervisor indicates to the supervisee that somehow these conditions should be changed, or that they will either preclude effective therapy or severely constrict it.

So you can see that tensions created in the supervisory bipersonal field can contribute to tensions between the supervisee and the administration. Such problems should ideally be resolved through more open communication between the supervisor and the administration, so as not to overburden the supervisee with these conflicts and anxieties. As you might guess, under such conditions the patient will more than likely suffer; the supervisee will somehow draw him into the area of conflict, will inappropriately burden the patient with his own anxieties, and will often unconsciously seek the patient's assistance.

I can see that I am already ahead of myself. I am suggesting interactions between the supervisory and therapeutic bipersonal fields without as yet having created a sufficient foundation for their investigation. So perhaps we should now return to this presentation, though it might be helpful first for me to summarize a bit. We have seen something of the role of the conditions under which the supervisor and supervisee first meet; we have touched upon some aspects of how we create a framework for the supervisory situation; and we have seen some indications that both the nature of the frame and the communicative properties of the supervisory field will be different in important ways from the therapeutic bipersonal field. We have discussed some factors in the supervisee's image of the supervisor, and have seen indications that the supervisee may experience a high level of anxiety in first coming to see him. This might well be based on conscious and unconscious fantasies of the supervisor's powers of perception, his role in determining the supervisee's future, concerns about what the supervisee might reveal to the supervisor, and the like.

It is well to remember that the supervisee is revealing both conscious and unconscious dimensions of his therapeutic efforts, that he is reporting experiences drawn from a highly sensitive and personal therapeutic experience, and that it is the nature of the framework and conditions of the therapeutic bipersonal field to create an interaction in which unconscious fantasies and processes within both participants are often exquisitely revealed. You can see then that supervision is a necessary but painful form of self-revelation, and you can sense the unconscious exhibitionistic anxieties, examination anxieties, and the like that are inevitably experienced by the supervisee and, to a lesser extent, by the supervisor. These are added, as I noted, to many inevitable fantasies about the supervisor himself, but I want to stress again that I do not discuss these issues with the supervisee unless they are either revealed in his work with the patient or become a major obstacle to the supervisory experience, creating what I have termed a *supervisory crisis* which necessitates a shift in the usual area of discourse.

Discussant: Since you're focusing on material that you've been given, I noticed that the supervisee first contacted Dr. A during the summer.

Langs: Right.

Discussant: It is usual practice with many of us; we don't start such work until the summer is over. You haven't said much about the feelings the supervisee might have had as regards the fact that at the time he called, he had a continuous case and yet could not be seen. It might be worthwhile to say something about that.

Langs: Yes, these are all themes and variations. Here the supervisee has a patient, apparently a twice-a-week case that he wants supervision with, and by the time the fall comes, no more patient. Yes, that too could contribute to his anxieties, in terms of his knowing that the patient was lost to therapy. That's one aspect, or he could be resentful toward Dr. A for having put him off. And, of course, whether there's something to his having contacted Dr. A during the summer, very possibly knowing that supervision wouldn't be available then, well that's something we just don't know.

And I want to stress how very speculative all this is. As sophisticated supervisors and therapists, we will of course form some preliminary impressions, but it is important to recognize that we will not, as a rule, have enough data from the supervisee to validate this type of hypothesis. And since, as has frequently been noted in the literature, the supervisee almost inevitably identifies with his supervisor, it behooves us as supervisors to use only clinical material that can produce meaningful and testable hypotheses—material such as the process notes of a session. We must resist the temptation to make formulations about the inner state of the patient or the therapist when we have only incomplete data and communications that cannot be validated. All of which amounts to refraining from what would, in the analytic situation, be termed *wild analysis*—which we certainly do not wish to encourage in our supervisees.

So. These are possible signs of excessive anxiety in the supervisee, and we will keep them in mind in some general form. But we will wait until these anxieties are reflected in his interaction with the patient before discussing them in supervision, and then only because the patient is subjected to them and on some level experiences them along with their consequences. By confining our supervisory efforts to the report of the process notes of the therapy, we teach by our example a very important lesson: Be a therapist in the therapeutic situation and with your patients, and recognize that this is essentially the only field in which this type of relating and interacting is feasible.

So here we touch on a debate concerning the supervisor's proper functions. There are those who feel that the supervisor is exclusively, or at least primarily, a teacher, and is in no sense a therapist. Others feel that he is clearly both teacher and therapist, and that he must make interpretive interventions to the supervisee. It so happens this is one problem I think I have solved in a rather unique way—though I'll save that for a little bit later on, once we have more material.

For now, this leads me to another very important aspect

of the supervisory situation: the specific manner in which the field is structured. After all, it is obvious that supervision is not defined or arranged in the same way that therapy is established. It has its own set of ground rules. Ekstein and Wallerstein (1958) emphasized the extent to which these ground rules determine the properties of the supervisory situation and the nature of the communications that occur between the two participants, but oddly enough, did not, so far as I can see, carry this concept over to the *therapeutic* bipersonal field.

Now perhaps the best way to define the *supervisory bipersonal field* would be to review the basic ground rules of psychotherapy and to compare and contrast the two frameworks. First, in therapy we have set fees, hours, place, and length of sessions. In supervision, were it done privately, there would be a set fee, but I would be far more open to modifying the fee if the financial situation of the supervisee called for it. Similarly, I would establish set hours, a place to meet, and length of sessions in the supervisory situation, but would more readily shift the time or extend the supervision to meet any special needs of the supervisee. In addition, in contrast to therapy, where sessions should occur in a separate professional office without unneeded changes, supervision may take place in the office or home of either party—again, one is far more flexible in the latter situation.

It is evident already that one does not attempt to create the same type of framework and therapeutic hold for supervision as for therapy. In many matters related to the framework one adopts in supervision a more realistic and noninterpretive attitude than one would in therapy, where the focus would be on unconscious meanings and the like. Again, I'm not suggesting that one should set aside possible pathological unconscious motives in the supervisee who requests a change in fee, hour, or the like, but I *am* suggesting that the supervisory field generally permits only the vaguest impressions in this respect, and that they can be seriously considered only when there is extensive coalescing data and a crisis situation.

Moving on, psychotherapy is founded on the fundamental rule of free association by the patient, with communications occurring while the patient is in his chair or on the couch, and the therapist in his place. The counterpart of this in supervision would be the requirement that the supervisee present to the supervisor the specific process notes of his sessions, doing so in strict temporal sequence.

I noticed in reading Ekstein and Wallerstein (1958) that the policy at the Menninger Clinic was for the supervisee to dictate notes on his sessions and send them to the supervisor, who would read them before the supervisory session. The supervisor would then ask the supervisee what he wished to discuss and would allow the supervisory work to unfold from there. It is my belief, however, that this procedure significantly interferes with the conceptualization by the supervisor of the therapeutic interaction, and that there can be no substitute for the direct presentation of process notes to the supervisor. This permits a grasp of the patient's experience, as well as that of the therapist, allows for predictions and efforts at validation, and generates a shared re-creation of the therapeutic experience.

If the presentation of process notes in strict temporal sequence is the supervisory counterpart to free association, it cannot be said that there is any such counterpart to the placement of patient and therapist, or to the use of chair or couch. I have never heard of the use of the couch for a supervisee and of course see no place for it in the supervisory situation, but other than that there are no hard and fast rules in this matter. As regards preparation of the process notes, allow me to inject a note of caution. There are some supervisors who advocate note-taking during sessions or even the recording of therapeutic sessions, justifying these practices on a variety of grounds. Let me just say that such practices significantly modify the basic framework of the psychotherapeutic situation, imply the presence of third parties and the lack of confidentiality, and prove extremely disruptive to the therapeutic interaction. And these are disturbances that are based on actualities and that therefore cannot be modified interpretively. So I strongly suggest that sequential process notes be the basic communicative medium of supervision and that they be written immediately after each session, or as soon after as is feasible.

The next rule of psychotherapy is that there be no physical contact between patient and therapist and no extratherapeutic gratifications—the rule of abstinence. It hardly needs saying that a supervisory experience should preclude a more intimate relationship between supervisor and supervisee, although I recognize that a supervisory relationship, especially one that occurs after the basic training of the supervisee, may lead to a more extended relationship which might even include some form of social contact. Nonetheless, this additional mode of relatedness may well have an important influence on the supervisory experience and may even modify that bipersonal field by creating constraints in both supervisor and supervisee. It may lead to unconscious collusion, to supervisory misalliances and bastions—split-off areas of communication that interfere with the necessary openness of both the supervisee's presentation and the supervisor's responses.

As for gratifications beyond the satisfactions of learning and teaching, it seems to me that there is room for the offer of a cup of coffee by a supervisor, direct support or praise and the like, so long as it does not replace the necessary, more usual interpretation-like interventions which are the supervisor's basic responsibility. Here, too, I believe there is no need for the stringency required in psychotherapy. The supervisory bipersonal field is grounded more in the realities of the supervisory relationship than in the unconscious interaction between supervisor and supervisee; by contrast, the therapeutic situation is designed to heighten both the unconscious dimensions of the therapeutic interaction and the communication of the unconscious fantasies, memories, perceptions, and introjects within the patient. I trust that as I proceed with this discussion you can see that the differences in the frameworks of therapy and supervision not only reflect the distinctive goals of each situation, but also differentiate the two bipersonal fields so as to generate rather dissimilar communicative properties.

Next we have the therapeutic rules of relative anonymity, physicianly concern, and use of neutral interventions geared primarily toward interpretation. In supervision, however, the supervisee may already know a great deal about his supervisor, who may from time to time volunteer additional information. I would place but one stricture upon such communications: the supervisor should make allusions neither to his own work with patients nor to other supervisory situations. No allusions to his patients, because I truly believe that all psychotherapy should be done under conditions of total confidentiality; none to other supervisory experiences, because supervision too should be undertaken in an atmosphere of total confidentiality. If the supervisor refers to another supervisory experience, he is implicitly telling the supervisee that the material presented to him will not be treated with full confidentiality, a factor that will then detrimentally modify the communicative properties of the supervisory field.

The therapist's physicianly concern has a rather direct counterpart in the supervisor's similar concern for both the supervisee and his patient. The therapist's use of neutral interventions geared toward interpretation has its counterpart in the basic neutrality of the supervisor—a dimension that is often overlooked, especially since there is a tendency toward proselytizing and the expression of biases in the supervisor's relationship with the supervisee. At times supervision becomes a situation in which the supervisor, who has scrupulously attempted to control his countertransferences and prejudices in his work with his patients, becomes far less disciplined and permits more direct expression of his underlying tendencies to countertransference—to use the term broadly, as I will throughout this seminar.

Thus in principle the supervisor should attempt mainly to give technical advice and to develop formulations and the neutral interventions and interpretations he would himself offer the patient. He should in addition offer critiques of the supervisee's communications to the patient—his interventions and efforts at managing the frame. From there, of course, the supervisor may wish to generalize, to refer to the relevant literature, and to offer broad conceptions of the theoretical framework for his comments. He should, however, stick closely to ideas generated by the therapeutic interaction under observation and should, by and large, avoid superfluous remarks, especially if they reflect some aspect of an unresolved countertransference problem.

Although I have already mentioned it in passing, we can now consider the final major ground rule in psychotherapy: the necessity of maintaining an exclusive one-to-one relationship with total confidentiality. I have said that supervision too should be undertaken in an atmosphere of total confidentiality, which of course implies that the ideal supervisory experience takes place in a one-to-one relationship. However, as we have already seen, these conditions may of necessity have to be modified. The supervisor may have to report to an administrator, though this is best done on the level of general assessment, without specific reference to the details of the supervisory experience. It is also true that supervision often takes place either in groups or in continuous case conferences, and though this is certainly a viable format one must recognize that the presence of direct observers may limit the openness of the supervisory field.

In this connection I would like to stress once again that since a supervisor's basic commitment is to his patients and to the patients of his supervisee, self-revelations by the supervisor should not include references of any kind to his own work with patients or with other supervisees. I must stress that point since it is quite common for supervisors to refer to their own clinical work and, at times, to other supervisory experiences. This generates an image of the supervisor as someone unable to maintain total confidentiality, especially with regard to his own patients, and this will render meaningless and hypocritical any discussion he might offer regarding the importance of the framework of psychotherapy and, in particular, the crucial role played by confidentiality. And frankly, I feel that little is lost in this way, because the supervisee is exposed to enough direct case conferences and presentations in the literature to get a sense of how others work, and because ultimately he must validate—in his own work, directly with his own patients—all of the ideas and techniques presented to him.

We are now in a position to draw important distinctions between the communicative properties of the therapeutic and the supervisory bipersonal fields. In the therapy situation, one creates a firm hold; to use Winnicott's term (1958, 1965), the framework establishes a *holding environment* which offers implicit ego support even while maintaining distinct boundaries between patient and therapist. Certain types of inappropriate gratifications are precluded in order to foster the communication—in both behavior and words—of derivatives of the patient's pathological mental world, this in a form that lends itself to analyzability and interpretation. The framework establishes the analyst's containing function as well, but let me now summarize the properties of the second field—that of supervision—as they have emerged in the comparison with therapy and its ground rules.

The supervisor offers a somewhat loosely though clearly structured bipersonal field that provides the supervisee with the implicit ego support—hold and container—that will enable him to undergo the very special, highly personal, and often painful learning experiences that are the only road to psychotherapeutic competence. The frame and boundaries of the field offer a sense of support and security for the supervisor as well; he will function best when the participants' roles are clearly defined and the ground rules well established.

Now the communicative elements within the field are, first, the supervisee's process notes and occasional side comments, which means that the primary materials from which the supervisory situation is built are the patient's associations and the supervisee's interventions. Secondly, there are, of course, the supervisor's interventions, which are geared toward understanding the material and the supervisee's work. These include a variety of communications that the supervisor feels necessary for the effective development of the student therapist. These exchanges, then, take place along an interface with inputs from both participants to supervision; the resultant amalgam is taken in—introjected—by the supervisee to become a significant vector or input in the first bipersonal field—his work with his patient.

But I would like to stress in particular that the supervisory field that I have created is one in which maximal confidentiality prevails, in which trust is implicitly encouraged. Both the holding-containing qualities and the trust are essential to the kind of direct teaching one must engage in to be an effective supervisor.

I hope also that you can see why I have suggested this particular framework. Within its confines, the main communicative medium is the patient's associations and the therapist's interventions. It follows that it is these elements on which the supervisor must rely; everything that he formulates will be derived from this data and will be validated from it as well. As you will soon see, this means that the patient's associations—his direct and indirect, conscious and unconscious communications—will be at the heart of the supervisory experience and will be the basic guide and yardstick throughout.

As for the therapist, the supervisor will have only his interventions to work with by and large, and he will respect the limitations this imposes. We will have to rely more on the patient's unconscious perceptions and introjections of the supervisee's unconscious countertransference fantasies, which the therapist communicates in his verbal interventions and managements of the frame, than on the therapist's own communications. And I state this now because it is an important principle, one founded on the fact that the supervisory bipersonal field is constructed so as to have all of the associations from the patient—the essential requisite for any assessment of unconscious contents and processes—and only highly selective, intermittent communications from the therapist. The supervisory field is therefore an actuality that precludes, for lack of necessary data, any full understanding of the supervisee's unconscious processes and mental contents.

Previous writers on supervision have often recognized these limitations in regard to data concerning the supervisee's countertransferences but, as far as I can determine, have not turned to the patient as a valid and important source of such data. In our work today I hope to demonstrate in considerable detail how the material from the patient provides definitive and validatable material in regard to both his own inner pathology and that of his therapist—though I hasten to add that there are, as we shall see, very definite limitations in regard to the patient's introjections of, and unconscious sensitivities to, the therapist's unconscious processes and contents.

Another point, though it remains to be seen whether I will be able to demonstrate it today, is that the patient will serve not only as a means of validating the supervisor's formulations to the supervisee, but that, as part of the interaction between the supervisory and bipersonal fields, countertransference-based communications from supervisor to supervisee tend to be communicated in some form and on some level from supervisee to patient. The latter may then respond, unconsciously but meaningfully and in a sense directly, to the supervisor's countertransferences. Unless the supervisor meets and interacts with the patient directly—a modification in the frame to which I have strong objections—the effects of the supervisor's countertransferences are expressed always through the medium of the supervisee. The patient often will introject this pathology and respond to it in a variety of ways, both exploitative and curative.

My last remark brings up another important issue in supervision, namely, whether the supervisor should have any contact with the patient apart from the supervisee's presentation of process notes. Such contact would include direct interviews with the patient, as well as observations through tape recordings, videotape, or one-way mirrors. By now you can probably guess my position on this issue. I of course object to such techniques, on the grounds that they seriously modify the framework by openly and directly altering the one-to-one relationship and the need for total confidentiality. They also call into question the position and responsibility of the supervisee as the patient's therapist. This is why I have advocated the use of process notes written after sessions, rather than during them, and why I believe it inadvisable to directly inform the patient of the supervision.

I would like to point out here, however, that most clinic patients are "clinic-wise," and that they know on some level that supervision is usually implicit in clinic therapy. The therapist should be able to intervene when derivatives appear that are related to this belief, or to the patient's extensions of it in fantasy. The therapist should implicitly recognize the reality of supervision, but should neither confess nor acknowledge it. Nor should he intervene in a manner that might suggest to the patient that his therapist thinks him mistaken—or even crazy—in his true belief.

To return to the case we began to look at, recall that the supervisee called the supervisor during the summer, lost the patient he wanted to present, got lost himself and was late coming to the first supervisory session. Now, though these are manifest and intermittent communications, you do not have, nor should you obtain, the supervisee's associations to them. And you are therefore limited in regard to what you can derive from them. If you attempt to be a therapist for the patient who verbalizes something like one association out of one hundred, you are in a lot of trouble—you're going to make a lot of mistakes and will often look foolish. And you will certainly be an ineffective therapist. Respect the limitations of the data you have regarding your supervisee, safeguard his privacy as much as possible, and avoid undue intrusions into his inner world. Use only the contents and processes reflected in his interventions to his patient and in his occasional extraneous comments. Be very careful with your speculations about him and try especially hard to avoid conveying them to your supervisee unless you are faced with a crisis situation. Even then, use utmost caution, humility, and tact.

In taking this approach, you afford the supervisee two excellent examples: a therapist who realizes that he can operate only within a clearly defined bipersonal field established by ground rules particular to the psychotherapeutic situation; and a supervisor who realizes that in the bipersonal field particular to supervision observations are made and conclusions drawn that are quite different from those appropriate to therapy. And so, following your double example, the supervisee will perhaps learn to focus in supervision on material derived from his patient. Here we encounter the reflection process that obtains between the first and second fields—therapy and supervision—based on the supervisee's presence in both situations. This aspect is touched upon by both Searles (1955) and Arlow (1966).

So we neither ignore nor overestimate whatever data we might have from the therapist beyond his behaviors in sessions with his patient. Of course, if he makes extraneous comments, appears anxious or relaxed, presents the material in a particular kind of way, shows a certain sense of affect or its lack—well, as therapists or analysts, we of course can hardly avoid attending to these communications. But we must fully recognize that we are restricted to manifest contents and behaviors, and some ready inferences that we make based on our general experiences. These inferences I term *Type One derivatives* (Langs 1978 h, j): the reading of manifest communications for possible latent meanings, without knowing the relevant adaptive context—and here, without benefit even of the supervisee's associations.

In fact, as I hope to demonstrate, you will learn a great deal more about the supervisee from the communications from the patient which prompt his erroneous interventions —and of course, from the way in which he intervenes and manages the frame—than you will from any other source. As therapists and analysts we want to make formulations based on free associations and observations of behaviors, on material that can be fully understood in depth, so that we can generate hypotheses and interventions that can be truly validated. In the psychotherapeutic situation I would almost never deviate from this principle, nor would I in most situations of crisis and emergency in supervision. What is called for is a study of the therapeutic situation under supervision for the sources of the disturbance and for clues as to both its underlying basis and the best means of resolving it.

But the fact of the matter is that a crisis in the therapy may occur that is related more to the supervision relationship than to the patient-supervisee relationship. We must recognize such a possibility and consider it at all times of emergency, since it is the one area that the supervisor, due to his own countertransference-based needs, is most likely to overlook. And when some aspect of the supervisory interaction has created a crisis that severely threatens either the therapy under supervision or the supervisory experience itself, the supervisor must make use of everything he knows. In addressing his comments to the supervisee at such times, he might well directly acknowledge the limitations of the data and therefore of the formulations he is about to make; the restrictions will be considerable and the supervisor must recognize that he is working in a field with many inevitable blind spots. That is why I virtually always confine my extraneous comments—that is, those not deriving from the presented therapeutic interaction—to crisis situations, and why I also make every effort always to proceed gently, with support and understanding, tact and compassion, so as to avoid such crises if at all possible.

Discussant: But aren't you touching upon some of the ways in which the teaching of psychotherapy does not follow the usual medical model?

Langs: Yes, that is quite true. Much of this difference stems from the nature of the material, the manner in which the patient's pathology is manifested in his verbal and behavioral communications—especially his interaction with the therapist—and, from the fact that the treatment itself, the curative factor, resides within the therapist himself and requires therefore not only a knowledge of techniques and methods but considerable self-knowledge as well. We also are dealing with two bipersonal fields within which the manifest communication and interaction is only a partial factor; here unconscious communications, structures, and processes play a far more significant role. Yes, the nature of our basic data, the very nature of the treatment process, and the nature as well of each component of the interaction is so distinctive that the usual medical model of teaching does not prove serviceable.

So getting back to the presented material, you can see from what I've said that I would not begin this first supervisory session by saying, Oh, I notice you are late; you called me during the summer and then lost the patient. I think you have some very serious problems. (Laughter.) As you can see, that's rather unempathic, hostile, even attacking. It is also very general and is calculated to increase the supervisee's anxiety as well as his sense of threat. Each of you have had experiences with supervisors, and I am sure that you can remember your own anxieties, as well as the manner in which your supervisor responded to them. Perhaps he ignored them; perhaps he was a bit reassuring. Or perhaps he directly commented upon your anxiety, or tried to interpret its basis. If the last, I suspect he only created in you a far greater sense of threat. But whatever the case, insights from such experiences should always be validated in your actual supervisory work.

I am reminded of my own supervisory experiences with Arlow, whom I mention largely because of his excellent paper (1963) on the supervisory situation. I can say that, in addition to all that I learned about clinical psychoanalytic theory and technique, it was Arlow who taught me the need for a psychoanalytic methodology and who helped me develop a sensitivity in this area. Now, he tended to be implicitly supportive—direct, workmanlike, candid, extremely perceptive—and yet respectful, sympathetic, empathic, and deeply committed to his work.

And while it takes me a bit afield, I had a remarkable experience in rereading his paper on supervision. I discovered that he offered there a rather extensive discussion of the important issue of unconscious collusion between patient and therapist. Now as you may know, I have written extensively on that subject (1975a, 1976a, d) and have developed a number of what I feel to be important concepts in that area. But in reviewing all the basic literature on the therapeutic interaction, I never looked at Arlow's paper on supervision, though I had read it some years ago. Needless to say, I was now quite astounded at Arlow's perceptiveness in this area and immediately recognized that both this paper and his direct supervision with me must have contributed to the development of my own ideas—though this all took place without my conscious awareness. So I am pleased to find in this workshop the opportunity to acknowledge publicly this source of my ideas.

And so once again I come back to the creative opportunities in supervision, opportunities Searles (1955, 1962) has also recognized. It is after all no accident that Arlow's discussion of unconscious collusion between patient and analyst appears in a paper on supervision. There are many clinical phenomena that can be identified, understood, formulated, and meaningfully validated in the supervisory situation, especially when the supervisee is having difficulty. And *most* especially, when his difficulties have their basis in countertransference. In placing the supervisor at a remove, in sparing him the immediate interaction with the patient, the supervisory situation affords the supervisor a special opportunity for new insights and creativity. The disadvantages of distance seem more than made up for by its advantages.

It is this bit of understanding that helped me feel a little less disturbed that most of my basic discoveries were derived first from the supervisory experience, and only secondarily confirmed in my own work—with but a few interesting exceptions. I kept feeling that, ideally, such insights should come from my immediate analytic and therapeutic work, most especially from the former. But I discovered that in reality this often is not the case. The psychotherapeutic situation provides a great deal of material for original thinking, and the supervisory situation allows a particular freedom for speculation quite different from one's more imaginative reactions in direct work with patients.

In supervision the pressures and anxieties, especially in regard to the disruptive aspects of the patient's material, are considerably less, perhaps allowing a greater openness to the patient's creative and curative thrusts. This affords the supervisor a relative serenity that allows him to convey to the supervisee—though implicitly—a sense of mastery in regard to the therapeutic bipersonal field. By this I do not mean to encourage in the supervisor any air of omniscience or omnipotence, nor any unrealistic and grandiose quality implying that as a therapist and supervisor he understands every communication from the patient and every aspect of the therapeutic interaction. Certainly it should be possible for you to indicate to a supervisee that you fail to understand a particular segment of a session, or even an entire session or two. In fact, if you are a rather sensitive supervisor, it will often turn out in such situations that the supervisee has failed to inform you of an important adaptive context—often something related to the therapeutic interaction, such as his pending vacation—information that almost immediately helps you understand what had been previously quite perplexing.

Still, there will be sessions where comprehension eludes

you, and, while you should make every effort to identify in yourself any countertransference factors in your failure to understand, there will be important occasions in supervision when you must admit that you find it impossible to understand the unconscious implications of the material and that you are unable to organize the patient's communications in any meaningful way. In fact, since in supervision we tend to overstress organizing and understanding, we may fail to recognize that at certain times patients unconsciously associate in a manner that makes comprehension impossible—the patient is in fact attempting to destroy all meaning. So there should be a place for not being able to understand the patient; but, I hasten to add, if this is indeed our formulation, it eventually should be validated through subsequent associations from the patient. We must not project into the patient a failure on our part to understand material that can, in fact, be comprehended. Such moments always call for self-scrutiny and for use of the validating process.

These caveats notwithstanding, conveying a sense of mastery in regard to your own therapeutic and supervisory work—and to the ideas that you present—can be quite important to the supervisee. During the course of my supervisory career, this point has been brought home to me on a number of rather painful occasions. In the course of teaching continuous case seminars and doing individual and group supervision I was making discoveries and developing concepts which, whatever their ultimate worth, I knew to involve dimensions of the therapeutic interaction my teachers had never clearly presented. And, in the process of sharing and even making these discoveries during the actual supervisory work, what I discovered, very much to my dismay, was that, instead of my students sharing in the excitement and gratification of the experience, it scared the hell out of them. Now some of this occurred because my findings contradicted their own experiences in personal therapy or analysis, but what I want to stress is that it became quite clear that the fact that I did not have full mastery over these new ideas and, consequently, over what I was teaching made a cogent and persuasive presentation impossible. To my supervisees a new discovery could therefore mean only that, previously, something had not been completely understood, and this proved quite anxiety-provoking for them. So to the extent that you have achieved relative mastery of the therapeutic situation—and I think that total mastery is an unreachable ideal rather than a realistic goal—to that extent the supervisee is able to identify with and incorporate your sense of confidence and your capacity to handle the therapeutic interaction. And I found that as my ideas became organized and finally fell into place the response of my supervisees was quite different; up to a point they were able to sense the security of the hold I offered in the supervisory situation, and they found it important to sense that I had both situations—therapy and supervision—largely under control.

Discussant: I am interested in your reference to the unconscious collusion between supervisor and supervisee. Perhaps you could comment further.

Langs: Yes, that is a very important issue. Actually, there can be conscious as well as unconscious collusion between the two, though in my discussion here, as well as in my writings (Langs 1975a, 1976a,d), I have stressed mainly the unconscious variety. It is important that the supervisor be constantly on the lookout for areas of unconscious collusion, and that the supervisee, as he listens to his supervisor and reflects on his supervisory session after such an hour, make efforts of his own to discover any shared defenses, prejudices, inappropriate gratifications—any split-off bastions or supervisory misalliances. It is quite important to acknowledge their possible emergence and to maintain a constant vigilance for their presence. This effort will rely on the self-knowledge of the supervisor—to consider this from his vantage point first—who may be alerted by any indicator in himself of uncertainty, discomfort, or unusual response to the patient or supervisee. These are subjective indicators of disturbing effects derived from unconscious countertransference fantasies and introjects (Langs 1974, 1976a,d); he should as well be alert to all objective signs of crises or disruption in the supervision or therapy. Once alerted, the supervisor proceeds to examine his interaction with the supervisee and attempts to discover areas of collusion. Here he will be greatly aided by a consistent use of the validating process. He should offer definitive formulations based on the material he is hearing in sequence and should attempt to validate these formulations in the patient's subsequent associations, as well as through the therapist's subsequent interventions. Since it is so difficult to detect the effects of an unconscious countertransference problem—and because such problems are especially refractory to discovery in the supervisory interaction—I have stressed the importance of creating a supervisory bipersonal field within which genuine and regular efforts at validation can be undertaken. And these efforts at validation should also be made by the supervisee, who should not simply accept as gospel the formulations of his supervisor, but should search for clear-cut validation or refutation within both his own subjective responses and the continuing material related to his interaction with the patient.

Discussant: Can you clarify what you mean by validation?

Langs: I hope to go into this further once we have some clinical material before us. I will then be able to offer a specific formulation and follow this with efforts at validation. In brief, we begin with a *silent (interpretive) hypothesis*, a silent formulation, developed from the patient's initial communications. This should then be confirmed through Type Two derivatives in the subsequent associations of the patient and, to a lesser extent, by the subjective experiences and additional associations of the therapist or supervisor.

Such confirmation takes place in two spheres in the

therapeutic bipersonal field: the cognitive and the introjective-interactional. The first refers to the manner in which a correct interpretation modifies repression and other defenses so that the patient subsequently communicates novel and quite unexpected material that helps reorganize the understanding of the patient's communications to that point—the emergence of what Bion (1962) has termed the *selected fact*. In the interactional realm, the patient inherently identifies with and incorporates the positive aspects of the functioning of a therapist who is able to offer a correct interpretation. This is reflected in associations related to individuals who are functioning constructively and helpfully, and often through some positive comment that the patient might make about himself. He might remark, for instance, that he has been functioning better lately.

In the supervisory bipersonal field, the supervisee's interventions should be validated in his sessions with his patients. As for the supervisor, his formulations and suggested interventions—and it is important to offer both as specifically as possible—can be validated in two ways: the first and most important is derived from the subsequent material from the patient or, more rarely, from the later interventions of the therapist in that session—associations and interventions that confirm the supervisor's formulation in a truly unique way. Direct agreement or the repetition, even with variations, of the same theme does not constitute cognitive validation. I must emphasize that point since all therapists and supervisors have a special narcissistic investment in their own formulations and interventions, and this creates considerable resistances to the recognition of nonvalidating responses.

The second form of confirmation of a formulation developed by a supervisor is interactional, and takes the form of some type of confirmatory response by the supervisee. As Arlow (1963) has described, the supervisee may sometimes recall a previously unreported or repressed fragment of the session that he is presenting—a segment that confirms the supervisor's comments in a fresh and novel way. This type of confirmation must be placed in a secondary position as against validation by the patient's material; that source must always take precedence.

Actually, there is a third form of confirmation for the supervisor's formulations, one that we would like to see more often. Unfortunately, I must say that experience has shown me that it does not appear as frequently as we might hope. Validation in this form occurs when the supervisee incorporates and integrates the supervisor's comments, listens to the material of the next new session with the patient, and finds an appropriate and valid opportunity to intervene—preferably to interpret or to manage the framework—in a manner in keeping with the supervisor's formulation. The intervention is then validated by the patient. Here, a formulation within the second bipersonal field—that of supervision—is validated in the first bipersonal field—the therapeutic interaction. This can be most dramatic and most efficacious for the patient, but there are many resistances and other factors that tend to disturb this ideal flow of insight and understanding—even though it is the ultimate test of any formulation.

As you can see, I am stressing the importance of validating both verbal interventions and one's management of the framework—the latter is relatively overlooked in this respect. I am also attempting to develop now a methodology for the supervisory situation, one in which the patient is not only the key to the formulations developed by the supervisor but is as well the ultimate source of validation. And you can see that this is a methodology that can be used by both the supervisor and the supervisee, and that it actually offers a means by which anyone in supervision can rather carefully and systematically evaluate the validity of the formulations being proposed.

Discussant: As I understand them, your comments concerning unconscious collusion relate to your concept of therapeutic misalliances (Langs 1975a) in the therapeutic bipersonal field. You are now suggesting—and it makes a great deal of sense—that there can be misalliances in the supervisory situation as well.

Langs: Yes. It is my impression, from personal discussions and from a selected consideration of the literature, that far too little consideration has been accorded the supervisor's teaching difficulties: his errors, blind spots, and invitations to the supervisee to form bastions and misalliances. In fact much of the psychoanalytic literature seems to take as its paradigm an analyst quite free, except for occasional and sporadic upsurges, of all countertransference influence; it shies away from viewing the analyst or therapist as under constant pressure from his unconscious countertransference fantasies and needs. But it is the latter view, surely, that is closer to reality, however experienced the therapist. And a funny thing: even a therapist prepared to surrender an overidealized image of himself in his work with patients clings to the overidealized image of himself as supervisor. He is doubtless encouraged in this by the tendency in supervisees to overidealize their supervisors and to all too readily accept invitations to collusion and misalliance.

Very few supervisees are taught a basic and critical methodology; even fewer can assess their own interventions or those of their supervisors with the validating process I have outlined. As a result, even when their work with a patient is not going well, they are seldom able to question or challenge their supervisor, to consider his possible contributions nondefensively, or to offer alternative formulations. We should teach our supervisees, as part of supervision, how to do such things; this can be done not only through direct presentation of clinical methodology, but also through offering ourselves as examples allowing positive identification with our own work. We must therefore consistently attempt to evaluate and validate our formulations and proposed interventions, and must discuss quite openly the extent to which subsequent material from the patient offers confirmation. Just as in his work as a therapist, the supervisor must be prepared for nonconfirmation. He must be ready to reformulate under such circumstances and to use the patient's subsequent associations as his guide. Ultimately, both parties to supervision must rely on the patient for all efforts at validation, as well as for important unconscious efforts to bring to the attention of his therapist—and the unseen and unknown supervisor—countertransference problems that exist in either of them. The patient, from time to time, unconsciously attempts to cure the pathology of both bipersonal fields.

Discussant: I don't want to complicate the issue unnecessarily, but I think that we must take into account what we're doing here. We have to appreciate that there are three bipersonal fields: the therapeutic, the supervisory, and now this conference. And your relationship with Dr. A, and any possible misalliance that it might generate, could influence everything else that goes on.

Langs: Yes, we're all in trouble. I know. (Laughter.) And what about the audience, why do you leave yourselves out as possible sources of misalliance? (Laughter.) But I agree, the situation is quite complex, and it is important to identify each pertinent interactional field.

Discussant: Can you elaborate on the validating process—and on listening to the patient?

Langs: Yes. I had planned to discuss each of these fundamental problems in terms of the material that will be presented to us. However, I can see from your questions, and from my own need to establish a framework for the conference, that it is important to at least outline some basic concepts in advance of hearing further material. It seems to me that we have already touched upon most of the issues related to structuring the supervisory situation, and to establishing a validating process viable in terms of the conditions of each field. But it is characteristic of me, and of virtually all analysts, to come last to the specifics of how we *listen* to patients—and to supervisees. We do it almost as an afterthought, as I do now only in response to the second of your two requests.

The development of my own writings is representative in this respect up to a point, and then is, I think, quite a departure. When I was writing my two-volume work on technique (1973, 1974), the last chapter I did was on how to listen to the patient. I had already written a chapter on the nature of material from patients, based on an earlier paper (1972), and had written something about the concept of derivatives and the adaptive context. But as I looked over the two volumes as my work on them neared completion, I realized that I had not offered any systematic discussion of how to listen to the patient and or of the basics of formulating his material. So I wrote such a chapter, one I consider entirely unique in the analytic literature. My initial avoidance, I think, was consonant with a more general human tendency to develop myths and to make silent, though unfounded, basic assumptions. Psychoanalysts silently assume that all analysts and therapists know how to listen to their patients, and how to formulate the manifest and latent content derived from the patient's associations and behaviors—a thesis that proves markedly unfounded. And it's quite interesting to me that that particular chapter is one of the few in the two-volume work that I would not essentially change.

And typically, only now am I about to turn to the writing of a small book (Langs 1978c) on this very important subject. It turns out that my development of a relatively unique set of concepts related to listening, and to all intaking aspects of the therapist's functioning, proves to be the key to every new perspective I have developed, as well as to the solidification and elaboration of many familiar ideas. Only in the last couple of months have I begun to concentrate on investigations of communicative properties of the bipersonal field, the nature of the communications from both patient and therapist, the concept of derivatives, and the like, and I have found that a great deal of so-called analytic work actually takes place entirely on the level of manifest content, and that almost everyone else works with what I call *Type One derivatives*. These are the sometimes clever translations of manifest contents into latent contents undertaken in some relatively direct manner, without any consideration of the adaptive context or the dynamic location and interactional meanings of the associations. I now classify the material from patients as *manifest content*, as *Type One derivatives*, which either patient or analyst offers as translations from conscious into unconscious contents, and as *Type Two derivatives*, in which the patient's associations are organized around an *adaptive context* to yield specific, dynamic, unconscious and interactional meanings reflecting highly individualized and currently meaningful unconscious contents, defenses, fantasies, and perceptions (Langs 1978c).

It is rather obvious that the manner in which one listens and organizes the material from the patient determines the level and scope of his understanding. Throughout this seminar I will use the term *listening* to refer to the entire intaking process of the therapist or supervisor. It has cognitive and interactional, sensory and nonsensory aspects, and is rather complex. I will stress the cognitive aspects for now, and will add other dimensions as they are suggested by the material. Cognitively, listening begins with hearing everything that is said and observing all the patient's behaviors; *listening* is in fact something of a misnomer since the intaking process includes both auditory and visual cues, as well as, on occasion, cues derived from the other senses—touch excluded. There is a stress on the patient's words, silences, and behaviors. The listening process, then, begins with the therapist's capacity to observe accurately and extends into his efforts at understanding, formulating, and organizing. This basic intaking process, with its less defined qualities, such as trial identifications, empathy, and intuition, blends into the therapist's—or supervisor's—efforts at synthesis and comprehension, which might be identified as a second phase. A third phase would entail the formulation of a potential intervention—what I have termed a *silent hypothesis* (1976a, d, 1978 c)—and ultimately leads to the offer of an intervention to the patient.

At the cognitive core of listening and comprehending is the adaptive approach: the effort to identify, for all sequences of associations from the patient, the central, intrapsychically meaningful adaptive context—the precipitant of the patient's responses. With the adaptive context one can understand the patient's associations and behaviors in a dynamic and actively meaningful manner, and, since most crucial adaptive contexts derive from the therapeutic relationship, one can also usually formulate the material definitively in terms of the ongoing therapeutic interaction. In the course of your supervisory efforts you should note the communications from the patient that prompt the therapist either to interpret or to make attempts at managing the framework. The patient's immediate associations are the adaptive context for the therapist's intervention, and, when a mistaken intervention is made, the preceding material from the patient offers important clues as to the unconscious precipitant of the error as well as to aspects of its unconscious meanings and functions. The supervisor should consciously identify these clues, especially since the patient will unconsciously but rather consistently be in touch with this aspect of the interaction. Further, the therapist's intervention itself is an immediate adaptive context for the patient's subsequent associations, which always have both a conscious and an unconscious bearing on that adaptive context and can be meaningfully understood within it. This applies to all interventions by the therapist: his silences, his verbal interventions, his management of the framework.

In discussing the adaptive context concept I have for the most part restricted myself to the bipersonal field in therapy or analysis; but I feel quite certain that, as material is presented today, we will find the concept equally appropriate to the supervisory bipersonal field.

Discussant: In regard to your comments about how the therapist listens, I can think of one reference to this subject, in a volume by Bion called *Attention and Interpretation* (1970). In it, he discusses how to listen to patients, and although he does it in his own way I find it rather interesting and really quite valuable.

Langs: Yes, I am familiar with Bion's work and would agree with you. His discussion in *Attention and Interpretation* contains one of the few truly original recommendations regarding the listening aspect of technique. In an effort to facilitate the analyst's search for new formulations and to counteract his tendency to discover in the patient's material only what is familiar to him, Bion suggests that the analyst or therapist enter each session without desire, memory, or understanding, thus permitting the patient's fresh associations to direct his recall and his understanding. I have elaborated this concept in my own writings (1976a, b, 1978c) and endeavor to apply it in my own clinical practice.

I also make use of this basic concept in supervision, in that I will, in a continuous case presentation, begin each supervisory hour with the report of the new sessions, without any summary of what had taken place in the previous hours or in the prior supervisory discussion. Similarly, in my own work with patients I make no notes at any time and try to enter each session relatively fresh and empty, allowing the patient's associations to direct me, fully believing that each session will be an entity to itself, and that any valid interpretation will be freshly created by both the patient and the therapist in the course of the session at hand. This concept I derived not only from my own application of Bion's thinking, but also by extending a rather beautiful paper by de Racker (1961) in which she stresses the extent to which the patient will in some derivative form place all the necessary ingredients for a valid interpretation into the therapist, whose essential function is to conceptualize the material offered him.

So for some time I had succumbed to the myth that we all know how to listen to the patient's material, and it took me a long while to become directly aware of my repeated observation that this was simply not the case—that, in fact, much of the confusion that has developed in response to my own conceptualizations has stemmed from the fact that many analysts do not consistently listen to the patient within the framework of an adaptive context. They do not consistently apply the validating process, either in their analytic writings or in their work with patients.

The efficacy of these methods is particularly evident when the adaptive context enables you to observe a most fascinating sequence filled with unconscious meanings. Let's take as an example a situation in which a patient suggests an alteration of the frame; let's say he brings in an insurance form after several sessions. If you take this behavior as an adaptive response to the previous hour and its contents, you will discover intensely conflictual material and increasing anxiety within the patient. You will find that the proposed alteration in the frame is an effort at what I have termed a *framework deviation cure* (Langs 1976a, d), a means of alleviating the anxiety in question and of disposing of the disturbing unconscious fantasies and perceptions related to it. If you then listen to the patient's material with the proposed alteration of the frame as the organizing and adaptive context, you will find ample confirmation of these unconscious meanings and functions of the proposal and, despite the patient's conscious preference that you fill out the form, you will find him unconsciously aware that such a step will severely modify and curtail the open and necessary communicative properties of the bipersonal field. That type of split between conscious and unconscious communication in the area of the frame is absolutely typical. But I am now getting into some of my favorite topics, long before we have the material from supervision that would justify this diversion.

Discussant: It seems to me that you are saying that there are many factors that influence a supervisory experience and that none should be overlooked. Included is the decision by the supervisor to present this particular supervisory experience to this seminar—whether he informs the supervisee or not.

Supervisor A: In this situation, because I began to take more detailed notes, I did tell the supervisee that there would be a presentation.

Discussant: I think we would all agree that this information would have an influence on the supervisory experience—as well as on the supervisee's work with the patient. Before commenting on that aspect, Dr. Langs, I wonder if you would first comment further on what you have called the *validating process*.

Langs: Yes. That would be more in keeping with these initial efforts to establish a basic methodology for supervision—one that must be closely connected to our clinical methodology and the psychotherapeutic situation itself. Let me say again, though briefly, since we need to get to the clinical material, that I have seen much to convince me that many psychotherapists work either without a basic concept of methodology and validation, or with one so loosely constructed and so narcissistically invested that all but the most blatant denials are seen as confirmatory of their interventions. In fact, basing themselves on Freud's papers on negation (1925a) and constructions in analysis (1937), some are able to view even blatant denials as a negative form of confirmation.

In brief, I would describe the validating process as follows: first, in therapy or analysis it entails listening to the patient's associations and observing his behavior; identifying the *adaptive context* and formulating a *silent hypothesis* which identifies the central meaning of the material from the patient—unconscious fantasies, unconscious perceptions, and the like; finding confirmation of this hypothesis in the ongoing associations from the patient; offering an intervention with the appearance of an appropriate bridge to your thesis, in the form of either an interpretation or a response related to the management of the framework; and listening to the material that follows for confirmation or nonconformation. Confirmation here takes the form of truly unique associations that permit a significant reconceptualization of the material and includes the striking revelation of previously unknown information. I term that *Type Two derivative validation* (Langs 1978c). Since I intend to elaborate once we have the clinical material, please accept this as a basic model. Those of you who are interested can clarify this area by reading my publications on this subject (1972, 1973, 1976a, b, 1978c, g, i).

The validating process in supervision is similar to that I have outlined for therapy or analysis, though it is distinctive because of the special conditions of the supervisory situation. Let me just sketch the basics: the supervisee's unfolding presentation of the process notes of the session, offered in strict sequence without extraneous comments; the supervisor's formulation of the adaptive context and a silent hypothesis related to the associational material, the patient's behaviors, and, sometimes, the communications from the therapist; the presentation of this hypothesis to the supervisee once it has been crystallized; and the continued presentation of the process notes with a search for confirmatory and nonconfirmatory material. At this point, two possibilities must be considered. The first is that the supervisee has intervened in the session; the second is that, though the supervisee has not intervened, the supervisor has identified a particular point in the session where he would himself have done so. In the first case, the supervisee's comment is evaluated in terms of the antecedent material of the session and compared with the supervisor's formulation. When these are in basic agreement, the supervisee continues with his presentation of process notes, and both participants examine the material for further confirmation or its lack.

When their formulations differ, a discussion must ensue in which the basis for these differences is explored in the context of the material from the patient up to that point. If the supervisor maintains his belief that his evaluation is correct or, alternatively, if it is his position that he cannot organize the material into a viable intervention even though the supervisee has done so, he then must examine the discrepancy between the supervisee's intervention and the patient's material. He may in this way be able to delineate the idiosyncratic or countertransference-based contributions of the therapist which are being communicated and projectively identified into the patient. To these the patient will respond quite extensively.

This latter type of formulation is quite important, since it is the supervisor's evaluation of the pathological component of the therapist's intervention and should be counterbalanced with an appreciation of the valid elements to the extent that they are present. Both aspects can be traced out in the patient's response, which will involve either an introjection of all the unconscious dimensions of the therapist's intervention—the most common reaction—or a refusal to contain some or all of these pathological contents.

Much of this will become clear, I trust, once we have some clinical material in front of us. I simply want to stress here that every formulation and assessment made by the supervisor must be subject to validation in terms of subsequent material from the patient. There is, however, a second type of validation in supervision, though one I consider secondary to confirmation derived from the original therapeutic situation. It takes the form of the supervisee remembering aspects of his session he had previously failed to report, or remembering some earlier material from the patient that tends to confirm the supervisor's synthesis. We should remember, however, that such seemingly validating responses are open to unconscious influences related to such matters as idealization of the supervisor, wishes to please him, and the like, and that they are not part of a continuous associational flow. They therefore must be viewed as a secondary form of confirmation, a form which, by the way, Arlow rather nicely describes in his 1963 paper.

The second possibility, to which I referred earlier, occurs when the material from the patient is such that the supervisor decides that he would intervene at a particular point in the session, although the supervisee has not. In this situation, the supervisor as a rule will have already presented his initial hypothesis to the supervisee, identified evidence for subsequent confirmation in the continuing associations from the patient, and then found a communicative bridge—a point at which he would have intervened. The supervisor then indicates the specific comments or management of the frame that he would have offered; once again, he searches the patient's subsequent material for confirmatory data.

Now please understand that this is a skeletal outline, that much of it must be fleshed out in the supervisory situation with extensive explanations, with references to the pertinent literature, and with full opportunity for questions and discussion. But I offer it as a basic methodology for the supervisory situation and stress the importance of developing definitive procedures such as these as a means of lending a systematic and even scientific tone to the supervisory experience.

Discussant: I was not clear as to whether the supervisor informed his supervisee of this conference.

Supervisor A: I would put it this way: our residents know everything.

Langs: That's excellent. And the parallel is, patients know everything too, up to a point. We should remember that. It's certainly true in regard to their unconscious sensitivities and their knowledge of the therapist. Take clinic patients. Before the therapist mentions a clinic holiday, the patient knows about it. Before the therapist can tell his patient he is leaving the clinic, the patient on some level seems to know. It is best to assume knowledge, and to recognize that if it is not conscious, it is often unconscious—though it is important too that we recognize that there are indeed some facts of which the patient is entirely unaware. In addition, I do not feel that this implies that it is the therapist's responsibility always to make such information explicit—though he should certainly inform his patients of holidays and forced terminations well before they can learn of them from other sources.

This has a direct bearing on an important issue for supervision, one I would like to introduce here so that we can discuss it as we go along. It is a problem that constitutes a real Scylla and Charybdis for the supervisory situation. I refer to the question as to whether the supervisee should directly inform the patient that his treatment is being supervised. There are some who advocate such a procedure on the grounds that the patient has a right to know. These people seem to overlook the fact that there exists a contradiction between this right and the influence of such a revelation on the treatment process. I will say this much for the moment: since my position is based on a conception of the importance of a secure framework to the patient and the therapy, and on an appreciation for the need to keep all modifications of the frame to an absolute minimum, it is my belief, supported by a number of specific clinical observations (see Langs 1973a), that it is in the patient's best interest that he *not* be explicitly told that there is a supervisor for the case. I have found that the direct reference to a third party severely compromises the therapeutic bipersonal field and generates in the patient quite disruptive and destructive negative introjects of his therapist.

On the other hand, I have found that in general the patient who comes for psychotherapy in a clinic is either quite conscious of the likelihood that his treatment is being supervised or has some unconscious knowledge in this regard that, for some reason, he fears to make explicit. In any case, the supervisee must strive to develop a capacity to recognize derivatives related to the patient's belief regarding the presence of a supervisor. The therapist must realize that the patient's impression or fantasy, though it may be distorted in the service of his pathology, is nevertheless based, if not always on reality, at least on something quite within the realm of possibility. And since it touches on an area of considerable vulnerability for the supervisee, who is bound to experience a considerable degree of anxiety in this respect, extensive countertransference-based difficulties are likely. The patient too is likely to be anxious and upset by the presence of a third party, although he will also unconsciously accept the intruder as a protector, as a means of curtailing the potential for therapeutic regression.

So since the situation asks a lot of both patient and therapist, the supervisee should always monitor the material from the patient for *commentaries*—fantasies and perceptions related to the therapeutic relationship and interaction. And when some adaptive context helps identify derivatives related to belief in the presence of a supervisor, he should interpret the patient's belief, and the fantasies that surround it, in a spirit that implicitly acknowledges its realistic core, that treats that component as undistorted, while at the same time he recognizes that the veridical core can prompt extensions into pathological and distorted unconscious fantasies—transference reactions—which can then be interpreted.

In this context I might mention a vignette from my technique book (1973, pp. 191-192). In brief, the therapist was seeing a divorced man in psychotherapy at a clinic, and the therapist would occasionally write notes. In one session, the patient chided the therapist, saying he thought the note-taking reflected a lack of interest. The therapist responded by telling the patient that he was a supervised case and that the notes were made in order to present clearly the content of the sessions.

In the following hour, the patient, who had silently accepted this answer, talked of not allowing his addict brother to be a leech who sucks off him, of being humiliated by a doctor who told his mother his penis was very small, and of a friend who had called him the previous night to offer him his wife for sexual relations. He then commented on not wanting to return to his previous career as a dancer because there were so many homosexuals around.

Now let's take, as the adaptive context for this sequence of associations, the therapist's informing the patient of the presence of the supervisor. And I stress to you that we should do exactly that: take any modification of the frame—here, a self-revelation that both modifies the therapist's anonymity and, by indicating the presence of a third party, alters both total confidentiality and the one-to-one relationship. Then we should, in principle, organize all the material that follows such a deviation—both in the session in which it occurs and in the hour following—around that adaptive context, and you can expect to obtain what I have called Type Two derivatives—indirect and disguised commentaries, mixtures of unconscious perception and introjection on the one hand, and unconscious fantasies on the other. All this in response to a simple alteration in the frame.

To perhaps underscore the obvious, I will give you a brief rundown of the Type Two derivatives yielded by this vignette. The therapist who uses the patient to learn from is in a sense a leech who sucks off and drains the patient—whatever other motives he might have, whatever other functions he might serve in the therapeutic relationship. Such a therapist is also behaving addictively and prostituting himself. He is dependent on the patient, using him for his own needs rather than confining the therapeutic situation entirely to the therapeutic needs of the patient. Also, the resident—or any therapist or analyst—who presents material from sessions to a supervisor or anyone else is exposing his patient and, in some sense, humiliating him as well. At the same time, the association to the leech-addict represents an introjective identification with a therapist whose therapeutic powers are so lacking and need for others so great that he must present his work to a supervisor for help. It is this aspect, of course, that might most readily be overlooked.

You can see, then, how these Type Two derivatives organized around a meaningful adaptive context contain delicate and fascinating mixtures of unconscious fantasy, unconscious perception, and unconscious introjection. There is a great deal of perceptiveness and, in addition, some degree of fantasy and distortion. But I would stress that one must respect the validity of the patient's fantasied experience here, and not shift immediately to the manifest reality with a claim that the therapist is simply trying to learn how to do effective work, and that all the rest is the patient's distortions. Both patient and therapist express themselves in manifest behaviors and communications and for both there are extensive unconscious reverberations. We must first recognize the validity of the unconscious implications of supervision for both patient and therapist before it will be possible to identify the truly distorted elements. As you can see, there is often more truth than fiction in a patient's response to a therapist-invoked modification of the frame.

To continue the vignette just briefly, the patient then went on to rather exquisitely describe a ménage à trois—and who is to say whether it is indeed the patient's psychopathology sexualizing the threesome, or whether it is a valid perception of the therapist's unconscious use of the patient in the supervisory, and even the therapeutic, relationship? Here, if we had a relatively well-analyzed therapist, we might truly believe that this is the patient's sexualization; but on the other hand, you can be quite sure that many therapists, of various degrees of inexperience, derive unconscious sexual gratification in the therapeutic interaction, at the expense of the patient. We must ask, too, whether this alteration in confidentiality inherently contains a thrust toward sexualization of the therapeutic relationship.

In any case, self-knowledge and an extensive examination of the patient's associations for valid and distorted communications would be essential to determining just how much of this is indeed a reflection of the patient's psychopathology—a primarily transference communication, based on unconscious transference fantasies prompted by a traumatic reality—and how much is an interactional sexualization—a shared and mutual sexual misalliance.

The same considerations apply to the patient's reference to homosexual dancers. Here again we see a condensation of the patient's own exhibitionistic and homosexual conflicts with those of the therapist, and it would take considerable exploration of both members of such a therapeutic dyad to determine the extent to which the therapist did indeed derive homosexual gratification in his presentation of this patient and the extent to which this was not the case, but largely a distortion by the patient. Incidentally, it is my belief that it would be impossible to resolve the underlying homosexual transference under conditions such as these, in which the therapist behaves in a manner that appears to gratify his own homosexual fantasies and provides a field in which the unconscious sexual fantasies and pathology of the therapist cannot be relatively excluded, so that the pathology of the patient in the same area can be clearly identified, explored, worked through, and resolved.

I hope that I have not taken you too far afield with that vignette. It was a dramatic experience for me as a supervisor to hear that material, and was pivotal in my learning about the impact of such direct revelations on the patient and the therapeutic field. And you can see too, from this rather blatant example, why I feel that the security of the frame is so vital to the therapeutic interaction and work—not because I feel the need to maintain an anxious secret, but because the therapist must create the best possible therapeutic field for the patient, however modified, as it must be in the case of supervised treatment situations.

There are many areas in which this type of conflict between the needs of the patient and the pressures of third parties, such as clinics and governments, will arise in the years to come. There are, for example, already some states that require specific notes and records on every patient seen by a physician—including psychotherapy and psychoanalysis. In contrast, it is my belief, and my finding, that it is best for the treatment of the patient to make no records at all, for the therapist to write no notes, and to enter each session as Bion (1970) advises—free of what we already know, so that we can get to what we don't know, free to listen creatively and to allow the patient to place into us, with as little bias within us as possible, the communications that we will need to understand his pathology in that particular hour.

So it is in the best interests of the patient for the therapist to not announce supervision, to not take notes, and to not maintain records. And as for the implicit presence of a supervisor when psychotherapy takes place in a clinic, you will find many well-disguised derivatives related to the presence of a third party in the material from all such patients—allusions to threesomes, to someone at work who has a supervisor, references to helping and observing figures, and, in situations where supervision begins to become effective, allusions to the fluctuations in the quality of the therapist's work as influenced by some type of observer or teacher. These references often appear in what I call *embedded form*, that is, as secondary qualities to some other major theme. For example, the patient is talking about his job and some particular problem he's having with it, and along the way slips in a reference to his supervisor that is not especially developed. Or he mentions in passing that he feels uncomfortable about being watched, while stressing some other aspect of the work situation. In any case, as I have indicated, there are strong needs for defense in this area on the part of both the patient and the therapist, and it is only when some major alteration of the frame serves as an adaptive context—one that evokes reactions to all insecure sectors of the framework—that some valid interpretive work can be done in this area, and then only so long as such efforts implicitly accept the reality of the situation, and move on from there to the patient's unconscious fantasies and eventual distortions.

Moving at last back toward the presentation at hand—

and I promise now to curtail further elaborations of what has become a rather extensive series of preliminary and orienting comments—I believe that the nature of the supervisory bipersonal field would permit an appropriate reference by a supervisor to the fact that he will be presenting aspects of the supervisory work to other professionals. It will create additional pressure on the supervisee; it will intensify those on the supervisor; and it will certainly modify that aspect of the supervisory framework that calls for the total confidentiality of supervision. Yet it should not seriously alter the communicative properties of the supervisory bipersonal field. You can see that I am suggesting—hypothetically, to be sure—that modifications of the framework in supervision do not have the same consequences as alterations in the framework of the therapeutic situation, and that many of the basic ground rules can be handled more flexibly in the supervisory experience. I do, however, believe that close adherence to the basic framework will produce the best conditions for the unfolding of the supervisory experience.

Well, it is time now to get some specific material with which to develop further discussions.

Supervisor A: I didn't comment on his being late. The thoughts that were going on in my mind were, indeed, that perhaps it did relate to his anxiety about not having the case he had originally called me about. But, in addition, there is some reality in the fact that we have the distinction of being in a building that is extremely difficult to find; the numbers are confusing, so mix-ups can occur.

Langs: Now, everything is in his unconscious: reality does exist, and yet—it may also be exploited unconsciously. But the point is that in a supervisory bipersonal field, it will be difficult to sort such things out. We should file them away pending further data and concentrate on the supervisee's work with his patient. At least for now.

Supervisor A: I felt that this was our first meeting and there might be some problem, and that I would wait and see.

Langs: Yes, but you are also presenting another aspect of supervision that I want to identify—every little element can have its implications. It is evident now that you are meeting in your office.

Supervisor A: Yes. He had asked to work with me, and our agreement was that he would come to my office.

Langs: That has an influence, and let me briefly attempt to identify it. As you undoubtedly know, there are many residencies where there is a firm requisite that supervision take place in the hospital setting. This is done so that the work is clearly experienced by the resident as part of his training. On a more practical level, it is an effort to protect the resident from having to travel all over town. Often, under special conditions, supervision would be permitted in the supervisor's office, but the requirement that it take place in the hospital setting also serves to foster the supervisor's commitment to the training program.

Now, going to the supervisor's office creates a certain ambience. There is, as a rule, a positive effect on the supervisee, although he can respond, too, by feeling rather inadequate by contrast, or even with envy. In any event, the supervisee will tend to experience more anxiety in a strange place, and of course the supervisor will himself generally feel more comfortable and secure in his own office. He will certainly be pleased with the saving in time occasioned by the supervisee's doing the traveling.

Now by and large, factors such as these tend to recede into the background, part of the framework and hold, unless they become an issue or happen to generate undue anxiety in one of the participants. The selection of the locale of supervision is therefore a secondary issue, one not fraught with the consequences locale has for psychotherapy. When, for example, a patient is seen in the therapist's private office, matters of anonymity and total confidentiality can be effectively secured; this is certainly not the case when a patient is seen in a clinic, or by a private therapist in a hospital setting complete with a secretary, charts, and all sorts of alterations in the frame. Let's hear more.

Supervisor A: I have one additional thought about my response to the supervisee's lateness. My own particular style of doing supervision is such that I don't make interpretations to the supervisee about his own personal conflicts. Nor do I attempt to explore possible indicators of such difficulties, such as the business of his lateness. So I didn't take up the lateness, and decided to wait to see what developed.

Now in this initial interview he spontaneously told me a few things about himself. Now here, too, I limit the amount of material that I permit the supervisee to give me about himself. I restrict it to just what I feel is needed to have an acquaintance with him, and I feel that any more personal information is best reserved for his own personal life and therapy, and does not belong in the supervisory situation.

Langs: You see immediately how endless the issues are in supervision and how quickly the material presented to us points us in an unexpected and yet important direction. Here, the supervisee comes in and wants to say something about himself on a rather personal level. How do we respond? Do we listen? Do we tell him not to bother? On the other hand, if he doesn't volunteer such information, do we, as supervisors, ask him about himself? And if so, what is it that we ask? Do we want a personal history? Do we want an outline of his professional experience? Do we want to know if he is in analysis or therapy, and with whom? How far do we go?

My own personal position is that I ask for no information about the supervisee at all. I will listen politely to what he has to offer, but if I feel he is attempting to use me as a therapist, or to dilute his own personal therapy, or to detract from the presentation of his therapeutic work, then I feel comfortable in interrupting him and suggesting that we get to his work with the patient. I stress that that should be the basic communicative material in the supervisory bipersonal field and should constitute our essential realm of discourse. I especially do not pry and do not ask for personal and confidential information, such as whether the supervisee is in treatment. I approach the supervisee as someone who wishes to learn the necessary techniques, and I tactfully and slowly try to teach him what he will have to know. I try first to develop his capacity to listen and organize the material from the patient, then to manage the framework, and, later, to intervene—interpret—effectively. But I will always modify this general sequence in keeping with the needs of the patient and the supervisee based on my observations of each specific therapeutic interaction.

I think we also have to realize that the therapist's own inner mental world, the extent of his positive capacities and of his own apparent inner difficulties as they are reflected in his work—his noncountertransference- and countertransference-based functioning—is probably the single most important influence on both his therapeutic work with his patient and his ability to learn in the supervisory situation. And, however tactfully and carefully this must be presented to him, based on his case presentation, I do not think it possible to spare the supervisee the painful awareness that much if not all of what goes wrong in therapy has to do with his own inner problems and his unresolved countertransferences. If he is in therapy or analysis, all to the good. If he is not, the chances are that he will quickly learn how much he needs to be in treatment, and he will soon wish that he sure as hell was (Laughter), that he had somewhere to take what he was working over, and someone to help him analyze it. You can believe that, and not because of me, not because of the supervisor I want you to be, but because of his patient, who will create intense pressures on him to resolve his inner difficulties and to become an effective therapist. The patient will himself make efforts to cure the therapist when he finds him in difficulty. In fact, these pressures can be avoided only through denial and through lacking the capacity to hear the patient in depth. Once you learn to listen to derivatives within an adaptive context you quickly come to recognize the extent of the patient's unconscious perceptiveness. You will also become attuned to his unconscious fantasies, memories, and introjects. And once this happens, you come to learn how much the patient unconsciously knows about your countertransference difficulties, and they become rather difficult to bear.

Once again, I am somewhat ahead of the material, but I have started to discuss the supervisee's countertransference problems. The question of the extent to which the supervisor should address such issues, and how he should go about it, has led to considerable controversy in the literature. At one extreme are those supervisors who feel that they have a responsibility consistently to identify the countertransference difficulties of the supervisee, and as much of their unconscious basis and implications as possible, doing so largely by forming impressions of the supervisee's work with the patient and confronting him with formulations. Some supervisors, in fact, actually attempt to do some type of what I would call bastard therapy—*lie therapy*—in the supervisory bipersonal field and, as you might expect, I do not think such work either feasible or desirable within the framework of supervision. It presents the supervisor as a negative and destructive introject and model of the wild analyst who intervenes inappropriately, without sufficient data, and with a distinctly aggressive and seductive tone, and who projectively identifies into the supervisee many aspects of his own unresolved unconscious countertransference difficulties.

At the other extreme are those supervisors who feel that there should be no allusions whatsoever to the supervisee's countertransference difficulties, that the supervisory bipersonal field is constructed as a learning and teaching situation, and that the exploration of countertransference belongs in the supervisee's therapy or analysis. These supervisors view the errors of the supervisee as manifest errors in technique and make no effort to identify or explore countertransference factors. Instead they respond primarily by indicating what they believe to be the proper intervention, and why they think it so.

There is, as always, a middle group, who approach supervision essentially as a teaching-learning experience, and who will on occasion suggest to the supervisee that a particular erroneous intervention appears to be based on countertransference difficulties. They leave the matter at that, for the self-exploration of the supervisee or for his treatment situation. I suspect that this is the most common approach; it is certainly the one that I was taught and that I experienced with most of my own supervisors.

My own approach is based on my model of supervision, and on my related model of the psychotherapeutic situation. Much of this stems from the bipersonal field concept, which holds that every experience within that field receives vectors from both patient and therapist, and that the contributions of each must be taken into account in understanding every experience—intrapsychic or interactional—within that field. I base all of my supervision on the communications from the patient and the therapist. Just as I endeavor to allow the patient to put into me and shape through his unconscious communications the interpretation or management of the framework that I should offer him in a particular hour, so I allow the communications from the patient and the therapist to shape my supervisory interventions. We begin by listening to the material from the patient and developing our formulation of the intrapsychically relevant adaptive context and of the unconscious fantasies and perceptions with which the patient has responded—Type Two derivatives. Or, we develop a thesis regarding either the absence of a clear-cut adaptive context or of Type Two derivatives, recognizing that the patient is for the moment communicating neither symbolically nor through illusion.

Here I have made a small but I think necessary detour in suggesting that the supervisor not only listens to the contents of the patient's communictions—and for adaptive contexts and the patient's unconscious responses—but that he attempts to ascertain the basic properties of the therapeutic bipersonal field and the basic mode of communication between the patient and the therapist. As I said earlier, the therapist is in a position to organize the patient's communications on three levels: manifest content; Type One derivatives, which are efforts at translations of the unconscious implications of that manifest content; and Type Two derivatives, which are organized around a specific adaptive context yielding dynamically meaningful unconscious fantasies and perceptions. Through studying the communicative interaction between patients and therapists, I have discovered (Langs 1978b) three basic communicative fields. Type A is the field tacitly assumed by classical analysts and analytically oriented therapists, a field in which symbolic, illusory communication prevails. This is the analytic situation as a transitional space (Winnicott 1971). Here there is a true quest for understanding and adaptive inner change, and here also, I must add, some of the more dreadful anxieties may be experienced, by either or both the patient or therapist—insight and growth do not come cheap.

The second type of communicative field, which I term Type B, is an action field characterized by the use of language and behaviors for projective identification, and for discharge and excretion. In such a field, interpretations of content are of little value, unless they are addressed to the projective identification and discharge qualities of the patient's efforts. I hasten to add that the therapist's countertransferences and his inappropriate alterations of the frame are critical contributors to the development of this type of field; the Type A field cannot be established or restored unless these errors are rectified.

The third type of field, Type C, is primarily a holding or static field, one in which either or both participants wish to confine communications to the manifest level, and in which there is little projective identifying or disturbance.

There is a great deal of relatively monotonous repetition. This is a field of barriers, falsifications, clichés, and the destruction of meaning. It is my preliminary impression that this type of field is constructed by patients and therapists who have been severely traumatized in their childhood and who have consequently developed a kind of rigid barrier to seal off a psychotic core which they dread experiencing and communicating, even in the treatment situation.

Now I mention all this because the basic supervisory task is not simply listening to the patient's associations and other communications, and attempting to formulate their unconscious meanings. Such a conception of the supervisory task, in which the basic principle of identifying resistances before other unconscious contents is well established, must be considerably extended, based on the model of therapy I have been developing. For example, you can now see that the supervisor must consistently monitor the therapist's management of the framework of the bipersonal field, and that he must do so both because of the patient's exquisite sensitivity to alterations of that frame and because of their importance in determining the meaning of words and actions within that field. Perhaps I could say it this way: The medium determines the message, and the medium is one crucial message among several—and a primary message, at that.

But you can see in addition how this requires that we get clear on the capacity of both patient and therapist for symbolic communication. We must be able to gauge the extent to which they use the therapeutic bipersonal field for discharge, action, and projective identification, and must be able to identify the basic qualities of the communicative amalgam they have formed. It is also more than evident that inappropriate or pathological shifts from a Type A to a Type B or C field may be initiated by the therapist, based on his countertransferences.

Now, having arrived back at the subject of countertransference, I shall briefly outline how I handle the supervisee's countertransferences in the supervisory situation.

I have taken my detour in order to establish the extent to which the therapist contributes to the nature of the therapeutic bipersonal field, and to the interaction and its meanings. I have also tried to make clear, and hope soon to clinically document, the extent to which the patient introjects the therapist's psychopathology as reflected in technical errors both in the verbal-interpretive sphere and in his management of the framework—a point nicely elaborated by Searles (1958, 1959, 1965, 1975).

But lest I be misunderstood as suggesting that this is the only type of introjective process that occurs in a therapeutic bipersonal field, before I trace out the influence of these pathologic introjects I want to stress, as I have in my *Therapeutic Interaction* (1976d), that patients experience adaptive and positive introjects when the therapist correctively manages the frame or offers a sound and meaningful interpretation. Here, for the moment, I am simply tracing out the influence of countertransference-based interventions—a problem that is, despite protests to the contrary, far more pervasive than most therapists and analysts are willing to acknowledge.

In any case, once the patient experiences the therapist's countertransference-based communications and projective identifications, he may either refuse to introject and contain them or, far more commonly, may take them unconsciously into himself, contain and experience them, and then respond. This introject—if I may oversimplify to present a model—is reflected in the patient's ongoing associations. And if we take the therapist's intervention as the adaptive context for those continued associations, we can determine what the therapist has unconsciously put into the patient—the valid core of the patient's perception that he may then go on to distort.

On this basis, then, the supervisor has an opportunity to identify and formulate the patient's experience of the therapist's countertransferences, and since this process is promoted by the supervisor's evaluation of the supervisee's intervention he should as a rule, after hearing an interpretation or observing an effort to manage the frame, attempt to evaluate the unconscious communications contained in the particular intervention. He should determine the extent to which they are in keeping with the patient's material and needs, and the extent to which they veer away from those functions and toward the inappropriate needs of the therapist—that is, the degree to which they reflect countertransferences.

The supervisor's conscious formulation of the pathological elements of the supervisee's intervention should be validated and echoed in the patient's unconscious communications, based on a pathological introject. This is material that will both confirm the supervisor's formulation and provide an opportunity to explore the supervisee's countertransference difficulties. I say opportunity, but really I believe this to be a necessity. The supervisor has no choice in this matter; he derives all his interventions from the material from the patient and from the supervisee's interventions, but he validates them largely through the patient's associations and, more rarely, through subsequent interventions from the therapist.

Once countertransference problems become central to the therapist's communications to the patient and have been introjected by the patient, their presence must be rectified, analyzed, worked through, and resolved before there can be interpretable access to the patient's psychopathology, before a Type B or C field can shift to Type A, before the patient can experience trust and return to stable therapeutic alliance, and before the essentially therapeutic communicative properties of the bipersonal field can be restored.

There are actually many more reasons that compel the supervisor to deal with the patient's introjection of the therapist's countertransferences and therefore with the therapist's countertransferences themselves, though essentially in terms of the patient's experience of them, but I think I have identified enough of them for the moment to convince you that this is not a matter of choice. This is where the patient is at, so to speak; it is the central problem of the bipersonal field for the moment, and its resolution is essential to the restoration of the treatment process. It offers the most meaningful—actually, the only meaningful—insights, positive introjects, and therapeutic effects available at that juncture.

Incidentally, it is this method of dealing with countertransferences that has gotten me into so much difficulty. There are many who feel that I am too confronting with my supervisees, that I communicate to them far more than they can handle, and that I'm preoccupied with the therapist's pathology to the point of being thought paranoid. I hope, once we hear some clinical material, to be able to clearly refute such criticisms by showing you that this method is an effort to identify exactly what the patient is unconsciously experiencing and that any avoidance of it will be detrimental to both the supervisory experience and the therapy itself.

So I am suggesting that the supervisee's countertransferences must be pointed out to him by the supervisor to the extent that they are introjected and metabolized by the patient, and reflected in his associations. I have also tried to indicate that this must be done quite gently, and that it is helpful if it is carried out predictively, through an initial assessment of the supervisee's intervention or failure to intervene, and through a full delineation of the unconscious meanings of an assessed error. This should all be presented as a means of anticipating the introjection and subsequent unconscious communications from the patient. Now this of course implies extensive confrontations of the supervisee, confrontations he may be quite unprepared for. But since this is significant to the patient's mental state, his experiences of the interaction, and to the conditions of the treatment, it is my belief that the supervisee cannot, however unfortunately, be spared such formulations. Later, when we have some specific material for illustration, I will be quite pleased to answer questions on this particular point. For the moment I would like to move on to some additional material from this supervisory interaction.

Discussant: Unfortunately, your comments do raise a number of questions, and I would appreciate some clarification. For one thing, I am not clear about your use of the term *projective identification*. For another, could you extend your comments a bit regarding your approach to the supervisee's countertransferences? I find these introductory discussions very provocative and illuminating.

Langs: Projective identification is a confusing and sometimes frightening term. Perhaps a better term would be *interactional projection*, an effort by the subject, whether patient or therapist, to place contents, processes, defenses, and the like into the object—aspects of his inner mental world with which he remains identified—and to evoke an introjective identification on the part of the object as well. These are communications that have evocative qualities. Not all behaviors and associations—nor all interventions—constitute projective identifications, though it is quite likely that any intervention by the therapist, because of its special provocative and evocative aspects, is likely to contain some degree of projective identification. This is especially so when the intervention is erroneous; correct interventions and proper managements of the frame are less likely to have such qualities, though they will often contain positive, constructive, nonpathological projective identifications, which are reflected in positive introjects.

For the moment, I am stressing the therapist's pathological projective identifications into the patient, largely because they are a topic much neglected, even by the Kleinians, and because they are so common in therapists-in-training. They are also far more common in sophisticated analysts than has been recognized in the literature. And since some readers have misunderstood *The Bipersonal Field* (Langs 1976a) in this repect, I want to stress that I am well aware that a balanced view of the therapeutic interaction would take into account the pathological and constructive projective identifications of both participants. The emphasis in that volume, and in this discussion, on the therapist's pathological projective identifications arises from the nature of the data presented rather than from any bias in my view of the bipersonal field.

I must add too that the patient is under no obligation to introjectively identify with the projective identifications of the therapist. He may be refractory, may refuse to function as what I have termed a *pathological container*—that is, as an inappropriate metabolizer or even victim of the therapist's pathological interactional projections. However, almost always, the patient will indeed introject such contents and defenses, and will then work over this introjective identification, in terms both of its actual nature and of extensions based on the patient's own needs, pathological as well as nonpathological.

In response to such introjects, the patient may create a misalliance with the therapist and enter into unconscious collusion with him as a means of maintaining his own neurosis or more severe pathology. But in addition, he will characteristically attempt, unconsciously, to cure the pathological therapist-introject, and to communicate these curative and corrective efforts to the therapist—a point developed by Searles (1965, 1975) and myself (Langs 1976a,d).

Here I am taking a position regarding the therapist's errors somewhat at odds with the few discussions of this subject in the literature, for example, those by Reich (1960) and Greenson (1971); they believe that technical errors may reflect either countertransference or ignorance and poor training. I feel that despite the latter factors there is *always* an element of countertransference in *any* erroneous intervention, in any mismanagement of the frame, and I have been able to confirm this hypothesis personally in every such instance.

I should also point out that technically the therapist must strive to identify the precise nature of a pathological introject derived within the patient from the therapist's errors. He must intervene implicitly and in a way that accepts the valid elements in the patient's experience, noting that the patient has taken in a particular intervention as a destructive or seductive pressure. Further, it is essential to identify the exact contents and mechanisms that have been erroneously placed into the patient. Once that is established, the therapist can proceed to identify the patient's reactions to the interactional projection—the unconscious collusion, the unconscious metabolism and interpretation, or whatever.

You will find that these unconscious interpretations take the form of indirect allusions to the patient's perceptions and fantasies regarding the presence and basis of the therapist's errors. And they usually are shaped as rather general indirect interpretations, such as the patient's referring to someone, even herself, who has a problem because she is so irrationally angry with her mother. And if we know the adaptive stimulus—the unconscious communications contained in the erroneous intervention—we can identify the unconscious meanings and communications directed to the therapist by the patient. You will soon discover that these unconscious efforts by the patient are usually very perceptive and constructive.

However, I must stress that I do not ask the supervisee to confirm either my formulations regarding his countertransferences—based on the material from the patient, of course—or the unconscious interventions of the patient. In the supervisory bipersonal field I believe that the supervisee should have no obligation to periodic self-revelation. I feel, as I have stated more generally before, that this is not the appropriate realm of the supervisory field, and that it cannot offer the conditions in which sufficient data is available for this type of analysis and its validation. Efforts in this direction are both intrusive and disruptive; they are a form of inappropriate prying that generates a basically destructive image of the supervisor and his work. Such efforts set a poor tone for the teaching of psychotherapy and would compromise the learning experience.

On the other hand, I do feel that it is crucial that every formulation offered by the supervisor be confirmed by the continued associations and behaviors of the patient.

Remember, I attempt in principle to develop my comments to the supervisee in a manner that contains initial—silent, if you will—validations. I listen to the patient's associations and then either indicate that I would have intervened at a given moment and believe that the therapist's silence is in error, or I listen to an intervention from the therapist and suggest that it is either ill-timed or incorrect in terms of its contents. I refer here, for the moment, to those interventions that are countertransference-based, and leave aside those interventions that the supervisor feels the therapist has made in a valid manner—situations where I expect significant validation from the patient.

So, I have my own formulation. I then indicate how I would have intervened or the nature of the therapist's error, in depth. And then I listen to the patient's subsequent associations. It is these associations that must validate my formulation through Type Two derivatives if I am to feel that I have made a supervisory intervention that is correct. If I fail to obtain such validation, I must, as I would in the clinical situation, be prepared to reformulate. Here too, by the way, the patient should be quite helpful to me as a supervisor, much as he would be with the therapist. But in essence I am indicating again that validation of supervisory formulations must be derived from the material from the patient—that they can be and should.

So, my suggestions regarding the handling of the therapist's countertransferences is based on the patient's needs, and not on some inappropriate model of supervision in which efforts are made to be therapeutic toward the supervisee even though such endeavors are essentially unfeasible. It is what the patient is dealing with, and the supervisee must be in touch with it too. Here it becomes quite clear that my model of supervision is derived from my model of psychotherapy, and that my understanding of the nature of the supervisory process and the responsibilities of the supervisor are similarly founded. And for the moment, I am stressing aspects of my interactional view of psychotherapy, and the patient's introjection of the expressions of the therapist's countertransferences.

Unfortunately, but I think quite inevitably, one of the major blind spots in analysis has been in the area of countertransference, and this was as true of Freud as of his followers to this day. This is reflected in Freud's relative neglect of the subject, and in the fact that one aspect of his momentous discovery of transference is that its very recognition undoubtedly served a defensive function for him—as it does for many analysts to this day. Often enough the analyst's stress on the genetic aspects of so-called transferences—on the seemingly distorted elements in the patient's responses to the analyst—serve as a defense against recognizing the current meanings of such communications vis-à-vis the analytic interaction, especially the valid components containing the patient's unconscious perceptions of the analyst's countertransferences.

In fact, it has occurred to me of late that one could state and fairly well document that Freud's discovery of transference was derived from material from his patients that was essentially nontransference-based—that is, primarily perceptive and nondistorted, rather than fantasy-based and pathological—though these perceptions and introjects were then, of course, intrapsychically elaborated (Langs 1976,1978d,e). And I think that Freud's shift from believing that his patients had been traumatized in reality—the so-called seduction hypothesis—to a position that emphasized the role of isolated unconscious fantasies and memories in neurosogenesis (the imagined aspects of the genetic dimension) has many similar qualities to his position regarding the patient's relationship with the analyst. In both areas he shifted away from the influence of actualities, past and present, and stressed the role of fantasies relatively divorced from the realities which evoked them and to which they were an inner response. Both Szasz (1963) and Chertok (1968) have made somewhat similar points. This is not, of course, meant to in any way discount the sheer genius reflected in Freud's unprecedented recognition that communications to the therapist could be both distorted and derived from an earlier important figure in the patient's life.

I am reminded too of an aspect of the discovery of transference that relates to the supervisory process. You may recall that it was actually Freud's observations of Breuer and his work with Anna O. (Breuer and Freud 1893-1895; see also Chertok 1968), in something of a supervisory capacity, that first enabled him to discover transference—a phenomenon he later identified in his own clinical work (see Freud 1925b). This is undoubtedly the first recorded instance of an aspect of supervision to which I alluded earlier—namely, that being removed from the direct therapeutic interaction enhances one's capacity to observe, formulate, and create, despite the limitations that stem from the lack of direct contact with the patient. This limitation undoubtedly has to be rectified through confirmatory observations of supervisory formulations in one's own therapeutic experiences. Still, creativity and research interests will disturb the therapeutic bipersonal field, while they have a less disruptive influence on the supervisory field—far more creative work should be done there.

Discussant: When you use the term *countertransference*, I gather that you are including the therapist's transference to the patient, as well as his countertransference more narrowly conceived—that is, on the one hand, the therapist's pathological predispositions toward the patient and, on the other, his responses either to the patient's transferences, to use the term in our sense, or to any other aspect of the material from the patient.

Langs: I had wanted to get to additional material from our supervisor, but I see that you share with me a need to clarify basic concepts and definitions. And your question is an important one. The literature is rather muddled in this area. Some have attempted to distinguish the therapist's transferences to the patient from his countertransferences.

The former, as you said, are seen as based on the therapist's own unconscious pathological fantasies about the patient. These are distortions based on the therapist's earlier pathological (genetic) experiences as they disturb his perception of, and reactions to, the patient. In this context, countertransference is defined as the therapist's distorted and pathological responses to the patient's transferences. This definition is sometimes extended, as you said, to inappropriate responses to any aspect of the material from the patient (see Sandler et al. 1973).

However, once you adopt an interactional approach to countertransference, the therapist's transferences to the patient and his countertransferences merge and cannot actually be distinguished. The two intermingle and the definition of which type of pathological response predominates come to depend on who is the prime mover: the therapist (his transferences) or the patient (countertransferences). In addition, the term *therapist's transferences* is not in common use.

As a result, I adopt a simple definition and use the term *countertransference* alone, defining it as all unconscious, pathological, and distorting fantasies and introjects which disturb the therapist's interaction and work with his patient. That definition stresses the basis of countertransference expressions in unconscious contents and defenses, and permits in turn a broad definition of the influence of these pathological inner tendencies. Actually, they may affect every aspect of treatment: the therapist's basic relationship to the patient, the therapeutic alliance, the management of the frame, the nature of his interventions, his actual perception of the patient, his work in general, and the like.

Such a definition of countertransference, in its adaptational sense, would require an adaptive context usually in the interaction with the patient, as the evocative factor in the countertransference-based response. It would leave room for secondary adaptive contexts in the analyst's outside relationships or in his interaction with his other patients—something that would be difficult to include in the definitions you gave.

My conception stresses the unconscious basis of countertransference. It creates a requisite for efforts directed toward self-awareness by the therapist, through the study of his own subjective experiences and derivatives, and, of course, through an analysis of the communications from the patient. As you can see, the interactional viewpoint enables us to recognize that the patient's material is a valid and extremely useful means of detecting one's own countertransferences, a point first made by Little (1951) and which both Searles (1965, 1975) and myself (1975a, 1976a,d; see also chapter 5) have elaborated.

My definition also establishes an area of non-countertransference functioning in the therapist. This includes all adaptive and appropriate conscious and unconscious fantasies that the therapist has toward his patient, and the entire realm of his valid and sensitive functioning in the therapeutic interaction. With all the stress that I have placed so far on the countertransferences of supervisees, this gives me an opportunity to point out that the supervisor should also be alert to the supervisee's valid and insightful functioning. He certainly should be prepared to acknowledge and discuss such aspects when they are in evidence. He must, as always, make efforts to validate his assessment, even when it is positive, doing so through the subsequent material from the patient. It is sometimes said that I am unduly harsh and critical of my supervisees, and that many of my interventions are too direct and even premature. But I would hope to soon demonstrate to you that I am well aware of the traumatic qualities of the necessary confrontations to a supervisee. I express myself not only with tact and concern, but also with appropriate and controlled humor and humanity; and essentially I offer the information he must have in order to work effectively with the patient.

So, to return at long last to our point of departure, personal data about the supervisee is not essentially relevant to the supervisory work as I conceive it. While a limited amount of information may help develop the supervisory alliance, it may just as readily create difficulties; one must treat such communications on an individual basis. I certainly would not attempt to elicit such material. I would thereby make clear implicitly that the structure of the supervisory field is somewhat different than the treatment situation, and that we will pursue the emotional difficulties of the patient, not those of the supervisee—except insofar as they are reflected in his interaction with his patient.

It may well be that, unconsciously, the offer of personal information by the supervisee constitutes either an appeal for help of some kind, a warning, or even an effort to have a supervisor go easy. It would be difficult to tell right off, though its implications would become much clearer in the supervisee's responses to the supervisor's interventions. This reminds me of Ekstein's and Wallerstein's book (1958) where there is a reference to the resident who comes to the supervisor and says, forget about supervision, will you take me as a patient? And here, I would emphasize that not only does the supervisory situation preclude any possibility of therapy with the supervisee, but also that, if you have met the supervisee in the context of a supervisory situation, it will not be feasible for you ever to be an effective therapist to him. The contaminants, and the unconsciously shared defenses and gratifications, will be relatively unmodifiable.

Discussant: It seems to me that much of what you are saying relates to the concept of transference. I wonder how you would relate your ideas to the problem of transference resistances?

Langs: Well, I don't believe that I have defined transference specifically, although I have offered some relevant concepts and have been making some implicit use of the concept. Again, I will offer a brief orienting definition, and suggest that those of you who are interested can read the relevant sections in my recent two-volume work, *The Therapeutic Interaction* (1976d). Basically, I believe that there are two types of transference: first, *classical transference*, which refers to all behaviors and communications from the patient to the therapist that are based on distorting and pathological unconscious fantasies, memories, and introjects. These unconscious contents and defenses lead to unconscious and conscious fantasies about, and responses to, the therapist that are inappropriate to the actualities of the therapeutic relationship, and yet appropriate to some past pathological relationship.

I would stress here that the core of a classical transference response is an unconscious fantasy about the therapist and that its elements may relate to wishes, defenses, superego components, and the like. I would also like to stress that the manifestations of this pathological unconscious fantasy may appear in direct, though distorted, references to the therapist, but may also appear in disguised form in communications about other persons and in direct interactions with them. Transference expressions are not confined to references to the therapist, nor to obvious displacements. The basic understanding should be that every communication from the patient includes a transference component, a point first specifically suggested by Klein (1952), although Freud (1900, 1925b) did make passing reference to it.

I also have found that every transference-based reaction is prompted by some adaptive context, most often within the therapeutic interaction itself. As a rule, those reactions in the patient that are primarily transference-based (and there is always an intermixture of transference and nontransference, distorted and valid responsiveness) are usually prompted by such hurtful inevitable realities as vacations and by the degree of inevitable hurt that may be found in every valid intervention. The core of classical transference, then, is a displacement onto the therapist from a past figure, and the main intrapsychic mechanisms are repression and displacement. It is, by the way, my finding and position that even within psychotherapy every communication and experience of the patient has a transference element, quite often a significant one.

The second basic form of transference I would term *interactional transference*. These responses are also based on unconscious and pathological fantasies and introjects within the patient, as they influence his interaction with the therapist; and they, too, have genetic antecedents. However, their main characteristic is the effort by the patient to actualize the transference expression in his relationship with the therapist. In this form of transference, the patient inappropriately uses projective identification, and becomes involved in unconscious efforts to evoke responses and roles in the therapist.

Certainly, the two forms of transference overlap. But I think it helpful to separate the interactional form from the classical, because we tend to think of the latter in terms of fantasy and symbolic communication, rather than in terms of effort at direct, interactional realization. However, Sandler (1976) has recently discussed efforts to actualize classical transference. So it may well be that we can return to a basic conception of transference in terms of its genetic roots, and then describe various efforts to actualize or otherwise express these unconscious transference fantasies and introjects. This would leave room for the role of displacement and fantasy formation, and for the use of projective identification and efforts to actualize transference contents and defenses.

But I must add this: basic to the definition of transference is the definition of nontransference. That is, it requires a full appreciation of the patient's nondistorted unconscious fantasies and introjects, and of his valid functioning and veridical conscious and unconscious perceptions of the therapist. These too are expressed in derivative and sometimes direct form in the therapeutic interaction, and secondarily in outside relationships. There are also nonpathological projective and introjective identifications.

Analysts have followed the lead of Freud in viewing transference as the basic medium of the therapeutic interaction, and nontransference as secondary. They have now also attempted to distinguish between transference and the so-called real relationship. Without going into the pitfalls of these two approaches (see Langs 1976d), I would like to suggest that the basic attitude of the therapist with his patient should be one in which he first assesses the patient's communications for their valid and nondistorted components. This process must be founded on his own capacity to know and test reality, including the actual unconscious implications of his own behaviors and communications to the patient and his own private inner reality. The second step in his assessment of the patient's material should be to identify what stands beyond these veridical elements: distortions, inappropriate defenses, inappropriate efforts at gratification, and all types of unrealistic fantasies, perceptions, and behaviors. That is the realm of transference, though it is never divorced from both its reality precipitants on the one side, and their influences on reality—especially the therapist—on the other.

As for transference resistance, much of what I am discussing with you pertains to the problem of resistances, with a full appreciation of its complexities. Transference resistances are those obstacles to therapeutic progress that derive from unconscious transference fantasies. Resistances to transference is a related concept which generally implies an avoidance by the patient of manifest or easily identifiable displaced allusions to the analyst or therapist himself. In my own work (1976a,d), I have stressed the role of what I call *interactional resistances*: obstacles to analytic progress and defenses shared, usually unconsciously, by both patient and therapist. However, many of these obstacles turn out to be complicated interactional and intrapsychic amalgams, with specific unconscious sources in the patient, the therapist, or both.

Discussant: Would you please state the goal of psychotherapy?

Langs: Yes. But I must be brief. It is the resolution of the patient's symptoms and characterological disturbances achieved essentially through insightful adaptive inner change and through the inevitable positive introjective identifications that accrue to a patient in his experiences with a therapist who capably manages the framework and interprets.

This leads me to state the goals of supervision, which I will define as the education of the therapist; as teaching him the basic techniques of therapy; and as involving him with the relevant background literature. Secondarily, the goal is to build a healthy investment in doing insightful psychotherapy and to implicitly encourage a constructive introjective identification with a well-functioning supervisor.

Discussant: Some suggest that the goal of therapy is to make conscious for the patient what is unconscious.

Langs: You can see again how every question raises complicated issues, and how we can continue to be sidetracked with many of them. In brief, it is my position that making unconscious contents and mechanisms conscious for the patient is indeed one of the means through which we achieve the goals I have mentioned, just as reconstructing past significant traumas and fantasies is another and related means.

But basically, there are two avenues of adaptive inner change for the patient: one derives from the cognitive insights gained by the patient through the therapist's interpretations, and here the shift from unconscious to conscious state plays an important role. The other is the patient's inevitable identifications with the well-functioning therapist; there, rendering unconscious contents and the like into a conscious state may not play a significant role.

And I want to stress a point that I have discussed extensively in *The Therapeutic Interaction* (Langs 1976d), to the effect that I have found that the patient makes continued introjective identifications of the analyst's conscious and unconscious communications and their implications. They are inevitable processes, but this does not mean they should not be analyzed. Rangell (1968) and Reich (1960) were especially critical of analysts who attempt to use introjective identification as a primary vehicle of cure, and who forgo the interpretive and reconstructive work that is so vital to the specific resolution of the patient's intrapsychic conflicts and the modification of pathological introjects. I would agree with them in part, but would also stress that all evidence of conscious or unconscious identification, admiration, idealization, or overidealization should be responded to with listening within the relative adaptive context and with interpretation where indicated.

So there are both cognitive and interactional aspects to the cure of the patient in psychotherapy. And I am suggesting that within the limits imposed by the psychotherapeutic situation, these are the basic goals and methods of therapy, as well as of analysis. Again, this does not imply that one can accomplish quite as much in therapy as in analysis, or work as deeply in therapy as in the analytic situation. But it does suggest that there is essentially one sound and basic model of treatment; that its proper application pertains to all types of psychotherapeutic situation; that patients themselves react negatively when a therapist or analyst deviates from this model; and that one applies the model in keeping with the patient's needs, pathology, strengths, treatment modality, and the like.

Incidentally, the identificatory processes offer general ego strengthening, while the cognitive insights assist the patient in resolving specific conflicts and pathological interactions.

Discussant: I am not clear, then, as to how you deal with resistances in therapy.

Langs: Much of this will become clear once we hear some

specific clinical material. I think that the fundamental principle is that we initiate the therapeutic work and interventions with the analysis of defenses and resistances, rather than with interpretations of instinctual drive derivatives; that is still a basic and acceptable tenet. I would suggest only that resistances are not mechanistic defenses, but are themselves built out of unconscious fantasies, introjects, and the like, as described by many of the Kleinians. On the surface they are an expression of the ego's defenses, while in depth they are derivatives of unconscious fantasies and introjects which, structurally speaking, have contributions from id, ego, and superego. Often, they are both intrapsychic and interactional; the latter implies significant contributions from the therapist, which must be both rectified and interpreted.

I would just add this: therapists should be cautious in working with resistances. Inappropriate confrontations with resistances may well be the single most extensive means through which therapists express their unresolved unconscious countertransference-based hostility toward their patients. At such times patients are viewed as the enemy, rather than as people with mixed intentions, both curative and destructive, directed both toward themselves and toward you as therapists.

Discussant: Coming back to the supervisory situation, I sometimes tell the supervisee a bit about myself and my background, and I now wonder about your position in that regard.

Langs: Well, as I said before, I do not make personal inquiries of the supervisee, although I will allow a moderate amount of such information to be communicated by him if he has the need. Similarly, I do not make a practice of informing the supervisee of my background or current position, although I do so in the course of the supervision, where it seems appropriate or helpful. I also allow room for occasional personal but not inappropriately revealing comments. I almost always confine these to the professional sphere, and will make them only when they seem pertinent to a problem at hand. Also, I do so only where I feel that such occasional remarks help solidify the supervisory relationship.

Discussant: I would like to ask the supervisor how he obtained the material he is presenting. Did he record these sessions? Did he take notes, or is he using the notes of the supervisee?

Supervisor A: I am using notes that I myself made both during and after the supervisory session.

Langs: You raised an important issue, and I would like to make a brief comment. As you may know, based on my understanding of the functions of the ground rules and framework, I maintain the position that the therapist should not record his sessions with patients. Such a procedure introduces the potential for leakage of material, and the possibility of modifications in total confidentiality and the one-to-one relationship. It implies the use of the patient and his session for some inappropriate need, however rationalized, of the therapist. And it generates extensive disturbances in the communicative properties of the therapeutic field, both on this basis and because of the inevitable negatively toned incorporative image of the therapist derived from this type of behavior.

Similarly, in the usual supervisory situation, the process should unfold based on the presentation of process notes written by the supervisee after the therapy hour, presented as I said, in strict sequence. The recording of a supervisory experience should take place only under extraordinary conditions, such as this conference, and with as full awareness as possible of its complicating influence.

Ekstein and Wallerstein (1958) describe a procedure in which the therapist would dictate a note on a given session and send it to his supervisor, who would then read it before the supervision. The two would then talk about the problems that either wished to explore. I can only iterate my belief that supervision should unfold as an interactional experience, as a description of the interaction between patient and therapist—in strict sequence. To the extent that the notes are confined to the patient's and supervisee's communications, the supervisor has a special opportunity to experience the process, the communications, and their conscious and unconscious implications. There is an opportunity to make predictions and to validate them, rendering an important quality to the supervisory work that has crucial implications for how the supervisee will work with his patient. This method also gives the supervisee an opportunity to validate his supervisor's comments, a process that we should not only be aware of, but which we should encourage.

Far too often there is an arbitrary quality both to psychotherapy itself and to supervision. It is generally taken for granted that the supervisor must be right; he is idealized, though sometimes the supervisee feels that he simply must be wrong. Disagreements are based on ill-defined impressions, and seldom on the sequential listening to the material from the patient, the interventions of the therapist, and the subsequent responses of the patient.

Every comment by the supervisor should be subjected to the validating process, and every similar or contradictory hypothesis offered by the supervisee, either directly to the supervisor or through his interventions to the patient, should also be so subjected. Supervision should be conducted in a manner that permits validation. We have a methodology and we must develop and use it to the fullest extent possible. In addition to teaching the supervisee the basics of listening, formulating, and intervening, we must also impart to him the essentials of the validating process. And we do this by discussing and developing it with him, and both by making consistent use of it within the supervisory situation in regard to our formulations of the patient's material, and by stressing the supervisee's use of validation in responding to every piece of supervisory work.

This means too that you should openly acknowledge those situations where the patient's material does not confirm your formulation, and that you should engage in efforts with the supervisee to understand the basis of your error—much as you would in exploring the factors involved when he makes a mistake. And while unexpected recollections of material and information on the part of the supervisee may sometimes, as noted by Arlow (1963) among others, confirm the supervisor's formulation, I want to stress that the basic realm of validation lies within the communications from the patient—in both the treatment situation itself and in supervision.

And finally, remember too that nonconfirmation from the patient is a directive to understand the basis of your error, and to explore its countertransference elements—the contributions of your own psychopathology—even in the supervisory situation. You should do that work within yourself, however, without burdening the supervisee. Technically, of course, nonvalidation is an indication of the need to reformulate, using the subsequent material from the patient as your guide. In contrast, as you would expect, if you do supervision arbitrarily and by fiat, unconsciously you are encouraging the supervisee to do psychotherapy in that way. And despite your verbal protests, this is the kind of introject he will derive from his work with you.

As there are for the moment no further questions, now would be a good time for our short midmorning break. We will take ten minutes, after which I would like to turn more extensively to the presentation.

Chapter 2

Some Basic Issues

Langs: Could you now take up where you left off?

Supervisor A: One of the things he told me was that he did not plan to enter analysis himself.

Langs: Well, you can all sense that even in a field not structured for the free associations of the supervisee, he will at times do just that, and will offer in the process validating personal communications in response to your own silent hypothesis concerning his anxieties and resistances. Some supervisors might respond with some kind of understanding and reassuring comment, as a means of trying to create a more positive atmosphere; others would recognize his anxiety and intense state of conflict, but would remain silent for the moment. Here I believe it is a matter of personal choice, so long as one does not attempt to shift toward a therapeutic or interpretive intervention and thereby inappropriately create a quasi-therapeutic field. Direct reassurance has essentially no place in psychotherapy, though it may serve a function in the supervisory bipersonal field. I have found that so-called supportive interventions prove quite destructive in the treatment situation (Langs 1973, 1976a,d), while implicitly supportive interpretations serve quite well. On the other hand, more direct support may have some small calming influence in the supervisory field, while interpretations will prove ultimately threatening and disruptive.

Notice the nature of his conflict: he wishes to be neither an analyst nor an analysand—yet he desires supervision from an analyst. I would anticipate that as a therapist and supervisee, he will similarly profess an interest in insight-oriented therapy but will be consistently frightened by the patient's inner mental world—the derivatives of his unconscious fantasies and the like. On this hypothesis, I would be alert to this aspect of his work. I would then expect to make efforts later on, when the material permits, to alert him to this inner conflict when it is adversely affecting his work with his patient.

Supervisor A: I then got into the question of what sort of patient he had been seeing. He told me that he is fairly well into his residency, and it was my impression that he is rather obviously a very capable, bright young man. The reports on him that I had heard up to that time indicated that he is respected in the department.

Langs: I wonder how you all reacted to hearing that the supervisor had advance information regarding the supervisee, third-party observations that apparently influenced his attitude toward him? Now I am well aware that the imparting of such information is quite common within training programs. But I am immediately struck by how it is bound to bias the supervisor, and how in some sense it contaminates the supervisory bipersonal field.

I really think that the supervisee should have the chance to present himself and his work with his patient on his own terms, so you may experience him on various levels without prejudice. This affords you the opportunity of an independent evaluation and, more important, of a chance to approach him without bias and as someone you look forward to teaching.

For some reason or other, administrators of training programs have a need to share their impressions and those of others with many of their supervisors. You hear them saying that they are sending you this one because he is the worst resident in the program and maybe you can do something with him. Or they apologize for sending you someone known to be cantankerous and difficult. Or they imply that they are sending you a very special gift in the form of their best trainee. Whatever.

And all of this seems grossly unfair to the supervisee. It deprives him of an independent evaluation through which you may well discover his assets or liabilities. And it could slant your supervisory approach to the detriment of both patient and therapist—toward expecting either too much or too little. Finally, it may lead you inappropriately to offer too much or too little to the supervisee.

Incidentally, the same problem exists in a far more destructive form in your direct work with patients. It should be possible for you to overcome prejudices placed into you in anticipation of meeting a supervisee. But secrets about a patient you see in consultation through a referral from a colleague who has told you about his own consultation with the patient create contaminants to the therapeutic bipersonal field destructive both to yourself and to the patient. In principle, I never see a patient in consultation if I do not have time for therapy or analysis. I don't go through this business of sending them to someone else. I think that practice is quite destructive to the patient, and I do not believe that there is any service that I can offer to the patient that cannot be provided by a well-qualified colleague. I in no way want to be a third party to a treatment, or someone who abandons the patient; such experiences are quite detrimental to the therapeutic process.

Similarly, if for some reason a colleague has seen a

patient in consultation and calls to refer the patient to me for treatment, I go through an elaborate explanation about why I prefer to see the patient fresh and without prior knowledge. I indicate that I want to allow the therapeutic interaction to begin and unfold without contamination, and discuss how any information that he could tell me about the patient is really not helpful or pertinent. I tell him too that I especially do not want to be party to a breach of confidentiality, someone with secrets about the patient, which I would then have to either confess or conceal at the very moment I am initiating a consultation and therapeutic experience. This practice is a modification in the framework that, despite the contrary belief of the offending parties, is not in the service of the patient, and is usually in the service of the countertransference propensities of both participants. It is only because I have so consistently established a countertransference basis for such alterations in the framework that I feel I can allude to aspects of their underlying basis. But I ask for forgiveness for having spoken without data, and for acceptance of my need to offer an important model that I have documented extensively elsewhere (1975a, b, 1976a).

In any case, I find that nonpsychiatric referring physicians are actually better able to tolerate and accept my position in this respect. And I go so far as to establish with them the fact that I will not at all communicate with them after they have referred a patient to me, adding that they can always be certain that I will either have seen the patient myself and initiated treatment, or made a suitable referral after speaking with the patient on the telephone.

So, returning to the supervisory situation, we should, as a matter of technical principle, see a supervisee without prior information, and should avoid all unnecessary contaminants of the supervisory bipersonal field. Please go on.

Supervisor A: He responded that he had a few patients whom he had been following for more than a year in psychotherapy. In particular, he had had a female patient whom he had been seeing for twice a week for over one hundred hours, but the patient had interrupted therapy just a few months ago and had returned to her native city. He had had a significant amount of supervision regarding this patient from various supervisors on the staff of this center, and he said that he could think of at least four different supervisors who had worked with him on the case.

Langs: I trust that this means in sequence, rather than simultaneously.

Supervisor A: Yes, but I sensed a note of upset or even resentment in his tone, and a hint of an effort on his part to blame the supervision for the loss of the patient.

Langs: This brings us to an important principle of supervision: there should be one supervisor to a case at a given time. I have had some personal experience in running continuous case seminars, and in doing supervision as a consultant, in which I was a second simultaneous supervisor for a supervisee and his patient. And without going into detail, I found that as a rule, this is a terrible contamination of the supervisory bipersonal field, that it sets up impossible crosscurrents, and that it creates turmoil and conflicts within the supervisee to the point where his work with the patient is seriously disrupted. After all, disagreements are all too common and both supervisors feel that they are intervening in a valid fashion, and the supervisee usually has not mastered the validating process, through which he might make a sensible choice. The result is an extended field of destructive rivalries, conflicting allegiances, efforts by one of the threesome to play the other off against the third, and an endless array of unmanageable complications.

In general, I would also propose that a change in supervisor be undertaken only under special conditions, such as when a case has been going badly for some time. A change may also be called for when there is a problem in the supervisory relationship or a strong feeling in either supervisor or supervisee that something irreparable and disruptive is taking place between them. The issue of when to change supervisors is very complicated, and for that reason we should address it toward the end of this seminar rather than at this point. For the moment I would, however, like to point out that the supervisor must maintain a realistic perspective regarding his responsibility to the supervisee and to the patient, and in respect to the extent of his influence on the therapeutic process he is supervising. It is rather obvious that this is not easy to assess, and that one could err either toward overstating the supervisor's responsibility, or toward understating it. Pathological residuals of narcissistic and other needs being what they are, there is a general tendency among supervisors to blame the patient or the supervisee when a treatment situation he is supervising does not go well. This is of course, the supervisory version of the tendency among many therapists to blame the patient when problems arise, in the patient or in the therapy, rather than viewing these difficulties as interactional products to which he might well have made a significant contribution.

In all of this, the material from the patient is the guide. You will be quite amazed to discover that, in a derivative form, the indirect associations reveal that the patient will comment unconsciously on the work of both the supervisee and the supervisor. These indirect communications can be used to alert you to your own possible countertransference-based contributions to a therapy in difficulty.

With clinic cases, there is also the added danger, especially after one comes to appreciate the crucial functions of the framework, to blame the altered frame that is inevitable in a clinic situation. But I suspect, though I'm still not certain, that despite these modifications, which may well be severely curtailing, one can strive to offer the best possible therapeutic experience to the patient and, within limits, accomplish something constructive.

In this particular supervision, I would be listening to these opening remarks on one level as a series of realities.

But on another level, I would quietly think of them as a sequence of associations filled with unconscious meanings, only a portion of which I will be able to determine. As a result, in the supervisory bipersonal field, I think of my formulations regarding the supervisee as tentative and limited, and as hunches rather than definitive hypotheses.

For example, in this sequence the supervisee goes from suggesting that he wishes neither to analyze nor be analyzed to mention of the premature termination of a woman patient with whom he had several supervisors. I would speculate silently to myself that this woman in some way frightened him so much, in terms of what it was that she stirred up within him, that he has every hope of never experiencing this part of his inner mental world in any form of personal treatment. And I would be concerned that he would have the strong unconscious need to protect himself from such frightening experiences with his other patients as well.

The so-called dread of "the unconscious" is universal in mankind, and in therapists no less. It must be mastered adequately in order to become an insight-oriented therapist, a point that I developed rather extensively in a recent paper on becoming a psychiatrist (1976c). In this regard, it is, of course, extremely useful to be sensitive to the anxieties, conflicts, and conscious and unconscious motives that supervisees have for becoming therapists, and, I must add again, to be aware too of the comparable anxieties, conflicts, and motives for your own wish to supervise. There is some literature on this subject, but I do believe that this is one area that deserves more extensive exploration and formulation.

One example of this type of effort is Greenson's extensive delineation (1967) of the unconscious factors in becoming a psychoanalyst. His commentary shows that there are factors on virtually every conceivable level, and that selection of crucial variables is quite difficult. Olinick (1969), for example, felt that the unconscious wish to rescue a depressed mother is an important dynamism in the selection of psychoanalysis as a profession, and I have seen some data that tends to support this formulation, however restricted it may be.

But rather than speculate, I want instead to stress what we can derive from the clues offered by the supervisee. We must be aware of the dread of the therapist's own countertransference reactions to his patients, of someone of the same or the opposite sex, of the patient's disruptive behaviors and primitive mental contents and mechanisms, and of his transference- and even nontransference-based reactions. Ultimately, the therapist's fears of his own inner primitive mental world proves to be the crucial factor in either an overinvestment in insight-oriented therapy, or discouragement and flight from that modality.

I would also, in responding to the communications to this point, wonder if the supervisee is struggling with an undue sense of guilt in having failed with this woman patient, and would wonder a bit about what actually happened; but I would be careful not to inquire, since clearly this is not the patient he will be presenting.

Some supervisees convey a sense of almost manic relish regarding the pursuit of unconscious contents and mechanisms, while others evince a striking dread; most are, on some level, quite fearful. It seems to me that this supervisee is a rather striking mixture of the two extremes: he seeks out an analyst as a supervisor, which itself suggests a wish to explore the depths, but then alludes to a patient who took flight. She may well be serving here as an unconscious representation of himself in his own unconscious fantasies vis-à-vis the supervisor. In this way he again expresses his reluctance to enter any type of analytic therapy, while showing other evident signs of anxiety. Still, he comes to the analyst for supervision; he seems stirred up and uncertain.

I would keep these kinds of anxieties and conflicts in mind. And at a pertinent moment later on in supervision—for example, at a point where he fails to understand and interpret an unconscious fantasy—I might gently suggest that he seems to have some basic conflicts in regard to this type of exploration. I would be careful not to overstate my evaluation, and would counterbalance it with some type of supportive comment. For example, I might refer him to my paper (1976c) so that he could see that this is a universal form of anxiety. He might also discover some clues to his own problems through the ideas developed in that paper.

After all, I know that he is not in therapy, and I also know that his patients will consistently be impinging upon his countertransferences. So, whatever minimal self-analysis he can undertake, with whatever outside sources as aids, he might be able to develop some kind of perspective that would help him better manage these countertransferences in his interaction with the patient.

He will soon become aware of the striking limitations of an approach to countertransference that excludes personal therapy or analysis, and I am very much aware of the very little that can be accomplished on this basis. But it is all that we have with this type of supervisee, and we must help him as much as we can without becoming his therapist. Clearly, he may attempt to use us as his therapist, and some of our supervisory interventions may have a dual function for him; they may be experienced as both efforts at teaching and at helping him to achieve personal insight. But I must stress again that I would not design an intervention for the latter purpose, and would see the therapeutic benefit as coincidental to a valid supervisory experience, though also as inevitable.

Supervisor A: At this point, he presented me a typewritten copy of the initial evaluation—the summary he had done on the patient he was going to present.

Langs: We are still at the point in this supervision where we have not heard any material at all from or about the patient. I state this because the comments that I will have to make about these behaviors can be validated only in an extremely limited way; so long as we do not have material from the patient during a session, the validating process is quite curtailed. As a result, my remarks may seem to represent personal opinions or even biases, and this is the very situation that I am trying to avoid by using actual supervisory material. I can only state, as a means of counteracting that impression, that the principles I am developing here have all been derived from validated explorations of the therapeutic situation itself, and that almost all of them have been confirmed as well, in some form, in the supervisory situation itself.

Thus, I now have the impression that my initial formulations about the anxieties within this supervisee are finding a weak form of validation. I had suggested that this supervisee would have a great need for defensiveness in his work with his patient and, I would now add, in his supervisory experience as well. And this movement of his away from the personal quality of the supervisory exchange and toward a more mechanical approach is in keeping with this assessment. Now I am well aware that this might be standard practice at this center, but I would simply say that, if that is the case, a more comfortable and creative presenter might well have by now dismissed the use of such notes and would talk directly to the supervisor.

For my part, I would rather cordially return such notes to the supervisee, and use such a moment as an opportunity to structure the supervisory situation. I would explain that I would prefer a direct presentation, from the notes if necessary, which would begin with a brief summary of the patient's main complaints and central historical and current facts, and of the status of the therapy to the point at which he will begin presenting, in strict sequence, the process notes of the last two sessions. I would stress the extent to which we will be focusing on the therapeutic interaction itself, and would make it clear that such matters as evaluation, diagnosis, dynamic and genetic assessment, and overall treatment plan will be considered, but only secondarily. My plan would be to incorporate comments in these areas as they become pertinent to the material, though when a supervisee presents an initial session I will consider them more extensively.

Incidentally, since my focus will be on the therapeutic

interaction, I am quite careful in listening to an initial hour to demonstrate to the supervisee the presence of interactional dynamics even in a first session, and I stress the importance of being in touch with such dynamics from the outset. Often they are crucial to impairments in the developing therapeutic alliance and are an aspect of initial resistances. I do all that I can to counteract the tendency among many therapists to think of the first session or sessions rather nondynamically, in terms of some cumbersome model of assessment and evaluation that excludes the developing dynamic interaction between patient and therapist.

As I am speaking, I become aware of the extent to which I stress the comprehension of the ongoing therapeutic interaction, and the intrapsychic repercussions for both patient and therapist. This may be because this is an area I have studied extensively, but I tend to think that it is based on my belief that this is by far the most crucial dimension of psychotherapy, as well as the most difficult to master. Beyond such a basic focus, I try to be consistently sensitive and responsive to the consciously and unconsciously communicated learning needs of the supervisee.

Often, in defining the framework of the supervisory situation, I will hear one or another comment or objection from the supervisee, who may from time to time allude to experiences with other supervisors. I find it better to avoid direct debates, and take everything that is said about another supervisory experience with a grain of salt. My basic approach is to delineate my own method of supervision, to present a brief rationale with special stress on the need to create a sequential unfolding that will foster the use of the validating process, and to say something in general about how he will be exposed to many different kinds of supervision, and how eventually he will have to decide upon the method he feels most valid and useful for him—recognizing that this choice will have very critical unconscious determinants.

The supervisee's offer of this summary brings up another common issue that arises, especially with clinic patients who are transferred from one therapist to another. The departing therapist will usually write a summary of the course of therapy and the like, and sometimes will even attempt to directly contact his successor. Basing myself on framework considerations I have already discussed, I stress the importance that the new therapist not participate in this modification of confidentiality. It is a contamination with no constructive function for the patient, one that can greatly prejudice the new therapist and disturb the initial unfolding of the new therapy. Often, this effort to communicate with the new therapist is, in part, an attempt to inappropriately alleviate the guilt and anxiety of the departing therapist. In addition to considerations of the framework, I adopt this position because it has become quite clear to me that the only meaningful understanding of the patient and the only valid therapeutic work with him derives from the actual and direct interaction between the therapist and his patient, and from no other source.

Supervisor A: Well, I accepted the summary. However, I did so without looking at it, and asked that he tell me his own impressions of the patient. He began by indicating that the patient was a forty-one-year-old man who was separated, and who came for evaluation of a problem the supervisee described as anhedonia. This was his own construction, and I asked him what he meant by it—what the patient had actually told him.

Langs: Yes, I specifically let the supervisee know that his presentation should be descriptive, and should reflect as closely as possible the exact words and behaviors of the patient. I add that the supervisee should separately indicate his own formulations of the material, doing so, however, only after we have heard the raw data, so to speak. The point I am making is that I not only request that he do so, but that in addition I use such opportunities to spell out the pertinent ground rules of the supervisory situation—just as I would use the therapeutic interaction not only to formulate a specific aspect, but also to develop general principles.

Supervisor A: He said that the patient had told him that he had difficulty forming close relationships, especially with women. The patient felt that he had been fortunate with women, but that he tended not to get emotionally involved with them. He said he was seeking psychotherapy because of this, adding that he was currently living with a woman, whom the resident characterized as hysterical. I again interrupted and asked him what the patient had said. The resident then explained that this woman tries to punish the patient through her other relationships, and that it seemed that to some degree the patient actually encourages her to do so.

Langs: You see again a very human tendency, one that is quite common among therapists and analysts: a propensity toward mixing direct description with one's own formulations and impressions. This could be quite prejudicial and even confusing for the supervisor; it also reflects an internal confusion in the supervisee, who may, in his very act of listening, freely intermix the communications from the patient with his own formulations. This can be done to the point where his interventions will be based far too heavily on his own conscious and unconscious fantasies and assessments, and far too little on the actual communications from the patient. This can be explained to the supervisee. But in addition, it is important that you identify each point in his presentation where he does this sort of thing, since even silent acceptance will reinforce and encourage it. Essentially, this is a matter of the therapist's maintaining an awareness of the different elements in the listening process (Langs 1978c), and of the sources of his impressions—the patient or himself, and specific mixtures of the two.

I would also want to be quite clear as to the source of this material: is this a description of the initial session with the patient, or is it a summary of a group of ill-defined early sessions? In the supervisee's introduction of the patient, I will accept such a summary, but it should be identified as such. Actually, if this is the first session, I would be thinking of saying something about how this material already can be organized as Type Two derivatives and understood beyond its manifest content or the obvious implications this has for the patient's own unconscious perceptions and fantasies vis-à-vis women—formulations that would constitute Type One derivatives.

What I have in mind is that we can take as a crucial adaptive context for every initial session the patient's anticipations of, and experiences in, the therapeutic relationship—his coming for therapy and its ramifications. Using that particular adaptive context, one can organize the patient's associations to this point as Type Two derivatives related to the therapeutic relationship. However, on the basis of this scanty material it would be difficult to indicate the extent to which it reflects unconscious perceptions of the therapist's distance and hostilities—if they have, indeed, been communicated—and the extent to which it reflects the patient's unconscious fantasies: the degree to which this is primarily nontransference or primarily transference.

The material does, nonetheless, organize nicely around this particular adaptive context related to treatment, and could be used to suggest to the supervisee that such meanings can indeed be conveyed in the patient's communications even in the first hour—even while he is manifestly attempting to report on his symptoms, his present life, his emotional history. But I would do this only briefly and tentatively—as a model of a *silent hypothesis* at best—since we will not be hearing this particular session in detail, and since I want to proceed to the process notes of the most recent hour or two, depending on the time available.

Incidentally, I stress to my supervisees the dynamics of the first hour because quite often their basic clinical teaching in this respect is quite nondynamic, focused on history-taking and the acquisition of data. I also try to make brief mention that one should look for initial resistances and problems in the therapeutic alliance in every first hour. In this way I try to stress the depth of the dynamic interaction from the outset.

Supervisor A: He went on to say that this woman was quite provocative; at times she threatened to hurt him or even to hurt herself. The patient has felt a responsibility to this woman, and because of that had decided to come to the clinic, which is an outreach center in his neighborhood.

The resident went on to say that it turned out that this woman, whom the patient called his girlfriend, had been seen in therapy at the same outreach clinic. At this point the supervisee asked the patient what it was that made her different from all other women in his life.

Langs: So he is actually describing the initial session then?

Supervisor A: Yes.

Langs: Well, I am still unclear as to how long the supervisee has been seeing this patient, and I certainly would have inquired about that. There is a tendency in many supervisees—and, I might add, in many supervisors as well—to want to avoid working with the current material, the most recent therapeutic interaction or session. This is reflected in the supervisor's acceptance of a lengthy past history early in the supervision, or in going back to earlier sessions, sometimes because the supervisee feels there is a special point to be made or issue to be explored, or in other types of avoidance reactions. Because I believe it is critical to get to the immediate therapeutic work, I would therefore have asked that he clarify how long he had been seeing the patient. I would suggest that he continue with this first hour in detail only if he had seen the patient once or twice, or perhaps three times, and I would be certain to have him shift to the most recent session after presenting that first hour. On the other hand, if he has been seeing the patient for a longer period, I would suggest that he very briefly review the initial hours, in perhaps three or four minutes, and that he proceed to a three or four minute summary of the next-to-last hour, so we could then focus on the most recent session.

For the moment, we will listen along with you, not knowing for certain how long the therapist has been seeing this patient. On this basis, and accepting the fact that you have decided to hear this material and to work with it, we are now faced with the first intervention by the supervisee. To me, this is a critical moment in supervision. With few exceptions, I always comment immediately after the supervisee has intervened, doing so before I hear the patient's response. This is essential to my method, since my evaluation of the supervisee's intervention will involve the prediction of various qualities of the patient's subsequent associations: the extent to which they will confirm the supervisee's intervention, the possible latent content, and sometimes even their likely manifest content—much of this based on an evaluation of the therapeutic interaction to that point, and on the unconscious communications contained in the intervention.

In essence, then, the point at which the supervisee has intervened is a crucial moment for teaching. His comment most certainly reflects his capacity to listen to the material from the patient, his formulation of that material, and the kind of associations from the patient that he hopes to promote. It also reflects his concept of indications for intervention, their timing and their nature. It is, then, a most telling moment, and one that deserves extensive consideration in supervision.

It is far easier for a supervisor to respond to the supervisee's interventions than it is to formulate a moment at which he himself, had he been the therapist, would have most definitely intervened—a point at which he therefore must discuss a missed intervention. This latter type of supervisory effort is, however, extremely important, and I most definitely put it on the line and state specific interventions when I feel they are indicated and have been overlooked. I hope that I will be able to illustrate this type of work to you as we hear more of these two supervisory experiences. Incidentally, I find the formulation of missed interventions more common in supervisory work with therapists who have some clinical experience and sophistication, and who have worked with me for a while. Most trainees, at least initially, tend to be overactive, to the point of becoming rather interfering, and most of my effort is concentrated on their interventions and errors. In that context, it is always necessary for me to tell them that, though I am an active supervisor, believe it or not I am relatively silent as a therapist.

Now while I do not as a rule approach a supervisory session with a specific plan in mind, or a specific area for discussion, I do have an overall concept of my basic approach. I stress, as I said, the comprehension of the therapeutic interaction, and its ramifications, its ties to the present and the past for the patient and, within limits, for the therapist as well. And certainly in every session a nodal point occurs at the moment the therapist intervenes, or at a juncture where I feel an intervention should have been made.

I want to stress again my belief that there are rather definitive points in a given session where the therapist should intervene. I hasten to add, however, that I am not suggesting that every single session will see the patient producing associations that call for an intervention. It is not incumbent upon the therapist to speak in every session, and there are some sessions where I believe that the most constructive response is, indeed, the use of silence.

So, an intervention or failure to intervene is a key point in both the therapy and the supervisory sessions. It is our basic responsibility as supervisors to assess what the supervisee has said, to check it against our own unfolding formulations, and to convey to the supervisee the result of these evaluations. Here, early in supervision, one of my goals is helping the supervisee develop what I call the *listening process* (Langs 1978c): the capacity to observe and sense all incoming communications, verbal and nonverbal, to foster their development through appropriate silences and interventions, especially through a sound handling of the ground rules and framework, and to evaluate and formulate these incoming messages.

For a long time I debated as to where the supervisory process should begin: with the crucial therapeutic interaction and relationship? With considerations of diagnosis and evaluation? With the ground rules and framework so vital to the creation of a meaningful therapeutic experience? It is clear that learning when and how to intervene must come later, and that it is inherent in proper listening. But listening, understanding the nature of the interaction, and creating a secure frame are all basic factors—and I certainly pay considerable attention to each of them from the outset. But I have decided, after long thought, that the listening process itself must come first, and along with it the validating process, because this is absolutely fundamental to conceptualizing and understanding every other dimension of the therapeutic relationship and interaction.

So I do have all three basic areas in mind from the outset—listening, the relationship, and the framework—and I will initially stress the factors in listening: understanding the concepts of derivative communication and unconscious processes in regard to both fantasy and perception; the processing of interactional mechanisms such as projective identifications and of role and image evocations; the organizing of the patient's material around its manifest content in terms of Type One and Type Two derivatives; and, above all, establishing the crucial role of the adaptive context in conceptualizing and comprehending derivative communication.

In fact, as I am about to demonstrate, these very basics of listening are not only formally taught to the supervisee, but also are demonstrated to him through your own supervisory efforts, which will be valid and effective only to the extent that you yourself are capable of making full use of the listening and validating processes. Your own supervisory work, then, reinforces your direct supervisory interventions; the coordination of verbal and nonverbal communication is essential in the teaching situation.

Now let's look at this particular intervention by the supervisee. Rather than asking a series of questions, I will present my own formulation and indicate how I would have intervened had I been the supervisor. In this way I will be able to demonstrate my basic model of supervisory work as a point of departure for further discussion.

I would begin, as a rule, by explicating the framework of both supervision and treatment. I would start at a very simple level, indicating to the supervisee that he had decided to intervene and asking him to identify the type of intervention. This would enable me to discuss with him the various types of interventions: silences, questions, clarifications, interpretations, reconstructions, and, I would add, efforts at management of the framework (Langs 1973, 1976a, d). At some point, I would refer him to Bibring's fundamental paper on this topic (1954), and to my own extension of this basic psychoanalytic approach to interventions, with its stress on their manifest nature (Langs 1973).

However, I would add that my position in this area has been greatly extended (Langs 1978b), and that, in addition to the initial step of identifying the formal qualities of an intervention, I now stress the extensive unconscious communications, projective identifications, and barriers that may be contained in any intervention from the therapist. I will soon demonstrate what I mean by this, and will speak of how I developed these ideas, but first let me outline a few other comments I might well make at this point in the supervisory session.

First, I might ask the resident if he was familiar with the goals of the first therapy session, and might ask him to clarify them for me. We could then discuss these goals as they pertain in general to the manner in which the therapist will intervene in an initial hour, especially because I do believe that he may respond a bit differently to the patient in the first session than he would throughout the remainder of a therapy. This would provide one framework for the evaluation of this intervention.

In brief, my basic position is to allow the patient to direct the unfolding of the initial hour—as I would at any point in treatment. With patients who are verbal and communicative, I will be relatively silent. On the other hand, with patients who are rather silent I will ask occasional, sometimes frequent, questions in the first session; in addition, as the material permits, I will also offer some initial and rather general interpretive comments regarding the unconscious meanings of their silences. I tend, then, to be a bit more active when needed in an initial session, and I discuss this with the supervisee, explaining my reasons and indicating that as treatment unfolds my stress is on interpretive rather than confronting or questioning interventions. In fact, for reasons that I hope will become clear, I no longer use questions or confrontations in my own therapeutic work, since I find they interfere with the patient's communications and his personal unfolding of the session; they interfere also with his efforts to put into me, as he always will, the necessary derivatives out of which I can develop an appropriate interpretation or management of the framework.

Because there are many models of first sessions, I will take some time to explain mine, doing so in the context of this particular intervention, which will help me document and validate my position. I stress the need to allow the patient to unconsciously direct the unfolding of the hour, my belief that the therapist need not pursue the details of the patient's history and that he can work with the data presented by the patient. Basically, the therapist is attempting to establish the need for treatment, and to create a sound therapeutic alliance largely through an initially concerned understanding, and an interpretive approach that is essentially devoid of manipulation. In the main, he will be deciding on matters such as frequency of sessions (I leave out, for the moment, considerations of fee and the question of recommending analysis versus psychotherapy) and attempting to define the ground rules or framework of the treatment situation. By and large, I believe that the basic model should be twice-a-week psychotherapy, unless extraneous realities in the life of the patient or within the clinic suggest an alternative—for example, the resident may wish to work more intensively with a patient on a three times a week basis, or clinic policy may direct that this particular patient be seen just once a week.

And I think that this twice-a-week modality is serviceable for all therapy patients, however disturbed. I am suggesting, then, that the essential model of psychotherapy is quite functional for all types of patients, and that the therapist's basic approach and the nature of the therapeutic interaction is fundamentally the same in all therapeutic relationships. This in no way denies the differences in the actual communications and therapeutic work in analysis as compared to therapy, or with schizophrenic patients as compared to nonschizophrenics. Similarly, it does not suggest that your interventions will lack important differences in these two treatment modalities or with these two groups of patients: the material will be different, their therapeutic needs will be different, the ways in which they communicate and test the frame will be somewhat different, but nonetheless, you will use the same basic principles in dealing with this material, even though the exact nature of what you say and do will be somewhat distinctive.

In respect to the first hour, I want to stress the importance of listening to the patient in terms of what he mentions and does not mention, of conceptualizing the associations not only on their manifest level—which is important, especially since you are hearing a good deal of historical material—but in terms of their latent content, especially within the adaptive context of the initiation of treatment. And it is also necessary toward the end of the hour to indicate the expectation that you, as a therapist, can help the patient resolve his symptoms or other problems, and to clearly define the explicit ground rules, thereby creating what Freud (1940) called the *analytic contract*—here, it would be the *therapeutic contract*—and establishing a well-defined framework (Langs 1973, 1975b, 1976a,d) which will then be reinforced implicitly through your own subsequent behaviors, and management and interpretation of framework issues as they arise.

Now let's come back to the supervisee's question: what made his girlfriend different from all other women in his life. Within the context of the general orientation that I have now established for the supervisor regarding the initial session—and having asked him to identify the formal nature of his intervention, and having discussed his response—I would now ask him to define the extent to which his comment was relevant to the goals we had defined for the first hour and in what sense it was based on the patient's associations, thereby trying to approach the definition of its unconscious meanings and functions. We can see that a patient's initial communications in an evaluation session can evoke a universe of questions; here, the supervisee selects a particular question and states it in a particular manner.

Discussant: It seems to me that we have to remember that the patient came to the clinic to be evaluated. This means about one or two diagnostic sessions in which the resident is required to obtain all sorts of information: the chief complaint, its history, his present relationships, his past history, and all the rest, so that he can generate a diagnostic impression and a dynamic and psychological formulation.

Langs: Yes. So we come now to the influence of clinic policy on the first session. But this approach stresses the needs of the clinic, rather than those of the patient, and it tends to fill up clinic record rooms with pages and pages that virtually no one is ever going to read or even look at. And if the supervisee is forced into such a position, he may decide to comply, but if he has the support of a supervisor, he may attempt a less directive initial interview—and, if need be, defend himself against the clinic administrator.

Incidentally, there are many clinics where the patient is evaluated by one therapist or social worker, and then recommended to a second therapist, who carries out the treatment. I simply want to point out that based on my explorations of the framework this is never in the best interests of the patient, and that it should be a basic policy to have the trainee who evaluates the patient available as the potential therapist. And it is the therapist himself who should telephone or write to the patient for the first appointment, if that is the policy, though you can sense that this is a bit seductive but necessary, since as a rule, the patient has already called the clinic and has been told that he will be hearing from the therapist at a later date. How nice it would be if the patient could be referred immediately to the therapist who would undertake responsibility for the entire unfolding of the treatment experience. It is terribly traumatic for a patient to be told that he has been assigned to another therapist for treatment, or to be informed that he will be evaluated for a session or two, and then be told whether he will continue with the evaluating therapist or be sent on to someone else—for reasons that are seldom, if ever, clear to the patient, and that cause him hurt and pain. This is in keeping with what I said about private practice: a therapist should be prepared to offer treatment to every patient who walks through his door, without exception, and he should not unnecessarily traumatize the frightened and often fragile patient in need.

Discussant: I must say that it seems to me that you are being somewhat unrealistic. How often will you know ahead of time whether you are going to take on a patient? You know nothing about him and yet suggest that, regardless of what he might present, all he need do is step through your door to become your patient.

Langs: Perhaps I was unclear: my emphasis was on

approaching the consultation with the expectation that if the patient so wishes you yourself will offer him treatment. This is really a side issue, so to be brief, I am simply stressing the needs of the patient and stating an ideal I feel we should all strive for. I am well aware that there are many therapists who make exceptions, who will not treat one or another type of patient, or too many of a particular kind, and that there are others who do consultations without any intention of offering either therapy or analysis. All of this reflects the needs of the therapist; many of these needs are countertransference-based, and all of them impose very special hurts on the patients involved. Here again, as this relates to your supervisory work, the model you have of a consultation clearly influences both your model of supervision and the way in which you supervise an initial interview. And the extent to which the needs of a trainee or the needs of a clinic run counter to those of the patient, and to the development of an ideal therapeutic field, one must strive to rectify such situations and to prevent their occurrence. And where change is impossible, the therapist should at least recognize the implications of his position so that he can understand the patient's reactions; he can then implicitly acknowledge their valid core, and yet interpret any pathology added to the response.

Discussant: Are you saying that you don't think that the significant parts of the patient's history, what is called the geography of their lives, should be understood before getting into the meat of the therapy? I can understand that the moment the patient walks into the therapist's office, treatment begins—or even before that point, depending upon the initial contact—but I am not clear as to your position regarding the life history of the patient.

Langs: Yes, that is indeed what I am saying. I do not feel that you need a detailed history in order to undertake treatment. In fact, I have found that the pursuit of such historical facts creates a particular type of bipersonal field in which symbolic communication and illusions are impaired. In terms of the field typology I mentioned earlier, active questioning can shift a patient capable of symbolic communication toward projective identification or intense defensiveness. It moves the patient to the surface of his thoughts, stresses manifest content, and is inimical to derivative communication, especially to communication of Type Two derivatives.

Of course, it is essential that you know enough about the patient—history, dynamics, psychopathology, assets and positive capacities—to recommend a treatment modality and a frequency of sessions. But it is my belief that you can develop such formulations from simply listening to the patient regardless of how much he communicates about his past. All of this can be done by observing how the patient communicates, what he says and does not say, sensing his ego capacities—reality testing and the like—and his resistances or receptivity to therapy, and using his communications, whatever they may be, toward such an assessment.

I am well aware that many therapists and analysts work quite differently. For example, I have recently discussed this very subject with a well-known analyst, who informed me that she takes a detailed history from every patient. She justifies her position by saying that she has seen many patients in second and third analyses with whom certain significant facts in their lives, important traumas and events, had never been discussed or worked through. In keeping with this, she takes notes throughout her sessions, and feels that she cannot properly hear the patient without writing.

In contrast, I accept the patient on his own terms, make no special effort to take a formal history, write no notes during any session, and make no record whatsoever. I would suggest that the analyses she cites, in which these significant experiences were never analyzed, were treatment situations in which poor technique and countertransference difficulties prevailed, in which the patient's defenses, to the extent that they contributed to this avoidance, were not sufficiently analyzed, and that these oversights had little to do with fact finding. In my experience, significant traumas always come up in some form: they may be signaled through a notable void, through a passing mention of something related to the traumatic experience, or in a variety of direct or derivative ways. It is a matter of having the sensitivity to recognize the clues, to analyze the relevant defenses and resistances, and to allow the meaning to unfold. Much of this has to do with the capacity to listen for and identify derivatives, and to establish each important adaptive context and to understand the material within that framework. This procedure permits interpretations that will foster the further communication of relevant genetic material—some of it directly, some of it in derivative form, and some of it enacted directly with the therapist.

I do want to indicate that I have a perspective on these matters. In an initial hour, I would like, if possible, to know something about major life traumas, for example, and I have found that most patients will offer a sampling of these important historical facts, though no patient will present all of them. In fact, it is extremely important subsequently to work along with a patient and see the extent to which insightful interpretive efforts and sound management of the framework permits an unfolding that includes the gradual modification of repressive barriers, and the eventual revelation, analysis, and working through of significant past traumas, many of which would not even have been mentioned in response to direct history-taking.

Discussant: At present, does the decision to use your model, as compared to a more medical model, depend on the situation up to the point of referral? For example, your patients may come to you already screened, whereas patients we see in the clinic may be seen for the first time. In fact, they may be suicidal and not reveal it spontaneously, unless the resident happens to ask. In that sense, I feel that we have to make use of a medical model rather than an analytic model.

Langs: I am very unhappy with the distinction you are proposing between the medical and analytic models of the initial interview. I am not suggesting that if a therapist senses, in any way whatsoever, the presence of suicidal impulses or fantasies, or a suicidal risk, that he not investigate this area in an initial interview and that he not be as active as necessary. What I am saying is that it should not be a matter of routinely asking every patient if he is suicidal. I feel that such a formality reflects an insensitivity on the part of the therapist, who should be able to detect the presence of depression and suicidal propensities, doing so as the patient's own communicative style and contents unfold. I am not suggesting that one always refrain from questions in a first hour, nor am I saying that there is never an urgent need for such queries. However, in emergencies, I do believe it is best to adhere to the basic interpretive model as a means of permitting the patient to communicate the crucial underlying derivatives. Still, sometimes—though more rarely than usually recognized—direct inquiry and confrontation may be necessary. All I am suggesting is that we recognize that this approach can sometimes entail an alteration in the framework, a modification in neutrality, for example, and that it will have ramifications for the patient and contain a variety of unconscious communications. As a result, in addition to the therapist's conscious intentions and their effects, the patient will respond to the presence of additional unconscious meanings and their implications. In essence, the therapist responds, as I said, to the patient's needs, rather than working from some type of rigid model of therapy—but these needs must be properly conceptualized and answered.

You are implying that some consultations unfold according to the usual medical model, in which a formal series of questions are routinely asked of the patient—a situation which resembles the usual nonpsychiatric medical practice. You would contrast this, I expect, with what you have called an analytic model, in which the therapist is relatively silent and nondirective, and is interested in unconscious processes and contents, and the like. However, for me both psychotherapy and psychoanalysis are distinctive forms of treatment, with requisites that are, in the main, quite different from any other medical interaction. And I think that these distinctions are crucial to successful therapeutic work, and that actually there is only one basic model of psychotherapy: it is medical in its intentions, in that it is designed to be appropriately therapeutic, and it is analytic in its form, in that this particular approach offers the patient the best opportunity for such a cure.

Incidentally, almost all of the patients that I see have not been screened. I think too that through the years you learn to not entirely trust a screening interview, regardless of who has carried it out. You rely on your own work. The model that I am proposing applies, then, to any therapeutic consultation, and is designed to develop the best possible therapeutic field, while most carefully attending to the patient's needs, not only for a valid therapeutic experience, but also in terms of any more emergency-related requirements.

In my technique book (1973), I do include as one of the goals of the first session the need to identify any life crisis or suicidal threat, and I do stress the importance of investigating such issues in the first hour. But here I would suggest that the more you allow the patient to freely communicate and produce meaningful derivatives, the better able you will be to understand the underlying factors in the patient's suicidal tendencies—far better able than if you ask a series of direct questions which will tend to exclude the underlying dynamics and will probably detrimentally influence the patient's unconscious perception of you in response to his suicidal tendencies. For example, undue questioning and focusing on the manifest content may unconsciously communicate to the patient a deep anxiety regarding your own capacity to take in, contain, manage, metabolize, and interpret the factors related to his suicidal wishes. In contrast, patient listening and an initial, however general, interpretation might well communicate a secure hold of the patient, an absence of any undue dread of his suicidal impulses, and a capacity to manage and understand their underlying basis.

To put all of this still one more way, I am often misunderstood as suggesting a total rigidity regarding the ground rules and framework. Actually, my position is that I believe that it is most therapeutic to maintin a stable and secure, relatively unchanging frame, and to limit alterations in the framework to those totally imposed by the patient or those dictated by clear-cut, thoroughly analyzed realities. I also believe that in an acute emergency, maintaining the framework offers the patient the best hold and implicit ego support available, the greatest opportunity to use you as a container for his pathological inner mental world, and the best opportunity for you to obtain the Type Two derivatives through which you can meaningfully interpret the unconscious dynamics of his suicidal impulses.

It is for those reasons that I believe so strongly in adhering to the frame, and I am critical of any therapist whose first impulse is to alter the frame, often because of his own uncontrolled anxieties and the like—that is, because of countertransference factors. Only extremely rarely will it truly be necessary in an emergency to alter the framework, for example, with an acutely and deeply suicidal patient who shows no indication of perspective or control. This may take the form of asking such a patient for direct assurances regarding the safeguarding of his life and requiring of that patient that he call you if he begins to feel hopelessly suicidal. However, you should be aware that the patient will react in a distinctly mixed way to such an alteration in the frame: he perceives something positive in your deep concern and in your offer of auxiliary controls and the like, and even in your insistence that he survive; while on the other hand, on another level and usually quite unconsciously, he resents the invasion of autonomy and the manipulation involved, even though it turns out to have been a lifesaving measure.

Coming back to the supervisory situation, my general

approach is quite comparable: I stick to the basic model of supervision, in which the supervisee presents in sequence the material from the patient and himself, intervene where I feel it indicated, and deviate from that model only when there is a crisis in the supervisory situation. On the other hand, when there is a crisis in the psychotherapy that I am supervising, I prefer to stick to the material of the presentation so that patient and therapist can together communicate to me the unconscious basis of the difficulty. Here, I allow them to lead the way and to help me in my supervisory work, and I will use the material not only to understand the contribution of patient and therapist to the crisis situation, but for the exploration of my own possible contribution as well.

Discussant: I gather that you are not implying that you tell the patient nothing in the first hour, that is, that you do establish a set of ground rules.

Langs: Yes, indeed. Toward the end of the initial session, I indicate that I feel that I can be of help, recommend a fee and frequency of visits, and spell out the ground rules. In essence, I let the patient know that the time is set aside for him, that he is responsible for his sessions, and that we will be working either face to face or on the couch. I let him know when I anticipate taking vacations, and in recommending a fee I try to select from within my narrow range of fees the one that seems fairest to the patient and myself, and one that he can handle on his own without insurance or other third parties. By and large, reductions in the basic fee tend to have quite detrimental consequences for the therapeutic interaction (see Eissler 1974), and should be avoided if at all possible. The remaining ground rules, such as the absence of physical contact, total confidentiality, the one-to-one relationship, the therapist's neutrality and anonymity, and the fundamental rule of free association, are in general conveyed implicitly, although they might have to be stated directly under some circumstances. And remember too that once you have structured the therapeutic situation, nothing should be modified, to the extent this is humanly possible, without first exploring the direct and indirect material. And you will find that, typically, patients are split when they ask for an alteration in the frame: Consciously, they seek it out or appreciate it when you make the offer, while unconsciously they are filled with anger and see the move as quite inappropriate and as entailing a disruption in the basic therapeutic symbiosis—to use Searles's term (1965, 1970, 1971, 1973)—and in the very basic hold that they require for an effective therapeutic experience. Therapeutic kindness lies in offering valid interpretations and proper management of the framework, and not in behaviors that would be acceptable socially.

But now, I would like to come back to this specific intervention, to the supervisee's questions as to what made his patient's girlfriend different from the other women in his life. I have already indicated that I would have responded to this question by clarifying my basic model of the initial interview. I would, in addition, have very tentatively suggested that the supervisee begin to realize that every one of his interventions is prompted by the communications from the patient—the immediate adaptive context—and secondarily by factors in the therapist's external life and internal mental world. The latter dimension I leave to the self-knowledge and personal sensitivity of the therapist, while the conscious and unconscious implications of his intervention, and the associations and behaviors of the patient, are represented in the process notes and can be discussed with the supervisee. In that regard, the most important adaptive context for every intervention is the preceding material from the patient, and the most immediate adaptive context for the intervention is the patient's last associations.

Using this model is extremely helpful in supervision. If we take the patient's material as the precipitant for the therapist's intervention, which it certainly is, we can then compare the explicit and derivative meanings contained in the communications from each participant. In addition, we can see the way in which the patient's communications may serve as a disturbing adaptive context for the therapist's intervention, in that an erroneous intervention will be evoked by the overall material from the patient and quite often will be made precisely at a moment of acute disturbance. This immediate adaptive context often illuminates the unconscious meanings and functions of an erroneous intervention, which tends, in general, to be designed as a defense against that particular communication from the patient or as an effort to create an appropriately gratifying misalliance (Langs 1975a, 1976a,d).

To briefly illustrate with this material, you may recall that the patient had been talking about his girlfriend's threat to both of them, and the feeling of responsibility that prompted him to seek therapy. He then mentioned that his girlfriend had been in therapy at the same clinic. Now it seems to me that this last piece of information could be loaded with meaning, and that it would be well to allow the patient to proceed in order to see whether he elaborates or changes the subject, goes on to associations that are indirectly illuminating, or clarifies some of this in a straightforward manner. I see no particular indication for a question at this time, especially for a question that changes the subject and shifts the patient from his associations to his girlfriend's treatment at the clinic to his associations about her as a different type of woman.

I might then suggest to the supervisee that he may well have felt threatened in some manner by the reference to the clinic, and that he had a need to shift the patient's thoughts and feelings away from the clinic, away from derivatives related to himself, and toward the girlfriend. I would be quite tentative in this regard, but it is an important issue in that therapists quite frequently, for reasons of anxiety and defense, ask a question or make a confrontation or seeming interpretation that unconsciously is designed to shift the patient away from communications related to themselves. These relatively undisguised derivatives related to the therapeutic relationship may be primarily distorted and fantasy-based or may on the other hand contain valid and hurtful unconscious perceptions of the therapist by the patient; in any case, the therapist tries to change the subject. In terms that I have discussed recently (Langs 1976a,d), this intervention reflects a refractoriness toward containing and metabolizing derivatives closely related to the unconscious fantasies and perceptions of the therapist. In regard to the qualities of the therapeutic field, the intervention directs the patient to communicate on a manifest level, rather than in derivative form, concretely rather than symbolically, and will foster the development of a Type B or Type C communicative field, rather than Type A—that is, an action-discharge or static field, rather than one of symbolic communication and illustration.

I guess you can see now why I am considered a tough supervisor. But I hope that you also have some insight as to why I will comment on seemingly innocuous questions: I do so largely because I am aware of their extensive consequences for both the patient and the therapeutic situation. If I seem hypersensitive, I can assure you that this is so because patients have taught me that, unconsciously, they themselves are extremely hypersensitive; as a supervisor, it is my responsibility to consciously state what I anticipate will be their unconscious reactions—or to put this another way, to explicitly state the unconscious communications contained in the therapist's interventions. With that in mind, let's now see what happened. In a sense, I have offered a formulation—what I call a *silent hypothesis* (Langs 1978c)—and would turn to the material from the patient, and to the therapist's subsequent interventions, for validation or its lack.

Supervisor A: The patient went on to talk about her being a very sexually active woman. This was the end of the first supervisory hour.

Langs: Well, there was really little opportunity for validation. Perhaps you could accept the communication about the girlfriend as a sexually active woman as possibly relating to an unconscious perception of this therapist, whom I suspect was rather more active in this session than he conveyed in the brief summary of his presentation. I am well aware that this is a description of this particular woman, but I would also say that it is shaped by the patient's unconscious perceptions of the therapist. Remember, the therapist's interventions are the immediate adaptive context for the patient's subsequent associations. The latter are to be viewed as *commentaries*, filled with both perception and distortion. They are to be treated as Type Two derivatives in the context of the intervention. In this way, this last association may be seen to be especially designed as a response to the therapist's curiosity about this woman's sexual problem. Certainly there may also be something about the patient and his psychopathology in all of this—perhaps related to his own sexual conflicts—but in principle it will be necessary to isolate first the valid unconscious perceptions and introjects of the therapist before we can securely identify those communications that derive primarily from the patient and his own inner mental world.

It also is important to intervene in the supervisory situation at a point that allows enough subsequent time and material for validation and further consideration. This may not always be possible, but it should be the basic model. The material here is not sufficiently detailed to clearly validate my hunch, but I do want to suggest tentatively that the therapist's sexual curiosity is unconsciously seen by the patient as a sexualization of the therapeutic situation, and that there probably is some validity to this unconscious perception, which will become an introject. If I had sufficent material to validate this hypothesis, I would stress several points to the supervisee. He should strive to get in touch with his unconscious communications to his patients and should recognize the extent of his communicative interaction with the patient. He should append every communication from the patient to the therapeutic interaction, and monitor it as a commentary with qualities of both fantasy and actuality. Finally, I would point out that the patient communicates along what I call a *me/not-me interface*—that he is referring at all times both to himself and to the therapist, and secondarily to others. Depending on time, I would select one or two of these subjects for extended comment. Overall, my goal would be to build a model of how to listen, and an accompanying model of how to structure and conceptualize the therapeutic situation and interaction.

In this situation, the material permits only a questionable confirmation, if any at all. I must stress here the extent to which the supervisor should acknowledge the absence of validation, should indicate when it seems rather tentative, and should clearly outline the form taken by truly validating responses.

Discussant: You are saying, in principle, that everything that this patient says and does after the therapist's intervention is a commentary on that intervention.

Langs: Yes. Once the therapist has intervened, it is the immediate adaptive context for the patient's ongoing associations, and I consistently organize these associations as Type Two derivatives within that adaptive context. And I must stress that I apply this not only to the therapist's verbal interventions, but also to his managements of the frame—an area quite neglected by most therapists and analysts. And I say that these are commentaries because I want to acknowledge the likelihood of both valid and distorted aspects. These responses are usually a type of what I have termed *transversal communications,* associations that embody both reality and fantasy, self and object (therapist), transference and nontransference, and the like (Langs 1978c). I do not assume in advance that these commentaries are essentially distorted; in fact, they often tend to be more unconsciously perceptive than distorted, especially when the therapist is in error. The reverse tends to occur when the therapist has intervened correctly: that is, a valid intervention will prompt distorted associations—the revelation of new genetic material and new aspects of the patient's psychopathology, emerging, as a rule, within some type of true transference context.

Incidentally, my comments here about the unconscious implications of the therapist's intervention also demonstrate in a preliminary way my approach to the therapist's countertransferences. And while I would not make an explicit comment to the supervisee at this juncture, I would very much suspect that his interest in this woman is a defense against unconscious homosexual anxieties and fantasies, and against narcissistic vulnerabilities related to his being a resident in a clinic. As I began to suggest earlier, he is offering the patient what I term an *interactional defense* (Langs 1976a, d) that will help to fend off derivatives closely related to the patient's unconscious perceptions and fantasies about the therapist. And I believe that if the session had continued—and it is not yet clear whether we have in fact heard the end of the first therapy hour, or simply the end of the supervisory hour, with more to be heard of the therapy session—in any case, I fully suspect that further material from the patient will demonstrate his introjection of the therapist's countertransference difficulties, and his unconscious working over of the relevant contents and defenses. He will tend to exploit them for his own neurosis on one level, but on another will unconsciously attempt to cure the therapist through unconscious interpretations and the like.

Discussant: Your concept that everything the patient says after the therapist's intervention is a commentary on that intervention is extremely illuminating. However, would you not consider as the exception to that rule, the patient who uses a given therapeutic hour to evacuate disturbing inner mental contents, using the session as a cathartic experience to get rid of disruptive material? And isn't it true that such patients do not introject anything that the therapist is trying to say, that they ignore it and will not respond?

Langs: You have raised some complicated issues which get us into a dimension of supervision that has not been conceptualized before. As you may remember, I had suggested earlier that there are actually three types of communicative bipersonal field, each created by an amalgam of contributions from the patient and the therapist. I also stated that with the therapist capable of symbolic communication, the most significant determinants of the field tend to be related to the communicative mode of the patient.

So far as I have been able to discover, all of the literature on supervision, as is true of the literature on the psychoanalytic interaction, has assumed the presence in therapy of what I call the Type A field: that of symbolic communication, the use of illusion, a transitional play space with the use of language directed toward insight and to express analyzable defenses—in sum, the use of derivatives of unconscious fantasies, memories, and introjects that ultimately can be interpreted. In addition, there is the related assumption that the supervisory field will be so constituted: that the therapist will be capable of symbolic communication with both his patient and his supervisor, and that the supervisor, in turn, will use language similarly.

But once you think about it, it becomes obvious that this type of therapeutic and supervisory field exists only for some patients and supervisees, and not for others. And it is true that for the moment I am assuming a Type A therapeutic and supervisory field in this presentation, but have insufficient material with which to validate my assumption. In fact, with the therapist's last intervention, I began to consider the possibility of a Type B or C field in the treatment situation.

Now your question raises the issue of what takes place in a Type B therapeutic field, one that is action-oriented and in which projective identification is the main mode of communication, and in which evacuation, immediate relief, direct and inappropriate gratification, discharge, and the like predominate. Here, language too is used for discharge and projective identification, and this may arise either out of propensities in the patient, or from tendencies in the therapist—through such interventions as unneeded alterations in the framework and erroneous interventions that constitute pathological projective identifications into the patient, even though language is the primary vehicle.

Similiarly, the supervisory bipersonal field can be constructed through the needs of the supervisee, the supervisor, or both, less for symbolic communication and understanding than for such activities as discharge, projective and introjective identification, evacuation, and the like—characteristics of the Type B field. There are serious problems when the supervisor is unable to recognize his own penchant for his operating in the Type B communicative mode, just as there are also major difficulties when it is the supervisee who is the prime factor in developing this type of supervisory field—problems that must be addressed and modified if meaningful learning is to occur. Difficulties of this sort may well require direct confrontations with the supervisee, and general efforts to help him shift toward a more symbolic mode of communicating—though your ability to do this will be severely limited. These are issues that we can delve into more extensively if they happen to come up in the course of these presentations.

Now, returning to your question, I would like to point out first, that the recognition of distinctive types of communicative fields requires of the supervisor that he identify the particular field that the patient and therapist have developed, that he identify the contributions of each, and that he, with full use of the material presented to him, gently and carefully demonstrate the therapist's contributions when they are present, doing so through the patient's unconscious perceptions and introjections. The nature of the communicative interaction is a first-order consideration in supervision, as it is in the treatment situation itself. And in keeping with a basic principle I hope to more clearly demonstrate as we go along, efforts in supervision to modify a pathological communicative field must always be based on the process notes of the therapeutic transaction, and must always begin with a demonstration of the contributions from the therapist, their form and their consequences. Then the supervisor can address the part being played by the patient. Once these issues have been clarified, the supervisor can also address the distinctive interventions required in each of these communicative fields, as well as the techniques through which the Type B and Type C communicative modes can be analyzed and modified. Incidentally, in dealing with the supervisee's contribution to these latter two fields, you have available not only the unconscious implications of his interventions, but the patient's unconscious perceptiveness, introjections, and curative endeavors as well. Many supervisees and present-day therapists and analysts unwittingly utilize their interventions as a major form of pathological projective identification into the patient, while others make use of what I have termed the *psychoanalytic cliché* (Langs 1978c) as a means of creating interpersonal and intrapsychic barriers for both themselves and their patients. Obviously, as supervisors, we should make every effort to call these tendencies to the attention of the supervisee, and to direct him toward the development of the Type A communicative mode—within the limitations of feasibility in supervision.

On the other hand, when it is the patient who is primarily responsible for a Type B field, the supervisor must help the supervisee understand the nature of such fields and teach him that his interventions must be shaped in accordance with this communicative mode. In general, such work must center around the defensive and inappropriately gratifying uses of projective identification, action, role and image evocations, and other discharge maneuvers—on what I term the *interpretive processing of interactional pressures* (Langs 1978b). Efforts at symbolic interpretation that do not focus in these realms will simply fail.

So you begin to see that teaching the supervisee how to listen leads to helping him learn to identify the particular communicative field within which he is working—his own and the patient's communicative styles—and that considerations of this kind open a whole new dimension of the supervisory experience. Incidentally, in the static-barrier Type C field, the therapist must learn to silently hold the patient, and to wait for moments of crisis when his massive defenses are momentarily modified, for moments when language is being used for communication rather than for anticommunication, and for metaphorical representations of the Type C communicative mode, before he intervenes. These patients use language for defense, for obliteration, for creating false impressions, and for barriers to interpersonal relatedness. They speak on a manifest level without underlying substance, and there is a lack of either an adaptive context or the unconscious responses to an adaptive context—an absence of Type One and, especially, Type Two derivatives. With these patients, there are as a rule no projective identifications to interpret, and no symbolic or latent communication, except at times of crisis when there is a shift to the Type A or Type B mode. The therapist can then intervene with his focus on the patient's massive defenses, the metaphors of the Type C style, and, secondarily, on the tumultuous inner mental contents that it is designed to seal off.

Supervisory fields of this kind are extremely static, and are usually generated by a supervisee and supervisor who both dread the inner mental world of their patients, and of themselves. There are, of course, all three types of supervisory communicative fields, and it is essential that the supervisor know his own style and that produced by his interaction with the supervisee. In the case at hand, I suspect some Type B and C propensities in the supervisee, and a Type A mode in the supervisor. Under pressure, styles may change; it is an important dimension to monitor in both bipersonal fields.

I still haven't answered your query, but I will do so now. It is my clinical finding that in a Type B field, the patient not only projectively identifies into the therapist, but he also remains open, in most instances, to the projective identifications of the therapist. He tends to experience the therapist's interventions as projective identifications and discharge products, and he has difficulty comprehending their symbolic qualities. It takes a good deal of therapeutic work to help develop in these patients a capacity to comprehend on a symbolic level.

As a rule, then, I have not found these patients to be refractory to the therapist's interventions, though occasionally they do prove refractory to containing what is placed into them, especially when there are pathological elements stemming from the therapist. In addition, they will always process these introjects in terms of their own pathological and nonpathological needs, and often will reproject this amalgam back into the therapist. The danger here is a sequence of unconscious pathological projective identifications, introjective identifications, reprojection, and further reprojection ad infinitum. It is here that I would like some clinical data for documentation, so, if we may, let's continue with the presentation.

Supervisor A: The next supervisory session was a week later. The resident began by telling me that the patient had missed an appointment with him that week. He continued to tell me something of his initial impressions of the patient.

Langs: The supervisory field seems poorly structured. As a result, it is not clear if the supervisee has another session to report from that particular week, or if this is a once-weekly patient and he therefore has no new session to report. It may also be that he still has some old sessions to review...

Supervisor A: Yes, he has the old sessions.

Langs: I want to examine here some of the chaos that occurs when the supervisory situation is not clearly structured and the supervisee is allowed to wander about, somewhat aimlessly, and is permitted to present old material rather than the most recent session or two. Much of the supervisee's approach seems highly defensive, and we are now faced with a situation where a patient has missed an hour and we have no idea of the prior session.

Under these circumstances, I believe that the supervisee—and his patient—is unconsciously communicating a need for structure and organization, for the definition of the supervisory field. Without these qualities, he continues his defensiveness by returning to a description of his initial impressions of the patient, rather than turning immediately to the hour prior to the missed session in order to explore some of the factors involved in the patient's absence. It is apparent acting out of this kind that justifies my sequential approach and highlights the need, even in an initial supervisory session, to allow sufficient time to get to the most recent session.

Supervisor A: Actually, this is not how I proceeded. It seems to me as I look over my notes that I did allow the supervisee to wander, and I see little promise in describing this particular supervisory session. I wonder if instead, since we are limited in regard to time, if it would not be more profitable to go to the last supervisory session?

Langs: Certainly: if this is where you want to take us, we will follow along.

Supervisor A: This supervisory session occurred this week. The supervisee by now had developed a bit of perspective; and there had been some work done in previous therapy sessions with this patient regarding his need to maintain control in his relationships with women, and his need to keep an adequate distance and not get too close to them. This had also been reflected in the way he allowed the therapeutic situation to be structured; that is, he would tend to be late or miss sessions, in order to gain some kind of distance or control in his relationship with the therapist.

Langs: I have several reactions at this point, but because you are summarizing, I will be brief. First, I am always suspicious of therapeutic work that arrives at general formulations such as those you have just described: a need for distance or control and a fear of closeness. In these situations I find, first, that there is a great deal of intellectualizing going on, and that it is usually bilateral, or interactional; second, that the specific unconscious fantasies and interactional mechanisms that are contributing to the lateness or absence are being missed; and third, that the therapist is not utilizing specific interventions developed through definitive adaptive contexts, and leading to the identification of dynamically active unconscious fantasies and defenses. There is a tendency, under these circumstances, to locate all of the factors in the latenesses and absences in the patient, when as a rule, there tend to be contributions from both patient and therapist—from transference and nontransference on the one hand, and countertransference on the other.

Along different lines, whenever there is an issue related to the framework, I would offer the supervisee a rather detailed discussion of the functions of the frame: its importance in creating a symbolic field and therapeutic regression, in offering a basic hold for both patient and therapist, and how modifications in the framework, whether initiated by patient or therapist, are often efforts at what I call *framework deviation cures*—symptom relief through an alteration in the frame (Langs 1975b, 1976a, d). I would add details in keeping with the most pertinent frame issue at hand.

Since we do not have the clinical data, I will leave it at that. I simply want to stress that in addition to identifying dynamic factors in the patient, I would explore the therapeutic interaction for contributions to these apparent forms of acting out or acting in. I would attempt to identify countertransference-based factors and study their influence on the communicative field, and to relate the relevant material from the patient to the basic functions of the framework. As you can see, we have far more to teach the therapist than how to interpret unconscious fantasies and memories—and much of that can be developed in response to a problem of this kind.

This reminds me too of Viderman's paper (1974), in which he stated that every patient brings to therapy his own frame, which is primarily designed to justify and maintain his neurosis. He will test out the frame that the therapist creates, as also his management of it. At issue is whether a therapeutic bipersonal field will be created, and whether the frame will be sufficiently damaged so as to preclude the insightful resolution of the patient's neurosis.

Supervisor A: I want to mention an additional factor that has come up in the previous supervisory sessions. The resident had asked if he could now discuss the woman patient who had left therapy. Apparently, she is planning to return to the area; she had called to make an appointment and he had made plans to see her. He wanted to know something about how to handle the situation with her, and whether he should agree to take her back into therapy. It soon became quite apparent that he was concerned about the extent to which she might have developed an erotic transference to him, and there was some question as to whether she had returned to this city just to be near the therapist.

Langs: In principle, I think it is best for the supervisee to work with a single case at a time with each supervisor. I have no objection at all to a shift from one patient to another when a supervisee requests it, although I will consider to myself the extent to which there is some wish to avoid supervision with the first patient, and will offer a comment along such lines if need be. I also think about the degree to which I feel that the patient can be treated without supervision.

However, when I sense a major need in the supervisee for supervision with a second patient, I am inclined to go along with his request. In fact, if the supervisee is capable of doing it, and there is no supervisor available for the first patient, I will even offer supervision for both patients. Unfortunately, in general, such an effort proves far too demanding for many trainees. I would therefore focus on the patient with whom he is having the greatest trouble and, perhaps, from time to time, spend the supervisory session on the other case.

In keeping with my strong preference for definitive data, I would have answered this supervisee's questions by suggesting that he present his last session with this patient, immediately before she left his area. From that material I would be able to formulate both her anxieties and his, her unconscious transference fantasies and unconscious perceptions of the therapist, and his countertransferences and noncountertransferences—suspecting, of course, that the erotic transference is actually a mixture of transference and nontransference, with a large measure of countertransference as well: an interactional syndrome (Langs 1976a,d).

In any case, on the basis of such a presentation I could help the therapist to structure the new treatment situation with this patient and to anticipate the material of the first hour.

Supervisor A: Well, I will now describe the most recent supervisory session; we were still working with this male patient. The patient wasn't on time, and he began by saying that things with his girlfriend weren't so good, that she had become a pain in the ass, and that she was calling him too much and coming over to his apartment too often.

In the supervisory session I focused somewhat on the patient's choice of words, and explored the possible dynamic meanings of the patient's language.

Langs: I must say that once again I am having difficulty in following this material, largely because we do not have a clear-cut sequence indicating the material presented to you, the point at which you intervened, and the nature of your specific interventions. As a result, I have little sense of either the therapeutic or supervisory interactions.

This is all quite fragmented, but I will share with you my own impressions. Applying the principles that all the patient's communications have some bearing on the therapeutic interaction, that they are a mixture of unconscious fantasy and perception, and that therapists-in-training tend to make more technical errors than correct interventions, I can treat this material as Type One derivatives since, after all, we do not have the specific adaptive context. I would infer from this material that the patient unconsciously perceives the therapist as prodding him, jabbing him in the ass—a latent homosexual image—and that he feels that therapy is not going too well, and that the therapist is being too invasive.

All of that is a broad silent hypothesis. I don't know if we will have an opportunity to validate it. I have simply monitored the material in terms of some possible general qualities of the therapeutic experience—and as probably containing primarily valid unconscious perceptions of the therapist. But for now, let's focus on what you said to the supervisee, and where things went from there.

Supervisor A: Well, I told him that I wondered whether there might have been some displacement from the transference, because there were some associations in the previous sessions that indicated that the patient felt that the resident was bugging him with certain interpretations, interventions, and the like. Specifically, the resident had made a comment about the patient's missing sessions, and told the patient that this interfered with his treatment. I therefore felt that there was some basis on which to suggest that the patient was talking about the therapist in the guise of his girlfriend.

Langs: Well, I am pleased to see that we are on the same track. It seems to me that you are suggesting a specific adaptive context for this particular session: namely, the therapist's noninterpretive intervention, in which he told the patient that missing sessions interfered with his therapy. He made this comment as an alternative to listening for an adaptive context and for a sequence of associations that would have yielded Type Two derivatives that would then permit an interpretation of the unconscious meaning of the missed sessions. Or if, as I am beginning to suspect, this is a Type B field, the therapist could have used this material to interpret the unconscious meanings of the patient's projective identifications and could have commented on this type of communication and behavior.

I was concerned when you said that you had approached this material by focusing on the patient's choice of words, fearing that you were about to offer some type of intellectualized comment rather than a formulation concerning the therapeutic interaction. Instead, I see that you decided to intervene at a point where you felt that you could formulate this material in terms of a particular adaptive context. As a rule, it is best to initiate such a discussion by asking the supervisee to evaluate this material first, a most valuable teaching method which may reveal additional problems in his listening and formulating functions. In addition to then discussing his assessment, you could develop your own hypothesis and tentative intervention, which could then be confirmed by the patient's continued associations and could serve as a model against which you would measure the supervisee's actual intervention later in the hour.

If I may, I would like to caution you against formulating this as a displacement from "the transference," because I feel that it must be stated as a displacement from "the therapeutic relationship"—and then defined in terms of pathological unconscious fantasies (transference) and veridical unconscious perception (nontransference). When you call the therapeutic relationship from the vantage point of the patient "transference," you are implying a predominance of fantasy and distortion. This stands in contrast to your own comment that the patient rightfully felt bugged by the therapist's interventions, and your implication that this was a primarily nondistorted experience, however exaggerated.

It is here that I also can show you how a valid unconscious perception and introjection is both defended against and elaborated in keeping with the patient's unconscious needs. On the one hand the patient shifts to comments about his girlfriend and away from the therapeutic relationship and the latent homosexual implications of the interaction, while on the other he unconsciously gives the experience a distinct homosexual coloring which may well arise from his own intrapsychic pathology. However, we have not ruled out the strong possibility that this communication nonetheless includes a valid unconscious perception of unconscious dynamics within the therapist. In fact, you may remember that based on my evaluation of his initial question about the patient's girlfriend, I suggested the possibility that the therapist was attempting to defend himself against unconscious homosexual derivatives related to himself. The congruence of these two independent formulations offers some degree of validation, and you will notice that it is based largely on the therapist's interventions and, to a lesser degree, on the communications from the patient—especially his reference to how the girlfriend was becoming a pain in the ass. We need more material from the patient to really be confident regarding the validation of these hypotheses.

It is, however, reassuring, and another secondary form of validation, that two independent observers—the supervisor and myself—have arrived at relatively similar formulations of this material. This type of validation can occur in supervision when both supervisee and supervisor are in agreement. However, I warn you against possible unconscious collusion and misalliance in this regard, and would stress the need for independent validation from the patient under those circumstances.

Supervisor A: So I asked the supervisee what he thought about the patient's choice of words and what he felt it was related to. The supervisee responded that he thought it involved the anal level of development and a struggle for power and control in the therapeutic situation. I agreed with him in this regard, and added the additional facet of the displacement from himself onto the girlfriend.

Langs: I am not clear again: you stressed the role of displacement; had the supervisee connected this material to the therapeutic interaction?

Supervisor A: No, I am sorry; I had presented what he had said and what I had added together. Actually, he had stressed the issue of anal control between the patient and his girlfriend, and it was I who had connected it to treatment.

Langs: Yes, I had sensed an ambiguity there. And it's actually a rather important point: I would have been quite impressed with a supervisee who would have recognized that these associations were derivatives related to the therapeutic interaction. Such thinking is quite the exception, even after a good bit of supervisory work—which I think testifies, unfortunately, to the limited quality of supervision as it is practiced in most centers today. And, even if he had simply treated this material as Type One derivatives whose manifest content alludes to the therapeutic relationship—and he undoubtedly would have thought of them primarily in terms of fantasy, rather than of unconscious perception—that would have been an important accomplishment on his part.

This discussion suggests that one of the goals of the supervisory experience is to enable the supervisee to develop a tolerance for dealing with the inevitable anxieties and conflicts that are stirred up when he consistently monitors the material from his patients in terms of commentaries on the therapeutic relationship, using the me/not-me interface and accepting every association as pertaining to himself and the patient—with varying mixtures of perceptiveness and distortion. This is a position that many analysts who have gone through a personal analysis still find difficult to adopt and manage.

So at best we can educate the supervisee in this direction, and leave the rest up to him: to attempt on his own the introjective identification of such derivatives—an almost herculean effort—or to pursue his personal therapy.

However, it turns out that this supervisee is really quite representative of therapists-in-training. He tends to formulate the material from his patients in terms of intrapsychic fantasies and issues, in terms of early developmental levels, and divorces it from the immediate therapeutic interaction, especially from himself. Interventions that are based on such formulations tend to be intellectualized and highly defensive—the common use of "transference genetics" as defense (Langs 1978c). This promotes a very common interactional defense in which both patient and therapist create sector of misalliance (Langs 1975a) and a bastion (Baranger and Baranger) 1966)—a split-off sector of the bipersonal field that contains derivatives and direct references related to the therapeutic relationship.

You can see that there are two common errors reflected in the material: first, the tendency, based on countertransference need, to exclude the therapeutic relationship, and to utilize the intrapsychic focus as a defense against acknowledging that the derivatives do indeed pertain to the therapeutic interaction; and second, to think of such material primarily in terms of fantasies and distortions, overlooking the specific adaptive context and the evidence that much of this material is actually made up of Type Two derivatives containing unconscious perceptions, with secondary transference-based elaborations.

I hope you can see now why I virtually never discuss intrapsychic and genetic issues without linking them to the therapeutic interaction; I do not promote this type of defensive position in my supervisees and I do not find it meaningful to use psychoanalytic jargon in this way. In addition, in keeping with the principle of allowing the patient's material to direct my supervisory interventions, I tend not to bring up the genetic dimension unless the patient has directly or indirectly raised such issues. At times, it can be mentioned as an educational device, but we must be careful to avoid unconsciously fostering any propensity with the supervisee to divorce the material from his own interaction with the patient, who for his part never makes that mistake.

By the way, it is quite common even among psychoanalysts to make use of intrapsychic and psychosexual-genetic formulations as a defense against elements in the present therapeutic interaction, especially those related to quite unconscious countertransference expressions. This is a defense that apparently was utilized by Freud in his own analytic work, and which even contributed to his discovery of transference through clinical observations that actually entailed in many instances nontransference-based reactions to himself that had important genetic antecedents—a point made earlier by Szasz (1963) and Chertok (1968).

I would also like to add a few comments about supervisory technique and methodology. Here the supervisor has heard a certain amount of material; he has formulated a hypothesis; he may then wait for the supervisee to intervene, or he might ask the supervisee for his own hypothesis at this point—especially since the supervisor seems rather confident that he has sufficient evidence for his own ideas. For me, this is a valid teaching technique. But I would not have approached this with a query as to the language the patient used, but would have asked for the supervisee's silent hypothesis and developed the discussion from there.

Now, what actually happened is that the supervisee then offered a formulation in terms of the patient's psychosexual development, implying too that he was viewing this material primarily in terms of the patient's relationship with his girlfriend: he was formulating Type One derivatives in terms of a relationship outside the therapeutic interaction. The supervisor then offered a hypothesis that this material was quite pertinent to what he called "the transference," and what I have identified as "the therapeutic relationship." We do not know whether the supervisor offered any clarifying comments at this point, but I would tend to delay my discussion of the pertinent conceptual and technical issues until we heard additional material from the patient—material which might validate the supervisor's hypothesis on some level, either through the development of closer derivatives related to the therapeutic relationship or through a shift to manifest references to the therapist or the therapeutic situation. Perhaps we will have an actual opportunity for such validation in a moment.

But what I am stressing here is that, methodologically, both supervisor and supervisee should state an initial hypothesis and should allow the patient's subsequent material to be the judge: to offer validation or nonvalidation. Then, if the supervisor's formulation is not validated, he should openly revise his thinking based on the leads from the patient's subsequent associations, and should discuss the possible reasons for his error. On the other hand, if his formulation is validated, this becomes an excellent opportunity to discuss the relevant topics with the supervisee. Here these might include the importance of appending all of the material from the patient to the therapeutic interaction, the distinction between transference and nontransference, the universal defensiveness in therapists and analysts regarding the patient's unconscious perceptions of themselves and their difficulties, the validating process in both therapy and supervision, the basics of the listening process as it is directed toward the detection of derivatives and unconscious processes—to name some salient topics—and much of it is shaped further by the patient's subsequent material. I would continue to stress the importance of identifying the critical adaptive context and the extent to which this is generally within the therapeutic relationship.

I am now stressing the need to be quite explicit in supervision, to continually develop basic principles as the ongoing material from the presentation directs you toward one area or another, and to explicitly identify for the supervisee the major factors that have a bearing on your own formulations and your assessment of his silent hypotheses or interventions. Here the supervisor implied that the adaptive context for this material was a recent traumatic intervention by the therapist. As you can see, I would have been quite specific in this regard, and would not only have identified the specific precipitant for this material, but would also have discussed the broader issue of the role of the adaptive context in the patient's communications and in the therapist's listening process. It is certainly the creative supervisor who is able to consistently and meaningfully shift from the specifics of a given presentation to the basic issues it touches upon; this continuous shift from the specific to the general is essential to sound supervisory technique.

We have now an opportunity to apply the validating process to this material, so let's see what happens.

Supervisor A: The patient went on to say that his girlfriend had once asked him, when he had called her and was getting ready to terminate the conversation, Are you forgetting something? Namely, that the patient should have said, I love you. The therapist intervened at that point and said, Now that she is seeing only you, how do you feel?

What had happened is that the patient had decided to begin seeing other women for a while, and the girlfriend was going to see other men. Then they had decided not to do that, and the latest understanding was that the girlfriend was going to see only him.

Langs: The leopard never changes his spots, right? The therapist did not modify his countertransferences and they continue to influence his interventions. This material is fascinating in a number of ways, and I think it demonstrates why I prefer, in general, to wait until the therapist intervenes before making my supervisory comments. It provides a better nodal point for the statement of contrasting hypotheses, since it will be the material subsequent to this intervention that will be most pertinent to the validating process. After all, the best reflection of a supervisee's formulation is found in his intervention to the patient; at this point he has in a sense committed himself to the patient, and it generates a very meaningful moment in the supervisory experience. It is here that I do my supervisory work.

I would proceed by asking the supervisee a series of questions: What are the formal qualities of this intervention? Let's look at it: Now that she is seeing only you, how do you feel? Clearly, a question. Next I would ask, What are its additional formal characteristics and what are some of its most evident communicative properties? (I will want to focus much of my teaching in this last area.) Here, we would first discover that it lacks an adaptive context, and that it also reflects listening on a manifest level. It addresses the manifest content without consideration of either Type One or Type Two derivatives and therefore disregards unconscious processes.

I would also ask the supervisee to attempt to identify the major unconscious communications contained in this intervention. And here, the stress would be on the manner in which he is inviting the patient to avoid any recognition that this material represents derivatives related to the therapeutic relationship or that it invites, as I said earlier, an interactional defense, a sector of misalliance, a bastion.

As a rule, though consciously designed to promote communication from the patient, questions almost without exception have these disruptive qualities and interfere with derivative communication. For this reason, I no longer use them as an intervention (Langs 1978b,c). I would, then, in supervising this resident, discuss my position in this regard, and touch upon the many related issues I have mentioned earlier.

Depending on the point in supervision, on my assessment of the supervisee's tolerance for confrontation, and on how often he commits this technical error, I would add some further comments. First, I would want to point out that this particular question is a new version of the query made in the first session. This point may help you—and the supervisee—to realize how very meaningful that initial question had been, and how tellingly it reflected the unconscious countertransferences of the therapist. I have to prove again and again that I am not nit-picking, and that there is no such thing as an inconsequential intervention. We are touching upon crucial countertransference issues that are introjected by the patient and that influence his therapeutic experience.

Now, as I was saying, depending on a number of factors, it would be admissible for me also to ask the supervisee if he has any notion as to the underlying basis for this particular intervention—as a means of predicting how the patient unconsciously will perceive it. Here I would be attempting to approach the therapist's unconscious homosexual anxieties as they specifically relate to his defensive need to deflect the patient's communications away from himself, and to do so, in part, by stressing heterosexual relationships outside of treatment. This is, of course, a difficult issue, as countertransference always is, but it is my consistent observation that patients unconsciously introject not only the unconscious defenses involved in an intervention of this kind, but also that they unconsciously sense aspects of its underlying basis. I would therefore anticipate—predict—that this patient unconsciously will perceive and introject the therapist's unconscious homosexual anxieties and defensive needs—and I have already cited evidence that he has done so based on the therapist's earlier interventions.

I therefore feel that this is a painful but necessary supervisory confrontation for two essential reasons: first, it is significantly influencing the therapist's work with this patient, which, in large measure, cannot be corrected unless at least some aspect of the underlying unconscious fantasies and anxieties are modified; and second, this identifies the essential qualities of the unconscious introject to which the patient has been subjected. This is, as I've said, very difficult stuff, yet it also is very crucial to the therapeutic process and to the true growth of the resident.

This material also prompts me to state my strong belief that the supervisor should take a definitive position in evaluating each intervention of the therapist—in terms of its nature, validity, and communicative properties. I firmly believe that there is such a thing as a correct or incorrect intervention, and that correct interventions are confirmed by the patient and experienced in terms of positive introjects, while incorrect interventions are not validated and are experienced in terms of negative introjects. I believe that there is far more science and methodology to both psychotherapy and psychoanalysis than is generally assumed, and that our neglect of clinical methodology has been unfortunate and defensive, whatever other factors may also be involved.

I think that it is crucial in supervision to take a definite stand when possible, and to then apply the validating process to the subsequent material from the patient. To do this in the most meaningful manner, the supervisor should, for example, not only indicate his judgment that a particular intervention is in error; he should also define its specific nature, the countertransference-based unconscious communications it contains, and the specific alternative intervention that he would have made, if any. Wherever possible, the unconsciously constructive dimension of a basically erroneous intervention should also be spelled out. This last is based on my finding, reported in *The Bipersonal Field* (Langs 1976a) that virtually every mistaken intervention has some constructive nucleus contained within it. I have found that identifying this element often counterbalances one's criticism of a hurtful, destructive, or seductive intervention.

Finally, I want to mention another thesis of *The Bipersonal Field*: namely, that every erroneous intervention, since it is not based on the needs of the patient, entails either an attempt to create a Type C barrier against some inner chaos, within himself or the patient, with which he cannot deal, or is an unconscious effort by the therapist to projectively identify into the patient his own pathological inner mental contents and processes, as a means of misusing the patient as what I have termed a *pathological container* and as a source of proxy responses.

To illustrate specifically, in regard to this therapist's intervention—asking the patient how he feels now that his girlfriend was seeing only him—once I had identified this as a question, I would have asked the supervisee to evaluate his own intervention. I would expect him to begin by trying to establish the central adaptive context for this session; it is the crucial determinant for deciding upon the validity of the intervention and its unconscious meanings. Here I would expect that we could eventually reach a consensus that the most meaningful adaptive context for this hour is the therapist's hostile and critical interventions in the previous hour. Whether the intervention described earlier—asking the patient how his girlfriend was different from the other women in his life—was made in that hour or not, I would expect that we could easily discover a series of similar interventions in the previous session. And I would endeavor to establish these specific communications and their unconscious implications—contents and functions—as the definitive adaptive context, within the broader, more general context of the therapist's repeated difficulties in managing the framework and in intervening with this patient.

Once the adaptive context has been arrived at, one can readily demonstrate that this particular intervention is essentially in error, as it totally disregards the most crucial adaptive context for the patient's communications. I would then ask the supervisee to attempt to understand the unconscious nature and function of this particular intervention. In this way, I would try to demonstrate to him that it serves to deflect the patient's communications away from himself, to defend against the unconscious homosexual qualities of the interaction—with elements of transference, nontransference, countertransference, and noncountertransference—and that it serves also to direct the patient to the manifest contents of his associations, thereby ignoring both Type One and Type Two derivatives and, more broadly, unconscious processes and contents.

This intervention demonstrates a very common split within supervisees, and within supervisors as well: on one level most will acknowledge the unconscious factors in emotional illnesses and problems, while on another level, in their actual work with patients, they deal with conscious contents and readily available inferences, failing to recognize the inherent and basic contradiction. It is here that the use of the adaptive context as the organizer of the patient's associations facilitates the understanding of derivatives and unconscious processes, of convoluted, neurotic communication (Langs 1978d), and permits of course, the therapeutic work to take place on the necessary and definitive unconscious level.

I would also propose to the supervisee that this intervention is an offer of an intellectualized and ruminative defensive sector of misalliance, and that it will generate what I call an *interactional resistance* (Langs 1976 a, d), in that the patient will in all likelihood tend initially to ruminate about the girlfriend and to accept the bastion related to the therapeutic relationship—though later I would expect him to undertake efforts at modifying the bastion and misalliance, as well as the countertransference difficulties of the therapist.

Finally, I would point to the unconscious positive core of this intervention: namely, its allusion to the one-to-one relationship theme. In this respect, I believe that unconsciously the therapist is identifying his one-to-one relationship with the patient as a source of mutual anxiety. He is, of course, in this way revealing an aspect of his own countertransference difficulties, but is at the same time suggesting that the patient is having similar problems. In identifying such an unconscious positive nucleus, however, I always stress that there can be only one unconscious interpreter in the psychotherapeutic situation, and that, unfortunately for the therapist, it must be the patient. It is the therapist's responsibility to translate unconscious communications and mechanisms meaningfully into the conscious sphere for both himself and the patient. Thus, while there is a positive core here, it will have only a minimal salutory effect on the patient. On the other hand, the conscious recognition of these anxieties, along with their mastery and the development of the appropriate interpretation, would have a far more positive effect. In general, the negative qualities of an incorrect intervention far outweigh the constructive nucleu, and as a result the latter can serve only as a small consolation to the supervisee who is struggling to clarify the nature of his therapeutic work and the underlying countertransferences.

Now all of these remarks would be embedded in a discussion of the type of communicative field that seems to obtain between the patient and his therapist. Here it seems that the supervisor and the supervisee, having developed between them a Type A communicative field, are endeavoring to understand, on a symbolic, insight-seeking level, the nature of the therapeutic interaction and its ramifications. When we turn to the therapeutic bipersonal field, however, the situation seems less clear. My formulation at this point—open, of course, to validation would be that we are observing mainly a Type B communicative field, in which the patient is grossly acting out and ridding himself of disturbing stimuli, while making, in addition, sporadic efforts at unconscious, symbolic communication. The therapist for his part is using language—verbal interventions—as a means of projectively identifying into the patient aspects of his own unconscious fantasies, conflicts, and defenses. Language is serving as a way of getting rid of disturbing inner stimuli within himself. It would be presumptuous of me, with the little data available, to suggest the scope of the contribution of each participant to the development of this apparently Type B field; but it does seem safe to say that so long as the therapist intervenes harshly, noninterpretively, and incorrectly, the patient will continue to utilize language and behavior for discharge and the essential qualities of this field will not be modified. In this context, I hear the patient's efforts at derivative communication as an endeavor to shift this field to a Type A field. And I would add, too, that the therapist's intervention has the additional characteristic of offering Type C barriers and falsifications—it may generate a field with both Type B and Type C qualities.

How much time I would devote to spelling out my evaluation would depend on many factors: the point in supervision, the time left in that particular supervisory hour, my estimation of the needs and tolerance of the supervisee, my assessment of the needs of the patient, etc. If it is early in supervision, I might elaborate as a kind of model assessment, to begin to acquaint the supervisee with the vast implications of his communications to the patient. Later in supervision, I might select for emphasis certain issues I believe relevant to major blind spots and difficulties in the supervisee, or areas I feel are critical to the apparent difficulties we see in this treatment situation.

In light of the common tendency to hold the patient almost entirely responsible for resistances and disruptions in therapy, it is important to carefully delineate both the patient's and the therapist's contributions to a major resistance. This is an interactional process that must be clarified on both sides. Now I am well aware of critics who feel that I concentrate on the pathological contributions of the therapist, far more than those of the patient. And there are also some who say that this approach is far too intense for the supervisee to bear. In response to the first criticism, I would submit that I am simply following the threads of the unconscious communicative interaction, and that often, under conditions such as these, the contributions of the therapist to the treatment difficulties is, indeed, far greater than those from the patient. In addition, it is critical to help the supervisee become aware of and resolve such tendencies and, if possible, their underlying countertransference-based aspects. In fact, he would have to make inner changes of his own before it would be feasible for him to identify, analyze, and interpretively resolve the contributions from the patient.

Remember, too, that it is the therapist's role in these difficulties that the patient is, for the moment, unconsciously concentrating on and working over. It is important to recognize that process, and to help the supervisee to understand that aspect of the patient's communications. For the moment, we can see that the patient has his own propensities toward acting out and living out, toward projective identification and action-discharge; but these are quite poorly defined for in the material because, to put it metaphorically, the interface of the bipersonal field has shifted toward the pathology of the therapist, and the work of the field is now concentrated upon his countertransference difficulties far more than on the transference problems—the psychopathology—of the patient.

And, by the way, this is rather typical when there are countertransference-based interventions as a factor in the field. Only the insightful resolution of these difficulties will shift the interface toward the patient's pathology and transferences, so the work of the field—patient and therapist—can become concentrated on the psychopathologyof the patient. I really want to stress that point, because my position does not represent a preoccupation with the pathology of the therapist, but is intended to convey a full, fair, and balanced appreciation of the actualities of the therapeutic interaction. Rather coincidentally, my position then stresses a major dimension of the psychotherapeutic experience that has, by and large, been greatly underestimated by previous writers.

As for the criticisms that supervision of this kind tends to be overwhelming and unmanageable for the supervisee, that it functions something like a premature interpretation, and that it may well be more disruptive than constructive, I must confess that this is an aspect of my work that has consistently caused me great concern. I have again and again examined this aspect of the supervisory experience in search of modulating considerations. But I have stayed with this approach because, as I said earlier, it seems of the utmost necessity because it identifies the specific impingements upon the patient, and deals with the true nature of the patient's interaction with the therapist—the state of the bipersonal field.

As therapists we are committed to a search for the truth, from the surface to the depths, and we must be aware of these truths in order to work effectively with our patients. I therefore believe that it is not I who am imposing burdensome interventions upon the therapist but, rather, that it is the patient. I believe that the problem is not in the nature of my supervision, but that it lies instead in the nature of the work the supervisee has chosen, and in his conscious and unconscious interaction with his patient.

In this context, I think that the supervisee who has some inkling of the nature of his own unconscious communications, and those of the patient, is actually in a far better position than otherwise to undertake efforts at rectifying and interpreting the pathology of the field, and in learning how to effect a valid, insightful, positive, and adaptive cure for his patient. Psychotherapy is an extremely difficult form of treatment; it weighs heavily on anyone who attempts to carry it out in its most valid and effective form. And the bipersonal field within which it occurs generates unending pressures on the therapist's vulnerabilities and countertransferences, and requires of him a therapeutic need for continuous mastery. This should be taken to imply neither the erroneous conception that the bipersonal field is designed for the cure of the therapist, nor the mistaken notion that the therapist should be preoccupied with his own problems rather than those of the patient.

In light of the very trying, painful, and anxiety-provoking qualities of this type of supervision, I make every effort to offer valid forms of support and understanding, and to convey an appreciation of the stressful qualities of both this kind of supervision and this kind of psychotherapy. And I maintain a sensitivity to the supervisee's capacity to tolerate this kind of work—with his patient and with me. I am well aware that for some supervisees this type of supervision generates intense threat to brittle defenses encapsulating extremely disruptive inner mental contents. Often this type of therapist works in a Type C field—in both therapy and supervision; at issue may well be some type of underlying psychotic or near-psychotic disturbance.

Unfortunately, however, the same danger of regression and disorganization exists in his work with his patient, the same vulnerability, and, in consequence, the need for similar efforts to maintain rigid defenses and to exclude all potentially disruptive stimuli. As you can see, then, such a therapist cannot function effectively with his patients, and his intolerance of the supervisory experience offers him a much-needed opportunity to recognize the extent of his own problems and, hopefully, to seek and find the necessary help.

I can assure you that I am not attempting to rationalize a destructive approach to supervisees, and that I have made repeated efforts at self-analysis in this area: my intentions are to the greatest degree possible constructive and truth seeking.

Perhaps you can continue a bit before we break for lunch; we could use some material for the validating process.

Supervisor A: Well, the patient went on and said, At times it's too much. (Laughter.) By the way, he said, I met a woman that you know.

Langs: There are times when I find the unconscious dimension of psychotherapy and supervision absolutely incredible, and this is one such moment. I have always said that a good question and a valid formulation will be clarified and confirmed in the material from the patient. And I am enormously relieved, having gone out on a limb, that the patient immediately validates so much of what I have just said. You can see now the kind of beautiful feelings, sensitivities, and interplay of ideas that can occur in the supervisory situation when you work in keeping with the model I have been developing. In fact, I came to this model by finding, reassuringly enough, that often a formulation or prediction that I would make in supervision was subsequently stated in derivative form by the patient. And I must say, in keeping with this experience, that it usually takes me a great deal of time to develop my ideas, while the patient is able to do almost as well in a few pithy and remarkably creative, exquisitely condensed phrases: it's too much; I met someone you know.

Both Arlow (1963) and Searles (1955)—among others—have written of the parallel processes that take place in the two bipersonal fields, supervision and therapy, stressing the manner in which the supervisor's interaction with the supervisee may mirror the interaction between the supervisee and his patient. And I hope to be able to demonstrate aspects of this type of parallel process with some later material; it will often provide important subjective clues to the supervisor as to what the patient is unconsciously experiencing in his work with the supervisee.

I mention this here, however, because I am defining another type of parallel process, one somewhat related to the type that I have just described. But here, the parallel lies between the supervisor's conscious formulations of the supervisee's communications to the patient, and the patient's unconscious assessment and response. In this area, we may make more use of our cognitive capacities than of those that are empathic and interactional. A supervisor's use of empathy and intuition is more immediately in the service of understanding and is a striking factor in the parallel process type of experience described by Arlow and Searles. It often takes the form of sensing something unusual about the supervisee's relationship and interaction with you as the supervisor—working over interactional inputs and even projective identifications that are processed within yourself toward conscious understanding and translated into what the patient must be experiencing. I am stressing in addition a more direct response and evaluation of the material presented by the supervisee, and a striking parallel between the supervisor's conscious understanding and the unconscious understanding of the patient.

The patient's initial comment—At times it's too much—suggests that my mini-lecture on the burdens of being a therapist derived in some meaningful way from an emphatic appreciation of important stressful qualities of this particular therapeutic interaction. And I feel that the patient is speaking unconsciously for both himself and the therapist, and that he is alluding to their shared sense of being overwhelmed in the therapeutic relationship. On the side of the therapist, this reflects the patient's unconscious appreciation that the therapist is unable to adequately contain, hold, and interpret, and that he feels overburdened. This point is amply validated by the patient's next association: I met a woman that you know.

In fact, I would wonder whether the therapist already knew of this meeting, and whether this was serving as a specific adaptive context for the therapist's defensive and deflecting intervention. On the other hand, what we have heard may simply be an aspect of an ongoing and chronic difficulty within the therapist. Certainly, the patient unconsciously senses that the therapist will be even more disturbed with this new bit of news. You can see too that the patient does not really accept the offered intellectualizing misalliance and the bastion related to the therapeutic relationship; he moves directly into this area in a way that validates my thesis that the central adaptive context lies in this realm.

Now this also helps to verify a point I made just a few minutes ago: namely, that at times the patient may function not only unconsciously as therapist, but also in ways that are evidently far more healthy and nondefensive than does the therapist. At this point it is clear that it is the therapist who is behaving defensively and the patient who is attempting to get to important issues. And I think that we can extract from this observation the likelihood that in supervision we must first help the supervisee to master his countertransferences before turning to the patient's pathology. We can see too that we have further evidence that the patient is prepared to communicate analyzable derivatives and, probably, to shift to a Type A field—if the therapist will permit.

As for the patient's feeling overburdened, some of this may well have to do with his meeting a woman who knows his therapist, a trying experience at best, and one that might well tax his defenses and prove disruptive intrapsychically. But much of this also alludes to the therapeutic relationship itself: to the patient's feelings that he is being used by his therapist as a pathological container and is being subjected to disruptive projective identifications. Some of this may also arise from a pathological introjective identification with the therapist's difficulty in mastering the unconscious homosexual fantasies, conflicts, and anxieties in the bipersonal field, and present in both patient and therapist.

Incidentally, I probably would not have intervened in supervision as yet, as I would want to hear more of the patient's associations. But I would, I must admit, be feeling quite satisfied and relieved—as I felt here just a moment ago—because it is no easy matter to attempt to be definitive, to commit yourself, to wait for validation, and to sometimes have to face nonvalidating responses. For me, validation of this kind confirms my basic model of supervision, and affords us the exact type of experience that I hope to generate through these presentations—as a means of developing a sense of conviction in each of you. This is what I have called "validation through Type Two derivatives" (Langs 1978 c, i)—a derivative form of unique and unexpected confirmation. Actually, every clinical psychoanalytic hypothesis should be validated in this way before it is accepted as sound and proven.

Notice too, that the reference to meeting a woman who knows the therapist brings us right back to the framework; it is a boundary issue and opens this area to further exploration. Finally, it is important to recognize that these associations do not confirm the therapist's intervention—they do not produce new and startling perspectives related to his intrapsychic conflicts, or to his pathological unconscious fantasies and introjects vis-à-vis his girlfriend. Instead they confirm the supervisor's interventions—and my own as well—in truly remarkable ways, and in a form that can teach the supervisee a great deal about basic methodology.

Moderator: We will now recess for lunch. I am advised that the group would like to return a half hour early so that we could hear additional material from this presentation, before moving on to the second supervisory situation.

Chapter 3

Interplay Between the Supervisory and Therapeutic Fields

Moderator: We will continue now with the presentation that we were following before our break. I turn the floor over to Dr. Langs.

Langs: Thank you. As you might expect by now, I have a few introductory comments—most of them based on a number of interesting questions that were asked of me during lunch. One point has to do with my comments on the special qualities of the interpersonal elements of the psychotherapeutic situation as compared to that in general medicine, and, in particular, of the supervision of psychotherapy as compared to supervisory work in general medicine. It seems I allowed room for an unwarranted implication that I want to correct: I was not intending to deny any of the important aspects of the interpersonal interaction between patient and therapist in any medical field, or between any mentor and his student. I was simply indicating that in a certain sense the interpersonal sphere is virtually the all of therapy, and that, while it is crucial in other medical situations, it is by no means the all. On a medical service, for example, teaching focuses on the patient's symptoms, diagnosis, and the rest, and the personal relationship between supervisor and supervisee, and between the trainee and his patient, which are of course, extremely important, are in general seldom discussed unless it becomes an obvious issue and the supervisor is sensitive to such matters. In general, in a medical situation there is a focus on the patient and his symptoms, rather than on the personal interaction, whereas in the psychotherapy situation the focus is on the patient and his symptoms as they unfold in the interaction—and the interaction itself must be subjected to study.

I will leave my comments at that for the moment, and as we hear additional material I trust that those of you who have developed questions and comments will speak out.

Supervisor A: I would like to begin by saying a few words about my thinking about the case up until the point that I described just before our luncheon break. My style of supervision is to pay a great deal of attention to the phrasing and technique of interventions the resident makes, and particularly in trying to get each supervisee to pay equal attention to instinctual drive derivatives, ego and superego derivatives, anxiety, and the like, and not to land too heavily on id-type interpretations, which I think is one of the most frequent errors that I see in supervisees.

Langs: It is quite illuminating to hear you describe your own style of supervision. With all that I have had to say, the presentation of the material that the supervisee offered to you, and the discussions in this seminar, you have had little time to present your own interventions and their rationale. There is little doubt that every supervisor has his own style of work, and, as I have said repeatedly, his own model of both therapy and supervision. Still, I do believe that we are attempting here today to develop a basic model within which individual styles can flourish constructively. That is, I do feel that efforts should be made to arrive at the best models of supervision and therapy available, and to back them up with both a theoretical understanding and direct validation in one's supervisory and treatment work. These are, of course, extremely difficult issues to clarify, and even more difficult to validate, but it seems to me that we are now at a point in the history of psychoanalysis and psychotherapy where such validation is just beginning to be undertaken and where the challenge to psychoanalytically validate one's position must be met.

In your comment, you also touch upon your own collective experience as a supervisor—and implicitly, as a supervisee—and its influence on your particular approach to supervision. Here too the factors are legion: they begin with your own personal experiences as a trainee and then later as an independent therapist, and extend into your observations in doing supervision. All of this is influenced by your own unconscious needs, positive capacities, and unresolved countertransferences, and there is an interplay between your particular model of psychotherapy and your evolving model of supervision.

And as you are indicating here, part of that model is based on your assessment of the most common and important problems in supervisees. Undoubtedly many of you have been struck by the fact that the supervisory policy offered by our presenting supervisor touches upon an area that I did not emphasize at all for the moment—even though certain aspects of my comments, such as the need to comprehend all dimensions of the bipersonal field, might be seen as an interactional form of your stress on the therapist's balanced listening to the material from the patient. In a sense, then, your emphasis is on a balanced understanding of the intrapsychic ramifications of the material from the patient, while mine has been on balanced listening of this material as it applies to the inner world of both patient and therapist, and to their unconscious communicative interaction. I state it this way so that it can become evident that your formulation, which I believe is representative of the classical psychoanalytic position, can be seen as only one small portion of the model I have offered. In this way, perhaps some of the implications of my particular interactional model are made clear. It is this very focus on the intrapsychic world of the patient that I have been attempting to expand, to document its inadequacy, in order to foster a more balanced approach to the contributions—even to the patient's associations—that are derived from both patient and therapist.

So your model of therapy and supervision is clearly influenced by your personal training, your healthy and unhealthy needs, your capacities to observe, experience, formulate, think creatively, and the like. And there is considerable influence from one of the main sources of learning, at least among psychoanalysts and many psychotherapists: their own psychoanalytic treatment and the implicit and explicit pressures of their training experiences. As you all must know, there are strong pressures to conform to models of therapy and supervision, and it is only after a therapist has completed his analysis and graduated from an institute that he is able to experience a sense of freedom previously lacking. But even then the pressures do not entirely let up.

As I was reminded by a discussion at lunch, there are additional anxieties that confront the therapist when he becomes a supervisor, including the common trend now to permit the trainee to evaluate his mentors. And even here, where you share with us aspects of your own concept of supervision, and I find striking differences from my own conceptualization, I think it will be useful to consider again some of the pressures with which a supervisor must deal.

So, let's think again about the supervisor: his concern for his self-image, his reputation, his place in the hierarchy of teachers, his hopes for referrals, and the like—all exert an influence on his functioning as a supervisor. Since much of this is rather obvious and beyond the scope of the data we will be exploring today, I will be brief. I only wish to point out such factors as his confidence as a teacher, his grasp of issues in supervision, his comprehension of the therapeutic interaction, his comfort with what he knows well, as well as with areas of uncertainty, his training, his own personal therapy or analysis, the place of analytically trained as compared to nonanalytic supervisors in a given department, the collective reputation of his particular group, the extent to which his work with the supervisee receives direct and indirect support from the established directors of the clinic and department, and the degree to which personal and ideological rivalries and disagreements lead a particular departmental or section head to undermine the work of a given supervisor—all of these are background issues that can influence the manner in which the supervisor works with the supervisee, as well as the ways in which the supervisee learns. I address these areas because any comprehensive study of the supervisory situation must take them into account, and any specific department attempting to study the supervisory work within its confines will similarly have to investigate these areas. And because they are filled with personal investments, they are often quite difficult to define, discuss, and explore. At times, especially when there is stress and disagreement, disputes over such issues can undermine the teaching qualities of the supervisory bipersonal field, and may occasion significant inputs into that field through interactions both between the administration and the supervisor, and between the administrator and the supervisee.

This leads me to identify some additional factors peripheral to the direct teaching relationship in supervision but which nonetheless exert an influence, often considerable. Again I will briefly catalogue some obvious dimensions, primarily as a means of identifying still other areas requiring investigation in our effort toward comprehensive understanding of the supervisory process. The supervisor's personal style of teaching; his total relationship with the supervisee; his feelings about him as a person and as a student; his reactions to the particular patient who is being supervised; his capacity to quickly tune in on the therapeutic interaction; the patient's assets and psychopathology; the supervisee's positive capacities and countertransference difficulties; the supervisor's reaction to the quality of the therapeutic work; the unfolding sense of development and progress; or, in contrast, the prevalence of unmodified major difficulties in both the therapeutic and supervisory situations—all are part of an enormous catalogue of factors that have a bearing on the supervisory experience.

Returning to your remarks on supervisory method, it is interesting to me that I have not found the trend you note among supervisees toward offering unnecessary id interpretations. In fact, my impression is that the very opposite problem prevails: namely, that trainees tend to make superficial interventions, to ask far too many questions and make too many confrontations, and that they have difficulty making true interpretations in which unconscious contents and processes are actually made conscious for the patient in a meaningful manner; they have special difficulties in interpreting unconscious fantasies, memories, introjects, and perceptions. In my experience, trainees back away from and dread the primitive inner mental world of their patients—and of themselves as well. They tend to remain on the surface, most often identifying superficial and evident defenses, and less often addressing id and superego issues.

Now this may reflect differences in our actual experiences, which are another influence on the approach of each supervisor. But I must add that I have now done supervision in a number of centers, and with presentations from all over the country, and these trends seem to hold up—as I believe they do in the current presentation, where the supervisee has confined himself to questions and to a surface reprimand, as reflected in the material presented to this point.

Well, I've gone on a bit, but perhaps I can conclude these comments by identifying what I feel are the major problems in supervisees. Unfortunately, they are the major problems of experienced therapists as well. They entail an avoidance, a failure to understand and interpret the material from the patient around organizing adaptive contexts—which inevitably lead to the therapeutic interaction, to the patient's intense involvement with the therapist, and vice versa, and to both unconscious perceptions and actualities, as well as unconscious fantasies and distortions. So, the greatest problems in doing therapy that I have observed relate to the avoidance of transference and nontransference, and the related avoidance of countertransference—that is, they involve ongoing issues related to the communicative therapeutic interaction and to the bipersonal field within which it occurs.

Now I can add a number of secondary problems, some of them related to your own remarks. For example, there is a very common difficulty among supervisees in conceptualizing how we work from the surface to the depths, and from the unconsciously defensive components of the patient's behaviors and associations down toward superego and id material—what it means to deal with the ego first, and where the self comes into play in the therapeutic work with patients. There is a tendency among supervisees to bypass defenses, to ignore them and to go directly toward the fantasy contents in the material; and here I would agree, that often they move directly toward instinctual drive content without exploration and interpretation of defenses. Still, there are many therapists and analysts who do not truly explore and interpret the unconscious fantasies and introjects on which complicated intrapsychic and interactional defenses are based, who tend to approach ego defenses in a mechanistic way. Others neglect the frame and its functions, actualities, and the communicative mode and medium, reducing everything to transference and distorted fantasy and neglecting their own countertransference-based expressions and effects.

Another basic problem, and it is implied in much of what I have already said, is learning how to listen to and formulate derivatives, and accepting them in terms of both unconscious fantasy and perception. It is here that the use of the adaptive context proves crucial, and therapeutic work with instinctual drive derivatives, as well as representations of the superego and ego—defenses and the like—start to take on specific and dynamic meaning, usually in the context of the ongoing therapeutic interaction.

I do not wish to impose my own conception of the major problems in supervision upon this group. Instead, I have simply offered, off the top of my head, my main impressions. And I would propose that it is important for supervisors to specifically delineate the categories of problems that appear in their work with each supervisee, and on that basis, to develop a collective lexicon of major problems. Clearly, such a study would rely heavily on the supervisor's model of therapy and supervision, and on his ability to identify both conscious and unconscious difficulties. This would be a far from simple investigation, yet one well worth undertaking, and well worth the effort needed to collect the necessary empirical data.

In regard to clinical investigations related to psychoanalysis and psychotherapy, there has been a tendency on every level to set aside basic methodology, to fail to collect definitive data, and to rely instead on general impressions or questionable generalizations from single case studies. Certainly, in investigating the various dimensions of the supervisory experience, such as attempting to identify major problem areas, one could readily develop sound methods for collecting observational material, for formulating the implications of that data, and for applying the validating process to it. I must say that I hope that in addition to fostering the development of each of you as an individual supervisor, I would be most gratified if we also generated an investigative model with which to study supervision—and further, if we were able to identify certain crucial issues well worth investigating.

Supervisor A: I would like to respond to an aspect of your remarks that actually touches upon something I was going to say, a point related to some of the special influences on supervision. I have felt for some time that a portion of the resident's intrusiveness with this patient was related to his awareness that this was a special kind of case situation, and perhaps to my own awareness as well that this was a special kind of supervisory experience.

Langs: Special in what sense?

Supervisor A: I am referring to his knowledge that the supervisory interaction was going to be used for this presentation.

Langs: Yes, for both you and the resident, this must have generated considerable anxiety and exerted a great deal of pressure.

Actually, your point touches more broadly upon the influence of supervision on a given therapeutic interaction. And while we all know that such influences can be quite extensive, this exchange, and the material presented to this point, leads me to a particular point: namely, that quite often a supervisee will develop an intense wish to please the supervisor, or to evoke some other special reaction, such as intense anger, extreme love, fear or dread, and the like. Such conscious attitudes are filled with complementary and contradictory unconscious feelings and fantasies, and are quite complex. However, on the surface they often lead the supervisee to respond to his patient in a somewhat uncharacteristic way—although this is never divorced from the influence of his own unconscious countertransference propensities. Still, your comment regarding the resident's intrusiveness suggests that this was rather uncharacteristic for him, and serves to remind us that often a supervisee will have some fantasy-model of how his supervisor expects him to respond to the patient. This fantasy-model, lest you misunderstand me, is based on his valid perceptions of the supervisor's conscious and unconscious communications, which interact with the supervisee's own valid and pathological conscious and unconscious needs and models of therapy—it is, as always, an interactional amalgam.

At times, this aspect of the *supervisor introject*—or if you prefer to state it more interactionally, the supervisory introject—can exert a salutary effect on the supervisee's clinical work, although it is my impression that quite often it can be disruptive and detrimental. This introject may lead to undue silence or, more commonly, I believe, to excessive activity on the part of the supervisee, at times prompting him to intervene more for the sake of the supervisor than for his patient. These are all aspects that must be considered in understanding the supervisee's interventions. Often he will alert us to this dimension by justifying a particular period of silence, or an effort at management of the frame or verbal intervention, by alluding to our previous supervisory comments.

You can sense now that there is an extensive interactional process that takes place in the supervisory situation; there is also a powerful unconscious communicative interaction. For the supervisee, it may be somewhat projective, but it is primarily introjective—a function of the supervisor's conscious and unconscious communications, as they reflect his cognitive knowledge, intrapsychic balances, assets, pathology, fantasies, introjects, and the like. Overall, his hope, on this level, is to generate a constructive and positive functioning supervisory introject, rather than one filled with anxiety, disruptive forces, and the like. As an introject, it may eventually be smoothly incorporated into the ego or self of the supervisee, and contribute to both his own inner mental world and his constructive functioning with the patient. But when the supervisor generates an essentially pathological introjective process, it creates significant disturbances for both the supervisee and his patient, and for the development of the supervisee in particular. Here too I would very much like to see specific studies. There has been a great deal of work recently in regard to the patient's introjective processes in his interaction with his therapist or analyst (see Lang 1976a); this should be extended to the supervisory situation.

So there is a danger that the fantasies, expectations, and anxieties regarding this presentation could create special burdens for both of you. And they might bring out the best or the worst in each of you, and might possibly accentuate the supervisee's countertransference problems in particular. Well, perhaps we can now hear a bit more.

Supervisor A: Well, as you may recall, the patient had been talking about his girlfriend seeing him exclusively, and the supervisee had said, Now that she is seeing only you, how do you feel? The patient had responded, At times, it is too much. By the way, I met a woman that you know. And the therapist responded, Who is she?

Langs: Well, in terms of your discussion, I can make this specific point: certainly, asking this immediate question reflects a great deal of anxiety in the supervisee, anxiety that is conveyed to the patient. Now while the supervisee might well feel quite anxious in this area because of his usual inner problems—after all, we have seen evidence of considerable anxiety and defensiveness on his part when the patient begins to encroach, even through indirect derivatives, upon the therapeutic relationship—we can all well imagine how the supervisee must have felt when he learned that the patient had met a friend of his. His heart must have dropped: now the whole world will know—whatever.

And this anxiety applies to the supervisory situation itself: the supervisor may be party to a secret of the supervisee. This concern is intensified by a second and larger supervisory situation, such as this conference. We can all empathize with the therapist who hears about his patient meeting someone he knows. Who among us knows what secrets lie in the heart of the supervisee, and what actual fears of exposure such a comment may have evoked. Perhaps, then, his immediate question—its urgency, its implied anxiety—serves to confirm how a contact with a third party known to the therapist may affect both the supervisory bipersonal field and the therapeutic situation. Not to mention the supervisee's responses in both places.

In this context, I also want to come back to my earlier remarks regarding the need to maintain the confidentiality of the supervisory situation. If this patient has met someone who might occasion some personal embarrassment for the supervisee, he would be in enormous difficulty in both bipersonal fields in attempting to deal with such material. And the situation would be quite impossible if the supervisee felt that the supervisor might discuss this material with anyone else. It leads me again to ask each of you to maintain the confidentiality of this material, and to respect our privilege in hearing it in the service of our needs to learn. And I can assure you that it will be extensively disguised for publication. Still, I hope you will all pause now, and reflect on the need for total confidentiality in both the therapeutic and supervisory fields—in response to the anxious question of the supervisee.

Supervisor A: Well at that point I suggested to him that curiosity did not have too much place in therapy. And I said that if he wanted to ask a question like that, it would probably be better to wait and see if the patient actually avoided mentioning the name of his friend for some reason, and that he could then perhaps bring it to his attention.

Langs: That's an interesting response, in that you discussed with us the influence of the conference on the supervisee's interventions, but discussed with him his own undue pathological curiosity. In a way, despite the elements of truth, your remark is unbalanced and is something like placing all of the blame on the supervisee, much as therapists sometimes blame their patients despite the presence of their own contribution, however unconscious, to his resistances or other pathological expression. Your comment implies a denial of a contribution to his pathological curiosity on your own part and on ours as the larger audience. It would have been far better if you had been able to adopt a broader perspective here, and had acknowledged this possible influence in any comment addressed to this intervention. This demonstrates rather clearly how at times such peripheral influences take on significance and should be briefly discussed by the supervisor.

Still, the positive element in your intervention is that you made an effort to implicitly suggest that his undue curiosity was based on a countertransference problem—a point I would have made quite explicitly. And further, you are by implication also suggesting that the supervisee should be silent, should allow himself time to observe the possible development of defensive avoidance, and then, as I understand your comment, possibly confront the patient with this defensiveness. Here you are dealing with one of the common problems in residents that we just discussed: the bypassing of defenses—even though here there was little time for the patient to establish them.

My own response would not only have been shaped by the extraneous conditions I have already identified, but I would also have attempted to be more definitive and to generate basic principles from this specific instance, covering the pertinent fundamental areas of teaching: principles of technique, intrapsychic formulations related to the patient's conflicts and dynamics, issues of countertransference, and especially a full consideration of the unconscious communicative interaction between patient and therapist—eventually everything should be funneled into that critical area. So, in principle, whenever a key issue arises we go from the specific situation to general principles, and from the intrapsychic to the interactional.

Much of what I would have said is an elaboration of your own comments. Formally, this intervention is a question.

It is also a premature intervention. And in terms of technical principles related to the intrapsychic happenings within the patient, it precludes the development of defenses and their analysis. Returning to matters of technique, it therefore calls for the use of silence in its place.

Next, maintaining an intrapsychic focus, I might suggest that it reflects undue curiosity and defensiveness in the therapist. I would also comment on the supervisee's anxieties regarding the person the patient had met, and his anxieties related to both supervision and the presentation here. Still, the main technical point might well be the importance of permitting the patient to free associate in order to see expressions of his fantasies, introjects, and defenses—in order to identify both derivatives and the defenses against them. It would be difficult, however, to separate this discussion from the therapeutic interaction, so I would soon shift from these more manifest and technical levels to the therapeutic interaction itself, and to the unconscious communications contained in the therapist's intervention.

I have already developed this model for you and here I will demonstrate it again. I always pay attention to the interaction and attempt to identify what the patient is experiencing. To state the same issue from the viewpoint of the therapist, I try to formulate what the supervisee is communicating and projectively identifying into the patient—pathologically, if the intervention is in error. Here, as a supervisor, I utilize empathy and intuition, a sensitivity to unconscious communications, a recognition of both reality and fantasy, and a series of cognitive operations.

In assessing this intervention as a specific instance of pathological projective identification, I would suggest that it reflects a difficulty within the therapist in managing his curiosity, and that it places into the patient his own sense of anxiety, his poor controls, his defensiveness, and his sense of disturbance as the material from the patient shifts to a very personal and uncertain area. And you can see how such a projective identification could influence the patient's own capacity for the management of anxieties, conflicts, and instinctual drive derivatives. The therapist for the moment, lacks a sense of patience and management. And precisely these qualities, which the therapist lacks, will be introjected by the patient, who will then suffer from them, inappropriately exploit them to justify his own psychopathology, and yet attempt also to heal the pathological introject—to cure the disturbance within himself and, interactionally, to cure the therapist. All of this, of course, largely on an unconscious level.

And it is here that the supervisor, if he responds sensitively and identifies the factors in this premature intervention within both the therapeutic and supervisory interactions, could serve as a model for the supervisee—not only of understanding but, more important, of management and control. This might then help the supervisee to better manage his anxieties in the therapeutic relationship, within whatever limits such gains are possible through the supervisory experience—through unconscious positive identifications without cognitive insight. The supervisor would therefore, based on the available material, attempt to indicate the most likely countertransference difficulties involved, allude to some of the possible factors, including a contribution from himself, and more broadly support the supervisee's general ego functioning and understanding.

In this respect, I would like to note another process that positive supervisory experiences, through constructive introjects and other means, can generate similarly constructive experiences in the therapeutic relationship. In this way, we can see that there is not only a process by which the primary therapeutic situation can generate its analogue in the secondary supervisory field, but that the reverse can also occur: the supervisory situation may generate primary experiences that are then paralleled in the supervisee's relationship with his patient. And while I have stated this in terms of positive potential, it is more than evident that this can occur in a quite destructive manner as well. Pathological and disruptive supervisory interactions will often find parallel expression, again through unconscious introjection and identification, in the supervisee's interaction with his patient.

In this context, one might suggest the following sequence: the existence of supervision and the announcement that this particular material will be presented to this conference; the incorporation of the related anxieties within the therapist and, possibly, the supervisor; their expression as a projective identification by the supervisee into the patient at the point when the patient brings in material to which the supervisee is especially sensitive in this context; and now, the introjection by the patient of the related anxieties and his working over of the projected contents—in ways we will soon hear. As a rule, this would then be followed by a reprojection by the patient through his continued associations and behaviors as they reflect his metabolism of the therapist's pathological projective identification. He has become an inappropriate, pathological container for the therapist's pathological contents, and will respond in terms of the projected contents and mechanisms, and his own inner needs, healthy and pathological. The communicated results will then be introjected by the supervisee, and they will influence his subsequent work with the patient, as well as his interaction with the supervisor.

This suggestion, then, that one important set of mechanisms among the many process generating parallels between the therapeutic and supervisory situations is that of projective and introjective identification. These interactional mechanisms may operate in either direction: the projective identifications may extend from patient into therapist into supervisor; or from therapist into patient back into therapist and then into supervisor; or this may occur in a reverse flow, from supervisor into therapist into patient. I am attempting to demonstrate that these parallel experiences—for example, when a supervisor subjectively experiences something comparable to what the patient is experiencing—not only rely on comparable communications from the supervisee to the patient and supervisor, but may also derive from complex interactions and elaborate interactional mechanisms.

Finally, in this particular supervisory situation, after having covered selected aspects of the points that I am developing in this seminar, I would probably offer some reassurance to the therapist by discussing the inevitability of countertransference-based influences in his work with patients, and similarly, the inevitability of supervisory influences as well. In addition, if I have now made several interventions in which I have addressed the countertransference-based communications and projective identifications of the therapist, I might extend these remarks by suggesting that the therapeutic bipersonal field creates a situation in which countertransference-based expressions are bound to flourish. I would discuss with the supervisee the difficulty of recognizing such unconsciously determined behaviors and interventions, and even more so of resolving them without therapy. I would be quite sympathetic, but there is little I could do to avoid generating some type of disturbance within the supervisee at this point. At best, I could help him recognize the universality of his plight. I must, however, prepare him for his patient's reaction to the unconscious implications of his intervention.

Discussant: I am especially struck by the influence of the resident's knowledge that his work was going to be presented to you and to virtually every member of the teaching faculty at this center; it was bound to be overwhelming.

Langs: Oh yes; you mean it wasn't merely anxiety, it was sheer panic! (Laughter.) But doesn't this help us recognize something of the experience of every patient who sees a therapist in a clinic, and who on some level, conscious or unconscious, realizes that the transactions of his sessions with the therapist will be presented to a third party. The patient is far more vulnerable in this respect, and often, far less resourceful. And yet, we can see that unconsciously the resident shares these anxieties with his patient. There is little room for denial or avoidance, since the supervisee is confronted weekly with his supervisor. This could also be extrapolated so that we include the supervisor who presents his work to others, and we then come full circle in recognizing some of the liabilities of the supervisory experience.

While not definitive, this material gives me an opportunity to make several additional comments and to touch upon aspects of supervision that I have not as yet clearly delineated. Your supervisory intervention in response to the supervisee's anxious and premature question—which, according to my formulation, placed the entire onus on the therapist and excluded any reference to your own contribution to his anxieties—can be taken as a model of a supervisor's countertransference-based blind spot. As I said before, this is a common form of defensive avoidance, and it is another version of the therapist's need to hold patients responsible for difficulties. This lack of insight in the supervisor can generate a shift of the supervisory bipersonal field from Type A, in which symbolic communication and the search for understanding prevails, to a Type B or C field—more likely, I think, to the Type B field, in which action, discharge, and projective identification predominate. Such a communicative atmosphere will promote and reinforce the action-oriented and projective identificatory tendencies of the supervisee, and his tendency to use Type C barriers. It will also generate pressures within the therapeutic bipersonal field that may shift it, too, from a Type A to a Type B or C communicative field. So this may seem a minor omission, and I will not belabor it. Just remember that repeated errors and blind spots in the supervior can have far-reaching effects on the supervisee and on supervision.

Among the implications of this discussion, I want to

stress the importance of the supervisor taking both the supervisee and the patient as mirrors to himself, as the recipient and echo of his conscious and unconscious communications and projective identifications. He should listen to the communications from both along the me/not-me interface, as pertaining not only to the patient and the supervisee, but as consistently alluding to himself as well. Further, I want to stress the importance of vigilantly monitoring the supervisory field itself for possible projective identifications or periods of static noncommunication on the part of either dyadic member. The supervisor should consider each shift in the therapeutic bipersonal field—its intrapsychic qualities and interactional dimensions, including the nature of the communicative field—as a possible indicator of some comparable shift in the supervisory situation. You can now see the importance of identifying the unconscious communications contained in every supervisory intervention, and the need to trace the influence of each supervisory intervention as it effects both the supervisee and his patient. In periods of crisis it is especially important to explore the possibility that you have failed to intervene or have erred, and to listen to the material from both patient and supervisee for the relevant clues.

In detailing the extensive influence of the supervisor and the supervisory situation on both the supervisee and his patient, I again would remind you of the importance of total confidentiality in the usual—that is, unsupervised—therapeutic situation. At this point, we can all sense the enormity of the grief and anxiety, the embarrassment, the intrusion and contamination, created by any alteration in the total confidentiality of the therapeutic situation. And while such deviations are indeed necessary, both in the therapist's supervision and in his personal analysis, perhaps you can all now grasp how very essential the ground rule of total confidentiality is to therapeutic progress and the creation of Type A communicative fields. And I must add that this is true of every other ground rule of therapy: every one of them secures the bipersonal field in a way that sets aside some version of this kind of chaos.

So all this serves as a reminder that these deviations impair the openness and flow of the communicative field, and that they can generate considerable anxiety for both participants. It is a reminder too that we are actually dealing with the secret life of the patient, and we see now that it can even intrude upon the secret life of the therapist. And we can recognize that, at the very least, an essentially secure frame can offer much-needed support as such secrets—interpersonal and intrapsychic—begin to unfold; it can provide the potential for a communicative field within which they can be expressed, analyzed, and their pathological aspects resolved.

I come back to my request that this presentation be treated with confidentiality, so that it does not extend beyond this room. Although I have asked and obtained in advance the privilege of publishing this material once it is fully disguised, I can assure you that I am well aware of the special burdens and responsibilities that such a request imposes upon me. I think that we must recognize and somehow set straight the therapist or analyst who neglects the patient's need for total confidentiality—who has his wife typing his notes, or who discusses experiences with patients at the dinner table or at cocktail parties. And in this regard, have we as yet ascertained the influence on patients, present or past, of writing papers on them? I think such practices reflect this very kind of chaos and insanity, and, sadly enough, it creates a pathetic and destructive image of therapists, analysts, and the very field we hold so dear. I will spare you a sermon, although I could not refrain from stressing the importance of the framework in the light of this material.

So. We see something of the mixed influence of the supervisory experience—its very necessary and positive potential, as well as its inevitable anxiety-provoking and sometimes clearly detrimental effects. Many analysts have noted the remarkable difference between analytic work while under supervision in an analytic institute and that conducted after graduation. The subject deserves more attention, but it might well lead us to conclude that every patient—training case, clinic patient, whatever—really deserves a period of treatment in the private office of the therapist or analyst, in a framework of total confidentiality and without supervision. This would provide both patient and therapist the crucial opportunity to rectify the inevitably damaging aspects of the initial conditions of treatment, to secure the necessary frame and to then explore the extensive, previously concealed implications of the initial modified situation, and to generate both a final positive introject of the therapist and the crucial insights unavailable in the first setting.

I have found without exception that an alteration in the frame creates bastions—walled-off sectors of communication which are not available for analytic work—and that this bastion can be resolved only with true rectification of the frame. In addition, my recent investigations of the communicative properties of the bipersonal field suggest that alterations in the frame are quite damaging to a Type A field, and that they generate pressures toward Type B and C fields; they influence the very basic conscious and unconscious communicative interaction of patient and therapist—the entire therapeutic experience and its outcome. As I say, the therapist may sometimes alter the bipersonal field out of true necessity, but he must be sensitive to the damage done to the therapeutic experience of the patient, and should rectify the situation as quickly as possible and interpret some of the consequences when they emerge in the patient's material. But so long as the alteration exists, some of its consequences cannot be undone. I agree with those who say that matters would be still worse if the therapist could not learn and develop; supervision is a necessity, but I do believe that we have tended to overlook its liabilities. I think now of Lewin's conception (1955) of the analyst as disturber of the patient's sleep, of his defenses and inner pathological equilibrium. And I think we can analogize to the supervisory experience, and recognize that the supervisor is a disturber of the privacy between patient and therapist, of the therapeutic bipersonal field—a helpful intruder, but a threat nonetheless. I could say more, but I think it would be helpful now to see what follows.

Supervisor A: The patient then identified the friend, and the resident said, How do you feel about this? Actually, the patient had reported that he was beginning to date this person.

Langs: A woman that the patient is starting to date; and you don't know anything about the relationship the resident has with this woman? Is that right?

Supervisor A: It's a professional acquaintance.

Langs: So, it's a professional relationship, as far as you know?

Supervisor A: An honorable profession, and an honorable relationship. (Laughter).

Langs: Is there any other? Still, we could begin to fathom the possibilities and the ramifications. We have a patient who is dating a colleague of the therapist, or someone he knows professionally—it's still a bit unclear and we lack the details. But it clearly stirs our imagination: it could have been a girlfriend, a former mistress, an ex-wife, even someone the supervisor knows; or, on the other hand, a distant acquaintance. One can empathize with the supervisee's anxiety, and we can see that it has increased his rate of activity: he intervened again, I take it.

Supervisor A: Yes. He asked the patient, How do you feel about this?

Langs: So—yet another question. And I think that here we can truly distinguish between conscious and unconscious communication, and between the therapist's wish to know and his wish not to know—and on what level he wants each to exist. And while I would have discussed many of these issues in connection with the therapist's previous intervention, I would have added a bit more at this juncture.

I might well have begun with an empathic comment such as, This information must have created a considerable amount of anxiety for you. And from there, I would try to help the supervisee see that his questions and their frequency are clearly a function of this anxiety. I could then stress that we actually learn a great deal about ourselves as therapists when we are conscious of our heightened anxieties and can then review our interventions in that context, we can learn something about our more pathological efforts at mastery, and how our interventions can be based on countertransference-based needs to master disturbing communications put into the field—and into the therapist—by the patient.

At this point I might suggest that there are probably a number of unconscious meanings and functions to the patient's communication of his meeting and dating an acquaintance of the therapist. This could include some type of unconscious revenge or some effort to initiate disruptive pathological projective identifications into the therapist—in part as a defense against similar projections by the therapist or for revenge for what he feels the therapist has been putting into him. We would want also to suggest that in addition to the possibility that the patient is living out some type of unconscious transference fantasy—some type of pathological defense and similarly pathological instinctual drive wishes—that interactionally this behavior might have a number of meanings vis-à-vis the therapeutic relationship.

For one, it brings up the issue of the frame, especially the issues of anonymity and total confidentiality, aspects of the frame that are usually poorly maintained in a clinic setting. This could then be this patient's working over of these frame issues, and in addition to its disturbing effects it could reflect his unconscious constructive effort to have the therapist experience the impact of an alteration in the frame: the anxiety that it evokes and the manner in which it impairs the communicative properties of the bipersonal field. Here we see a likely shift from a potential Type A field to one that appears to be a Type B field, in which projective identification and discharge of inner tensions prevails; language is used not so much for symbolic communication or understanding as for getting rid of such tensions.

And I would stress this point to the supervisee, since he is bound to feel on the spot, threatened, and endangered by this liaison, and angered and frightened—or perhaps even stimulated. It is therefore crucial to show him that whatever the destructive qualities or seductive elements, there is a nucleus of constructive intention—an unconscious attempt to cure the therapist who is unable to maintain his distance, who has had difficulty in working with the patient's unconscious homosexual fantasies and perceptions, and who has been unable, for whatever reason, to secure a therapeutic frame for this bipersonal field.

On another level, this is a form of interactional enactment or living out in which both patient and therapist have promoted the expression of the unconscious sexual transference and nontransference in an outside relationship, a reflection of the type of interactional defenses we have discussed earlier: the behavior could serve to foster the avoidance of such contents and qualities in any direct connection with the therapeutic relationship. The patient also may be attempting to spare the supervisee the intensity of his countertransference-based homosexual anxieties. Still, to permit this type of maladaptive resolution would be to forgo adequate analytic work directed toward insight and true mastery.

Since there is much to be said here about the therapist's countertransferences, it would be helpful—even though we have so little material as yet—to begin with a few tentative hypotheses regarding the possible mixed qualities and unconscious implications of the patient's behavior, offering them in the form of preliminary formulations to be validated by the subsequent material, and as models related to important dimensions of the therapeutic situation. There is both possible harm and cure contained in this behavior, and a constructive analysis would depend on a full comprehension of its implications, and ultimately on the therapist's capacity to contain and interpret its relevant meanings in terms of both unconscious perceptions-introjections and unconscious distortions-transferences—it is a powerful transversal communication.

Shifting now to the supervisee's intervention, you could show him how the threatened presence of a third party to treatment has affected his communications to the patient, and has prompted him to be overactive and to ask questions that direct the patient to the surface of his thoughts and away from derivatives and unconscious ramifications. This can then serve as an important model of how alterations in the framework significantly influence the communicative properties of the bipersonal field, sometimes permanently altering these properties to the point where analyzable derivatives of unconscious fantasies and perceptions are no longer available and either a static field or one filled with projective identification and discharge prevails.

By showing the therapist how his communications have changed, we can help him to better empathize with his patient and come to realize how his patient's communications are altered under comparable conditions. I would stress this at some length, because it is often said that modifications in the frame can be meaningfully analyzed, and that such work can yield valuable insights. And while this is true up to a point, it is just as crucial to realize that these very alterations in the frame create bastions—split-off sectors of material—and alter the basic communicative properties of the field to the point where whole sectors of important material will simply not be accessible for analytic work. The derivatives will not appear and there will be marked limitations to therapeutic outcome. It is these actual consequences of modifications in the framework that have been so neglected by classical analysts, and in fact by all analytic writers. Analysts are loath to acknowledge the realistic consequences of their countertransference-based interventions and mismanagements of the framework, and I feel that it is important to take every opportunity to help a trainee understand this very basic issue and area of confusion.

To continue, I would suggest to the resident—again, as tentative formulations to be validated—that his active inquiries are designed to restrict the patient's communications in this area, and that his intervention unconsciously is designed to constrict the communicative field and to protect himself against the unconscious derivatives related to the patient's date with a professional acquaintance of his. So, while his conscious communication is Tell me more, his unconscious communication is, Let's restrict what you have to say—in essence, Tell me nothing more. Further, at the very moment at which the therapist is attempting to suggest his openness to contain the relevant associations, he is actually conveying his anxiety through his excessive activity, unconsciously asking the patient to limit himself, and communicating his difficulties in containing this material and his own feelings and fantasies about it.

I suspect too that the supervisee, probably quite unconsciously, senses that there may be something rather primitive about this piece of behavior, and that it may well be connected to unconscious sexual and aggressive fantasies and perceptions related to himself; he seems to be experiencing an intense need for protection. And one of the more common ways of seeking safety is to ask enough questions to keep the patient on the surface of his thoughts, and to not allow the indirect derivatives to unfold—material that would be far more revealing and have, in all likelihood, an intense impact on the therapist. It will be quite interesting to see how this mixed message—tell me, but don't tell me too much—is perceived by and influences the patient.

Incidentally, it is at moments like this, when the material gets so close to the therapist that he can't help but be aware of his anxieties and, usually, of his conscious fantasies, that a supervisor can help the supervisee to understand the impact that the patient has upon him: the inevitable fears that he experiences regarding the therapeutic relationship and the patient's sensitivities and primitive fantasies, and the type of defenses that he utilizes to protect himself from such inputs and the related anxieties.

It might also be possible to help the therapist understand that subjectively he is experiencing not only a verbal communication from the patient, but also a projective identification. I think that it is important to develop a subjective sensitivity to communications that have such qualities—interactional pressures (Langs 1978c)—but one must always stress the importance of validating such an introjective experience from the verbal material from the patient. Interactional formulations are extremely vulnerable to countertransference-based influence and must always be validated on some other level before they can be a basis for intervening.

It is because these associations touch upon such basic issues and vulnerabilities that I have embarked upon such an extended discussion in response to so little data. It is an important teaching opportunity, and much of what I would say would be offered as suggested silent hypotheses to be validated as the material unfolds.

Supervisor A: The patient responded to that question by saying, The world is a small place. At this point I made a comment to the supervisee that, as is true for the child, there are not many places to go. The resident continued: the patient had gone on to tell him that he felt close to the girlfriend, but that he is kind of afraid of her—she is too pushy. I then pointed out to the resident that this also might have been a reference to himself. I did not, however, go into further detail.

Langs: Well, I believe that here, as I indicated before you intervened, I would have said much more. I certainly would have made an attempt to acknowledge the supervisee's anxieties and their influence upon his intervention.

In another vein, I would like to stress again the importance of making your supervisory interventions as specific as possible. Here I feel that it is far too general and ill-defined to simply suggest that the patient's communications about the new girlfriend are displaced from the therapist. I must emphasize again the importance of being as specific as possible in your work with patients, as well as in supervision.

And here, I would stress that in alluding to this material as derivatives related to the therapeutic relationship, it would be important to identify the specific adaptive context which evoked these associations, and from there, to sort out those elements that are transference-based and those that fall into the realm of nontransference. Here too we are touching upon a common problem for supervisees, and for therapists and analysts: a tendency to work intellectually and ruminatively with the patient in terms of isolated contents, a failure to develop the material around specific adaptive contexts and in terms of Type Two derivatives, and, further, a failure to distinguish between transference and nontransference.

In tracing out the sequence of the therapeutic interaction, it is important to emphasize that the patient's communications at this point are a commentary—a mixture of valid and distorted responses—on the therapist's intervention. That is, on one level I would stress that this material is a response to the adaptive context of the therapist's intervention and must be organized around it. This effort would reveal that much of this is essentially nontransference (and covers over possible transference elements), in that it contains an unconscious perception of the therapist's being too pushy, and an unconscious introjection of the therapist's anxieties vis-à-vis his intimacy with the patient. All of this would have to be modified and resolved before we could determine the extent to which the patient himself experiences anxiety in close relationships; that is, the pathological inputs from the therapist must be rectified before we can determine the nature of the patient's pathology. The patient tends to embed and conceal his own pathology within parallel problems in the therapist, and they will be unanalyzable until the countertransference difficulty is brought under control and no longer influences the bipersonal field. Without such rectification, interpretations of the material from the patient as transference-based and distorted constitutes a pathological denial of the therapist's true unconscious communications to the patient.

On a second level, it is extremely important to evaluate the extent to which the patient's subsequent communications validate the intervention by the therapist. Here, the therapist asked a question, and the patient begins to offer something of his conscious feelings, though unconsciously communicating a variety of unconscious perceptions as well. It would be important to hear more material so we can determine the extent to which the patient's subsequent associations are more a response to the intrusiveness of the question than to its manifest content—it would largely be a matter of tracing out the influence of the intervention, both consciously and unconsciously.

So, think sequentially in supervision; take each intervention as the adaptive context for the subsequent material from the patient. And, in addition, apply the validating process to each intervention by the supervisee, as well as to any of your own proposed interventions. It is important to be explicit, and forgive me for repeating it again, but it is also important to work consistently around an adaptive context.

Discussant: Even if it means repeating some of the points that you made earlier, could you elaborate a bit?

Langs: Well, in brief, I use an adaptational-interactional viewpoint of what goes on in and between human beings—patient and the therapist. And I am saying that effective therapeutic work requires a vantage point, so we do not treat the material from the patient in isolation and solely as fantasy and distortion. By maintaining an adaptational sequence, beginning with an adaptive context—the day residue or precipitant—we can understand the dynamics of the manifest and latent content of the patient's associations and the therapist's interventions. If we begin with the conscious and unconscious communications of the therapist, we can then examine the intrapsychic responses of the patient—his associations and behaviors—and organize them not so much around their manifest themes or our immediate impressions of possible latent contents—Type One derivatives—as around that specific adaptive context which gives the associations that follow a very specific meaning—as Type Two derivatives. The responsive material is a commentary, a form of indirect communication in which both unconscious perceptions and valid introjections are intermixed with evoked unconscious fantasies and distortions.

Now the same model applies to the therapist: for him, the most crucial day residue is the communications from his patient, material that he works over within himself toward an interpretation or a management response related to the framework. His interventions reflect his unconscious sensitivity to the material from the patient and his capacity to metabolize the inputs from the patient toward conscious realizations that lead to appropriate interventions. If the adaptive context, as represented by the communications from the patient, evokes a pathological response in the therapist, he will then intervene idiosyncratically on the basis of his countertransference-based needs and defenses and will thereby generate a traumatic experience for the patient that will evoke a new adaptive sequence.

Ultimately, with clinical experience and mastery, in both therapy and analysis, we would expect that most of the pathological inputs into the bipersonal field will come from the patient, with only occasional major inputs of that type from the therapist—though more subtle expressions are part of the continuous communicative interaction. Our supervisory work will then center around the intrapsychic and interactional pathology of the patient. However, in working with the residents and other trainees, we must expect a significant proportion of pathological inputs from the therapist, and it will be necessary to do a considerable amount of supervisory work in keeping with this reality. Such supervisory work does not represent the view that the main function of psychotherapy should be the cure of the therapist—or that its main focus should be his countertransferences. It is quite easy for the supervisee to develop such a criticism, part of it being quite defensive, and it becomes important to stress a balanced view of the psychotherapeutic situation and to emphasize that one must supervise based on the realities of the field under consideration. It is a painful truth to face: that therapists often place significant pathological inputs into this field. We must have the tools for recognizing such inputs and for working through their traumatizing effects on the patient, so that they can, to whatever extent possible, be transformed into some degree of therapeutic gain.

The adaptive context, then, is an intrapsychically significant event for the patient. It has manifest and latent content, and is the evoker and organizer of his reactions, both conscious and unconscious. It is the essential organizer for the therapist as well; he must correctly identify its presence and its meaning in order to understand that patient's communications as Type Two derivatives. And clearly, I am suggesting that it is Type Two derivative responses that significantly relate to the patient's activated psychopathology, to his maladaptive reactions, to his symptoms, and to his characterological disturbances. It is in this realm that the unconscious meanings and functions of these very symptoms can be clarified, and this relates not only to unconscious fantasies, but also to unconscious perceptions—to introjects with essentially valid cores, as they influence the maladaptive functioning of the patient.

In addition to considering the formal qualities of our endeavors as therapists, I also want to stress that, ultimately, one's capacity to understand the patient—to formulate and to intervene—relies heavily on the therapist's ability to resolve his countertransferences and to know the truth about himself. Self-knowledge clearly is an absolutely essential prerequisite for knowing others.

Now I could extend these comments in many directions, but I would like to move toward this particular supervisory situation and suggest that this therapy is representative of one type of clinical interlude that is extremely common. It shows us a sequence in which the interface of the bipersonal field has shifted toward the pathology of the therapist, and the resolution of that disturbance must momentarily take precedence in the efforts of both patient and therapist. This will generate a shift of the interface back toward the pathology of the patient and return the field to its central function: the cure of the patient. And while many are prone to think of the therapeutic situation as distorted and even artificial under these conditions, my own position is that one can learn a great deal from such experiences. Their analytic resolution, which includes rectification of the frame and *implicit* acknowledgement of the error, can be therapeutic for both patient and therapist—even though the therapist's errors, depending upon many factors, will leave some residuals of trauma and disturbance within the patient.

In fact, under these conditions we learn a great deal about both patient and therapist, and about the bipersonal field and its frame, far more than we do when the field is secure and the therapeutic work is unfolding, as we hope it will most of the time, in keeping with the patient's strengths and pathology—interactionally with inputs from both patient and therapist, but largely on the patient's terms. This is, of course, the ideal therapeutic situation, and it is one in which the frame is stable and issues related to its management arise only infrequently. When they do, they are adequately handled by the therapist in a manner that maintains the stability of the frame while generating insights to the patient in regard to his efforts to alter it. Under those conditions, the therapist spends most of his time listening to the patient, formulating the nature of his communications, attempting to identify the types of available derivatives and the prevailing nature of the field, and intervening accordingly. All such work should, however, begin with an adaptive context related to the therapeutic interaction, and should unfold from there. All the while, the relationship itself—the therapist's hold, manner of responding, and basic attitudes toward the patient, is also fairly stable—is in keeping with the patient's appropriate and necessary needs, and with the nature of the communicative field. As such it offers a steady framework for the interpretative work.

Again, coming back to this particular clinical situation, I would be formulating the patient's associations around the adaptive context of the previous hour (which we have not heard), the liaison with the therapist's friend, and, especially now, the precipitants contained in the therapist's recent interventions. In principle, I would be organizing this material in terms of the patient's unconscious perceptions and introjections of the therapist's interventions and their unconscious meanings and functions. And I would be making every effort to utilize self-knowledge and the patient's unconscious working over of these introjects to understand what has transpired, and to understand the nature of the therapist's countertransference difficulties and the patient's reactions to them. And I would be waiting to see whether the patient's continued associations strengthen and deepen my formulations, or direct me toward revisions. I would be making consistent use of the validating process, and if I am able to define continued validation, I would expect that the patient's material would produce closer, less disguised, derivatives related to the therapeutic relationship—to a point where the nature of this entire sequence and its unconscious meanings, expressed in terms of perceptions and perhaps, if available, fantasies as well, could be interpreted to the patient. At times such as this, the therapist can make extremely important interpretations of unconscious perceptions and introjections that have considerable bearing on the patient's psychopathology, which is influenced by these essentially valid experiences, as well as by inner distortions and disruptive unconscious fantasies.

Perhaps most essential for this work, then, is a growing capacity for true self-knowledge, and the development of the technical skill that I would term the *capacity to listen*—to observe on every level, and to formulate—an ability that readily translates itself into a capacity to intervene. Here today, I have been trying to stress the nature of that listening process and of the validating process which is an essential component of such efforts, and attempting to show how they apply not only to the therapeutic situation, but to the supervisory field as well.

I hope that I have clarified some of the uncertainties that have arisen. But I must say that I do not hope to accomplish total clarity and resolution in a conference such as this. My main goal is to touch upon the basic issues, to demonstrate their relevance and meaning through the clinical material, and to give you a basic framework within which you can work over these problems again and again. I am well aware that I am covering far too much for you to absorb and digest; I can only hope to initiate a learning process that can unfold over the months or even years to come. Let's now have some more material.

Supervisor A: The patient had just said, I am close to my girlfriend, but I am afraid of her—she's too pushy. In supervision, I had commented that the remark also referred to the therapist. The supervisee went on, indicating that he had intervened at that point in the session, saying, Does this closeness problem remind you of something?

Langs: The therapist continues his excessive activity, creating a kind of staccato that almost binds the patient to the surface. In addition, with so many interventions, we learn almost more about his unconscious processes and contents than we do of the patient's for the moment. And the unconscious truths about the therapist contained in this intervention—whatever its other implications—are almost directly stated. If the therapist had said, Does this closeness problem remind you of some*one*, he would have been unconsciously acknowledging that he shares with this patient an aspect of his psychopathology.

In a way, then, this is a nice example of both projection and projective identification on the part of the therapist. We have already developed evidence that the therapist has some sort of difficulty with intimacy, especially in his relationship with the patient. And you can see how this shapes his intervention: it is one factor in why he does indeed address the surface of the patient's communications. The intervention once again lacks an adaptive context relevant to the unconscious issues. And in the very pushy manner that the patient is unconsciously experiencing, it places the closeness problem entirely within the patient. On one level, it constitutes a denial by the therapist that he has a similar difficulty, and it prods the patient to work over this difficulty in a manner that suggests the evocation of a proxy, a concept developed by Wangh (1962) which refers to the manner in which a projective identification may be an unconscious request that the object mobilize adaptive resources and responses unavailable to the subject.

Now I am well aware that this is a conjecture on my part, a formulation to be validated. You'll notice that the therapist does attempt to make use of a conscious communication from the patient. As a result, it seems that he is exploring a problem that the patient has stated. Still, his question is arbitrary—it is his own association, rather than the patient's. It is part of a sequence of interventions with pressured, premature, and selective qualities. It is for these reasons that I am suggesting it is countertransference-based—and both a projection (of his own fears of intimacy) and a projective identification (of his inner state of tension and fears of further revelations). Once again, after offering such a formulation to the supervisee, I would suggest that we turn to some more material from the patient for validation.

Incidentally, to the extent that my formulation proves

valid, it gives me an opportunity to point out how objects—that is, others—invite and facilitate projections and projective identifications, and to comment that this is true in all types of relationships, including that between the patient and the therapist—and there as elsewhere, on both sides of the relationship. Here, the patient's problems with closeness—whatever that means—facilitates what I believe to be a projection and projective identification by the therapist of similar problems. Efforts at projective identification, as I said earlier, are almost always among the unconscious motives for premature and incorrect intervention. More broadly speaking, such opportunities for pathological unconscious projective identification into patients constitutes one motivational system for the selection of psychotherapy and psychoanalysis as a profession (Langs 1976c). I might, at some relevant point, point this out to the supervisee.

Supervisor A: My unspoken hypothesis at this point, by the way, related to the supervisee's mentioning that he had had trouble dealing with this other patient, who had developed an erotic transference. I had also taken note of the fact that he had chosen to present a patient who had problems with lack of feeling toward women.

Langs: Yes, your remark reminds me that I have wanted to add an important comment related to the supervisory process in the context of this material; it had escaped me in my preoccupation with the therapist's possible projective identifications into the patient. I think it is important, as I am now actually demonstrating to you, to continuously monitor the presentation of the supervisee for commentaries on the supervisory interaction and yourself as supervisor. Because of the intimate interaction between the supervisory and therapeutic bipersonal fields, valid commentaries and mirrorings may come from either the patient or the therapist. But we must constantly struggle against the human tendency to blame—and I use the term here not as a pejorative—to place problems and issues, sources of disturbances, and sectors of psychopathology, outside of ourselves, into other and into other interactional fields.

It is therefore important, in observing that both patient and therapist are somewhat helplessly, and on the surface, working over an ill-defined problem with closeness and intimacy, that the supervisor at such a juncture ask himself whether these communications apply to himself as well, and to his interaction with the supervisee. As you can see, it is far easier to pay lip service to the notion that the therapeutic field is a mirror to the supervisory field than it is to apply that principle consistently in our work as supervisors. And let me stress too that I am suggesting a silent monitoring of this type, pointing it out as an opportunity for the supervisor to acquire some self-knowledge and to resolve possible countertransference-based inputs into the supervisory field. He is under no obligation to consciously and directly work over his difficulties with the supervisee; his main responsibility is to recognize the pertinence of these communications to himself, where this is the case, and to quietly, and on his own, resolve the relevant countertransferences.

On selected occasions, with discretion, humility, and honesty, especially in a crisis situation related to the therapy or to supervision, the supervisor may acknowledge the role of his own countertransferences and also indicate that he is making efforts to resolve it. (This is the sort of remark I do not explicitly make to a patient, though it is implicit in my attitude.) The danger there is that the supervisor might use the supervisory situation inappropriately, shifting the interface too close to his own pathology and thereby making the supervisory field a therapeutic place for himself, and using the supervisee as his therapist. These efforts are not only bound to fail, but to be markedly disruptive of the supervisory experience.

Still, if such remarks are made on rare occasion, with discretion and tact, and within appropriate limits, they can provide the supervisee an important and meaningful model that contributes to his capacities as a therapist.

However, if the subject is broached in a more pathological way, it constitutes an effort by the supervisor to use the supervisee as a pathological container, it will include pathological projective identifications into the supervisee, and it will greatly distort the nature and functions of the supervisory field, impairing its qualities as a growth-promoting, teaching medium. It could also generate on some level a crisis in supervision that would have to be dealt with through rectification of the frame—that is, a discontinuance of this sort of inappropriate use of the supervisory situation—and a long period of self-analysis on the part of the supervisor, all as the dust settles, so to speak, and efforts are made to return the supervisory field to its essential functions.

Now, in regard to this specific situation, I offered these comments only as a model, since I have no evidence that the supervisor does indeed have problems with intimacy or that this material in some way reflects an introjection of his difficulties into either patient or therapist. On the other hand, what you have heard about the plight of the supervisee is well taken: he may have wanted to present a patient who would not stir up his heterosexual conflicts, and here the material is doing just that, and stirring up homosexual problems as well. This is all quite inevitable; it's in the nature of the therapeutic situation and the communications from the patient to expose, sooner or later, all of the vulnerabilities of both participants, and there is, for the therapist, no escaping his unconscious anxieties and conflicts.

And to the extent that your observation has validity, it reminds us that attempts by the therapist to be selective with the patients he takes into treatment, and to manipulate the communications from his patients, are bound to fail—there is no substitute for personal therapy or analysis. It is under conditions such as this that therapists will unconsciously make powerful efforts to create misalliances with their patients, and to generate bastions into which contents that are anxiety-provoking for themselves will be split off and sealed away. And while a patient may well cooperate up to a point, this does not happen in a lasting way and sooner or later the therapist is intensely exposed on some level to the very contents that he dreads and finds so unmanageable—an attitude that is unconsciously communicated to the patient in a host of ways, including excessive interventions and efforts to focus on manifest content, as we see in the work of this supervisee.

In this context, too, I would once again suggest great caution in commenting on a supervisee's countertransference problems on the basis of data of this type—that is, on the basis of inferences drawn from the comment about another patient as it may shed light on the present case. A supervisor must use all sources of information as sensitively as possible. But in a manner that is similar to our work with patients, he must also be able to recognize when his formulations are tentative and not well founded, and when they are quite secure, clinically based, and susceptible to validation through process note presentation. I would therefore agree with you that your last formulation should be maintained as a silent hypothesis, though I would be prepared, when the material from the present therapeutic interaction permits, to indicate to the supervisee how his own sexual anxieties—heterosexual and homosexual—are interfering with his work with the patient. Such comments would be based almost entirely on the patient's unconscious perceptions and introjections of these anxieties and their underlying basis, and the patient's communication of these processes in his own associations. Wherever possible, I want to use the material from patient-therapist interaction as the basis for my supervisory comments, since such hypotheses can be validated in the therapeutic bipersonal field. We must try as much as possible to intervene as supervisors in a manner that permits sound validation.

This material can also be utilized to emphasize again the need for the supervisor to consistently search for possible misalliances and bastions in the supervisory field, and to constantly ask himself what it is he might be missing or inappropriately sharing with the supervisee. In fact, whenever there is evidence of a misalliance or bastion in the therapeutic bipersonal field, the supervisor should make a special effort to search for not only similar, but distinctly different sectors of misalliance and bastions in his work with the supervisee. The single greatest obstacle to cure lies within the countertransferences of the therapist and the supervisor, because it is here that they have the greatest resistances to overcome. It is here too that we need a catalogue of formal indicators of difficulty, as well as a clearly defined process that serves as a means through which we may consistently search for countertransference influences.

In this regard, as I have commented earlier, I have already attempted to develop the necessary models for the therapeutic situation, based on my own clinical observations and the work of others (Langs 1974, 1976a,d), and the basic principles carry over quite well to the supervisory situation. Thus, the presence of any type of disturbance in either the supervisory or therapeutic bipersonal fields, the experience by the supervisor of any type of discomfort or unusual feeling or fantasy—anything unusual—should call for an exploration of the supervisor's countertransferences and their possible expression in his relationship with the supervisee. Of course, a more acute crisis in either field would also direct the supervisor to examine his unresolved pathology and his interaction with the supervisee, but it is important to stress that resistances would have to be overcome in order to maintain an attitude of this type consistently. I want also to remind you that, in addition to efforts at self-scrutiny and self-analysis that can be undertaken by the supervisor at such times, he should also make use of the communications from both the supervisee and his patient—these communications represent on some level possible introjections of the supervisor's difficulties. He may use such material as a means of detecting clues to the specific nature of his countertransferences and, often, of some of the underlying motives.

Supervisor A: The patient responded to the therapist's question about the closeness problem, and whether it reminded him of something, by saying, When I was married, I was never close to my wife; I don't think I knew what love was. And the resident intervened again, by saying, How about the feeling you had of not being close to your parents?

So I intervened, and I suggested that the value of the patient's current and more immediate associations might be considerable, and I advised the resident not to push the genetic material too much, because it might lead to excessive intellectualization and a lack of emotional conviction within the patient.

Langs: This is becoming quite interesting, and I must say that I can envision myself intervening rather extensively with this supervisee. I would not be happy with a rather simple directive which stresses the relevance of these associations to the current situation—quite ill defined—and the danger of overintellectualization. I would instead consider myself faced with a chaotic therapeutic situation, and now, true to the principles that I have been developing, my first questions to myself would be: Am I contributing something to this chaos? Does this reflect some type of supervisory countertransference problem on my part? And, does all this mirror, in some way, a chaotic and defensive state of the supervisory interaction?

For me, this is becoming a crisis situation in which the therapist appears to be extremely anxious, and has now become not only inordinately active, but also is endeavoring to direct the patient away from his own associations to those of the supervisee, and as you indicated, from the present into the far distant past. This is a very common misuse of the genetic hypothesis: when the current therapeutic interaction becomes too anxiety-provoking for the therapist, he invokes a link to the past. This is far different from identifying the nature of the unconscious interaction—reality and fantasy—and then, based on the patient's associations, defining ties to the past—in terms of both actual repetitions in the here and now, and pathological displacements from the past into the present.

I think that most supervisors would see these incorrect interventions primarily in terms of the countertransference problems of the supervisee. I very much doubt that many supervisors adopt the basic principle of approaching every crisis in treatment with an initial exploration of their own countertransferences and possible disturbances in the supervisory bipersonal field, and only then moving on to a study of the disturbances in the therapeutic bipersonal field and within both patient and therapist.

Actually, the approach that I am suggesting is a variation on my remarks about understanding the material from the patient: my stress is on identifying valid unconscious perceptions and introjections—nontransferences—before defining distortions and transferences. We must establish the truth about the therapist before we can know the truth about the patient; similarly, we must establish the truth about the supervisor before we can know the truth about the supervisee and his patient. patient.

At this point, I would also apply to the supervisory field another essential principle derived from the therapeutic situation: namely, I would search for an adaptive context related to supervision, and use it as a basis for organizing the first part of my supervisory commentary. And here, since I feel that we are faced with a crisis situation in the therapeutic field, even in the absence of an apparent crisis in supervision and even in the presence of a powerful external stimulus (the new acquaintance), I would be inclined to share my impressions in this area with the supervisee. And, as you might have anticipated, all of this would have led me, as supervisor, to the fact that I was presenting this material at this conference. And it would have strengthened my conviction that the supervisee is quite frightened that the patient might reveal information related to this colleague that could be embarrassing to him, that he feels quite endangered in the therapeutic situation, and that he is actively and massively attempting to protect himself from the patient's spontaneous associations. At the same time, he is massively projectively identifying into the patient his own anxiety and his own fragile defenses, on the simplest level, using shifts to the surface and to the past—the far distant past at that.

I might at this juncture ask the supervisee if he had any sense of how excessively active he had become, how anxious he seems, and how inappropriately manipulative he had become. I would ask too if he had any sense as to what could have been evoking these anxieties and inappropriate interventions, and a positive, insightful response would be a favorable sign. I could then comment further on the effects of the pending presentation of his supervisory work, not so much as a means of blaming and projecting, but as an honest effort to identify an important source of anxiety for which the supervisor must take some responsibility. Allowing the supervisee to express himself in this area, and acknowledging the valid aspects of his anxieties—again, first recognizing whatever is not distorted before attempting to identify what is—I might even go so far as to offer to not present this material to the conference, so long as I had another possibility in mind.

In taking this approach, I believe that the supervisor would be offering himself implicitly as a sound model of a therapist, one that could profitably and constructively be introjected by the supervisee. In addition, the supervisor would be following the very basic principle that I established earlier: that efforts at rectification must precede all other therapeutic work. And in a supervisory field, the rectification of disruptive inputs by the supervisor must take precedence over teaching. In this way, you restore the necessary communicative properties to the teaching field.

Without rectification—and here, I allude to the offer to withdraw the presentation—the supervisee's anxieties will remain quite intense, his therapeutic work will be erratic and essentially countertransference-based, and the supervisory interaction will be infused with disruptive influences. Efforts to teach in other areas could hardly prove fruitful under these conditions, and either the supervisee becomes capable of mastering some of these anxieties on his own, or you would indeed have to find some means of restoring confidentiality to the supervisory field. I think here you can get a feeling for how important the communicative properties of the field are, and how, so long as the contaminant—the break in the frame—remains, its influence disturbs the usual therapeutic or teaching experience.

At this point, it might well be that you could honestly reassure the supervisee that this is the last session relevant to the seminar. And here you might even suggest that you would not present this session if it proves too revealing, but would focus on earlier presentations. This might have been a very nice way of rectifying the field, and of restoring the necessary trust and security that the supervisee needs in his relationship with you as his supervisor. You must remember that the patient's and supervisor's needs must take precedence over your own.

In a rather strange but typical way, the supervisee's anxiety and the supervisor's problems are the source of considerable insight for us in this seminar. They provide us the opportunity to study a crisis situation in a therapeutic bipersonal field, and to offer a compelling hypothesis—open to validation, of course—regarding a significant input from the supervisor—one that here, fortunately, is not especially countertransference-based.

Now, having rectified the supervisory bipersonal field, or at the very least, having stabilized it by addressing the presentation issue first, I then might have gone on to discuss the therapist's interventions, doing so in a context that would emphasize how much we can learn when we step back from countertransference-based interactions with our patients. In brief, I would address my remarks to the therapist's defensiveness, to the ways in which interventions can be designed to create misalliances and bastions—and to serve the defensive needs of the therapist—and to a characterization of the communicative properties of the bipersonal field that may develop when the therapist uses language primarily for projective identification and as a means of getting rid of his own inner tensions. I would stress the likelihood that the prevailing field is a Type B field at the moment, and would outline contributions from alterations in the frame, such as the therapist's lack of neutrality and his propensities toward action and discharge. I would suggest too that one consequence of such a field is the heightening of tendencies within the patient toward living out. Unfortunately, the therapist is so active here that it is difficult to determine the exact nature of the bipersonal field. Basing my formulation on the supervisee's activities, there is reason to believe that it is indeed mainly a Type B field, though, for the moment, the patient seems to be attempting to communicate through Type Two derivatives related to the therapist's interventions; he is using some symbolic communication, whatever else he is doing.

Much of what I would add I have already discussed based on the therapist's earlier interventions. I would stress the extent to which he is attempting to create interactional resistances, his dread of the immediate experience and his defensive use of genetics and manifest content, and I would mention again his efforts at projective identification into the patient. Here, I would emphasize his attempt to put into the patient an intensely defensive need.

On a simple technical level, I would discuss the importance of obtaining the patient's free associations and of allowing the patient to shape the session—to put into the therapist, in the form of derivatives, all of the communications that he will need for his neutral and interpretive interventions. I would try to help the supervisee develop a technique that neither leads the patient nor directs him away from his own communicative flow. While I am quite sure that the supervisee could justify his intervention as a genetic interpretation, I think it would be quite important to demonstrate how superficial and lacking in substance this entire sequence is, and how he is dealing with clichés and superficialities to the point of using language for noncommunication—as a means of creating falsehoods and deceptions suggestive of a Type C field. In fact, if the patient were to proceed to talk about his childhood, I believe that it would take the form of further clichés and emptiness, and that it would constitute not only an interactional defense, but a further use of Type C communication designed as an impenetrable and essentially meaningless barrier against unconscious processes and contents, and true relatedness. In this context, we can view the therapist's effort to make use of generalities and clichés, at a time when the specific associations from the patient might greatly disturb him, as an effort to create a Type C barrier through which the underlying derivatives are no longer expressed and cannot penetrate.

This material enables me to demonstrate what happens in either the therapeutic or supervisory bipersonal fields when the therapist or the supervisor becomes the main source of associations and offers the major pathological inputs. In therapy, we can now tell little about the patient's psychopathology, and even less about his immediate reactions to the therapist, though some of that does seem to be coming through. In supervision, similarly, we would lose sight of the supervisee's problems and find the field flooded with those of the supervisor. You must be quite careful to work closely with the material that is being presented to you, to work with silent hypotheses that are validated as the supervisee proceeds, and to tailor your interventions to the needs of the patient and the supervisee—concepts quite easy to state, but not so simple in their explication.

Discussant: Would you address your comments to the resident in the exact words you have used with us today?

Langs: Yes, this is exactly how I fashion my supervisory interventions. Oh, they might take a slightly different form in a one-to-one relationship, with an emphasis on the teaching needs of the supervisee, while here I am addressing a large group and stressing general principles. But on the whole I think my comments today faithfully reflect my style of intervening as a supervisor. I believe in candidness, precision, the explicit and specific use of the material from the patient, and a tactful, sensitive, and basically supportive approach. I try to use simple language, allowing my comments to be fashioned by the patient's associations and behaviors. I will, to facilitate communication and help the supervisee learn to conceptualize, use agreed-upon, clearly defined technical terms, but will in the main avoid the use of jargon and clichês.

I would also stress the importance of using language in keeping with derivatives of unconscious fantasies and introjects—daydreaming language that comes as close as possible to our conception of the raw material out of which fantasies are built. In this way, supervision is shaped by the language of the patient, and is more likely than otherwise to be in touch with unconscious processes and fantasies within thc patient.

I have already described in some detail the specific interventions that I would have made throughout this supervisory hour, and because we are now pressed for time, I will not attempt any sort of reiteration. I think it would be best to hear the end of this particular supervisory hour.

Supervisor A: Yes, we are near the end of the session that the supervisee was presenting. The patient did not take up the resident's question about closeness to his parents...

Langs: Well, the patient really seems to have little interest in the misalliance being offered him. As I said earlier, there is no such thing as a bad patient, only bad therapists. (Laughter.) And even then, if I had the free associations of the therapist, I would say there is no such thing, ultimately, as a bad therapist; as a human being, on some crucial, unconscious level, there is always a constructive hope and an effort at cure—a point that Searles (1965, 1975) too has made. Unfortunately, a supervisor must judge and evaluate the supervisee based on his interventions to the patient—his manifest behaviors and communications—and we are kind of stuck with that, just as the patient is.

Discussant: With the supervisee, then, are you not limited to manifest content? I wonder to what extent that limits and even shapes your comments to the supervisee. Should we, as supervisors, make efforts to identify the latent content of his intervention? This is especially pertinent, I think, because it has a bearing on how we handle the difficulties that the resident is having within himself.

Langs: Yes, this is a very basic issue and I will respond briefly since I have already attempted to discuss how the supervisor approaches the countertransference problems of the supervisee at several earlier junctures in this conference. The main principle I follow is that the supervisor should, among his many functions, make manifest what the patient is saying latently, indicating quite openly the nature of his unconscious communications to the therapist. I allow the patient's communications to guide me; I use the patient's unconscious supervisory efforts. And I attempt to demonstrate their validity, in addition to whatever distortions I also detect.

And so I state it again: it is through the material from the patient, and because of the patient's introjection of the therapist's countertransferences, that I approach this area as directly and supportively as possible with the supervisee. And in general, I confine myself to manifest statements based on the patient's derivative and, more rarely, direct communications. I therefore believe that in principle you have a responsibility to both patient and supervisee to use the material from the patient to define the therapist's countertransference problems. In doing this type of work, you must recognize that there is bound to be an initial heightening of the supervisee's anxieties, that you will generate a disequilibrium that will disturb his pathological defenses; you must indicate your appreciation of these very difficult aspects of learning how to do psychotherapy.

This leads me to a principle implicit in much of what I have been saying; I want to state it quite explicitly and elaborate it now: *the ultimate supervisor for the therapist is the patient*. One of the important lessons to be taught each supervisee is that sooner or later he must forgo formal supervision. Still, he must always maintain a listening attitude that on one level accepts and appreciates the patient's unconcious functions as supervisor and mentor, whatever other dimensions of the therapeutic interaction exist. And in a sense, my own supervisory work is shaped by this same principle: I allow the patient's unconscious supervisory efforts, as they are unfolding in the therapeutic interaction being presented, to be my essential guide. In a sense, my supervisory efforts are basically the translation of the patient's unconscious supervisory work into conscious statements offered in a teaching context as endeavors to help the therapist learn his trade.

The patient's unconscious supervision is one dimension of his unconscious efforts to cure the therapist. When you listen to a patient's responses to an incorrect intervention, you will readily discover that it will quite often take the form of pithy commentaries—via derivatives—that meet the criteria of valid supervisory work. At times, these efforts may be far more perceptive than those of the supervisor himself. After all, it is the patient who is most immediately experiencing—unconsciously perceiving and introjecting—the totality of the supervisee's communicated countertransferences, and who carries within him an extensive need to both exploit and modify these difficulties. Their ultimate modification, then, sometimes relies quite heavily on the patient's unconscious supervisory work. The therapist's failure to appreciate these unconscious efforts by the patient will generally lead the latter to be quite hurt and depressed—feelings that can be properly understood and interpreted only if their true adaptive context is recognized. In all, the recognition of the extent to which the patient is able, unconsciously, to quite validly function in this area offers the therapist an important opportunity to experience the extent to which the patient functions validly and constructively in the therapeutic interaction, no matter how sick and disturbed the patient happens to be in regard to the pathological parts of his personality.

In this way, I once again arrive at a recognition that a therapist can quite often benefit from his therapeutic work with his patient—benefits that must, as I have stated before, remain secondary and, hopefully, quite peripheral to the prevailing functioning goals of the bipersonal field. And I would simply extend this to the supervisory situation as well, and suggest that both patient and supervisee often unconsciously function as supervisors to the supervisor, who need only listen sensitively on this level to learn a great deal about the therapeutic and supervisory experiences—and himself. These principles are fundamental to my position on dealing with the supervisee's countertransferences: it is in this area that the patient offers his most intense supervisory comments, and I think that the supervisor himself has no choice but to follow the patient's lead, and to do much of his own work in that area—always with the basic tools of the patient's and therapist's communications within the session under supervision.

Supervisor A: As I said, the patient did not take the genetic escape route, but went back to talking about how he never felt emotions toward his wife—it was just a lack of feeling, maybe. He went on, I was afraid that jealousy might develop; sometimes I think it is better not to have any emotions at all because I feel that I would get jealous.

Langs: How nice: because whatever else this association communicates, it constitutes an introjective identification of the projective identification and unconscious communications from the therapist, a valid core that is influenced too by the patient's own inner fantasies and propensities. This association reflects the patient's evaluation not so much of the therapist's manifest interventions as of their latent implications: his over-activity is based on unconscious jealousy. And I would suggest that this association nicely demonstrates what I have termed *unconscious interpretation* (Langs 1976a,d), through which the patient is suggesting that the therapist's excessive activity and efforts to close off further associations to the meeting with his colleague is based on unresolved jealousy. And I can assure you again that in the supervisory situation with this supervisee I would offer a similar commentary. In addition, I would note that the patient is also unconsciously offering the therapist an interactional defense: the use of isolation and the suppression of all emotions.

I trust you can see that the patient is suggesting, unconsciously, that the therapist is jealous of the dating relationship between himself and this acquaintance. It is quite interesting too, to see that there is room here to think that the therapist may be jealous on both counts—that there is both a heterosexual and homosexual basis for this reaction. I hope you can also recognize that this unconscious communication from the patient meets all the criteria for general interpretations. All the therapist need do is apply the me/not-me interface and relate the patient's associations to himself; he might then consciously recognize what the patient is trying to say in derivative form and benefit from it—not so much by explicitly thanking the patient for his assistance, but more by silently considering his implicit intervention and attempting to bring his inappropriate reactions to the material about the colleague and the patient under control. Hopefully, the therapist could accomplish this through some quick self-analytic efforts.

And you can see again that knowing the adaptive context—and taking the therapist's intervention as the precipitant for the next set of associations and searching for the unconscious communications it contains—enables us to formulate this important level of the patient's associations, a level that must be understood, rectified, and resolved before we can return the bipersonal field to the treatment of the patient and the resolution of his own inappropriately jealous feelings and fantasies, his pathological defenses, his need to act out, and the rest: the "me" part of the communicative interface.

I would also like to say at this point that I realize I have been excessively active in my supervision of this resident today, largely because I am attempting here to develop in some detail a particular model of supervision. I would therefore stress that while I would have made many of these points to the supervisee, I would also try to avoid overwhelming him and to be gentle and relatively supportive in the face of such massive difficulties. I certainly do not want to overburden the resident and would try to confine myself to the basic issues, the main problems within the therapist, and the therapy, and the main avenues of potential resolution.

When a particular presentation has been especially revealing in regard to either the patient or the therapist, or both, I will sometime suggest to the supervisee that he reread the session on his own. One other point: I do not ask the supervisee to confirm or discuss with me the patient's unconscious interpretations. Instead, I have been able to validate such interventions with my own patients based on my self-knowledge. My principal effort is to teach the resident and to alert him to possible countertransference difficulties, and to ultimately undertake sufficient self-examination to determine the extent to which the patient is correct.

In some ways, despite the epochal significance of Freud's discovery of transference, it is unfortunate that he was vouchsafed this insight only on condition that he view nontransference as the exception. That gave us a dangerous heritage that can all too readily be enrolled in the service of countertransference. With my approach, nontransference is the assumption one starts with; transference, to the extent it is present, is whatever remains after the valid aspects of the patient's responses have been identified (in this regard, I think I have never encountered an example of "pure transference"). Methodologically this translates into the principle that self-knowledge must precede understanding the patient, and that your own projective identifications as a therapist must be considered before those of the patient, as must unconscious communication before manifest content.

All right. I gather that you are almost done with this particular supervisory hour.

Supervisor A: The patient finished the session by saying, Maybe it would be better not to have emotions because I feel jealous, but then again maybe it is good that I can begin to recognize and experience some of these feelings—things have been going better at work.

That was the end of the session. I said nothing for the moment, and as the supervisory hour was also drawing to a close, the resident told me that he had seen the female patient again—the one who had moved back into the city—the week before, in a first reevaluation session. He had been reasonably comfortable in dealing with her, and she had not decided what she was going to do—if she was going to stay in this area or go back to her home.

Langs: In this context, I want to mention that I would allow the resident to decide which patient he would like to present to me. I am glad to serve his needs; I feel that this should be his choice.

Incidentally, as I hear this last bit of material, I think of the problems and burdens of being a psychiatric resident—let alone an analytic candidate. It staggers the imagination: here he has a problem with this woman possibly returning to therapy, this other patient meets a woman he knows and begins to date her, and he is faced with a supervisor who is an analyst and who is presenting to me and to a large audience—to name a few factors that we know about. And once again, I must express a sense of sympathy regarding the burden that supervisors and patients put into residents; it is remarkable that we can indeed learn to do psychotherapy under such conditions.

Are there any final questions based on this last segment of the presentation?

Discussant: It seems to me that the patient's last comments—to the effect that things are going better at work—could be based on something that happened in the therapeutic interaction toward the end of the hour. As I heard it, the resident had begun to keep quiet, and it may well be that the patient felt quite relieved.

Langs: Yes, I had not commented because I felt that there were several possibilities in respect to that last segment of material. In the supervisory hour, I would have suggested to the resident that this final remark clearly challenged my repeated formulations that his interventions were essentially countertransference-based. I would encourage him to question my hypotheses when contradictory material appears. I would also suggest that this positive comment can be made only on the basis of a review of the last part of this interaction, with some help from the material of the following hour, especially the patient's initial communications.

And though several possible reasons could be given for this last communication, it is difficult to choose among them since this particular presentation—and I am not sure whether it is the therapist's or the supervisor's condensation we are hearing—is far too abbreviated: there is too little material with which to fully formulate the unconscious interaction and communication here. It is important to have an adequate summary of the session. You will find that some residents condense too tightly, and it is essential that you recommend that they offer more detailed notes. Others will want to offer verbatim notes, which as a rule are far too much to handle; with them, you must recommend some degree of condensation.

Since there is little antecedent material to the patient's positive comment, I will briefly identify my working hypothesis: First, if the therapist had indeed become relatively silent, the patient may well have felt a sense of relief. Another possibility is a misalliance cure based on shared and interactional defenses, in which disturbing emotions are avoided and denied, and the entire subject of the patient's date with the therapist's associate is sealed off in a bastion providing them mutual and temporary relief. If this is the case, I would expect to find the patient rather depressed at the beginning of the following hour, and that is why I feel we need subsequent material in order to clarify this particular communication.

Incidentally, I am suggesting here that I will try to predict aspects of the initial communications from the patient in the hour that is to follow. More important, I try, when I can, to prepare the supervisee for that particular session. Here, for example, I would suggest that he sit back and allow the material to unfold, and that he try to work through his anxieties about the patient's date with his colleague. I would reassure him regarding the restoration of total confidentiality in supervision, and suggest that he allow the derivatives to unfold as they relate to this particular date or to any new material that might emerge. And I would stress the need for the therapist to identify important adaptive contexts in the next hour, and to attempt perhaps one or two interpretations on that basis, consciously slowing down his rate of activity and modifying the randomness of his interventions.

Discussant: I felt that the very last remark the resident made regarding the female patient—to the effect that things went fairly well—was a way of attempting to reassure himself and of seeking some reassurance from the supervisor.

Langs: Yes, but he then added that she was uncertain whether she would stay here and resume treatment; that certainly modified any positive quality to that communication. It may well be that the resident was attempting to find some reassurance after his most difficult session with this patient—and with the supervisor as well. But I would not make too much of that in my work with him. Enough is enough, and there is no crisis for the moment. I make special efforts to avoid comments that are unrelated to the case presentation at hand.

Now I see that our time is up, and I want to thank our presenting supervisor—and his much beleaguered supervisee—for his courageous presentation. I am deeply appreciative, and I am sure that we all are.

Chapter 4

A Supervisory Crisis and Its Resolution

Moderator: We will now have a presentation of the second supervisory experience.

Discussant: Before we begin, Dr. Langs, I would like to ask a question. How often do you supervise a resident? And does that decision have anything to do with the frequency of the sessions that the resident has with his patient? Also, how much time do you give to the resident, as a rule?

Langs: I appreciate questions related to the basic structure of the supervisory bipersonal field. I make it a general practice to see a resident—or any supervisee—once a week in supervision, regardless of the frequency with which the patient is seen. Based on my experience, I believe that once weekly supervision is optimal for any therapy or analytic patient, and I prefer a supervisory hour that lasts from fifty to sixty minutes. In the case of supervisory seminars, I prefer meeting for an hour and a half once a week. I have experimented with other durations of supervision, and find these about right—though, as I said earlier this morning, I am quite prepared to extend the supervisory hour in an unresolved emergency, so long as I have the time available.

I use the same basic model of supervision and of therapy in all of these situations, whether it is a once-a-week patient or someone in analysis. My goals are comparable: to teach the supervisee essentially the same basic principles regardless of the therapeutic interaction he is presenting—although I do in addition shape the supervision in terms of the specific needs of a given patient, therapist, and therapeutic situation and am careful to note the few distinctions that do obtain between the therapeutic modalities.

I state all of this because there is a tendency to advocate artificial distinctions between analysis and therapy, and between so-called supportive treatment, which actually does not function supportively in the form in which it is advocated, and insight-oriented therapy or analysis. There is a tendency also toward inappropriate modification of fundamental therapeutic techniques on the basis of this fiction; the patient, by the way, does not at all share this tendency, as his derivatives always indicate.

And again I must state that I am not suggesting that within these same basic principles we do not actually make somewhat different interventions with, say, a once-a-week schizophrenic patient, as compared to a relatively more intact analytic patient. Our interventions are, of course, guided and shaped by the communications from the patient, and by both his psychopathology and his assets. There is always considerable confusion when I state this position; to put it succinctly, I am advocating individually tailored therapeutic techniques within a basic, relatively constant setting in accordance with a basic set of therapeutic principles.

Discussant: Dr. Langs, it seems to me that you have been rather outspoken about your concerns regarding the influence that the therapist might have on his patient. And yet you yourself make predictions to the supervisee, anticipations that I gather you present to the therapist and which then must influence his perceptions of the patient and his later interventions.

Langs: Yes, there is no doubt that the predictions that I make influence the therapist and the course of treatment. There are, in fact, some parallels between the influence of the therapist on his patient, and that of the supervisor on both the supervisee and his patient. Our conceptualization and understanding of the supervisory and therapeutic processes must take these effects into account. As I have already indicated, rather pathological interactions can develop between supervisor and supervisee, and when they are embedded in the character structure or blind spots of the supervisor, they are quite difficult to detect; the supervisor should constantly monitor the material presented to him for such factors.

To the extent that you are suggesting that my predictions may generate self-fulfilling prophesies, it is here that careful use of the validating process is most important—both in supervision and in therapy itself. As you undoubtedly know, there is a sense in which every interpretation is not only an evaluation of the unconscious elements within past material but is also a prediction and directive regarding the future communications of the patient. Every intervention has predictive qualities and will influence the future of both therapist and patient, or supervisor, therapist and patient. And it is here that self-knowledge, the continual search for countertransference-based influences, and the validating process are all applied as checks and safeguards.

In this context, I want also to stress the fact that I strive to make predictions that can be validated by the material in the session that is being presented to me at the time. This type of validation is, of course, less encumbered by the influence of my immediate supervision and predictions, since the session has already occurred and is, of course, quite fixed. Still, I must also point out that once the supervisory process has been initiated, each supervisory session will affect the subsequent hours between the patient and the supervisee, and it can influence the validating process as well. I have found that the latter is very much open to countertransference-based influences, and that one can hardly relax one's vigilance in this area—either as supervisor or as therapist.

Sometimes, the ideal goal is stated as the hope that the therapist will not influence the patient in the therapeutic interaction—not disturb the so-called unfolding of his transference neurosis—and that the supervisor too will not unduly bias the supervisee or the supervised therapy. Such ideals are very much based on the myth of the closed inner mental system, and the notion that interaction essentially distorts. In actuality the goal is first to recognize the inevitable interplay between the intrapsychic and interactional realms, and the inevitable influences of the supervisor on the supervisee, the therapist on his patient. Then we may strive to minimize the countertransference-based factors and to maximize the capacity of the therapist to be aware of these effects.

I have tried throughout this discussion to identify these interactional realities, to indicate ways they can be monitored, and to define their inevitable influence. These are conscious and unconscious, gross and subtle dimensions of both bipersonal fields. And it is the supervisor who has the responsibility of becoming conscious of their presence in the supervisory situation, far more than the supervisee.

Returning to your question about the use of predictions in supervision, I want to point out again that this technique helps the supervisee considerably in developing a sound clinical methodology and a sense of conviction as to its value. In a way, predictions carry with them in the supervisory situation an impact comparable to that of valid and well-timed, affect-laden interpretations or reconstructions in the therapeutic relationship. We need tools that will generate an awareness of sound therapeutic principles and support cognitive learning in the supervisee. And the validated prediction is one of the most important interventions of this kind available to supervisors. I do not believe that predictions validated and dramatically confirmed by the patient through Type Two derivatives can be viewed as prejudicial, because prejudice suggests distortion and confirmed predictions are nondistorting and constructive. They are therefore a different kind of influence—one that is basically sound.

Predictions are, of course, one means of generating a supervisor or supervisory introject (the former term stressing the introjection of qualities of the supervisor himself, the latter introjections of the supervisory interaction and process). And here we have one of the greatest assets a supervisor may implicitly offer to a supervisee, though at the same time, it may create one of his largest burdens. Such introjects do tend to have extensive effects and may generate pathological biases. Every intervention related to therapy and supervision contains the potential for countertransference-based misapplications; this does not preclude their constructive use . It is important to help the supervisee make full use of their valid core, and yet to enable him to be sufficiently free of these introjects to recognize new themes, contents, and defenses in his patients—and, more broadly, to discover for himself in a subsequent session the actual nature of the patient's conscious and unconscious communications. There is the danger of the supervisee's overidentifying with, and blindly submitting to, the supervisor.

On the other hand, we must be prepared also to evaluate a supervisee's negative response to our supervisory interventions. These may be valid or pathological, and while the material from the therapeutic interaction must decide the issue, it is well to recognize that envy and hostility toward his supervisors may lead a supervisee to make conscious and unconscious efforts to destroy the validity of a given prediction. He will try to prove the supervisor wrong, often by intervening on the basis of a prediction, but doing so prematurely or in some other, essentially erroneous way.

Conversely, some supervisees tend to overidealize their supervisors—and beware there, too, of underlying envy and hostility—and they may tend to rather emptily repeat the supervisor's formulations in their subsequent work with their patients. They will have difficulty, however, in truly integrating the supervisor's commentaries into their own understanding and style of working with the patient. These are all factors that the supervisor must attend to, and occasionally he may have to intervene in this area because it is disturbing the supervisee's work with his patient. Quite often you will be able to do so rather directly, because the patient unconsciously suggests to the supervisee that factors in his supervision are interfering with the therapeutic experience.

In this context I can't help but stress again the importance of generating an independent attitude in the supervisee, and of helping him develop his own capacity to use the validating process and to genuinely voice his objections to your discussions when he has some reasonable basis to do so. You should welcome disagreement and challenge from him; this is in keeping with the spirit of valid psychotherapy and supervision.

Discussant: It might help orient us for this next presentation if you could clarify the difference between Type One and Type Two derivatives, and offer an example of each.

Langs: Well, I will try to do it from the material that we just heard, and will keep it in mind as we move on. First, the Type One derivative: take the patient's utterance about his girlfriend being intrusive or pushy. If at that point we knew nothing about the therapeutic interaction, and could not identify a specific adaptive context but were simply monitoring the material in terms of the therapeutic relationship, we might wonder if this material alluded in some way to a fantasy about the therapist. If we were a bit more sophisticated, we might even go so far as to read into this material a possible unconscious perception of the therapist as well—inferring that the image of the girlfriend relates to some image of the therapist. In all, our formulation would be tentative, flat, nondynamic, and without substance or context.

Similarly, on hearing that the patient had had a date with a colleague of the therapist, we might speculate that unconsciously this colleague represents the therapist—that is, that unconsciously she is a substitute for him in some way, based on the patient's fantasies and, possibly, perceptions. In general, when we hear references to teachers, doctors, authority figures, and the like, we are bound to infer that the material in some way unconsciously alludes to the therapist, and we then try to derive the relevant meanings largely through direct translations from the manifest content related to the other person to a latent content involving the therapist. In this type of effort, we make rather direct translations, and much of the disguise is simply in the form of displacement. There may also be more complex situations, in which defenses have rendered the derivatives far more unintelligible on the surface, and which require quite sophisticated efforts at decoding. There, a specific adaptive context would prove to be a much needed key to the understanding of the latent meanings and functions involved.

In contrast, the Type Two derivative is always organized around a specific adaptive context. For example, in the material that we just heard, we observed that the therapist had intervened excessively. And if we take his overactivity as a specific adaptive context, the reference to the pushy girlfriend immediately suggests latent contents involving the patient's unconscious perceptions of the therapist's intrusiveness and, in addition, deeper unconscious homosexual fantasies and perceptions. Certainly, in making Type One inferences we might also suspect unconscious homosexual fantasies, and even perceptions, but having the opportunity to organize the manifest material around the specific adaptive context, which yields us Type Two derivatives, gives far more definitive clues.

Let me turn things around and show you this in regard to the therapist's interventions. If we simply take his excessive questions as Type One derivatives, it would be difficult to detect their latent content and unconscious meanings. We would be left with global indicators of anxiety and perhaps some clue that these reside in the current therapeutic interaction, since the therapist is attempting to move the patient both away from himself and into the past—though even that formulation reflects some concept of an adaptive context in the material from the patient. On the other hand, in terms of Type Two derivatives—and you can see that the same concepts apply to both therapist and patient—as soon as we become aware that the adaptive context for these interventions is the patient's date with the therapist's colleague we comprehend much more—all of it in terms of the ongoing unconscious interaction. What appears at first to be a relatively random set of questions, directing the patient this way and that, now organizes itself quite meaningfully, first, as an effort to direct the patient away from the deeper aspects of his responses to this specific experience, and, toward the end of the session, away from it entirely; and, second, as a means for the therapist to projectively identify into the patient his undue anxieties and fears of exposure.

The therapist's relatively ambiguous questions about how the patient felt about closeness to women, as a Type Two derivative, takes on specific meaning as a reflection of the therapist's own unconscious conflicts and anxieties about closeness and intimacy, and conveys the sense of threat generated by the social contact between the patient and the colleague, and by the therapist's relationship with the patient. This way of organizing the material begins to give substance to possible homosexual fantasies and anxieties in both patient and therapist, and leads us to suspect, in the light of the adaptive context, that the therapist's interventions are also intended as massive defenses against the homosexual qualities of the therapeutic interaction.

As a rule, then, the identification of the adaptive context for the communications of either patient or therapist will generate a series of specific formulations with far more definitive and dynamic qualities than we can attain through manifest content alone, or even through global efforts to read into the manifest content possible latent themes and meanings. In this context I would propose that any psychoanalytic clinical hypothesis, to achieve the status of accepted tenet, should be validated through Type Two derivatives, and that ideally these should follow an appropriate and well-timed interpretation based on the hypothesis in question. While such a criterion would lead to the rejection of almost the entire clinical psychoanalytic literature, it might produce a most refreshing cleansing process—and a crucial opportunity for rediscovery and true validation.

In essence, then, I am suggesting that every interpretation offered by a therapist or analyst to his patient, and every generalized formulation derived from such work, should be validated by the indirect communications of the patient, in a form that generates a reorganization of, and a set of new insights into, previously observed material that had resisted conceptualization until the new material emerged. My stress is on the importance of indirect validation, and I would go so far as to suggest that manifest agreement—or even agreement through Type One derivatives—does not truly constitute validation. These lack the quality of what Bion (1962) has called the *selected fact*—the insight that provides truly unanticipated meaning to previously known material.

Discussant: Are you implying that there is only one kind of derivative, but that there are different levels of understanding it?

Langs: That is not exactly what I am trying to say. In part, you are correct in that I am saying that Type Two derivatives are, in a sense, the true derivatives of neurotic conflicts and problems, while Type One derivatives are generalizations without specificity and do not meaningfully illuminate present neurotic functioning. Manifest content alone is, of course, not a form of derivative at all.

When I first investigated the area, I saw this primarily as a means of conceptualizing the material from the patient on three distinct levels of organization and implication, and of understanding manifest communications in terms of their possible latent meanings. More recently, as I have come to conceptualize the three types of communicative field, I have come to believe that this classification also relates to styles of communicating within patients and therapists, and within the bipersonal field. I will therefore now say that certain patients communicate almost entirely on the manifest level—they use the Type C mode—while others permit the therapist to experience Type One derivatives—they may be Type B or C—and still others far more consistently communicate in terms of both adaptive context and related associations, thereby communicating through Type Two derivatives using the Type A mode. I could say more, but since time is getting late, I believe that it is time to turn to the second presentation.

Supervisor B: Thank you. I will begin by saying that this resident didn't know she was going to have her supervisory sessions presented to this seminar. That's already a bit different from the first presentation.

I will first offer a brief outline on the patient, a twenty-eight-year-old married man who complained of depression, anxiety, an inability to express anger, problems in interpersonal relationships, and obsessive thinking—each for varying periods of time. I don't know how much more you want.

Langs: Very little; while it all would prove helpful, I think we should now concentrate on the supervisory sessions. Along with the way, where it is relevant, you can fill in with historical material and any other relevant information you might want to mention, and we will ask questions if we need to know more for our purposes.

Supervisor B: The material that was presented in this supervisory hour is from the fourth hour of therapy.

Langs: And from which hour of supervision?

Supervisor B: I believe it is the second hour. The patient is being seen once a week, and I am seeing the resident once a week.

The patient started this session by saying, I started school today (here the patient is referring to a graduate school that he is attending). He went on: But I don't know what to say. I'm feeling okay; I still have trouble with thoughts, especially before going to sleep. It always passes, but sometimes I get very nervous. I remember bad things, things I've seen on TV or in the movies, and they make a deeper impression on my mind.

Langs: As I scan this material, I feel very much at a disadvantage. We are lacking information regarding the previous session and we have no adaptive context. I hope that you are all experiencing the sense of uncertainty and the difficulties in organizing the material that arise in the absence of such a context. At best, we might attempt to work with manifest content and Type One derivatives. But the former will be of relatively little value regarding the structure of this patient's emotional illness, while the latter will tend to be quite general. For the moment there seems little we can do to organize this material around any latent theme or to tie it to the therapeutic interaction—though we could try to do so in a very tentative way. For example, when I hear about school, I often think of the patient's conscious or unconscious awareness that he is in treatment with a student therapist. I gather that this is true here.

Supervisor B: Yes.

Langs: As you can see, I always monitor the material from the patient for commentaries on the therapist and the therapeutic relationship and interaction—not only for the use of displacement, but for general themes that might have specific application to the treatment situation. For example, the reference to school may have something to do with being in treatment with a trainee, and in general I take such themes as an unconscious indication by the patient to the therapist that he has something to learn.

Then we hear that the patient is feeling all right, but that he is still having symptoms. And we hear something about television and movies, a theme related not only to exhibitionism and voyeurism, but also to public exposure—again, a possible reference to the clinic situation and to breaks in confidentiality.

We hear too of bad thoughts based on things he's seen and we might wonder if this relates to the tone of the therapeutic interaction. We sense a poor hold—a bad scene; inner contents are not well managed. But the question remains: how much of this is realistic and perceptive, and how much fantasy-based and distorted?

As you can see though, without an adaptive context these are relatively random thoughts and speculations; there is little sense of organization or of the coalescing of underlying meaning for the moment. And it may well be, if we had heard the prior hour, that we would have been able to identify a specific adaptive context that would serve as a selected fact—a true organizer—to these seemingly divergent associations.

Remember too, in hearing about school and about television and movies, that these may be commentaries related to the supervisory situation, to the patient's sense that the therapist is in supervision. This material may therefore reflect mixed feelings about the influence of the supervision on the treatment. Again, this is clearly quite speculative, but as supervisors we must first monitor the material in terms of the ongoing therapeutic situation between the supervisee and the patient and, second, in terms of the supervisory experience. We must be prepared to find the patient, the supervisee, and ourselves as supervisors in the patient's ongoing associations.

One last point: even if we take this material as Type One derivatives related to the therapist and supervisor, you can see how difficult it is to sort out those elements that are fantasied from those that are realistic and perceptive. We can do little to distinguish transference from nontransference, or countertransference from noncountertransference, I mention this because it once again demonstrates the importance of the adaptive context, not only for organizing the material from the patient into dynamically meaningful clusters, but also to make the crucial distinction between reality and fantasy in what the patient is conveying.

Supervisor B: This patient has had prior short-term treatment at another clinic. He also was in therapy in another city for a while.

Langs: There are more and more patients like that: they go from one clinic to another, having difficulty at each center and unfortunately never finding quite what they need.

Supervisor B: Returning to this session, the patient had been talking about remembering bad things that made a deep impression on his mind, and here, the resident intervened and asked, Like what? The patient responded, Most likely—well, hostile thoughts at night, thoughts before I go to sleep. The patient went on to describe how he ruminates about these thoughts, and the resident asked again, Like what? Well, the patient said, Like the other day I saw...

Langs: In the model of supervision that I proposed earlier today, I suggested that whenever the supervisee intervenes, the supervisor too should consider making an intervention. I did not comment on the supervisee's first question, primarily because I would very much like to get through this supervisory hour, so that we will have the opportunity to follow a sequence of two or three supervisory sessions. But when the supervisee intervenes again in the exact same fashion, I am reminded that the needs of the patient and the therapist must always come first, even above the needs of the participants in this seminar. And so I must comment briefly, and I would have done so with the supervisee had I been carrying out this supervision.

This particular intervention supports a thesis that I suggested earlier today, to the effect that trainees do not tend to offer deep and primitive premature interventions, but instead lean toward making extensive efforts to steer clear of precisely such primitive inner mental contents and to keep the patient on the surface of his thoughts and in the realm of manifest content. In this context, I must remark that in my initial investigations of the communicative properties of the bipersonal field—during which, I realize in retrospect, I was actually considering only two of the three fields I have identified, the Type A and Type B fields—I had stressed that symbolic communication could occur only in a field in which there was a secure frame and a symbolically interpreting therapist. I also noted that alterations in the framework and erroneous interventions always constituted a projective identification by the therapist into the patient and, in my present terms, a shift to a Type B field.

However, once I recognized the Type C field, with its major qualities of noncommunication, falsification, manifest content in a frozen state, and lack of meaning and deep emotional relatedness, I realized that many alterations in the framework and erroneous interventions can also promote a Type C field and could serve as a means of sealing off the patient's inner mental disturbance and that of the therapist, as well as the turmoil in the therapeutic interaction. Such interventions constitute what I would call *negative projective identifications*—

perhaps something like negative hallucinations, they constitute efforts, in the falsified name of seeking further understanding, to place into the patient a void, an absence of meaning, and suchlike.

Repetitive questions such as those being offered by this therapist characteristically have such qualities: they ask for further meaning, while unconsciously they convey the wish not to know, to destroy meaning, to stay on a manifest level, and, especially, to destroy clusters of Type Two derivatives. If I am correct, we will see a Type C field unfold, unless (1) the patient's psychopathology is so poorly defended and so disruptive that even the most massive efforts at falsification and negation on the part of the therapist will fail to prevent this expression, (2) the patient undertakes symbolic corrective and curative efforts, or (3) he reacts with active and powerful positive projective identifications of his own.

So, in my discussion with the supervisee, I might begin by telling him that I virtually never ask a question of a patient, and that I have no need for such interventions: they address the surface and interfere with derivative communication. I would go on to stress that the patient will spontaneously put into the therapist in derivative form all that he needs for his understanding and interventions, and that it is essential to allow the patient to free associate, and for him, as therapist, to seek both meaning and absence of meaning. My initial stress would be on the listening process—its nature and, here, how the therapist's interventions actively affect the material available from the patient for listening and processing.

From there, I might briefly offer a lecture on neuroses and borderline syndromes—the latter because this may well be what this patient is suffering from—and would stress the crucial role of unconscious processes and contents. I would emphasize that the therapy situation must be designed to help both patient and therapist gain access to the patient's disturbed inner mental world, and that after all this is the only means through which true insight and adaptive resolution can occur.

I would probably then go on to indicate, as I said, that questions stress manifest content, that manifest content is essentially a barrier to latent content when deprived of its derivative quality, and that repeated questions will create pressures toward a Type C field. I would review the features of that field and discuss the common countertransference-based needs in therapists to create static situations. I would also add here that the therapist should not be deceived by thinking that with a patient like this, who appears to be quite anxious and to be filled with disturbing conscious thoughts, he is obtaining latent and unconscious contents from these questions; instead he will be hearing primitive manifest contents. In this context, I would bring up the concept of the adaptive context, and the crucial importance of allowing it to emerge from this material before intervening, stating the basic need to organize the material around these day residues and precipitants.

Now I really don't want to hound the resident, so my exact remarks would depend a great deal on the nature of the prior supervisory sessions, the clinical situation with which we are dealing for the moment, the supervisee's receptivity and resistances, and just how much I feel she can tolerate. Since this is a once-a-week therapy, there should be enough time to cover most of these issues, but we would want to dose them out slowly so that the therapist can absorb them and work them over.

Supervisor B: So the therapist inquired more deeply, and the patient responded: Well, I saw a rock concert, and there was one guy slapping another guy.

Langs: While I would not intervene with the supervisee here, I would like to show you the repetition of a theme: the reference to a rock concert, to exposure, possibly something to do with therapy. These are further Type One derivatives, derivatives that we still can't organize around a specific adaptive context and with which we still cannot generate a specific and dynamic meaning.

I would also take note of the aggressive image. And here, my first hypothesis would be that this is an unconscious perception of a quality of the therapist's questions—an initial indication of a negative and hostile introjective identification. Here, I am shifting to a Type Two derivative in the adaptive context of the therapist's repeated questions. The present unconscious communicative interaction begins to attract my attention.

Supervisor B: He was saying: One guy slapped another guy. Sometimes I feel, he went on, like I have too good a memory. I have thoughts of hurting my wife, Darlene. It's like an obsession, but God I love Darlene and I wouldn't want to hurt her.

Here, the resident inquired, How often during the day do you have these kinds of thoughts?

Langs: Let's focus first on the supervisory process. A moment ago I offered you a silent hypothesis related to the adaptive context of the therapist's two questions, and I suggested the presence of a hostile introject. And now we hear that the patient has thoughts of hurting his wife. On one level, this association can be taken as tentative confirmation of my silent hypothesis—in the form of indirect, Type Two derivatives—and as a further indication, then, of the aggressive qualities of the therapeutic interaction.

In addition, it's rather striking that the patient also offers himself as a model of control: he loves his wife and does not want to hurt her. At the same time, it seems to me that he is indicating to the therapist that there are also positive introjects being derived from this therapeutic experience, though he is struggling to maintain them. In all, he is apparently experiencing mixed qualities in the therapist's interventions.

I would submit to you that this material also reflects conflicts over aggressive impulses and fantasies within this patient. But long before you could analyze and resolve these intrapsychic aspects the therapist would have to rectify her contributions, the destructive introject based on them, and the communicative qualities of the bipersonal field which are being disrupted because of her frequent questions.

Here too, you can see how the supervisee, for defensive purposes, makes use of a medical model: How often do you have the pains? How often do you have the fantasies? And there are mixed qualities to her intervention: on the one hand, she seems to validate my hypothesis that she is making efforts to create a Type C field, because it seems evident that information about the frequency of these thoughts is essentially a truth designed as a Type C barrier to more painful truths—a concept developed by Bion (1977) and extended by myself (Langs 1978g). That is, I think the therapist is unconsciously attempting to distract the patient from his unconscious perceptions of her own aggressiveness, as well as from the mounting aggressive conflicts that are being stirred up within the patient. And even though the question pertains to this area, it asks for facts that are designed to generate an interactional obsessional defense that could serve as a means of pathologically detoxifying the aggressive qualities of the bipersonal field and rendering them meaningless—though, paradoxically, they are bound to heighten the sense of destructiveness that now prevails.

Supervisor B: While I did not say anything to the resident at this time, I thought that her interventions were related to her own anxieties about what was going on in the patient's mind. She had already told me that she was wondering how severely ill this patient is.

Langs: I gather that you haven't intervened as yet in this session.

Supervisor B: Right, I hadn't said anything. In fact, I didn't intervene a great deal in this supervisory hour at all.

Langs: Well, I must say that my own model of supervision would call for a number of comments and extended responses to the interventions made by this therapist. It seems to me that when you have a therapist who is asking so many questions, who is becoming hyperactive, that unconsciously she is asking both the patient and the supervisor for help. There are indeed anxieties and fantasies that she is unable to manage or contain, and her interventions are now unconsciously designed to generate bastions, and possibly even the absence of meaning and relatedness—the Type C field. I want also to mention that the frequency of the therapist's interventions suggests a possible thrust toward a Type B field as well. And I expect that we will see something of a compromise, although I would now anticipate strong Type B field qualities, largely because it is my impression that patient and therapist can neither of them contain their inner primitive mental contents. The relatively rigid defenses needed to create a static and noncommunicative field of a more empty kind—the Type C—are available to neither of them. So there may well be extensive use of projective identification as a means of unburdening each of them of their inner tensions and primitive unconscious fantasies and perceptions—it will stir up a great deal in both participants.

I also get a rather uncomfortable and disquieting feeling that the questions of how severely ill this patient is has its counterpart in a comparable question about this supervisee—take that as a silent hypothesis for the moment. The frequency of her interventions, the sense of pressure, her efforts to destroy meaning—all raise such questions in my mind. And this brings up the very delicate issue of how to shape supervision when one senses rather severe pathology in the supervisee. This must be taken into account, and one must become considerably more supportive and take great pains to be tactful and yet direct, and to try to stress conceptualizations that might help the therapist manage her inner anxieties and disturbance.

In this context, I would like to make a brief additional

comment about the type of supervision that I do. I have found, largely through the reactions of my own supervisees, that my supervisory work is quite unique—inordinately compelling, demanding, and especially confronting—and that it is always a rather disturbing experience for them, however educational and productive they feel it to be. It is my belief that most supervisors approach the supervisory situation far too casually, and without sufficient regard for such basic matters as methodology, definitiveness, interaction, the crucial role of the therapist and countertransferences, especially when one is dealing with a trainee. I believe too, as I said before, that the supervisory experience has a far greater potential than is generally recognized.

I say this largely because my own supervisory work has such a dramatic impact upon my supervisees. It is so very different, so specific and detailed, that the contrast with other supervisors may add to the burden of the supervisee. Despite the fact that I meticulously validate every major comment I make, this type of supervision may generate such a degree of emotional turmoil that one must repeatedly come back to supportive comments. But it must be stressed again that some degree of turmoil is inevitable, though the ultimate rewards—the personal growth of the supervisee, the distinct improvement of his therapeutic techniques, and the resultant benefits to his patients—are considerable.

Returning now to this particular supervisory field, I would have to say that your formulation that the supervisee seemed concerned about how severely ill this patient is reflects an approach to supervision that tends first, and most important, to rather neglect the intricate realities of the therapeutic interaction. Second, it tends to reflect an effort to rationalize what would otherwise be viewed as countertransference-based excessive interventions. Unconsciously your formulation might reflect an unrecognized concern regarding the extent of your supervisee's pathology, but, as in the therapeutic situation, it is your responsibility as a supervisor to be *consciously* aware of such perceptions and anxieties on your part.

In terms of my model of supervision, your silence as a supervisor reflects failure to recognize the intensity of countertransference-based inputs into this therapeutic situation, the extent to which misalliances and bastions are being developed here, and the degree to which pathological introjects are being generated within the patient. This brings up the important issue of developing specific criteria for supervisory interventions, using a concept similar to the *therapeutic context* in the clinical situation (Langs, 1973, 1978c). Just as there is a hierarchy of requirements for interventions in therapy, so is there a hierarchy of demands for supervising interventions: roughly, the presence of countertransference-based silences or interventions; next, any alterations in the frame; then the presence of interactional resistances and symptoms; and so on. Certainly, acute crises come first—in the supervision or in the therapy—but you often must wait for process note material before intervening. For the moment, I am trying to define a hierarchy of immediate indications for supervisory interventions.

So, all of this suggests that we do not simply wait for the therapist to intervene, but also have a responsibility to maintain a continuous flow of silent hypotheses and unspoken formulations so that we are prepared, should there be any apparent, major disturbance of the therapeutic bipersonal field, to intervene and begin to formulate the basis for the chaotic situation—or moment of progress, to cite the other extreme.

In essence, then, I am suggesting as a basic principle the tenet that the supervisor has a responsibility to intervene whenever he observes a significant disturbance in the therapeutic bipersonal field, whether the supervisee has done so or not. I have formulated some major indications for supervisory interventions, and while my listing is undoubtedly incomplete it may, I think, serve as a valid model.

Here I would like to remind us that any formulation

regarding the growing chaos of this therapeutic situation must take into account the influence of the supervisory situation and the supervisor. Let's be reminded of that potential blind spot, even though we do not for the moment have sufficient data with which to formulate any possible contribution. For that, we would have to hear the prior supervisory hours. Still, it's a hypothesis that we may be able to validate as we proceed, and one well worth stating at this moment. The supervisor's silence to this point may be taken as an initial clue that he may be contributing something—we'll see.

We are now faced with a more disturbed therapeutic situation than in the first presentation. In addition, we may be observing a supervisory situation which, by the standards I have proposed, seems not to be performing its essential functions. I would expect that all of you, and especially our presenter, are beginning now to experience the kind of painful confrontations that my own supervisory work can create. With this remark, I am attempting to be supportive. And this is precisely how I work at the point at which I begin to realize that what I am saying must be disturbing for the supervisee. I try very much to offer a perspective and conscious help, fully aware of the limitations of such endeavors; I nonetheless see that as a necessity.

So, I must apologize for the moment for being so candid. But I would also suggest that any failure of candor on my part would support unresolved problems within this supervisor, in all of his work related to therapy. And that while my remarks may evoke a painful upheaval, it is the only possible road for personal growth, and for the enhancement of his supervisory and therapeutic work. It is, of course, unfortunate that we are working this over within this conference. But I also feel that everyone present in this room could become a bit more humble through observing this particular supervisory situation; I suspect we can all see a bit of ourselves in this supervisor.

And in this context I would like to make one final point. It touches upon an aspect of my work that I feel has been greatly misunderstood by some of my critics, and it reminds me of something that Freud said in his paper on the Wolf Man (1918): we will learn more from this presentation than we will from the first one. That is, if indeed, we will be finding major problems in both the therapy and the supervision, it will prove far more revealing and informative than the first presentation. And you will all have a chance to see that Freud was right when he stated that we learn very little from analyses that go well, and a great deal from those which do not.

The Bipersonal Field (Langs 1976a) has been criticized because the therapists were relatively inexperienced, and because they made so many errors that their work could not be taken as representative of the kind of therapy being done by most therapists. The conclusions drawn from such work were therefore seen by these critics as open to question. Without belaboring the issue, it is precisely because of their inexperience and errors that I learned so much, and was able to derive so many unique hypotheses. In addition, I seriously doubt that their work is anything but more representative than not of much of the psychotherapy being carried out in this country today.

Coming back to this particular therapeutic situation, I want to caution all of you regarding an assessment that the patient is suffering from a borderline syndrome. Often this immediately means that the therapist will deviate from basic ground rules, alter the frame, and modify the basic principles of therapy. I simply want to stress that such patients have an explicit need for a secure framework, and for treatment carried out with the same basic principles one would apply to any patient. Unneeded deviations will be destructive of treatment. This does not imply, as I said earlier today, that a therapist will not intervene somewhat differently with such patients than he might with the so-called neurotic.

I must mention that I agree with Green (1975) and others, many of them Kleinian like Bion (1977), who suggest that at the core of every neurosis is a psychosis. It is my clinical impression that we are dealing with patients who have dealt with this psychotic core more or less effectively—the more effective patients appearing relatively neurotic and with relatively integrated character disorders, and the less successful patients appearing as borderline and psychotic patients. In any case, I wanted to stress that as therapists we intervene in keeping with the patient's needs, and will shape the frequency and nature of our interventions accordingly. But this is not to be equated with modifying basic principles of technique, including maintenance of the framework and a basic interpretive approach.

In another area, considering all the allusions to public exposure, I would be developing two silent hypotheses: first, that there is some disturbance in the clinic situation that is making the patient especially concerned about lack of confidentiality in his treatment; and, second, that the therapist may have unconsciously exposed aspects of her countertransference difficulties to this patient through a variety of technical errors—themes of exhibitionism are quite common under these conditions. This second thesis is somewhat supported by the references to going to school and learning. It must be supplemented, however, by some concern that there are, in addition, problems in the supervisory situation.

Here again, I maintain the principle of the primacy of countertransference over transference if I may just once use these terms in their broader sense to allude to both pathological and nonpathological components, as a means of expressing myself quickly, though somewhat inaccurately. I would therefore be concerned with the patient's nontransference reactions and introjects before attempting to deal with his own clearly enormous problems with aggression and with the general management of his inner impulses.

I see here too the kind of typical unconscious message that we get from patients when the therapist has done a poor job: she is a nice and well-meaning individual who has nonetheless intervened destructively in some way. Much of my formulation here is restricted, of course, to Type One derivatives, since we do not know anything of the previous sessions. And incidentally, if this were a beginning supervision, I would probably have asked for a brief summary of the prior hour at this point, so that I could identify the adaptive context for this material and work with it far more meaningfully in the form of Type Two derivatives if at all possible. Lacking that material, I hope that you can all sense the limitations of manifest contents and Type One derivatives. We are still restricted to formulations that are generalities, and that are not specific to this therapeutic interaction; they are derived largely from one's own previous clinical experience and sensitivity to what we might call *universal themes*—except for the little we are beginning to discern from the specifics of this hour.

And I would apply these universal themes, I might add, to both the patient and the therapist. Her interventions reflect a rather common tendency among trainees to concentrate the patient's thoughts on the manifest level. This interferes with the likely flow of derivatives that would move more and more toward the therapeutic relationship, to what I have termed *closer derivatives* (Langs 1973) in which the allusions to the therapist become less and less disguised—often, even manifest. This is not only the offer of an interactional defense; it is also an attempt to create a barrier to derivatives related to the patient's relationship with the therapist, to negate their presence and generate a Type C field.

This is one advantage, by the way, of the supervisory situation: the supervisor does not, as a rule, share with the supervisee the personal need to obliterate the patient's unconscious fantasies and perceptions of the therapist. Many supervisory interventions—perhaps the single most frequent category—relate to the supervisor's recognition that the therapist is, indeed, attempting to actively discourage and destroy the patient's growing direct and indirect communications pertaining to his relationship with the therapist, in terms of both transference and nontransference. Finally, there is a reflection here of the frequent effort on the part of therapists to deprive the patient's communications of their unconscious meanings, and to shut off the patient's primitive inner mental world, not only because of the therapist's dread of its contents, but especially because these primitive contents allude in some way to herself.

So, these would be my hypotheses, and they might lead me to some initial questions of the therapist regarding the previous hour and regarding her thoughts about the nature and frequency of her interventions. Depending on her responses, I might then discuss some of my silent hypotheses, suggesting that we hear additional material to see whether they are borne out.

Supervisor B: So the therapist had asked this patient how often he had these fantasies during the day. The patient responded, Well, sometimes it's different; often I am aware of it all day. In general, I am not aware of it while I'm doing something physical like jogging. Darlene works occasionally, and then I have these ridiculous thoughts. At this point the resident spoke again, and asked what happened. The patient went on: Sometimes I drive her to work or pick her up, and I have these thoughts much more intensely when I am not with her than when I am in her presence. It is not only Darlene that I have these hostile thoughts about; it might just be women in general.

Langs: I hope that you can all see how nicely my model of supervision develops here. Having defined a series of silent hypotheses, we then listen to the material from the patient for confirmation or nonconfirmation.

So, I might intervene with the supervisee—as I am doing here—by pointing out that the patient's comment—"It might just be women in general"—serves as an important unconscious bridge between the patient's wife and the therapist. We still need a more direct bridge, but it should be in the offing. This is what I mean by the development of *closer derivatives* (Langs 1973): the gradual shift by the patient from relatively well disguised derivatives of his perceptions and fantasies about the therapist in the associations about his wife toward communications that permit a more definitive formulation, that provide a clearer clue to the latent content, and that would eventually more clearly suggest that we are indeed dealing with a displacement away from the therapist.

And in keeping with the data available for the moment, I would simply suggest that this comment supports my thesis in the form of a Type Two derivative, and would ask to hear more. For the moment I would stress the importance of listening for latent content in the patient's manifest material, and the clues that we can get, even with limited Type One derivatives.

Supervisor B: When Darlene was living in the Southwest, I would feel superior to all the other men I met. Here the resident interjects, Had you met anybody else yourself?

Langs: That intervention, which, again, is formally a question, seems almost a non sequitur. My silent hypothesis would be to the effect that no sooner does the patient offer a closer derivative to his relationship with the therapist—a potential bridge from his wife to the therapist—than the therapist once again becomes active, attempting to negate these derivatives, to destroy them, and to deflect material away from the therapeutic interaction.

This I think convincingly demonstrates the defensive function of questions; and in my experience, by the way, almost all questions serve such purposes, even when the therapist consciously believes they are designed to evoke derivatives of unconscious fantasies and perceptions. They disrupt the spontaneous flow from the patient and tend to focus on conscious thoughts and realities. In any case, I trust that you can also see that these inquiries constitute offers of interactional defenses, and are actually in the service of the destruction of derivative communication, rather than its development.

These qualities are also typical of interventions that are made without an adaptive context. In principle I virtually never ask questions or intervene without an adaptive context, unless it is to play back a series of themes which, as a rule, I suspect are related to the therapeutic relationship, but which lack a defined or stated adaptive context in that regard. I have found that often such an intervention will enable the patient to provide the missing adaptive context—the necessary organizer for the material (see Langs 1978b,c).

Supervisor B: So the resident asked the patient had he met anyone else and the patient said no. Now the resident asked him if he had had any dreams.

Langs: That's a typical question from someone who purports to be searching for unconscious contents and processes. You will now have a chance to see that it serves to disturb the patient's flow of associations and to move him away from critical, dynamically relevant material, especially as it pertains to the therapeutic interaction. Yet despite this I must say that this query—which is yet another non sequitur—may contain an unconscious nucleus or message to the effect that the therapist realizes that she has been attempting to fix the patient at a manifest and reality-oriented level, and is now attempting to modify that fixation. In this way, even though the inquiry is somewhat destructive and technically poor, it may have a positive effect in that the unconscious communication might well be, Okay that's enough defensiveness, for me at least, I am now prepared to hear something of what you really mean to say—about yourself and our interaction.

Technically, the preferred approach would be to sit back, to rectify the frame by desisting in these frequent and unneeded questions—efforts that clearly modify the therapist's neutrality and express her countertransference-based needs—and allow the interface of the bipersonal field to turn again toward the pathology of the patient, who would then, because of his own inner disturbance and therapeutic needs, eventually get around—in derivative form—to whatever is bothering him.

Supervisor B: I think that this question came because I had been speaking to the resident about dreams in the prior supervisory hour. I said that I would like to have some dreams to work with, and suggested that it is good to have such material to work over.

Langs: Well, that is quite interesting; I must now make a number of points. First, we must be careful to not overvalue dreams as a means of getting in touch with unconscious fantasies and perceptions. Remember that they can be used for both Type B discharge and projective identificatory purposes, and for Type C static functions in which they are shorn of all of their possible associations and offered as false communications and barriers to the therapist. Even in a Type A field, dreams may primarily serve resistances, though they would, in this case, be analyzable and interpretable. So you must teach the supervisee to work with the defensive aspects first, whatever form that may take. More broadly, though, any overestimation of the communicative function of dreams will tend to be accompanied by an underestimation of the communicative functions of all other types of associations from the patient.

Next, while I might at some time point out to a supervisee that a patient is not reporting dreams, I would also state that this is usually a function of two interacting factors: as you would expect, the propensities of the patient on the one hand, and those of the therapist on the other. I take the absence of dream reports as an interactional product. I then discuss the possible role of the patient's dread of his own inner mental life and world, and therefore his dread of remembering his dreams, a suggestion that I try to make at an opportune moment when I can base it on data related to the patient. But in addition, I attempt to identify as well any contribution to this phenomenon from the trainee. Here, for example, it appears to me that this is a patient who might well report dreams if allowed to express himself; and, at least based on the data to this point, a major contribution to the absence of such material—if this is the case—appears to be coming from a therapist who is attempting to focus and fix the patient on a reality level and to discourage the communication of derivatives of the patient's inner mental life and interactional experiences. This is an excellent example of how the model of supervision which takes into account interactional factors generates supervisory interventions that are somewhat different from the model of supervision focused primarily on the patient's intrapsychic pathology.

Next, you have here a good and concrete example of a supervisor introject, and I must say in all candor that it has more the qualities of a pathological introject than of a constructive one—recognizing that both types are possible in the supervisory experience and that, in addition, such introjects are often quite unconscious and not nearly as explicit as the one we see here. That is, it seems to me that your supervisory intervention, while perhaps seemingly innocuous enough, failed to take into account the interactional factors related to the patient's not reporting dreams, and was not based on a study of the therapeutic process. As such, as I implied before, it is not an especially sound supervisory intervention.

And this impression is somewhat validated through the manner in which the supervisory introject was expressed in the therapy situation. Granting that a supervisee may well distrot and misapply a sound supervisory intervention and the resultant introject, I think that once again we must adopt the principle of reality before fantasy, truth before distortion. This would lead us to examine the possibility that the supervisory intervention itself was somewhat sudden and stated out of context, and that the therapist's use of it validly mirrors these qualities, however much the supervisee, based on her own psychopathology, misapplied it. Thus I am suggesting that the supervisee took in this request from the supervisor, not only in terms of its manifest content, but also in regard to some of its unconscious qualities and functions. And her sudden application of this introject in her work with the patient reflected some of the disruptive qualities of the supervisory experience.

However, this interlude also provides me the opportunity to demonstrate that incorrect interventions by the supervisor may also contain hidden nuclei of valid meaning. That is, unconsciously contained within an essentially erroneous supervisory intervention can be found kernels of positive understanding and directives. Here it may well be that the supervisor had been unconsciously concerned about the level of the material from the patient, about the supervisee's and the patient's needs for this defensiveness; unconsciously, he may have been suggesting one possible means of modifying this difficulty. Again, however, I must stress the importance of the supervisor's conscious recognition of this problem; he must trace out its roots and intervene directly, rather than unconsciously, to the supervisee. Still, the kernel of unconscious constructive effort that I formulated for the supervisee with her patient seems also to apply to this supervisory intervention—at least as indicated by the data at hand. For the moment I will not especially concern myself with efforts to clarify that point, but welcome the chance to use it as a model for discussion.

I cannot drop this subject without stating that my own position in regard to dreams is that they are indeed special communications—experiences in an altered state of consciousness that we term sleep, and reported by the patient while once again awake. Understood in terms of their day residues or specific adaptive contexts, dreams do tend to be filled with derivatives of unconscious fantasies and perceptions—though they are but one, however special, means of conveying such communications. Before getting some more material, I want to make the point that asking this particular supervisee to bring dreams from her patient into supervision might well have created a great burden for her. Such a request and introject might have very anxiety-provoking qualities for her, especially since she appears so frightened of the patient's inner mental world and under such considerable defensive pressures of her own.

Supervisor B: The patient said, Yes, I had a dream: it was like being at war. I was fighting with the other guys. . .

Langs: You can see that we are faced again with some repetitive themes and variations: now, being at war. We are still limited largely to Type One derivatives. But if we adhere to the principle of monitoring every communication from the patient in the terms of his relationship and interaction with the therapist, and of searching for both realities and fantasies, we would continue to be concerned about the destructive qualities of this therapeutic interaction. And I suspect now, based on my observations of the therapist's interventions in this session, that the patient is—and has been—experiencing her interventions as attacks. This material may well contain a kind of unconscious interpretation to the therapist, in regard both to her poorly managed hostile impulses and to her related unconscious masculine identification. The patient's battles are with both men and women; the former battle suggests an unconscious perception and introjection of phallic qualities from this therapist. At the very least, it directs me to frame a silent hypothesis, to which I would add considerations of the patient's own inner anxieties and conflicts.

Now, at a second level, these may also be allusions to the supervisory bipersonal field. And we must keep this possibility in mind: is there some kind of hostility—conscious or unconscious—present in that field, some type of battle taking place within the supervisory situation that is somehow unconsciously being communicated to the patient? These tentative formulations may demonstrate how dreams often tend to be important conveyors of crucial qualities within the therapeutic and supervisory interactions. As a rule, the communication of a dream should help us generate more concentrated and specific silent hypotheses. And often, especially when we know their day residues or adaptive contexts, dreams help us synthesize and organize impressions and hypotheses we have been developing from other material. These often fall into place when we have an integrated understanding of a dream communication. But there too, remember to monitor this material for both unconscious perceptions and unconscious fantasies, and for allusions to both the therapeutic and supervisory interactions.

Specifically, when a supervisor hears a dream of this kind unfolding, he might ask himself if he has been too abrasive, has pushed the therapist too far, or has in any way generated a "state of war." It is only after we have worked over such possibilities that we then approach the therapeutic interaction and explore this material for perceptions and fantasies. And while we have some rather tentative adaptive contexts in the supervisor's and therapist's interventions in the respective bipersonal fields, we are still working largely with Type One derivatives. We lack the specific adaptive contexts that might really fit all of this together into a single major hypothesis, one that might lead us to modify our supervisory work or to suggest corrective interventions from the therapist.

Supervisor B: So, the patient said it was a dream like being at war. I was fighting with the other guys, he said; we were on a battlefield. I have dreams like this often, but one night, in one of these dreams, I had the feeling I was swinging at the wall. To this the resident responded with a question: What was the dream?

Langs: Whatever the fantasied element, this appears to be a valid unconscious perception of the therapist, and of the Type C field as well. This resident is like a wall, and she is attempting to build impenetrable walls between the patient, with his inner mental world, and herself, and, undoubtedly, between herself and her own inner mental world as well. Common metaphors for the Type C field include dead ends, vacuums, iron tanks and other such containers, walls, and the like. The patient unconsciously senses and represents this quality of the therapist and the field.

And you can see too how this tends to confirm my hypothesis that reality-oriented questions are designed as barriers, as impenetrable defenses, and that judging by the patient's imagery he is attempting to modify these barriers while the therapist is continuously reinforcing them. And this may well be the case: the Type C field is being generated for the moment more by the therapist than the patient, though I think we can now sense unconscious efforts on both their parts to modify this field.

Supervisor B: She asked, What was the dream? And he said, I don't recall. I just know I hate to go to bed at night. I'm afraid I might lose control. My mother is religious and says I should turn everything over to God.

Langs: How nicely the patient directs me. I had meant to ask whether this resident had told the patient directly that the case is being supervised, and here the patient speaks of turning everything over to God. Whatever else, I take this as a derivative related to supervision, a directive if you will: they both need God's help.

Supervisor B: The patient had not been told of supervision.

Langs: I see. But of course he might well have had his suspicions. This patient is suffering from pathological introjective identifications that undoubtedly reinforce his own psychopathology, and repeat in the reality with the therapist some version of the earlier childhood experiences that generated his pathology. We have here what Racker (1957) termed a *vicious circle:* an actual repetition of the past on some level, through which the patient's pathology is reinforced and intensified. It lacks, then, the essential qualities of an actual interaction which could generate nonpathological and pathology-modifying introjects, as well as specific, interpretive-cognitive insights. The patient is introjecting the therapist's unbridled aggression, her fears of losing control, and her desperate efforts to find suitable defenses—another possible meaning of the reference to God.

And you know, I now feel quite frustrated in not knowing the prior supervisory hours and sessions. I am quite convinced that there is a specific adaptive context for this material, or a series of traumatic precipitants that have generated these introjects which the patient is so intensely working over—in part, because they are being repeated in the present hour. All this is true in addition to whatever more private inner struggles this patient is engaged in—and whatever pathological projections and displacements are involved here as well.

Now, in the supervisory session, I would acknowledge the lack of an adaptive context and ask the supervisee if she could identify one. I would suggest that this material communicates the patient's unconscious perceptions and introjections of her intrusive interventions and their underlying basis, and would stress that we must identify the realities before we can know the patient's extensions of these communications within his own mind and through his own pathological fantasies. I would apologize for being so direct and candid, but I would point out that this is exactly what the patient himself is doing in derivative form. And I would add something to the effect of how important it is for this therapist to get in touch with both the patient's and her own unconscious communications.

These are, of course, painful confrontations for the supervisee: telling her that she is phallically intrusive, hostile and attacking, creating walls and barriers. But this is a serious situation; the patient is under great disruptive pressures. The supervisor must stress the importance of getting in touch with our own realities if we are to do valid psychotherapy—and if the patient is to get well.

Supervisor B: Could I add this? The patient did say to me, when we brought up transference and countertransference, that. . .

Langs: The patient or the resident?

Supervisor B: The resident. She did tell me that she does

have difficulty with positive transferences when she deals with men patients. And it somehow alerted me to the idea that she was acknowledging something about a problem, that she was indicating that she tries to defend herself against male patients' having positive feelings toward her; so this was her way of alerting me to one of her problems.

Langs: Was this in a previous supervisory hour?

Supervisor B: Yes.

Langs: The term *positive transference* has always struck me as something of a muddle. It implies something constructive, something loving, and yet as transference it is bound to have both loving and hateful, constructive and destructive elements. Here you are suggesting that the therapist alerted you to difficulties in handling positive feelings from male patients, conflicts in the area of being loved. In this light it is interesting that to this point my entire discussion has been in the area of what would have been termed *negative transference*—what I would term *destructive nontransference and transference* and *hostile countertransference*. And while that all might well be a defense against positive and loving feelings on the part of both patient and therapist, it is an area that the therapist would have to work over, analyze, and rectify if she wants to be capable of doing sound therapeutic work. In fact, all of this shows the extent to which destructiveness and lovingness can be intermixed, and how we must begin our work—in therapy or supervision—with whatever is on the surface, and from there work our way inward.

However, it is important to note that this therapist is capable of acknowledging a problem. This awareness of ours might provide us just the insight we need to develop and clarify many of the patient's unconscious perceptions and introjects of the therapist, in a manner that she might be better able to tolerate.

In addition, whatever the limitations of the supervisory bipersonal field, you should observe the timing of such a revelation and not simply think of it in terms of its manifest content. Attempt to understand it as an unconscious communication related to the supervisory relationship as well. And even though here you get into an area that you probably won't be able to sort out and validate, such a communication should alert you to the need to undertake a bit of self-scrutiny for any possible introjective identification of your own difficulties as a supervisor that the supervisee may be communicating. I am well aware that I am stressing the interactional aspects of much of what we are hearing, but this is what has been neglected; the intrapsychic elements are far more immediately apparent. Such considerations make supervision a far more difficult undertaking than has been previously recognized. Still, it is quite necessary to maintain a maximum degree of self-awareness in the supervisory situation; your supervisory work is bound to be enhanced by such careful monitoring and self-scrutiny.

Discussant: This seems to be the first time in the two presentations today that a therapist has talked about feelings; there has been up until now a great stress on words.

Langs: I believe that I mentioned the absence of feelings previously. But in any case, you are quite right: we must not neglect the area of affects and must tie it in to the cognitive dimension.

If I may return briefly to the model of supervision: the point at which the supervisee acknowledges a particular kind of problem should not, I feel, lead to a surface discussion of this difficulty. Instead it should be recognized as a most significant communication, one that is bound to be filled with extensive unconscious meanings, and that in general should alert the supervisor to the presence of extensive countertransference difficulties. However, these are problems that should be identified almost entirely through the presentation of the treatment experience—through the communications from both the patient and therapist, with occasional use of extraneous comments from the supervisee if these are especially pertinent. Often this kind of self-revelation is associated with a crisis in therapy or supervision. It should also alert the supervisor to a special need to carefully formulate the material and to be prepared to intervene, rather than not; the supervisee's communication expresses a special need for assistance. It is a high level indication for a supervisory intervention, and the process note material will more than likely facilitate such efforts.

In terms of this specific material, we hear the patient talk about his fears of losing control, and we recognize that the therapist herself is concerned about controls, about managing her responses to this patient, and that her questions are almost a desperate effort to control both the patient and herself. One senses, in fact, a danger that the entire therapy may be in jeopardy, and on the verge of becoming uncontrolled. And we must, on principle, wonder if similar concerns should be applied to the supervisory situation; at least we should be prepared to ask ourselves such painful and searching questions in the face of such material.

In this context the reference to God may well express a hope that the supervisor can be all-knowing and all-controlling, and that he can generate a very necessary settling and managing influence. As supervisor, I would take this communication from the patient as an unconscious directive to design an intervention that would serve this function for both patient and therapist, without sacrificing the search for insight and interpretations.

In fact it is only through interpretations that reflect the supervisor's and the supervisee's capacity to manage the patient's—and the therapist's—communications and projective identifications, to metabolize and understand them, and to return them to this supervisee and this patient detoxified, that would give the two of them the *management introject* they both so desperately need. This would enhance their inner controls and capacity to deal with their disturbing inner mental worlds and their mutual interaction. Remember again that there is no such thing as supportive therapy as it is usually conceived, and that the same is true of what might be termed supportive or noninterpretive supervision. Proper support comes from correct interpretations and sound management of the framework, directly in therapy and through such formulations of the process note material in supervision.

In this particular supervisory situation, then, I would be prepared to intervene, and I would share with the supervisee the insights into this therapeutic interaction that I have offered here. I would show her the indications of her anxieties and countertransferences and the patient's introjection of them; if necessary, I would in addition ask her if she feels that we have been engaged in any way in some kind of unconscious battle or struggle in supervision, or if she is experiencing me in some manner as also out of control and unable to manage. I think it is crucial to rectify the supervisory field and the supervisee's introjects of the supervisor as a means of initiating a sequence that could help get the therapeutic situation and relationship under control.

Supervisor B: The patient continued: I can't accept turning things over to anybody; I feel like I am losing my mind.

Langs: It would be disastrous for the therapy of this patient to simply listen to this material in terms of his own pathology and anxieties—as merely intrapsychic—since a failure to recognize the unconscious perceptions and introjects involved here would only further destroy his capacity for reality testing and the remnants of his ability to manage inner and outer reality; it would further intensify the vicious circle that I described before. This latest communication is true of both the patient and the therapist, and the patient certainly cannot be helped until this statement is no longer true of the therapist. So we must work in that area first. This has all the signs of a crisis situation in therapy, and, again, it is therefore a definitive indication for supervisory interventions.

And here, we are dealing with a supervisee who is having difficulties holding on, problems in understanding and managing herself, so we must proceed cautiously, tactfully, and yet candidly. And so, using a variety of supportive comments to the supervisee, I would discuss the issues that I have already brought up as this material has unfolded. And I would add here that there are indications that the patient has unconsciously perceived additional qualities of the therapist, and that he may well be commenting on her failure to understand and appreciate the help he has unconsciously offered her. In addition, the patient may be suggesting that she is not listening to her supervisor.

We have here an example of what I have called an *interactional symptom:* a fear of losing control in the patient to which both he and the therapist have contributed. And I fear that the patient has sensitively identified a dread within this therapist as well: namely, her fear that she too might go crazy. This thesis is supported by her massive efforts to focus on reality, in part as a means of not being overwhelmed by the crazy stuff inside both her patient and herself.

It seems evident that many of my initial hypotheses are now being supported and borne out especially in terms of the unconscious functions of the therapist's interventions and the nature of the therapeutic interaction. And incidently, while as a rule I would not directly suggest to such a supervisee that she seek therapy, I would very much hope that she would be honest enough with herself to recognize her almost desperate need for treatment.

And stressing how painful it must be for her to experience these anxieties with the patient, and to acknowledge his unconscious perceptions and commentaries about herself, I would outline the implications of this material. I would stress the importance of this supervisee's recognition of their meaning and of her eventual mastery of these problems as essential to her development as an effective therapist. Sound therapists are not born, but must develop through the difficult mastery of their own countertransferences. And I would be able to show the supervisee that her work with patients would be relatively disastrous were she not to master these anxieties and resolve their underlying basis. Conversely, this mastery, once achieved, would free up her creative capacities to a level probably never before experienced by her.

Incidentally, this is the kind of session that is so filled with information about the therapist herself, that I would recommend that she review the hour on her own as a means of getting in touch with herself. Remember too that the patient is telling you as supervisor to be quite sensitive with this supervisee, to be careful about overburdening her; in fact he is suggesting that she is quite fragile. And yet I feel that the most constructive and ego-building interventions that you could make as a supervisor will center around helping her understand herself and this therapeutic interaction, and that efforts at avoidance would be unconsciously perceived as conveying your own anxiety in response to the disorganization of both the patient and the therapist.

In terms of projective identification, the supervisee is putting into the supervisor a frightful and uncontrolled therapeutic situation, terrifying and unmanaged pathology from both the patient and herself. And it is essential that you understand and metabolize this introject, and respond constructively, thereby conveying both cognitive insights and a sense of your own capacity to tolerate and manage such primitive and uncontrolled inner mental contents and processes.

With this as your model, you might even advise the therapist to sit back a bit more, to try to settle down and get things under control, to try and tolerate what the patient wants to tell her, and perhaps to even avoid intervening for a while unless there is a crisis situation. She should let the dust settle, so to speak, and see if she can begin developing some initial understanding of the basis of this patient's anxieties and difficulties, and of her own. In this way you might, in a relatively concrete way, offer the supervisee a management introject and a chance to gain perspective, which, since this is not a therapy situation, is all you can do other than offering the necessary understanding of the interaction. Remember too that in principle it is important that you maintain both the frame of the supervisory bipersonal field and an interpretive-explanatory approach. Unneeded deviations will be taken as indications of your own anxieties and incapacities to manage. So I stress again how crucial it is to maintain your principles as you adjust the nature of your communications in keeping with the needs of the patient and the supervisee.

Supervisor B: I have to confirm what you're saying, because at the end of this hour. . .

Langs: Wait—don't tell us, please: nothing in advance of the actual sequence. It will spoil my opportunity to predict and to experience this as an interactional unfolding. So, please simply continue in sequence.

Supervisor B: The patient went on: I feel like I'm losing my mind. And here, the resident asked, Have you felt this way since last week?

Langs: At this juncture, we might have the type of clue Arlow (1963) refers to, where the supervisee shifts from saying, "The patient said she was afraid of losing her mind," to saying, "I might lose my mind." That is, the resident shifts from indirect to direct discourse, thereby revealing an overidentification with her patient. Now we should not make too much of such observations, but on the other hand, if this did indeed occur at this juncture, it would lend support to my hypothesis that this therapist is indeed overidentified with this very disturbed patient, and that in addition she is as concerned with her own going crazy as with his.

Now you can see again how this particular question

constitutes not only the offer of an interactional obsessive defense, but is also a type of clichéd inquiry designed as a barrier to the patient's craziness. That is, I would postulate that here, at a moment when the patient is attempting to reveal his own primitive and disturbing inner mental life, the therapist is attempting to seal off that entire realm, largely because of her own fears of disorganization and possibly because she lacks the interpretive ability to help the patient understand these contents and to defend himself better in that regard. In a sense, the patient is attempting to generate a Type A or Type B field—there are elements both of symbolic communications and of projective identification—while the supervisee is attempting to create a Type C field: the use of language as a falsification and barrier that could seal off the underlying disturbance.

This is an extremely fragile and sensitive situation. You have here a Sylla and Charybdis, in that if you on the one hand, continue to suggest to the resident that she is deeply disturbed and afraid of losing control, and that she is offering inappropriate barriers and meaningless defenses to the patient, you risk a further disturbance in this supervisee's fragile and brittle defenses and inner equilibrium that might evoke an intensification of anxieties and even uncontrolled panic. On the other hand, if you fail to sympathetically and gently discuss these issues with the supervisee—doing so in a manner that resembles interpreting upward—so as to offer her some general indications of her difficulties and of how they are influencing her interventions, you leave both the resident and her patient at the mercy of her uncontrolled pathology. You would also be neglecting your responsibility to both educate the supervisee and to exert a stabilizing influence on the therapeutic situation. Here one should slowly, gently, and with compassion acquaint the resident with her difficulties and their influence on her work with the patient. As I have indicated throughout the seminar, this is especially necessary since these anxieties and some of their underlying contents are being placed into the patient, as are pressures to generate a nonmeaningful, obliterating

Type C field. The patient will thus be introjecting and working over these very issues. As a supervisor, one would be remiss in failing to recognize and deal with this aspect of the therapeutic interaction; the patient will most certainly not fail to do so.

Discussant: Dr. Langs, when the resident says, Have you been feeling that way since last week? Doesn't this constitute an unconscious communication to the patient that she feels responsible for the patient's disturbance?

Langs: It is difficult to know the specific unconscious communication here, without knowing the contents of the session of the previous week and something of the supervision. Your point is well taken in that these questions are, indeed, rich in unconscious meaning, some of it undoubtedly quite personal, and this may include feelings of guilt and responsibility, concerns about erroneous technique and its influence on the patient, feelings of inadequacy and an inability to manage the treatment situation, and a sense of helplessness that is related to the use of these falsifying interventions as a kind of last-ditch effort to offer some temporary, albeit fragile, defenses to the patient—and to herself.

Discussant: It seems to me that the therapist's intervention suggests a state of undue anxiety and a sense of responsibility for the patient's losing control. I wonder if you take this as further confirmation of some of your initial ideas?

Langs: Yes, tentative confirmation and I will wait now for additional confirmatory material from the patient. The point to remember here is that as supervisors we develop silent hypotheses, share some of them with the supervisee, and listen to the conscious and unconscious communications from both patient and therapist as commentaries on these hypotheses. We seek validation or its absence, expand correct formulations, and revise those that prove incorrect.

Supervisor B: The patient answered the question about whether he had felt this way since last week by saying, I felt I was slipping, and I went for a walk. The therapist asked: What were you doing when you felt you were going to lose your mind? The patient responded: I was watching TV with my mother and father, and sister; I felt like hurting Darlene. I walked outside and felt better.

Langs: Now I can again demonstrate how a supervisory formulation can be confirmed by the subsequent material from the patient. I had suggested that on one level the therapist was attempting to generate responses to questions that would involve detail without meaning—that she was trying to create barriers and fabrications—a Type C field—rather than promote the unfolding of this patient's primitive inner mental world and his relationship to her. The patient supports this formulation, and I suspect that he does so because he has experienced this type of questioning from the therapist in previous sessions. He does so by handling his emerging destructive impulses toward his wife by leaving the house, absenting himself, removing himself from the stimulus, erecting a kind of empty barrier, and thereby feeling better.

This is not only the patient's introjection of the therapist's form of defense and his acceptance of a Type C communicative field; it is also an unconscious bit of supervision to the therapist: the patient is suggesting to her that she cool things down and get them under control, that she get some distance and thereby enable herself to better manage her aggressive impulses.

Perhaps this sequence can also help you see that so long as the therapist generates countertransference-based inputs into this bipersonal field, endeavors to invoke a Type C communicative mode, attempts to put interactional defenses into this patient, unconsciously communicates in a provocative way that suggests relatively uncontrolled hostile impulses—for just that long the patient himself will be unable to develop more appropriate defenses and will be unable to better manage his own aggressive impulses.

Valid verbal interpretations are not possible in this field, and the therapist's words will have little positive meaning until she is able to tolerate her own unconscious fantasies and impulses, to better manage them, and to tolerate them in her patients. On one level, this therapist is offering the patient highly pathological and inadequate defenses, and these are all that the patient himself can muster. On another level, the therapist's behaviors and communications not only tend to confirm the contents of this patient's inner mental world—pathological fantasies, perceptions, and introjects—but also reinforce his lack of adequate management capacities. This generates a vicious circle in which the patient's disturbed inner mental world corresponds to the outer world within the therapeutic bipersonal field, and the pathogenic past is repeated in the present. Under such conditions the therapist is incapable of changing the vicious circle because she is so blindly a part of it. As you can sense, it is based in part on her own pathological unconscious needs, and she seems quite unable to become aware of her rigid and fragile defenses, or, in all likelihood, her underlying pathological aggressiveness.

It therefore becomes the responsibility of the supervisor to intervene, to step in and enable the supervisee to become aware of the true nature of this therapeutic interaction so that she might begin to rectify the situation, to undertake self-analytic measures, and to do the management and therapeutic work necessary to break the vicious circle with the patient to renounce the misalliance and the bastions, to desist in repeating the pathogenic past, and to begin to allow the patient's pathology to unfold as central to the therapy and available for analysis.

As you can see, this is an enormous task for the therapist. But it is a true reflection of the nature of our work and she cannot be spared these confrontations, though they should be made slowly and gently. I can assure you that the patient will not spare her, and that she cannot change without such efforts.

I want to stress here a basic principle: when there is an unconscious misalliance and bastion between the supervisee and the patient—the presence of pathogenic vicious circles and a pathological communicative mode on the part of the supervisee—it is the responsibility of the supervisor to identify these disturbances and to undertake the necessary supervisory work, always based on material from both patient and therapist, to initiate corrective steps by the supervisee. It is also important to recognize that for the moment the influence of the therapist's countertransferences precludes the cure of the patient. There can be endless talk, but so long as these realities are not rectified there will be no adaptive inner change in the patient. And you can see how a therapist who offers pathological but relatively benign introjects to the patient, and who shows a distinct propensity toward the Type C communicative mode, is essentially incapable of cognitive insight or of generating valid interpretations and reconstructions. And you can see how unaware a therapist can be of these communicative propensities and their implications. We must also not forget to monitor this material in regard to the supervisory bipersonal field.

Discussant: Yes, I had begun to wonder whether the supervisor was not himself using avoidance mechanisms.

Langs: Yes, it may well be that the silence of this supervisor reflects avoidance—of relatedness and meaning—and a broader need for a Type C communicative field. Whatever the true situation, this serves as a reminder that not only as therapists but also as supervisors we must be fully aware of our communicative mode and preference. And we must undertake sufficient therapeutic work to modify any propensity toward pathological projective identifications or barriers and nonmeaning in our work in either role. It must be our goal to achieve a Type A communicative mode in all of its fullness in both bipersonal fields. It is the responsibility of the supervisor to foster the Type A communicative style in the supervisee, and to help her learn the specific techniques for analyzing within a Type A field, and for analyzing and resolving the patient's possible need for the Type B or Type C mode.

Discussant: I am struck by the fact that the supervisee does not ask yet another question at this point.

Langs: Yes, but this is the moment at which the patient is now unconsciously offering himself as a constructive model to the therapist. And further, for now he is accepting a Type C form of defense which fits quite well with the therapist's needs. In addition, this is a possible unconscious interpretation and the offer of a curative introject to the therapist, especially since it occurs at a point in the session where the supervisee has been extremely active in her questioning. Unconsciously, this communication from the patient seems designed to help her get the underlying aggression under control and to establish some necessary distance.

Incidentally, this material from the patient could also generate an hypothesis regarding supervision, to the effect that the supervisor is pushing the therapist too hard and should himself slow down and achieve some distance. However, we are reminded that we must check such unconscious communications against reality and for fit with the available data. Here we find, of course, that the supervisor has been relatively silent and that our hypothesis does not apply—at least not to this supervisory hour. On the other hand, had I been doing the supervision I am sure we would all have thought otherwise, and I would have taken the patient's communication as a directive to reconsider the pressures I was creating for the supervisee. In principle—to state it again— we listen for unconscious implications for both bipersonal fields in the communications from both patient and therapist, and these must be checked out against all known realities—those that are subtle and possibly unconscious as well as those that are relatively apparent.

It occurs to me, however, that we could fit this

unconscious communication from the patient with the supervisor's request for dream material—it could be a matter not of quantity, but rather of quality. You can see now that my thesis that this request could overburden and generate anxiety in this therapist is borne out a bit, in that she asks for dreams but quickly moves away from them, as does the patient. This too is typical of the Type C field: dreams are reported and quickly sealed off; they remain undecipherable barriers.

This demonstrates why I follow the lead of the patient in doing supervision. I think that here he is quite right in suggesting that his therapist lacks distance and controls, and I would shape my supervisory interventions accordingly. Allow the patient to supervise not only the supervisee, but the supervisor as well; unconsciously, he knows best.

Supervisor B: The patient said that he had been watching TV and had had thoughts of hurting his wife. Then the resident asked, How much younger is your little sister?

Langs: Well, she really did not hold off too long, and she derived little benefit from the patient's unconscious interpretive efforts. Instead she continues to confirm my hypothesis by asking questions that are increasingly irrelevant, and by offering distractions clearly designed as impenetrable barriers.

To my mind, this is a very pathological bipersonal field. And I would feel the need as a supervisor to continue intervening, rather carefully and sensitively of course. Here the supervisor's silence can be taken only as a negative indicator: possibly he too needs a Type C field; possibly he too is overwhelmed; possibly he is unable to comprehend and interpret; and clearly he too is unable to serve as a modulating and interpreting factor.

Now this puts me in mind of the therapist's containing functions, which have their counterpart in supervision. Just as the therapist must be open to contain the psychopathology of the patient, so the supervisor must be able to contain that of both the supervisee and *his* patient, Here there is a failure in the containing function of both therapist and supervisor.

It is the therapist's function to incorporate, contain, metabolize, comprehend, and interpret the patient's projective identifications and cognitive communications as one major vehicle for understanding and generating structural change. We have a most interesting situation here in that the therapist appears to be almost totally refractory to these projective identifications and communications; she lacks entirely what Bion (1962) has termed *reverie*. And the patient will suffer because of it, experiencing this refractoriness and the therapist's own projective identification into him of meaninglessness and destruction.

Bion (1977) wrote of the container's fear of the contained. Here you are witnessing a clinical illustration of such a dread, which Bion describes in terms of denudation and annihilation, and which appears to be based here on the therapist's relatively severe psychopathology and her dread of its intensification through potentially destructive introjects from the patient. I can assure you too that this is an extreme example of an anxiety and dread in every therapist, one that must be mastered in order to do effective therapeutic and analytic work.

The supervisor, then, must himself be capable of reverie, or there will be no hope. He must be able to introject the disturbing projective identifications and communications from both supervisee and patient, and metabolize them to the point of helping the supervisee understand the nature of the disturbed therapeutic interaction. In addition to its importance in the cognitive sphere, this is one essential component of the supervisee's ultimate constructive unconscious introjective identification with the supervisor's capacities. Interactionally, failures by the supervisor to contain and metabolize, and to reproject detoxified contents, will further intensify the supervisee's difficulties in this area and will further weaken her general ego functioning as well. Such failures suggest difficulties within the supervisor in regard to his containing and management capacities. Identificatory processes are inevitable in any interaction, especially within the therapeutic and supervisory bipersonal fields, and the literature on supervision is filled with ample references to the importance of these processes. However, few writers, if any, have attempted to clinically investigate this dimension in any detail.

Supervisor B: The patient responded to this question by saying that his sister is eight years younger than himself. The therapist then asked, Do you have any recollection of when she was born?

Langs: These are sad but extremely striking illustrations of the erratic and almost senseless quality of therapy when one tries randomly to lead the patient, rather than allowing the patient to lead the way. It all constitutes the offer of interactional ruminative defenses, and the use of genetics as a defense. More broadly, you can see how a therapist can unconsciously create the Type C form of communication, and Type B as well, using her interventions as a means of sealing off underlying meaning within the patient, and creating elaborate fictions designed as opaque defenses and as pathological projective identifications into the patient. The answer to each of the therapist's questions takes the patient further and further away from his dream and his own associations—his dreaded inner aggressive fantasies and the rest, his currently disturbing inner mental world. The therapist's queries in no way function as a means of developing derivatives of these inner contents, but serve instead, on the pretense of seeking information, as a means of entirely changing the area and style of communications.

Incidentally, you can see why this patient would dread the spontaneous recall and report of a dream to this therapist. Whatever his own inner reasons, unconsciously he must know that it would just scare the living daylights out of her. He is in some ways kinder than the supervisor who asked her to pursue dreams; he protects the patient from the inner mental turmoil that she dreads experiencing and containing. You can recognize now the extensive factors involved in the type of material a therapist hears from his patients; it is not a subject to be broached naively in therapy or supervision.

In the supervisory field, the supervisor's silence continues to imply acceptance of these interventions and a denial of the patient's and supervisee's pathology, and suggests again his own need for a Type C communicative field. It is here that a knowledge of indications for supervisory interventions, a recognition of signs of nonvalidation of silence (in therapy and in supervision), and self-scrutiny by the supervisor might help redirect the supervisory work. When a therapy is going poorly and a supervisee continues to intervene badly, the supervisor must intervene. Within the therapy, direct answers to the supervisee's questions are in no sense confirmatory responses, and the therapeutic interaction is quickly becoming overintellectualized, stalemated, and filled with the provocative pathology of the therapist.

Supervisor B: The patient went on: I remember when she was old enough to walk: she fell and cut her forehead. My cousin was there and he was crying, and I remember crying too. The resident asked, How did you feel? The patient responded, I don't really know. What did you think had happened to her, asked the resident. The patient responded that there was a lot of blood on his uncle's shoulder. He had picked her up. The patient remembered having the responsibility for looking after the sister, and he was in junior high school at the time. But he really never wanted to be there with his sister; he was afraid that something bad would happen to her and he was scared.

Langs: This material certainly reflects bodily anxieties in this patient, possible hostilities toward this sister, a dread of inner contents, and a fear of being unable to manage. Still, it would be virtually impossible to interpret these conflicts and contents to him, since on another level, so much of this material reflects an unconscious introjective identification with the therapist, and with his own comparable anxieties and the rest.

These associations seem to validate the hypothesis I developed just a moment ago: the patient describes his anxieties about being a caretaker and his incapacity to be protective, adding that he has no wish to carry out that role. There are unconscious interpretations here: the patient is pointing out that the therapist is failing to protect him, exposing him to danger, and he is suggesting that unconscious bodily anxieties within the therapist are a factor in these difficulties. I might add, by the way, that I used the me/not-me interface to derive that formulation.

I think too that it is marvelous how a patient, under the pressure of direct and limiting questions, and in the face of massive efforts to render the communicative field essentially meaningless, nonetheless maintains his capacity to communicate symbolically—in derivative form—now around the adaptive context of the therapist's excessively active and inappropriate interventions. So we have here Type Two derivatives and a determination by the patient to shape the field along Type A lines. I have little doubt, however, that, should the resident continue to intervene in the manner in evidence here, the patient will fluctuate in this regard, sometimes making efforts to communicate symbolically and at other moments becoming depressed and succumbing to the Type C mode. Sometimes patients in this predicament resort also to Type B communications—the use of traumatizing projective identifications and reprojections into the therapist that are designed to modify the barriers she has constructed and to place back into her the hostile and abrasive, possibly seductive projective identification to which he is being subjected.

So, despite every effort by the therapist to generate a meaningless session, this patient unconsciously and quite creatively adapts himself to the limited vehicle of communication offered him, and uses his early memories to convey both the nature of his unconscious introjects and his curative efforts. The manifest pressure is toward the patient's past and his family relationships; still, the latent communicative threads stay exquisitely in touch with the unconscious communicative interaction.

Notice too how well this patient communicates his unconscious perception of the therapist's anxieties: being a caretaker can be dangerous, someone can get hurt, you can get blood on you, it can be very frightening and you may attempt to deal with it all by turning away from the caring role. I hope I have shown clearly today how extensive the patient's unconscious constructive functioning is; it is a most neglected resource and an unappreciated dimension of the patient's functioning.

Finally, there may well be unconscious allusions to supervision here—most of it in a negative sense that might alert the supervisor to possible failings in his work with the supervisee. There are third parties present in this recollection, all of whom seem unable to prevent harm to the sister. The uncle who is soiled may represent an idealized, though empty, image of the supervisor. The patient himself is functioning as a caretaker—perhaps as a supposed help to both the therapist and the supervisor—and he fails in his protective functions. There is also a reference to school—probably to the need for all parties to learn. However speculative, these are Type One derivatives that should be followed up.

Supervisor B: I really thought here that the patient was afraid of damaging his little sister, and that that was why he didn't want to be left alone with her.

Langs: Yes, that is an important comment; it enables me to repeat several points. First, it gives us a chance to compare an effort to understand this material in terms of a particular genetic constellation and its manifest contents, as compared to its comprehension in terms of the unconscious unfolding of the therapeutic interaction—a study of sequential adaptive contexts and responses to them in both patient and therapist. That the patient is attempting to control his hostility toward his sister is undoubtedly true, but the crucial question is whether this particular truth is for the moment being used as a barrier to far more important truths about the therapeutic interaction, as a derivative of those underlying and more basic truths.

Now in some seminars this would be merely a matter of opinion. But here I believe we have the methodology with which to decide the issue. As you may have realized, this touches upon the question of whether we work in psychotherapy with the therapeutic interaction or with the patient's outside life. And while one instance can't decide the entire question, the resolution of the basic issue here may go a long way in helping you understand the basis on which this debate can be truly resolved.

Turning now to our methodology, I would suggest that you are here treating this material largely as manifest content and Type One derivatives—using available inferences from these associations, derived without an adaptive context. This is a common type of formulation, and often Type C patients offer material of this kind and Type C therapists develop such conceptualizations. But this thinking is based on a series of conscious thoughts and obvious indirect connections—a direct and linear sequence that lacks convolution and shifting, indirect, derivative, and truly symbolic communication.

This discussion can help me stress the importance of indirect and derivative communications in defining symbolic representation, at least as I use the term in the psychoanalytic sense, to refer to neurotic communication. We have a situation here where the patient's associations do indeed rather openly imply Type One derivatives related to aggression by the patient against his sister. But the true symbolic qualities of this communication do not reside in that relatively obvious inference; instead, I propose that they stem from their relatedness to the adaptive context involving the therapist's repeated hostile and destructive questions. It is here that disguise is in evidence, and derivative expression, and it is here that the me/not-me interface proves useful: interactionally, these associations unconsciously refer to both patient and therapist—and, in light of the adaptive context, primarily to the latter.

This discussion touches upon a basic clinical issue because a great deal of so called psychotherapeutic work is done on exactly this level, based on manifest content and Type One derivatives, rather than Type Two derivatives in terms of current adaptive contexts which lead only eventually to the past—in terms of both actual repetitions in the therapeutic experience and distortions based on the past introduced by the patient largely because of evoked pathological inner needs.

And you can see too that this is not simply a matter of cognitive confusion. The nonadaptive, superficial focus serves the countertransference-based needs of the therapist—and I think the supervisor as well—in that such formulations by and large tend to shift the focus away from the therapeutic interaction, away from the patient's unconscious perceptions of, and fantasies about, the therapist, and away from the therapist's countertransferences and errors.

As I have tried to demonstrate many times today, errors in analysis tend, as a rule, to have important dynamic meanings whether they are conceptual or are directly related to the treatment situtation. And these are all the more difficult to detect because there is a certain element of truth in the isolated genetic formulation—as compared to seeing the genetic reference as an allusion to unconscious aspects of the actual therapeutic interaction. This is a good example of the use of a psychoanalytic cliché (Langs 1978c)—the use of such apparent truths as an active and dynamic means of concealing more pressing and anxiety-provoking truths related to the therapeutic interaction.

So you have taken this material at its manifest level and as Type One derivatives related to the patient's aggression against his sister. And I would suggest that an alternate formulation would entail identifying, as I said, the therapist's excessive activity as the adaptive context—her aggressive and misleading questions—around which we could then organize these associations as Type Two derivatives, as indirect, derivative communications with true symbolic functions—transversal communications, if you will, mixtures of reality and fantasy, transference and nontransference. It is this level of meaning that is pertinent to the realm of the neuroses and more severe emotional disturbances.

I must stress this last point because therapists quickly forget that psychopathological syndromes are not based on conscious fears, or even on readily inferred anxieties and fantasies; they derive from distinctly unconscious contents and processes. And it is our responsibility as therapists to create the conditions under which these truly unconscious contents can emerge. We also must be capable of listening, organizing, and interpreting such material, and of interactional efforts on this truly unconscious and relevant level. So far as I know, no one has effectively challenged the importance of unconscious fantasies, memories, introjects, and interactional mechanisms in the development of neuroses, borderline syndromes, narcissistic disorders, psychoses, and the rest. What has happened instead is that such factors, accepted theoretically, are relatively ignored in the actual treatment situation.

As I said earlier, the adaptive context of the therapist's interventions—and the unconscious communications they contain—helps us to organize these associations in terms of her unconscious hostility toward the patient—and the patient's toward her—her fears of harming him and of being harmed, her anxieties as a therapist and caretaker, and the like. This formulation gives a quality of convolution and depth to this material that is lacking when one simply suggests that these associations reflect unconscious hostility toward the sister, and it includes both unconscious perceptions and unconscious fantasies, rather than being confined to superficial unconscious fantasies alone.

So, methodologically, I would submit that my

formulation has a quality of depth and pertinence that is lacking in your conception, and that it is, in important ways, an assessment in keeping with earlier conceptions of this material and with certain predictions made earlier about the nature of this therapeutic interaction. But the true test would come if the therapist would intervene on the basis of our respective silent hypotheses, while some indirectly validating material should help us decide as the session proceeds. And here, of course, I would speculate that an intervention based on your thinking would lead to further rumination and to no true validation. Alternatively, the patient might add sufficient but superficial and nondistinctive material to lead the unwary therapist into feeling that his intervention had indeed been confirmed. In contrast, an intervention based on my thesis would, I submit, lead to what Bion (1962) has called a selected fact—unexpected associations, including indications of both a widening cognitive awareness and a positive introject, that would help reorganize this material in a new and original way, and extend and deepen it.

Discussant: Perhaps the therapist is working with the thought that the patient's hostility toward his wife is based on aggression displaced from his sister.

Langs: Your comment demonstrates the extent to which therapists can rationalize and justify work with manifest themes and Type One derivatives. Of course, there is indeed some truth to your thesis: the patient's aggression toward his wife on one level undoubtedly relates to his conscious and unconscious hostility toward his sister. But I would propose that this is not the active unconscious issue that primarily concerns the patient at this time. It is all too direct and transparent. However, the test would come in seeing whether interpretations on this basis lead to validating responses and, ultimately, to the resolution of the destructive impulses toward the wife. In general, formulations of this kind are used as a kind of genetic defense—a flight from the current therapeutic interaction into genetic formulations that are either entirely divorced from that interaction or seen solely as a basis for its distortion in the patient's mind. This is quite different from starting with an aspect of the therapeutic interaction, identifying its realistic and distorted elements, and then tracing out genetic connections.

We must remember too that symptom relief need not be based on insight. For example, here I would suspect that interventions along the lines that you have proposed would unconsciously communicate to the patient the therapist's dread of her own contribution to his aggression. As a result, the patient could react either by further displaced hostility toward his wife—and here I mean, of course, displaced from the therapist—or he could respond by mobilizing his defenses in the face of the therapist's utter helplessness and lack of understanding, to the point where his destructiveness would diminish.

And we could distinguish these two underlying factors in any lessening of his hostile impulses by simply listening to the patient's associations in the session in which he reported such a change. It is crucial always to formulate the underlying basis for symptom alleviation, rather than taking the nonanalytic attitude that the patient seems to be feeling better, so why bother to understand the factors involved. In general, as you would expect, symptom alleviation based on a sector of misalliance is far less stable than that based on valid insight and implicit positive introjects.

It is my belief that in this situation superficial interpretations that relate the patient's hostility toward his wife to earlier feelings toward his sister would have little effect, other than to further distress the patient, who on some unconscious level knows that a central source of his mounting aggression and failing controls is from his interaction with this therapist, who is behaving and communicating in just that way. It seems evident, to me at least, that only true rectification of these countertransference-based imputs—their actual control and modification—along with the relevant interpretations the patient's unconscious perceptions and secondary fantasies, could provide this patient a sound basis for ultimately understanding the multiple sources of his aggressive symptomatology: first, as it derives from this therapeutic relationship, and only then, secondarily, from his earlier life history. Only work that would unfold along such lines could provide him the kind of valid symptom alleviation and controls he needs.

Remember, it is a basic principle that actualities must take precedence over fantasies, and that the current therapeutic interaction must also take precedence over the past. The past can only be modified and interpreted when the present differs significantly in regard to its pathological components. So much of this is overlooked by therapists and supervisors, and can be applied to the supervisory situation as well as to therapy—not only in terms of establishing important principles for supervisory work, but also in considering the qualities of the supervisory bipersonal field itself. Each field must be sound and secure in reality, or the therapeutic or supervisory work will be of little constructive help.

This material is so extremely rich; it offers me an opportunity to make another point: to the extent that this supervisee was indeed attempting to develop a formulation that the patient's hostility toward his wife was based on earlier hostilities toward his sister, and to the extent that the supervisor agreed, we have the making of a misalliance in the supervisory bipersonal field: a shared erroneous formulation which the patient could either accept or refute. In the former instance, the supervisory misalliance would lead to a misalliance in the therapeutic bipersonal field, while in the latter case, the patient would unconsciously attempt to cure both the therapist and the supervisor through derivative communications. As a rule, patients fluctuate, accepting misalliances one moment and attempting to modify them the next. I suspect that, unconsciously, supervisees will do the same: accept erroneous formulations from a supervisor at one point, and in some way unconsciously attempt to generate inputs that would correct the false thesis at a later juncture. I have no doubt that unconsciously the supervisor would be involved in similar struggles. But again I state that his responsibility is to be aware of errors and misalliances, and to repeatedly check out the material that is being presented for such possibilities—in essence, to make continuous use of the validating process in regard to any formulation that he, the patient, or the supervisee develops.

Supervisor B: The patient said, I was afraid that something bad would happen to my sister. The therapist asked, How did you feel? The patient responded: Well, I didn't like it, but I didn't have any choice.

Langs: How true. Perhaps you can see here how these comments continue unconsciously to illuminate themes related to the therapeutic interaction, doing so in a rather deep and moving way, and in exquisite derivative form that offers a coalescence of derivatives related now to one unconscious aspect of the interaction, earlier to another—building into a remarkably multifacted whole. In contrast, listening to this as material related directly to the sister conveys something of a flat sequence, some denial of unconscious need, some vague sense of anxiety, and little else.

Statements related to having no choice are extremely common in clinic patients. Some of this arises because they are often pressured by the therapist in a manner similar to that we are observing here, to the point that they have little choice regarding what the therapist will permit them to communicate. More broadly, we hear this theme because they truly have nowhere to go, nowhere to turn: as a rule, it is therapy at this clinic and with this therapist or nothing.

Supervisor B: The resident asked, What were you scared about? The patient went on: Well, I just felt uneasy that something would happen while my parents were away. My uncle was there, but on that occasion . . .

Langs: It's a bit uncanny, but this may well be another allusion to the supervisor; but please continue.

Supervisor B: My uncle was there, but one time she fell and fractured her nose, and they blamed it on me: they said I had pushed her. But my mother didn't go along with it and said that it was really not important, it was just an accident. That was all at the time that my mother and father were having frequent fights. My father wanted to leave her, and he was running around with his friends and with other women. And my mother threatened to commit suicide, and my sister was sent off to my aunt and I didn't have to care for her any more. My younger sister had appendicitis, and they called the doctor and took her to the hospital.

Langs: It would appear that the therapist at this point sat in stunned silence; she hasn't interrupted him for a while. The material conveys an enormous sense of chaos and confusion, and a lack of any sense of security—of a secure frame and hold. And unconsciously, as a mixture of perception and fantasy, the themes of poor caretaking and its consequences touch upon failures by both the therapist and the supervisor to exert an interpretive and holding, and therefore moderating and protective, influence. There are references to pathological denial, to depression and self-destructiveness, to safety through absence or flight, and to the danger of further emergencies. It would be defensive to think of this material solely as reflecting the terrible events in his past life or his current intrapsychic state, without realizing that it refers as well to the terrible qualities of the present therapeutic interaction, and possibly the supervision as well.

And perhaps those of you who felt that I was being harsh in my evaluation of this therapeutic situation can now see that I was attempting an honest appraisal, and that in fact the patient is being far more harsh than I had been. But of course the patient has experienced it far more intensely and has far more at stake; in any case, we now both share a sense of hopelessness, depression, and disaster in respect to this therapy. And I suspect that we both feel as well a need to undertake, consciously or unconsciously, some therapeutic work on behalf of the therapist. In the supervisory situation, this would mean a gentle but integrating discussion of the factors that are disturbing this therapeutic relationship, in a manner I have already outlined.

Supervisor B: The therapist asked, How did you relate to your little sister after that? Well, the patient said, we played together for a while, but in our teens we got involved with other friends. She became withdrawn after a while and would sit around the house.

Langs: Another allusion to protective withdrawal.

Supervisor B: The resident inquired, How do you get along with her now? The patient responded, Pretty good. Sometimes she infuriates me: she is selfish and insensitive; she doesn't recognize how other people feel, and she can yell a lot.

Langs: Perhaps this makes my discussion even clearer. Here, the patient is aware of his anger at this sister and of her pathological qualities. But this is merely manifest content, and quite direct. And while you might say that the therapist's questions enabled him to express these feelings more directly, I would respond that this may well be so, but there will be little, if any, therapeutic gain. These are, I suspect, feelings of which the patient has evidently been aware for some time, and while they undoubtedly are disturbing to him, they are not the significant factor for the moment in his own uncontrolled aggression.

On the other hand, in the adaptive context of the therapist's interventions in this session, you can hear this material as Type Two derivatives filled with valid and sensitive unconscious perceptions related to the therapist's selfishness, insensitivity, and provocative questioning. This is the patient's derivative way of supervising and attempting to help the therapist; indirectly, he has stated what I developed quite consciously, and this is one form of Type Two validation in the supervisory situation.

Supervisor B: Well, the resident goes on: she asks, Does it upset you when she yells at you? The patient answered, Yes, but I've never said anything to her because I can't handle my own anger.

Langs: It is so remarkable how the same themes come up again and again in situations of this kind. The patient says that he never said anything to his sister, that he feared losing control of himself—touching now on another aspect of this unconscious communicative interaction. And this reminds me that I have spent a lot of time attempting to understand why the patient, in the face of such latent aggression and distraction as we see reflected in the questions from this therapist, and in light of his own extremely sensitive indirect and derivative communications, seldom expresses his perceptions, feelings, and fantasies directly. And there are many reasons for this; the patient refers to one of them, his own fear of losing control. On an unconscious level, along the me/not-me interface, this conveys his fear that the therapist too will lose control if he were to speak up.

After all, there is every indication that this therapist is quite unable to handle her own aggressive impulses. In response to a direct confrontation from the patient, there is every reason for the patient to be concerned about a total loss of control on the part of the therapist, and a destructive, vengeful response. The patient can't trust the therapist, can't rely on her capacity to manage, and this mixture of mistrust and fear is certainly one factor in his communicating indirectly through derivatives, rather than directly. Whatever additional intrapsychic motives there may be for this defense, there are pressing interactional motives as well. And you can sense here, too, how nonneutral interventions alter the open and positive communicative properties of the bipersonal field. Undoubtedly, there is much that this patient will not tell this therapist, even in derivative form.

Discussant: If I may ask at this point, I am wondering how you feel about verbatim process notes, and whether you would comment on this material. Do you feel that it is too detailed; do you prefer more or less?

Langs: Well, to this point, it seems to me that this is a rather good presentation, with just the right amount of information. It may be a bit too detailed, but I have no sense of that since I do not know how far we are into this particular session. So I can't assess whether we are being inundated with excessive detail to the point where we will not be able to cover the entire session. For the moment, these notes permit a reasonably sensitive and I believe relatively complete appraisal of the implications of this material, and of the nature of this therapeutic interaction.

Discussant: Are these verbatim notes?

Supervisor B: I would say that they are.

Langs: How much more do you have?

Supervisor B: There is a great deal more.

Langs: Yes, so while this is all quite meaningful, it is somewhat over detailed. Did the supervisee write these notes during the therapy session?

Supervisor B: Yes.

Langs: You can see that it is important to establish these facts. And perhaps I should have inquired at the very outset, since it is basic to structuring the supervisory bipersonal field and to the supervisor's timing of his interventions. It is essential too that you discuss note-taking with the supervisee, that you establish a preference for writing sequential process notes *after* a session and for the absence of note-taking *during* the session, and that you deal with process notes written during the session in part by demonstrating the patient's unconscious perceptions of, and sensitivity to, this procedure. It is an important alteration in the frame and an adaptive context that requires first-order attention.

In this context, you may remember that, based on the initial material, I was concerned about the theme of public records, public exposure, and the like. And now we find out that the therapist was busy during these sessions taking notes. It is amazing that the therapist can intervene so actively and write at the same time, but that's exactly what she is doing. And it seems to me now that this contributes not only to the patient's anxieties about exposure, but also to his unconscious concerns about the therapist's supervision and its failures to exert a moderating influence. In addition, it seems to me that the note-taking adds considerably to the sense of chaos and to the patient's impression that the therapist is having considerable difficulty managing her own contributions to the treatment process.

Discussant: It seems to me that while verbatim note-taking or even recordings will have an effect on the patient, it is there in front of him. It therefore can be explored and even analyzed in the course of the therapy, and that it needn't be detrimental.

Langs: Your comment touches upon an important issue, what I consider one of the myths of psychotherapy or psychoanalysis. You are suggesting that this reality, and by implication, perhaps any reality, can be maintained so long as it is explored and what you call "analyzed." By implication, you are also suggesting that such understanding will modify the conscious and unconscious detrimental effects of the reality. I simply have not found this to be so, nor would I expect it to be so in principle.

After all, the presence of note-taking or a tape recorder is a reality, and one cannot verbally resolve a reality: one can only rectify it. It is for this reason that in my work with the frame of the bipersonal field (Langs 1975b, 1976a,d) I have stressed the importance of two therapeutic measures in this sphere: rectification and interpretation. Without the former, the latter is meaningless; in its extreme form, it is tantamount to a therapist having intercourse with his patient, and then exploring the patient's feelings, as if this would in any way modify the true unconscious meanings and implications of such an experience.

Similarly, the tape recorder or notes are a reality, and they convey something of the therapist's pathological conscious and unconscious needs. They modify the nature of the therapeutic relationship, the communicative field, the way in which the patient experiences and introjects the therapist, and the entire meaning of the therapeutic experience. In such a context, efforts to analyze, in the sense of resolve and make disappear, actually constitute a Type C endeavor: an attempt to generate seeming truths that are essentially designed to falsify and deny. Unconsciously, tape recording or note-taking means to the patient that his right to total confidentiality is being violated, that the therapist has a need to take him in and capture him, that the therapist is using the treatment situation for some selfish purpose that is not in the interest of the patient, and, often, that the therapist is in supervision or that he cannot manage the treatment situation as it unfolds spontaneously—to name just a few of the more general implications, without attempting to identify more primitive inferences that would have strikingly blatant aggressive and sexual qualities. All the so-called analytic work in the world could not genuinely modify these unconscious beliefs, perceptions, and introjects, or correct the communicative properties of the bipersonal field or the image of the therapist. They would only add to the destructive qualities of this image by generating an experience of the therapist as someone who, in addition to his note-taking, attempts to falsify or deny the true implications of his own behaviors. I hope that I have said enough about this point to make my position clear; it is a source of considerable misunderstanding. And as I hope you can see, a review of this session in light of this particular adaptive context, strongly supports my formulations through a series of coalescing Type Two derivatives.

As for the effect of the verbatim notes, I personally now feel somewhat overwhelmed. And it is, in part, a function of the great detail being offered by the supervisee. I begin to feel that it would be important now to sit back and move on to the next session. The input is too great to handle; it's something like an overwhelmingly massive projective identification that taxes one's capacities as a container and, here, as a supervisor. The mass of detail becomes a way of placing into the supervisor the extensive anxieties of the therapist, and it has a certain protective function: it offers far more than the supervisor can handle, in contrast to the supervisee who offers too little material as a defense. This is now a second level form of validation of my thesis that this supervisee makes extensive use of chaotic and destructive projective identifications herself—in both bipersonal fields. It becomes critical for the supervisor to contain and metabolize them, or they will continue unrecognized and unmodified.

Discussant: In addition to the resident's verbatim notes, are we to assume that the supervisor was himself taking verbatim notes during the presentation?

Supervisor B: No, these are not my notes; I simply borrowed the notes from the resident to present them here.

Langs: Yes, it is important that supervision, as a rule, be carried out without note-taking by the supervisor—as a means of maintaining the greatest possible openness and confidentiality for the supervisory field. Now, as you may have gathered, I myself sometimes take verbatim notes during supervision, and I even record supervisory seminars, but never the sessions of patients. And I do that knowing that it is a contamination, but justifying it in terms of the needs of the field at large, and the importance of generating definitive data for my publications. So, I make this exception knowing that it is a contaminant, but hopefully one whose influence can be kept to a minimum, though I do not expect it to disappear. And I do it only when it is essential for the ideas that I feel are important to present to others, and with the full permission of the supervisee.

Well, we do not have too much time left; could you proceed a bit more quickly so that we can hear out this supervisory hour, and perhaps hear a bit about the following hour as well?

Supervisor B: Well, the resident continued to ask questions about the background of the patient, and then she said, I thought your parents were separated now. The patient responded, No, you can never tell what my mother is going to do, but they battle and I guess they like it.

Langs: I am really struck with the extent to which a session of this kind raises all of the basic issues regarding what I would have to characterize as poor psychotherapy. And I say this rather humbly, because after all this resident is trying to learn, and she has been influenced by all kinds of supervision. But I do think that we can take this as an important model of poor therapeutic technique.

And I say this now because another very basic and somewhat intriguing question is why patients stay with therapists who are not only unhelpful, but also downright destructive. And here too I have found that there are many reasons: some patients unconsciously prefer so-called treatment with someone who is actually sicker than themselves; in an unfortunate way, they find this reassuring. Other patients—and this may be the situation here—stay because they find some type of masochistic gratification, some pleasure in fighting and being fought with, and some kind of punishment perhaps. Still others dread their inner mental world, and find maladaptive relief with a therapist who helps them to avoid it. There are other reasons as well, but time does not permit an extended discussion. Just remember that it would be very important with a supervisee of this kind, at some point in the supervision, to demonstrate these pathological unconscious motives to the supervisee. Without such supervisory efforts, she might feel that she keeps a certain number of patients in treatment, and that must mean that she is doing reasonable therapeutic work. It is hurtful and sad to demonstrate that the situation is quite otherwise, but it is absolutely necessary, for both the supervisee and for her patients.

Supervisor B: Well, the resident continued to ask about the sister, and how she clings to her parents. And then she finally got around to asking the patient specifically about his dream. The patient then responded that he was somewhere on a battlefield. He had a rifle and was shooting at someone. He was confused, in that he may have been shooting into a crowd somewhere. And there were people shooting back, and he remembers hitting two of them. Here the resident said, You haven't dreamed about your wife.

Langs: In the adaptive context of the qualities of this therapist's interventions and treatment interaction, the dream conveys a valid unconscious perception and introjection, and extension into fantasy, of the nature of this therapeutic interaction and experience. And we have to wonder, in this context, who the two people are that the patient shot: one has to at least suspect that it is the therapist and her supervisor.

And you can see how the therapist, in addition, persists in her Type C maneuvers: now she drops the sister and pursues the wife. And she says it so beautifully: "You haven't dreamed about your wife." She is interested in what the patient does not dream about, rather than what he does dream about. She is interested in destroying the actual dream, and in suggesting a fictional dream that will serve as a barrier to the real one. And lastly, she thinks only of manifest content and lacks a conception of latent content and functions. This too could be rather nicely demonstrated to her, along with all the additional support that she very much needs.

We could also pause at this point and derive a few generalizations from the two superivisory experiences we have observed. You can immediately sense that there is a range of residents; some will be relatively intact and have some degree of control over the psychotic part of their personality—as I call it—or their basic underlying disturbance, while others will be grossly disturbed and in considerable difficulty. And you can see too that there is also a range of supervisors. Each has his own distinctive style, his own capacity to respond to the supervisee's and patient's needs, his own level of activity, his own need for defense or lack of it, and the rest.

This particular session also brings up the issue of therapeutic and supervisory crises. We had no sense of acute crisis in the first supervisory presentation, but here I feel the matter is quite different: the therapeutic situation seems so disorganized that we have a major indication for supervisory interventions. In this context, I think of Searles's paper (1959) regarding unconscious attempts to drive the other person crazy. There, he wrote of unconscious attempts by therapists to drive their patients crazy. And I think that we are seeing here one such attempt. The unconscious thrust of these interventions can be characterized as offering the patient Type C barriers and falsifications, as well as interactional defenses, but there is also a quality of disorganization and distraction that would relate to unconscious efforts to drive the patient crazy: as soon as he gets started in one area, she shifts him into another; there is no sense of reality or stability. And it is crucial that the supervisor intervene to help the therapist get these efforts under control, that he serve not only as teacher and model to the supervisee, but also as a modulating factor for the treatment.

Supervisor B: Maybe I can summarize a bit here. The patient went on and talked about his experiences in the infantry, where he had been taught how to kill people silently by sneaking up on them. He then talked about two recent friends who died, of funerals, and his sense of identification with one of the victims—he felt it could have happened to himself. The resident asked about his emotions at these funerals, and he said that he had very little feeling; he didn't know the other people at the funeral and he had had thoughts about how people can be mugged and killed. The resident then asked how he is relating to his wife at present, and the patient said that he is not making her happy. He is on medicine and he is coming to a psychiatrist; it's like trying to climb a very high mountain.

Langs: Does this mean that he is receiving medication from the resident?

Supervisor B: Yes.

Langs: That too is a modification in the frame—a first-order issue. And among its many implications, for the patient it often means that the therapist is unable to be sufficiently helpful through his interventions in the therapeutic situation, and must draw upon pharmacological assistance. Medication will also promote the development of a Type C field: it functions as a barrier to underlying unconscious truths. For me, it is further confirmation that this resident is unable to manage the therapeutic situation, and that the patient is well aware of that—perhaps even consciously, although certainly on an unconscious level. I see no indication for medication with this patient at all. In fact, his communications are so rich in Type Two derivatives, he appears to be quite analyzable, using that term in its broader sense. That is, I believe that he communicates in a manner that permits significant interpretive work.

Notice too, how the patient confirms my formulations regarding the therapist's efforts to drive him crazy.

Unconsciously, this implies his destruction or annihilation, and the patient characterizes it as sneaky and unexpected. In addition, he describes his sense of frustration through the reference to climbing a high mountain: he senses that he is really getting nowhere.

Discussant: I wonder why you suggest that there is no indication for medication with this patient.

Langs: It may well be that this therapist cannot do otherwise than to prescribe medication. But with a therapist who is capable of establishing and maintaining the frame, and of Type A communication and interpretation, and who is quite able to manage his own inner impulses and convey an implicit sense of inner control, there would be absolutely no need for medication. And as I said, this patient communicates richly in derivative and symbolic form—much of it, for the moment, because of the many alterations in the basic frame—and would benefit from rectifications of the frame and interpretive work. Medication undermines interpretive work, regardless of the propaganda from the drug companies; it suggests that relief can be obtained through drugs rather than through understanding—and certainly not through understanding and the human resources of patient and therapist alone.

Perhaps you are concerned with dangers of suicide or homicide. But any modification of the frame, including the use of medication, tends to increase such dangers rather than decrease them. Such possibilities are significantly lessened through the development of a sound bipersonal field and therapeutic alliance, and through the presence of a therapist capable of controls and helpful interpretive interventions. They are among the means by which the therapist generates trust and inevitable introjects based on his valid containing and management capacities; that and cognitive insight are what help the patient with his suicidal or homicidal impulses.

Often the use of medication suggests a mistrust of the patient in his capacities for management and control, and a similar mistrust within the therapist that she can prove helpful—and all of that only increases the patient's anxieties, further impairs his ego functioning and capacities, and, as I said, increases the danger of some type of disastrous act.

Supervisor B: The patient had been tried on several drugs, and had experienced some serious side effects. Actually, I had not gotten into the issue of medication.

Langs: Yes, some supervisors separate this from their teaching efforts, just as many therapists disregard the crucial implications that requests for medication, and the actual prescribing of drugs, have for the patient in the therapeutic interaction. This gives me an opportunity to stress the importance of these ramifications of medication, and to suggest that the supervisor has a responsibility to explore this area in supervision—it is a basic frame issue of first-order importance. And again, it will be quite unnecessary to simply and arbitrarily suggest that the therapist discontinue the medication; one need not modify basic principles of supervision in this situation. If you listen to the presentation with the medication as an adaptive context, you will have ample opportunity to document from the unconscious communications from the patient the detrimental and destructive effects of the medication, and will find numerous unconscious directives from the patient to discontinue it. In the therapy situation itself, one would similarly follow the unconscious lead of the patient in rectifying and interpreting the deviation.

Supervisor B: The patient continued by describing a battle with his wife earlier, on the day of the session, and he told her that if he didn't get better, they should break up.

Langs: This is also characteristic: for some strange

reason, he won't terminate the treatment; he'll end the marriage instead. And the therapist who for any reason feels this to be a destructive and unhealthy marriage will take this enactment related to the unconscious and destructive dimensions of the therapeutic interaction as a sign of progress. And such a therapist will either ignore or misunderstand the patient's associations related to his behavior—associations that if examined would reveal their basis in the pathology of the therapist and the therapeutic interaction, as well as within the patient. Both patient and therapist in such a situation would maintain a bastion that will consist of never talking about or analyzing the therapeutic relationship and this will then generate what I have termed *interactional living out* (Langs 1976 d), in which the patient lives out the unconscious and shared fantasies, defenses, and introjects of both himself and the therapist.

Supervisor B: At this point in the supervisory situation, I said to the patient—I mean to the student . . .

Langs: Well, there is truth to your slip of the tongue: this resident should be a patient. And I can only hope that she recognizes that need, and that she does indeed get some help.

Supervisor B: Well, at this point I asked her if she wanted me to interject something. And I talked to the patient—I mean, the resident—about the fact that I'm more a consultant than I am a supervisor. And that she has the responsibility for the patient, and I don't have the responsibility for what the end result of this treatment will be. And that she, the resident, has been a doctor for a number of years, and she is my colleague. And that I am not going to, whatever happens to the patient—if he commits suicide or whatever happens to him—it is her responsibility. And I want her to feel free to do what she feels like, despite what I say. I emphasized that it is really her ultimate judgment that must prevail, because ultimately, he is her patient.

The next week she came back and said, I think that the best thing to do with this patient is to cut down on the therapy. (Laughter.)

Langs: Cut down on the therapy—the human principle of displacement—she won't say cut down on the supervision, just cut down on the therapy. And I am clearly implying here that she fears being direct and open with you, for reasons not unlike those of her own patient, who feared being direct with her.

I am quite impressed with your intervention. And here I must apologize for being very candid, but I think that you have provided us an opportunity to study some specific problems of the supervisory field—the psychopathology of the supervisory field, if I may use that term broadly and even a bit out of context. And while it is rather a delicate issue to delineate this appraisal in a conference of this kind, I think that it is crucial to the learning process. And I think that it will show us too that we can learn far more from errors and disturbances than we can when things go well in either therapy or supervision.

Let me say this in response to your intervention: I don't make superfluous lectures as a rule, and in particular I do not attempt to deny or negate my responsibilities to the supervisee and to the patient. And while I see that consciously your motivation was to provide the therapist with the ultimate responsibility for the patient, your unconscious communication is filled with additional meanings and implications. Thus, while it is true that you are the supervisor and she is the direct therapist, your need to disclaim responsibility and at the same time allude to the possible suicide of this patient can only be experienced by this supervisee as a reflection of your own anxieties, your feelings that you are unable to manage this situation, unable to offer an explanatory cognitive formulation and a series of technical recommendations, and that you feel an urgent need to protect yourself from responsibility in the face of some kind of acute danger.

Your intervention indicates that you were, on some level,

aware of the crisis nature of this therapeutic situation, but this should have been stated directly to the supervisee, rather than being conveyed within an intervention through which you disclaimed any responsibility for the consequences of this therapy. In addition, I am struck by the fact that you made no effort to formulate this material, to help this therapist, to teach her. Instead, you suddenly deny your responsibility and cast her off on her own—all in the face of her own evident anxiety, lack of control, disorganization, uncertainty, and defensiveness.

In terms of projective identifications, I would suggest that this supervisee placed into you a chaotic therapeutic situation and that rather than metabolizing and understanding these projected contents, you on one level refused to contain them, while on another you apparently unconsciously experienced something of the chaos and threat placed into you, and reprojected it back into the supervisee—but failing to detoxify the contents, to understand them, and actually generating an even more threatening reprojection, to which the supervisee immediately responded with a sense of hopelessness and a wish to get out of the situation.

To put all of this another way, I think that this supervisee was now under unbearable and destructive pressure from both sides—from both the patient and her supervisor—and that, lacking sufficient integrating capacities of her own, she had almost no choice but to reduce or stop the therapy. Your intervention has strong Type B communicative qualities, and the therapist responds in kind: you acted, now she wishes to do so. You dumped her and placed your uncontrolled anxieties into her, and now she wishes to do the same thing to the patient. She is also reprojecting the contents and mechanisms you placed into her back into you—letting you know the hopelessness, despair, and helplessness involved. This is a striking exchange of unmetabolized projective and introjective identifications—a rather destructive spiraling interaction.

You can see, then, that the supervisor does have a

responsibility to the supervisee and the patient, that this should not be disclaimed, that a supervisor should become consciously aware of a crisis situation in treatment or in supervision, and that his efforts should be developed along the lines of generating silent hypotheses and making efforts to formulate and understand the basis for the crisis, and to help the supervisee accordingly.

In addition, should you make an intervention of this kind as a supervisor, it would be well for you to reflect upon it afterwards. Hopefully, you would be able to recognize that it reflected some undue anxiety and confusion on your own part, and you might be prepared to undertake some self-analysis and to rectify the situation by offering some necessary formulations and technical advice. In addition—and this is quite important—as soon as the supervisee came in and suggested that she cut down on the therapy, this should have served as an immediate signal to you that not only is there something terribly uncontrolled and wrong with the treatment situation, but that there is something terribly the matter with the supervision as well. This communication suggests that the supervision is not being helpful to the supervisee, that it is not enabling her to master the therapeutic situation or to deal with the patient, and that the reduction in therapy is being suggested as an alternative to better supervision. It is a kind of acute therapeutic context that should lead you to an intense reevaluation of your supervisory work.

If time had not been so short, I would have attempted to predict the consequences of this supervisory intervention. It must have generated such an additional sense of chaos for the supervisee that she must have felt quite overwhelmed—and, I suspect, quite angry and disappointed as well. So, however painful, we now have an opportunity to study the influence of the supervisor's countertransference-based reactions on both the supervisee and the patient. I think that we are all about to learn some very important lessons.

Notice too that this is a kind of extraneous comment, that it is not based on the material of the presentation, and that it particularly does not derive from the patient's associations. It illustrates that extraneous comments are in principle especially vulnerable to countertransference influence, and that they require considerable self-scrutiny in advance before being offered by a supervisor.

So it seems you are reacting to the chaos and lack of control of the whole situation, to the destructiveness and uncontrolled aggression in both the patient and the therapist, and that for some reason you are unable to offer helpful and modulating supervisory interventions. Instead you unconsciously conveyed your own sense of alarm: "if he commits suicide."

Supervisor B: Actually, those were not my words to her; I was paraphrasing my intervention and included what, as soon became clear, she though I had told her—that her patient may commit suicide.

Langs: Yes, but in saying this is what she *thought* you had said, you seem to imply that you felt that you had said otherwise—and consciously, it appears that you believe that to be the case. But the resident was quite sensitive to the obvious implication in your comment: you were in a way warning her that this patient might commit suicide, and yet not helping her with this enormous danger. I might also add that your inclusion of her impression, without comment, in your paraphrase suggests that on some level you accept it as valid. So it would be important not to deny the implications of your remark; that would only generate even more anxiety in the supervisee. Let's hear how this unfolded.

Supervisor B: Well, the resident came in and said, I think that we should cut him down because he's too sick, and we should do a short-term psychotherapy on him. Here I asked why, and she said, Because he was going to commit suicide.

Langs: So, you can see how she experienced your comments, and how she now, in a sense, confronts you with them.

Supervisor B: Yes, I can see what she read into my remark.

Langs: Yes, but "read into" seems to suggest that it is still the supervisee's distortion the predominates here. I think, since it is always difficult to distinguish valid perception from distortion, that a more cautious and self-searching approach might be in order. You can also see here how some important myths develop regarding psychotherapy. For example, the myth that a patient with severe psychopathology should not be treated with insight psychotherapy, and that medication should be used in preference, along with some type of short-term treatment. The decision to shorten therapy here is clearly based on shared countertransference difficulties in both supervisee and supervisor; it is a defensive effort on the part of the therapist that is certainly not in the interest of the patient.

I am reminded of some of the remarks that I made earlier about factors that motivate trainees to move away from insight-oriented therapy toward drug therapy, behavior therapy, and the like. And you can see that unconsciously the supervisor can have a great influence in this respect. In this situation, we have a therapist who is greatly burdened by the insight-oriented treatment modality, who then experiences an equally great burden in her supervisor. Under these conditions, it is little wonder that she wishes to alter the therapeutic modality, because neither she nor the supervisor are capable of its constructive use. And I have found that it is rather typical to take flight from the inner mental world related to insightful treatment when one feels overwhelmed, and this may apply to patient, therapist, and supervisor alike.

And you can recognize too that the supervisee's introjective identification with the supervisor has qualities of dread, of being overwhelmed, a fear for the life of the patient, and a sense of utter helplessness. In such a context, the decision to move toward short-term, drug, and manifest content-oriented treatment, whatever its unfortunate consequences, has distinctive adaptive elements; it is probably the best that the supervisee can provide under the circumstances—however much it lacks as an ideal treatment modality.

However, if the supervisee would initiate such measures with the patient, she would run the risk of generating a sense of overwhelming anxiety and even loss of control in the patient, who would undoubtedly experience the change as reflecting the therapist's fear of his own inner mental world and her total inability to manage and interpret it. While the patient might welcome the additional Type C defensive barriers offered in this way, there is a great risk of precipitating uncontrolled living out, especially since the therapist herself is involved in an interactional enactment. There are great pressures here toward a Type B field with massive projective identifications and action discharge by both patient and therapist. This is matched by a comparable Type B supervisory field and interaction, and as a result there is no insight, no adequate metabolizing figure, no relief for anyone, and a consideration of desparate measures by the therapist. Still, her wish to act is unconsciously designed to evoke a proxy from the supervisor (Wangh 1962), to alert him to his failings, and, hopefully, to mobilize his adaptive resources. I could add considerably more, but I think we should get additional data.

Supervisor B: I told the supervisee that she had misunderstood what I had said.

Langs: So, you disclaimed the unconscious meanings to your remarks; unfortunately, this is the typical attitude in therapists regarding their interventions: their conscious intentions are what count, in contrast to the patient, whose unconscious communications are critical.

Supervisor B: I did that because I was responding to the fact that the therapist had started this patient on medication. And I felt that the patient didn't need medication, but I wanted her to go ahead and do whatever she needed to do.

Langs: That was not clear from your original presentation. But nonetheless, embedded in your acknowledging the therapist's responsibility to her patient were distinct unconscious communications of your own anxieties and sense of being overwhelmed, communications to which this therapist was quite sensitive.

In principle, in both the therapeutic and supervisory bipersonal fields, one must look for the kernel of truth in every communication from the patient or supervisee. That is, you should have accepted her remarks as a commentary—a possible mixture of perceptiveness and fantasy—and sought out your own contribution to how she played back your intervention. In addition, at the point at which you felt misunderstood, you should have been prompted to examine the nature of your supervisory interventions, and the status of the supervisory bipersonal field and its communicative qualities. And actually, first and foremost, you should have searched for the valid core in the supervisee's representation of your comments. In a manner quite comparable to what occurs under similar conditions with a patient, you will very often find that the supervisee has consciously or unconsciously detected valid communications of which you were unaware. The basic principle remains: reality before fantasy—a search for valid components before deciding that a communication is wholly or partially distorted.

However problematical and distressful this situation might be, you are actually offering us an excellent opportunity to discuss important and neglected issues related to supervision. In my introductory comments, I had spoken of crises, in supervision and in therapy. And I had suggested that a supervisor might modify his basic approach under certain conditions. I tried to stress that the first step should be to maintain the principle of using the material presented by the supervisee to deal with any emergency. And now, faced with an actual crisis in supervision, I would attempt to maintain that principle, perhaps adding sparse extraneous comments as needed, but taking great pains not to deny the perceptions of the supervisee. Instead, I would try to appreciate their actual basis and to attempt some quick self-analysis, and initiate efforts to rectify my errors and restore a positive quality to the supervisory situation.

If, at some point, even though I would move on to hear the session of the past week, you were to review in some appropriate context the material of the prior supervisory session, and if you were to use it to help the supervisee understand the crisis in therapy and supervision, it would be absolutely essential that you do this in a manner that would acknowledge your own detrimental contributions as a supervisor, rather than in a way that would be designed consciously or unconsciously to place the source of the crisis in the therapeutic bipersonal field and in the therapist or patient.

Remember, too, that supervisory crises must be dealt with before crises in therapy. And at the point at which the supervisee confronts you as the supervisor, it is essential to deal first with your own contribution to this situation, now of necessity, using the material from the prior presentation to shape your remarks, but clearly delineating your own errors and rectifying them. Only then can you turn to additional contributions to this crisis from the therapeutic field, and to the acute problems in the therapy situation itself.

Thus, you might here have acknowledged that your comments, without your having been aware of it, apparently reflected your concern about the chaotic state of the treatment situation, an issue that she and the patient unconsciously had been working over. You now realize you had failed to help the therapist to organize and understand what was happening, and that you had thereby added to her sense of helplessness, which had apparently prompted her to wish to reduce the frequency of the patient's session—and which may, in its broader sense, be a factor in the therapist's use of medication. You might then go on to indicate that, for the moment, rather than undertaking a reconsideration of that prior session, it would be well to get into the material of the present session, since you would expect it to be a reworking of these very issues. You could also promise an approach that would be designed to define for the therapist contributions from supervision, from herself, and from the patient, and add that you hope to suggest specific rectifications and interpretive interventions that should begin to get the situation under control. You could also indicate that you fully expect that slow, careful, and patient therapeutic work could have such an effect. In this way, you would be not only offering cognitive support to the supervisee, but also inherently conveying your own capacities to recover and to mobilize controls and understanding, and providing her a much needed introject as well.

Supervisor B: In my own reponse, I gave her reassurance. I stated that I wondered why she had reacted in that fashion, indicating that after all I was trying to reassure her, and yet she saw it as the opposite.

Langs: "As the opposite"—well, as I am sure you realize (and this often happens in my own supervision when the patient and I are in agreement, while the therapist feels otherwise) that I am in full agreement with her: I, too, experienced and formulated your effort at reassurance as quite the reverse. This certainly demonstrates the importance of the tenet that the supervisor should know the nature of his unconscious communications to the supervisee, and demonstrates as well that these unrecognized messages can have a major influence on the supervisee—and possibly, even on the patient.

So, the supervisee's communication is a directive for self-exploration, at the very least. Instead, you treat her response as distorted—in therapy, this would be as if it were entirely transference-based—and you disclaim your own contributions and deny her valid conscious (and unconscious?) perceptions. This is so very common among therapists with their patients: a denial of the valid core of their perceptions. And we see now that it may happen with a supervisor and his supervisee. This is an important lesson in the defensive misuse of the concept of transference.

Supervisor B: Actually, I was shocked. And I remember saying to myself, I guess I scared her to death.

Langs: Yes, that thought could have initiated the important process of self-scrutiny, which might have enabled you to understand in retrospect the nature of both your unconscious communication to the supervisee and of your own anxieties. In fact, this is the kind of thought that you might have shared with the supervisee in some form, somewhat apologetically indicating your recognition that you had frightened her and proposing now to get in touch with what is happening both in supervision and in the therapy—and to undertake some corrective measures.

So, your almost total silence during the prior supervisory session, and your final anxious and disruptive comment, combined to convey a sense of helplessness to this supervisee. It helps us to see that, first, the supervisor must indeed intervene to the best of his ability when faced with a chaotic therapeutic situation. Second, he must recognize that the level and frequency of his interventions in supervision may well be quite different from what is ideal in the psychotherapeutic situation. I do not believe in being a silent supervisor, especially with trainees, with whom a great deal of work has to be done in virtually every session. Whether the supervisee is relatively silent himself, overactive, or intervening rather adequately, there are many more indicators for supervisory interventions than for therapeutic ones. In addition, when a supervisee is so active herself, that is an unconscious appeal for activity from the supervisor: for interventions that would both help her to understand and to rectify, and to control her anxieties so that she can intervene less frequently and more effectively.

By the way, I suspect, as I said before, that this is not at all atypical: that most beginning therapists, and many experienced ones, tend to be overactive, concerned with manifest content, to unduly utilize questions and the like, and to have considerable anxiety regarding primitive mental contents. While this supervisee represents an extreme, you can learn a great deal about the average therapist from this material. In the face of such inevitable anxieties, it is important that the supervisor have a real mastery of the situation, even though it might include an occasional moment during which he must acknowledge his own sense of uncertainty and his own inability to offer an adequate formulation. But on the whole he should be capable of considerable understanding and teaching throughout the course of a supervisory hour, especially in the face of a crisis situation in the therapeutic or supervisory bipersonal field.

It is important to allow you to continue, because there can be no doubt that this disturbing experience in supervision will influence the work between the patient and the therapist, creating a communicative flow that could only be described as the initiation of a countertransference-based disturbance by the supervisor into the supervisory bipersonal field and supervisee, and then passed on through the supervisee to the patient.

I must therefore stress again, because some have questioned my work in this respect, that I fully believe that we are learning far more from this supervisory presentation than from the first one, largely because of the destructive inputs of the supervisor. These inputs enable us to trace out and formulate crucial aspects of the supervisory bipersonal field that are usually relatively silent and difficult to document. So I want once again to apologize for my candidness, and trust that you understand the importance of these formulations and the many extremely critical insights we are deriving from them. I very much appreciate your sharing this material with us, and, while I am trying to use this supervisory situation as a model and as a point of departure for some general comments, I am well aware that my remarks are undoubtedly having a personal effect on you as well. But I can assure you that everyone in this room can find something of himself in your supervisory work, and that they will learn far more about themselves from this experience than from the first presentation, in which these factors were not nearly as prominent.

Supervisor B: The supervisee went on to describe the next session. The patient came in and said that he felt sad and rejected. The supervisee immediately asked, What kind of things do you want from your wife?

Langs: Now, this is really most interesting. I will hardly comment on the double meaning of the patient's initial associations, and the manner in which they reflect his growing depression and sense of rejection because of the way in which the therapist has been intervening. I will also have little to say about the supervisee's continued efforts at questioning and at maintaining a bastion in which communications regarding herself and her interaction with the patient are sealed off, or about her continuing to offer the patient Type C barriers.

I want mainly to concentrate on this first communication from the supervisee in the adaptive context of the supervisory experience. In principle, if you identify an important adaptive context, whether it is in the therapeutic or the supervisory interaction, its influence will be reflected in the communications from both the patient and the therapist. Here, I am using an adaptive context drawn from supervision—the supervisor's silence and single comment—as a means of understanding the communication from the therapist. I see it as an intervention that is manifestly directed at the patient, while latently directed at the supervisor. Certainly in the adaptive context of the supervisor's traumatic intervention, this question by the therapist takes on unconscious Type Two derivative meaning. In fact, since this supervisee is still quite active, we will have a special opportunity to trace out the influence of the supervisory experience in her work with this patient.

Specifically, this supervisee came to the supervisor filled with needs to learn how to become a therapist. I have offered the hypothesis that the supervisor failed to meet these needs, and that he placed the therapist in a painfully deserted, anxious, and helpless position. And we can readily recognize the influence of this input from the supervisor in this initial question: the supervisee, her needs unmet, asks the patient what he wants from his wife. The supervisee is concerned with what is appropriate to ask of those who fulfill your needs; unconsciously, she is asking the patient to work over this question, and to help her with her own sense of frustration regarding the things she wanted from the supervisor. And while some of you might suggest that this question was shaped entirely or mainly from the communication from the patient, I would respond that this was probably a secondary influence, and that the question was beautifully shaped by countertransference-based inputs from the supervisor. These inputs that have left the resident wondering what she could justifiably want of supervision, and possibly, how she might convey her needs and ultimately obtain satisfaction in supervision, in the form of appropriate teaching interventions.

Unconsciously, then, to this resident, the supervisor is something like a caretaker and need provider—a spouse. And there is a certain amount of truth in that conception—the supervisee is entitled to appropriate forms of care and gratification. One could develop a similar unconscious analogy between the therapist and his patient, a husband and wife, or a mother and a child—so long as we recognize that in each situation there are specific appropriate needs and specific appropriate forms of gratification. In therapy, these take the form of valid management of the framework and interpretations, while in supervision they are expressed through some degree of management of the framework and, especially, proper supervisory interventions. Let's hear more.

Supervisor B: To the question of what things the patient wanted from his wife, he answered: Friendship, company, and love. The supervisee then said, Looking back into your past, is there anyone else you wanted those things from?

Langs: Well, I hope that the principles of exquisite fit, of parsimonious explanation, and of validation through Type Two derivative communication help you all to see that, using my formulation as an organizer, these questions from the resident take shape as extremely meaningful unconscious communications—in significant part, designed as adaptive reactions to supervision. Her interventions actually constitute projective identifications by the supervisee into the patient of her own problems with the supervisor and the pathological introjects derived from the supervisory experience—introjects she is having difficulty managing. They disturb her to the point where she turns to the patient, attempting, as Wangh (1962) so nicely described, to evoke proxy responses: to have the patient help her with her pathological supervisory introject.

And the clue is, of course, her asking the patient was there anyone else that he wanted those things from. Incidentally, this is a pathological use of the patient as a container for the therapist's and supervisor's psychopathology, and in no sense is it in the best interest of the patient to burden him unconsciously with these problems. These are introjects that the supervisee should be working over on her own, either in her own treatment or through some effort at self-analysis. Burdening the patient with these problems will only generate additional chaos, even though it will afford the patient an opportunity to be unconsciously interpretive and helpful. Therapists with unconscious needs of this kind almost never realize the underlying nature of their interaction with the patient, and they fail to recognize or understand his therapeutic responses if they do occur.

Supervisor B: To this, the patient responded, From my mother and sister. The supervisee said, Females? And the patient said, Yes, I remember my mother babying us, giving us a lot of attention, constantly telling us how much she loved us. Despite all of that, my sister felt that my mother had failed us.

Langs: I will refrain from further extended formulations of this material in terms of the patient's introjective identifications of the therapist's manifest indications of wishes to be helpful, and her underlying failure to do so. As we listen, each of you can attempt to further monitor this material in terms of the adaptive context of the therapist's continued excessive questioning.

For my part, I will concentrate on the interaction between the supervisory and therapeutic bipersonal fields. On that level, it is the supervisor who is experienced by both supervisee and patient as attempting to be helpful and yet failing. In particular, note the patient's wish for friendship and love from both his mother and sister—this may well allude to the therapist and her supervisor. I would propose that as a tentative hypothesis awaiting further confirmation.

In the actual supervisory situation, had I responded as this supervisor had in the prior hour, I would use this material to acknowledge my having failed the supervisee. And I would then develop a series of formulations related to the therapeutic interaction itself, and indicate ways in which the supervisee could begin to intervene, beginning with a rectification of the frame by bringing under control her excessive use of questions. This would require a further discussion of the model of neurosis, the nature of the patient's communications, and the concepts of adaptive context and derivatives. But since I have already described much of this supervisory work, I will, as I said, try now to concentrate on the fate of the pathological supervisory introject.

Supervisor B: The patient said: My father, on the other

hand, tried to show attention, but I turned him off. I had a lot of bad feelings toward him; I keep my distance and I'm quite cold. The supervisee inquired, What happens when you don't get attention?

Langs: Okay, do you hear it? Now we have a sequence of interventions: "What do you do when you don't get what you need? Who do you turn to? What happens when you don't get attention?" You can see how this supports my formulation that the therapist is attempting to place into the patient her conscious and unconscious problems with her supervisor, and aspects of the pathological supervisory introject, and that she is, indeed, asking for proxied responses—for the patient's assistance. I must say that I have seldom seen such efforts, which are virtually universal, so clearly expressed. As a rule, the supervisor seldom knows the nature of the therapist's problems or the specific adaptive contexts and traumas that he is inappropriately working over in his therapeutic interaction. Usually, we are limited to recognizing the inappropriateness of an intervention, to suggesting that it is based on some countertransference difficulty in the supervisee, and to defining its nature and function as the patient unconsciously experiences it, and we leave it to the resident to work over the problem.

By contrast, this is really an extremely unique opportunity to demonstrate the fate of introjects, the manner in which they get reprojected, the use of the patient as a pathological container and as a proxy, and other interactional mechanisms of this type. It demonstrates too that countertransference-based interventions can be derived not only from adaptive contexts directly involving the patient, but from those stemming from outside relationships, especially with the supervisor. And I very much hope that you can see how the defined adaptive context related to supervision so clearly illuminates one unconscious dimension of the supervisee's communications to the patient, and demonstrates their Type Two derivative qualities. In that context, her question is a moving one: Where do you turn when you don't get the help you need in supervision? This supervisee feels quite helpless, and her own answer, unconsciously, is that you turn to your patients. And let all therapists be wary of such propensities; they are ubiquitous and need to be recognized and controlled.

Supervisor B: The patient continued, saying he feels bad when he doesn't get attention, and then he turns to his wife. He feels jealous when he doesn't get attention; it happened often with other women before he was married. Once he was engaged and was afraid that he would lose his fiancée's attention, but when she finally broke the engagement he was not devastated, he didn't die. Here, the resident intervened: Tell me more about your need for attention.

Langs: This is really quite exquisite. In the face of early formulations of just how sick this patient appeared to be, we can only marvel at his unconscious capacities, and the extent to which he functions as an extremely capable proxy. Unconsciously, he tells the therapist that she should not be jealous of those who receive attention, including possibly even himself at a point where he may get help from this therapist. But he goes on to quite movingly state that these are unrealistic fears, that if someone fails the therapist, she won't be devastated or die—she should be able to handle it. And so he tells her to seek substitutes, but to recognize her own capacity to survive, offering her models that might help her manage the disruptive aspects of the supervisory situation.

Supervisor B: The patient continued: Sometimes I feel that I would be better off if I was not married. I need attention. I liked it when I was a child, and I got a lot of attention from an older brother, but then he left and my mother gave all of her attention to my sister. The resident said, But you were a child then. Yes, the patient responded, I used to get punished a lot. The resident said, But you are not a child now. And the patient said, But I still need attention.

Langs: On the level on which I am formulating this material, we hear the supervisee attempting to mobilize a model that would foster her own capacity to manage the pathological supervisory introject: You are not a child now, although you were a child then. Remember what the supervisor said to the resident: You are a doctor, you have been in practice for several years, you have responsibility. This may have been one of the positive kernels in this otherwise destructive and anxiety-provoking supervisory intervention, and the patient now attempts to draw upon it in her discussion with the patient.

I must pause briefly to remind us of my earlier discussion of supervisory introjects, because here we are studying a negative introject evoked by a failure to intervene and an anxiety-provoking comment. And you can see the unconscious influence of this introject, how much it shaped the supervisee's questions to the patient. And I hope you can thereby recognize the influence of the supervisory bipersonal field on the therapeutic field, and of the supervisor on the supervisee as it is then passed on to the patient. Make no mistake about it: the handing down of pathological introjects from analyst to analysand, from patient to therapist, and from supervisor to supervisee, is an all too common occurrence.

And you may remember too that I mentioned Searles's discussion (1955) of parallel processes in therapy and supervision, although his stress was on the manner in which the supervisor's experience of the supervisee can provide clues to parallel processes taking place in the therapeutic bipersonal field. This material provides an opportunity to demonstrate the presence of a process initiated in the supervisory bipersonal field, which then creates its double in the therapeutic field, and it shows something of the complexity of the interactional mechanisms involved.

Discussant: This sounds to me like an alliance between the supervisee and the patient to be supportive of each other, in terms of what each of them feels he isn't getting. The therapist seems to be responding in a directive kind of way in this situation.

Langs: I would call this rather a *mis*alliance because alliance means essentially that the two are working toward cognitive insight, while here we are observing a misalliance and unconsciously shared problems—shared fantasies and shared needs—that are not being processed toward insight, but which involve exchanges of projective identifications, and what I would call a Type C form of so-called support—the use of clichés as a barrier to disturbing underlying truths.

So while I believe your comment is on a somewhat superficial level, it does touch upon a deeper truth. The therapist is not getting what she needs as a professional in supervision; the patient is not getting what he needs as a patient in treatment; and despite their respective and shared helplessness, they are attempting together to mobilize their available resources, even if on a level of a Type C cliché and barrier.

Supervisor B: The patient continued to describe his feelings of being jealous of others, of being left out, and how his parents' fighting made him feel left out. The patient only saw his father on Sundays, because he worked six days a week and late hours, and often the patient was stoned on drugs or something. Still, when his parents went out, he didn't feel quite so alone. Somehow, after his mother threatened suicide things were strange; she was different and often lost control. Here the resident stated, I don't know how we got into all of this.

Langs: Once again this is a remarkable representation of the supervisor's communication, and of the introject based on it. It is a disclaimer of responsibility and an expression of confusion; the therapist now puts this into the patient, much as the supervisor had placed it into the supervisee.

Unconsciously, it also conveys a request to the patient to change the subject, to move away from these disturbing communications, based again on the implication that the therapist is unable to manage the relevant introjects, fantasies, and perceptions. But this too reflects the response of the supervisor to the supervisee's disturbing communications. Notice that the intervention followed the mention of a suicide threat—neither therapist nor supervisor feel prepared to deal with that subject, and the therapist took in the supervisor's anxieties in this area and now offers a pathological defense to herself and the patient designed to foster avoidance. After all, this is almost a direct appeal to the patient to serve as both therapist and supervisor, to help anchor and understand what is happening in the therapy—largely because neither the therapist nor the supervisor has been able to do so. So much of this material is uncanny in light of what we know about the supervision. Notice, for example, the reference to the parents' fighting, and how the patient suffered because of it. We must wonder about how much is conveyed to the patient through unconscious communications from the therapist—it seems like a great deal comes across.

Supervisor B: Well, the patient's response was, We were talking about getting attention. Next the therapist said, Are your thoughts any better lately? Here the patient responded by saying, Yes, I am going to night school and I have a daytime job. I don't have those obsessive thoughts about hurting my wife any more, and I don't have so much of a fear of losing control.

Langs: Well, whatever this is based on, it cannot be founded on cognitive insights and an introjection of an understanding and well-managing therapist. This may well be a mobilization of the patient's resources in the face of a significant lack of help from the therapist, and from her supervisor. Some would call this a flight into health, and others might term it a misalliance cure, but I believe that for the moment the basis of this symptomatic change eludes understanding largely because the therapist has been so hyperactive; it is almost impossible to follow the unconscious threads from the patient. This is why I have offered a rather general and uncertain hypothesis that this symptom relief constitutes a mobilization of the patient's resources and, possibly, an unconscious curative thrust directed toward the therapist, undertaken by offering himself as a model of control in the hope of rectifying the therapeutic bipersonal field so that he could again attempt to deal with his underlying problems. Perhaps too this is the patient's offer to the therapist of a model: go to school, obtain adequate supervision, and matters will improve. This is a not uncommon response under conditions such as these.

Supervisor B: So, the patient said that he felt he was in control. However, he added, In school sometimes, I am nervous. Somehow, I feel now that I am getting better, but that we will have to reach some further conclusions about these thoughts and maybe then I'll be able to put them away. And here the resident said, Who will have to do it?

Langs: Now the associations from the patient suggest symptom relief through the development of Type C barriers and clichés, through the mobilization of massive defenses. But without dwelling upon that, let's look again at the therapist's intervention: "Who will have to do it?" And I must say that if I could have written a scenario for this seminar, I could never have written a better one. Just look at the variations on this theme of who will help, and how? And just look at the expressions of this supervisory introject: Who will take responsibility, she asks; who will do the therapeutic work?

This intervention certainly reflects her confusion and self-doubts, and her belief that the supervisor too is incapable of the necessary therapeutic understanding and work. But is also plays back as a Type Two derivative the unconscious supervisory introject based on the supervisor's comment, though once again she projectively identifies it into the patient. Based on this intervention, I see the patient's symptomatic relief as a mobilization of barriers against the psychopathology of the patient himself, the therapist's and the supervisor's. His response is something like, I'd better get better and get the hell out of here before I am destroyed. (Laughter.) It is as if for the moment the patient is the healthiest member in the two bipersonal fields, but frankly, I do not believe that he will be able to maintain the mobilization of these rigid defenses for very long. And unless the therapist herself introjects some strength from these communications, and unless the supervisor does something similar and begins to offer helpful interventions, I very much feel that this therapeutic situation would soon deteriorate again.

Supervisor B: This is how the session ended.

Langs: Had you said anything to the supervisee in this session?

Supervisor B: I am sure that I had. I certainly saw the material quite differently than you, but I really can't put it all together.

Langs: Can't you remember anything? You can see how it would be virtually impossible to understand what follows without knowing your intervention.

Supervisor B: Well, I think that I pointed out to her that she was pushing the material away from herself, and that she was trying to close over material, to cover it up. I can also remember giving her some information about transference, and suggesting that the patient was beginning to transfer onto her, and that's why he was settling down more: because he now felt he had her attention. And I suggested that prior to this, he felt that he didn't have his wife's or his mother's attention, and that I think that he now felt that he had a stronger relationship with the therapist, and that she was controlling him in the sense that he was experiencing less fear of his own thoughts—largely because he felt that there was someone there helping him. And I added that I felt that he was entering into a positive transference and that he was feeling that he was getting something from her, and that therefore he didn't have the murderous thoughts against his wife.

Langs: Well, that is an interesting alternative formulation. And if time would permit, we could review the material from the patient to see whether it documents your hypothesis, though frankly I do not believe that it would do so. It seems to me that you are confining yourself to some general impressions, and that you are working without a specific adaptive context. But despite that, it is evident that you had responded to the supervisee's confrontation, and probably to the material of this particular session, recognized the need to intervene and had attempted to do so, alluding to countertransference-based defenses in the therapist and trying to delineate some positive elements of the therapeutic relationship and of the treatment situation. The effect of the supervisory interventions will depend very much on their validity, though I would expect that the supervisee will in any case respond more positively to your efforts to now be helpful.

Without going back over this session, I would like to hear the opening of the following hour to see whether it validates your hypothesis of the development of positive transference, or my hypothesis that the patient had been forced, so to speak, to work over hostile and negative introjects projected interactionally into him by the therapist, based on her own difficulties and those of the supervisor.

For the moment, I would stress the manner in which the supervisee's and patient's material and responses had a curative effect on you. I would even suggest that there is a sequence here in which you placed some of your pathology into the supervisee, who placed it into the patient, who responded in a curative manner, enabling the supervisee to confront you, and you to mobilize your resources. In brief, the patient seems to have cured both his therapist and her supervisor. But it is important to be open to such influences, and to recognize supervisory failures and to modify your approach when needed.

There is certainly a kernel of truth to your focus on the therapeutic relationship, even though I would not have discussed this material primarily in terms of transference, but in terms of both transference and nontransference. But the main point is that at least you have begun to show the supervisee that she is experiencing anxieties about her interaction with the patient, and that she was being overly defensive. You initiated some of the supervisory work that she very much needed, and perhaps she will now have less of a need to use the patient for such purposes.

All of this can serve as a reminder that, while it is not the main purpose of supervision in any sense, the supervisor in the course of his work may not only learn a great deal, but may actually benefit therapeutically—so long as he is open to such possibilities. The supervisor should not in any sense permit the supervisory bipersonal field to become a medium for his own therapy, nor for that of the supervisee, but such benefits may accrue in the course of appropriate teaching efforts.

Well, I see that the hour is drawing to a close. Let's just hear a bit of the next session and we will stop.

Supervisor B: The patient began this hour by saying that he felt insecure while he was growing up.

Langs: Well, I suspect that this reflects the continued influence of the therapist's inappropriate interventions, and that it may forebode a return of his symptoms. Certainly, it does not seem to point toward any sense of positive transference. Perhaps too this is an immediate effort by the patient to reassure the therapist: your problems with me will pass; they just reflect growing pains.

Supervisor B: Here the resident asked, What was the insecurity about? The patient responded: Well, my mother kept threatening to leave us all the time. And now I am dependent on my wife as I was dependent earlier on my sister, even though I would like to be self-reliant. Here the resident said, But on the other hand, what holds you back from being independent? No, excuse me. The resident actually said, What holds you back from becoming more self-reliant? The patient said, I don't know.

Langs: Here I believe we have evidence of a somewhat different tone in the therapist's interventions: now she says, why can't you be more self-reliant? This may well reflect a supervisory introject based on your more positive interventions—a point that I can only offer as a tentative hypothesis for the moment. Still, as a model, you can see a new sequence: constructive efforts by the supervisor, a positive tone in the therapist's nonetheless premature intervention (perhaps for the first time), and now we need only a positive response in the patient to complete a cycle of more constructive projective and introjective identifications.

Supervisor B: The patient then responded, I would really like to be more self-reliant, but I am afraid to be; I don't like to go out and I don't enjoy meeting new people. The resident asked, Is this something new? The patient said, I was never very close to women, but I did begin to depend on my wife, and that's how I am now. The resident asked, What would happen when you went on a date?

Langs: I think that the supervisee's interventions are, indeed, while still countertransference-based and intrusive, directed much more now toward independence, adequate functioning, and being on your own. It's actually a curious mixture, in that it is a continuation of the offer by the therapist of Type C barriers—of defenses against communications more directly related to the therapeutic relationship—yet still, the contents of the barrier have shifted from being frightened, uncontrolled, childish, and helpless to being far more positively toned and self-reliant. Again, I would stress that this is an influence of the new supervisory introject. The patient seems to be responding to this change in the therapist with clearer use of the Type A mode.

Supervisor B: I remember now that when the supervisee said that she thought that the patient should cut down, I had asked her why. And she said, I think that the patient is too sick. And I said that I didn't think that the patient was that sick, and I told her that I was not quite sure why she had the patient on medication. And it was that comment that seemed to have stirred the supervisee up: here I was saying that I didn't think the patient needed medication or was that sick, and she took the other position that he is too sick, and should be out of therapy.

Langs: In that connection, the patient gave the therapist an opportunity to explore the meaning of the medication and to eventually terminate its use, when he said something in the earlier hour about being on medication and how his wife doesn't like it. It is important to allow the patient's unconscious derivatives, understood within the therapeutic and adaptive context of the prescription of medication, to lead you to the cessation of medication and to the relevant interpretations. In principle, never direct the patient or introduce any concept arbitrarily. Once you have structured the treatment, let the patient be the guide; he will put into you all of the elements that you need for any intervention.

Well, I could go on with additional comments about medication, but I want to leave a few minutes for final questions. I've said a great deal today, and I certainly do not expect you to absorb it all. Still, I hope to have initiated an extensive searching process. And I've tried to show you in a very real and live way the kind of issues that actually come up in supervision, the truth of its influence on the supervisee and patient, and the importance of conceptualizing supervision in terms of these realities.

Discussant: Dr. Langs, how might you have handled the situation if the supervisee, at this point, had asked for a new supervisor?

Langs: Well, I would have taken that as an indication of a crisis situation and as a sign that I have been failing the supervisee in some important way—undoubtedly based on some unresolved countertransferences. Much would depend on my evaluation of the factors involved in this request. Under the conditions that we have seen here, I would discuss openly and directly with the supervisee the nature of her dissatisfactions, in the hope of recognizing my own contributions and of rectifying them—thereby modifying my supervisory approach so that it would be more satisfying and helpful to the supervisee.

In general, I think that it is best to maintain the supervision if at all feasible, and to work things out rather than initiate a change that could seriously cover over the contributions of both the supervisee and the supervisor to the crisis that had led to this request. I would therefore attempt to frankly indicate an awareness of my own failings, and suggest to the supervisee that I am now more aware of these difficulties and that I feel that I can, indeed, be more helpful. I would add that while I appreciate her wish to consider another supervisor, I would suggest that she attempt to continue to work with me for a while in the hope of generating a far more satisfactory supervisory experience.

Time is short, but I must quickly add some qualifying statements: First, if we are thinking of general principles, a request to change supervisors must lead to an appraisal of difficulties in both supervisor and supervisee. As you would expect, there would be a natural tendency in the supervisor to blame the supervisee—for example, to feel that the supervisee is frightened of sound supervision and sound therapy. All of that may be true, but nonetheless, it does not preclude a personal investigation by the supervisor for his own countertransference-based inputs. Then, in discussing the request with the supervisee, I would attempt to openly and honestly identify all of the factors that have contributed to this request, and would make every effort to work them out with the supervisee. Much will depend on the state of the supervisory alliance: if there is a positive tone to the supervisory relationship, much can be endured and then worked out.

Secondly, I think that it is important to acknowledge and accept one's failures when they are indeed unresolvable. While I do feel that in general the resolution of the supervisor's countertransference difficulties should take precedence over a change in supervisor, one must face his limitations and recognize that he may not be able to master certain anxieties and difficulties related to a given supervisory situation—as they pertain to either the patient or the supervisee, or to both—and then it would be quite appropriate, after the necessary effort has failed, to arrange a transfer to a new supervisor. That is certainly a painful experience for both supervisor and supervisee, but it is the kind of pain that can also generate growth.

Well, I see that we are nearly done. I would therefore like to point you now to the future with two very brief comments. First, I very much hope that this conference has provided you a basic framework not only for your coming individual supervisory efforts, but also for the investigations into the supervisory process that you plan to undertake as a group. I think it was extremely courageous of you to undertake a conference of this sort and I do hope that what you have experienced will motivate you to pursue additional meetings of this kind, even without an outside chairman. I would add only this: I also hope I have demonstrated that not only are conferences of supervisors essential to maintaining the vitality and validity of the supervisory work at any teaching center, but also that the actual, sequential presentation of supervisory process notes is really the only means through which such conferences can come to life and enable its participants to become aware of the difficult but realistic problems and issues that arise day after day in the supervisory situation, all the while providing clinical data with which to investigate and clarify these areas.

Finally, it has really, interestingly enough, just occurred to me that we have said nothing of self-supervision. That in itself is an enormous and neglected topic, well worth separate investigation. Certainly, it should be self-evident that every therapist has a fundamental responsibility to himself and to his patients to maintain a continuous self-supervisory attitude as part of his therapeutic position in every session. Basic to these endeavors is the predictive-validating methodology that I have developed with you in today's seminar, as is the coincidental use of, and benefit from, the patient's unconscious supervisory efforts. Just as self-analysis is a never ending task for every therapist and analyst, self-supervision is a necessary variation on this theme.

Moderator: Well, our time is up, and we certainly want to thank Dr. Langs and our two colleagues who have presented here today.

Langs: Yes, before we conclude, I want to express my deepest appreciation to both presenters. Perhaps more than they realize, it took considerable courage and strength to present their own supervisory work and to help us to break what has been in general an unnecessary taboo in the field. We are all indebted to them. And I am certain that we will all respect their own need for confidentiality, and that in addition, we will all respond with a sense of humility: There but for he go I.

Moderator: Yes, I think that we all have experienced something very moving and informative, and perhaps even a bit curative. You have given us a great deal to consider, and we all hope that this will be the initiation of many similar kinds of growth-promoting experiences. Thank you very much.

Part II

Chapter 5

The Patient as Unconscious Supervisor

This paper is an attempt to outline a basic and specific model of supervision founded on clinically derived principles. Its main thrust is that there is a set of fundamental tenets through which the supervisory situation may be established and explicated, and within which a given supervisor and supervisee may work in keeping with their respective therapeutic styles and the particular needs of the patient under supervision. Once the basic model is delineated, I will discuss a series of important but relatively neglected supervisory issues, with an eye toward their resolution. Stress will be placed on a methodology founded on prediction and validation. A brief clinical illustration will be offered, and the interested reader may turn to a series of publications in which I have discussed some of my views on supervision and presented in detail my own interpretation and application of the principles to be described here (see Langs 1973, 1974, 1976d, 1978c).

A Basic Model of Psychotherapy

It is self-evident that a supervisor's model of supervision—and hence his functioning as a supervisor—is founded on his conceptualization of the psychotherapeutic situation.* In brief (see also Langs 1973, 1974, 1976a,d, 1978c,g,i), insight-oriented or psychoanalytic psychotherapy may be conceptualized as taking place within a bipersonal field which is defined by the ground rules or framework that establishes the therapeutic situation and the conditions of its unfolding. With the patient at one pole and the therapist at the other, their communicative interaction takes place along an interface which ideally is determined primarily by the psychopathology of the patient, and by the adequate interpretive and management capacities of the therapist, although not infrequently the patient's (largely unconscious) valid functioning and the therapist's psychopathology play a major role, as they do in some small measure throughout the treatment. Most vital is a spiraling and unfolding communicative interaction, in which unconscious processes and mechanisms play a central role. These unconscious transactions provide the central adaptive stimuli and contexts for the two participants, and is the major realm of the therapist's interpretive work—to which are appended links to outside relationships and to the significant genetic past.

Basic to the therapeutic situation is the establishment and maintenance of the framework, which is essential for a sound therapeutic alliance, and which establishes the therapist's basic hold and containing capacities, as well as the communicative properties of the bipersonal field: the nature, function, and implications of the behaviors and

*The principles discussed in this paper are, by and large, equally applicable to both psychotherapy and psychoanalysis. Since most of my previous studies and reported supervision are drawn from the former situation, I will use therapy as my model for this paper.

verbalizations of each participant. In addition to managing the framework, the therapist strives to offer essentially interpretive and reconstructive interventions which are determined by the patient's communicative style, the nature of the communicative field, and the available derivatives of the patient's pathological unconscious fantasies, memories, introjects, and the conflicts to which they are related. The basic goal of psychotherapy is that of adaptive, inner structural change, based on cognitive insights and the inevitable positive introjective identifications that accrue to the patient by virtue of the therapist's adequate management and interpretive functioning.

Both the therapist's silence and his application of the listening process (Langs 1978c) are among his most fundamental tools. The material from the patient may be organized in the cognitive sphere in terms of manifest and latent content. The latter may be classified as Type One derivatives, readily available inferences postulated from the manifest content, and as Type Two derivatives, which are organized dynamically and interactionally around the prevailing neurotic adaptive context (which usually refers to some aspect of the therapeutic interaction). On this basis, three communicative styles and fields can be identified: Type A, which is symbolic, illusory, and uses an imaginative play space; Type B, in which projective identification and action-discharge prevail; and Type C, in which intrapsychic and interpersonal barriers, falsifications, clichés, and impenetrable defenses are characteristic. Listening must be geared to the nature of the patient's prevailing communicative style, and must be directed to both the cognitive contents of the patient's material and to its interactional aspects: identification of role and image evocations (the object relational sphere), and recognition and processing of interactional projections or projective identifications (the interactional mechanism sphere). In addition to yielding understanding on the cognitive and interactional levels, these conceptualizations permit the identification of six types of interventions, which together constitute a complete armamentarium (Langs 1978b): silences; establishing and managing the framework; interpretations and reconstructions; the playing back of derivatives in the absence of an identified adaptive context related to the therapeutic interaction; the interpretive processing of projective identifications; and the interpretive playback of metaphors of the Type C communicative style and field.

The Basic Model of Supervision

The structure and nature of the supervisory situation is determined by its ground rules and framework (Langs 1975b, where these are set out for the therapeutic situation). To be specific, supervision should be defined in terms of set fees, hours, and length of sessions, though there is latitude and flexibility with each of these aspects. The discussion of the supervisory situation here is based primarily on individual supervision, though clearly supervision is feasible within a group format; it should, however, be realized that the presence of even necessary and agreed upon observers influences the supervisory interaction between supervisor and supervisee. The relative anonymity of the supervisor is a valid tenet for supervision, though minimal and carefully selected personal revelations are acceptable as long as they are pertinent to the clinical work and are not unduly self-exposing. On the other hand, total confidentiality is a sine qua non and should be strictly observed; it is vital to a sound supervisory alliance in which the supervisee is safely and securely held and may freely speak and expose his difficulties, and is equally necessary for the supervisor, who must be candid, though tactful, and able to speak without fear of the public misuse of his teaching efforts.

The counterpart in supervision to the fundamental rule of free association in therapy is the structuring of the supervisory experience around the *strictly sequential, direct presentation* of the process notes of the therapeutic transactions of the sessions under consideration. This method, for which there is no viable alternative, provides the supervisor the opportunity to experience the unfolding therapeutic interaction with some sense of how it actually took place, and in a manner that fosters his empathic understanding of its influence on both patient and therapist. More important, however, this procedure is essential to the predictive, validating approach that is basic to the supervisory model proposed here.

It is a procedure that requires either a remarkable capacity for remembering on the part of the supervisee, or the writing of notes immediately after each therapy session as a means of providing the necessary material for the supervisory process. While note-taking does indeed alter one of the basic aspects of the optimal approach to each therapy session—characterized by Bion (1970) as entering each hour without desire, memory, or understanding—it is nonetheless one of the necessary alterations in the fundamental framework of the therapeutic situation that arises under conditions of supervision, along with modifications in confidentiality and the one-to-one relationship (the supervisor becomes a third party to treatment).

These changes, justified by the fact that psychotherapy cannot be learned without supervision, will affect the psychotherapy, and both patient and therapist, in major ways that are as a rule difficult for supervisees to appreciate and handle interpretively. As modifications of the frame, however, they come up repeatedly in derivative form throughout such a therapy, and constitute a major adaptive context for the listening process of both supervisor and supervisee (see Langs 1975b, 1976a,d, 1978c).

The conditions of the supervisory bipersonal field preclude the psychotherapy of the supervisee: the situation does not call for or permit his free associations, nor is a framework created that would permit analysis of his manifest and derivative communications. On the other hand, conditions are established for supervisory interventions directed toward the analysis and understanding of the therapeutic interaction under study, and toward the theoretical and technical education of the supervisee. To this end, each supervisory session should begin without direct recall of the prior therapy sessions or supervisory hour—the equivalent in supervision to approaching the treatment hour without desire, memory, or understanding.

One final quality of the supervisory alliance must be mentioned: the supervisor's commitment must be primarily to the patient in therapy and only secondarily to the trainee; physicianly responsibilities precede all else in any type of therapeutic situation. Supervisory interventions for which the supervisee may be unprepared are thus at times indicated, in the interests of securing for the patient a sound therapy situation. As might be expected, it is therefore especially crucial for the supervisor to the patient, tactful, careful in his explanations, and even, at times, directly supportive, because of the difficult discussions and confrontations he often must have with the supervisee.

Within this basic framework, I must again stress, a predictive approach is essential. Virtually all of the supervisor's interventions should be derived directly from the process notes of the supervised therapeutic interaction, should be couched as formulations with definitive and predictive qualities, and must be open to validation from the subsequent material from the session—from both patient and therapist. While incidental comments from the supervisee, or his unanticipated recollection of previously repressed aspects of a session or of forgotten information about the patient, may be taken as second-order validation, first-order validation must always take the form of the communication of Type Two derivatives from within the therapeutic situation under study.

A first type of supervisory situation arises when the supervisor develops a formulation before the supervisee has offered any intervention that might suggest, or have been predicted by, the formulation in question. If the formulation is correct, subsequent material from the patient should, in indirect, derivative, and coalescing form, provide otherwise unanticipated illumination and elaboration of the conception. As a rule, a correctly developed supervisory assessment should be "echoed" by the patient in the form of Type Two derivatives which communicate in disguised form (and the patient's own language) the supervisor's ideas and their implications. Ultimate validation occurs when the supervisee reports having intervened to the patient in a manner seen as consistent with the supervisor's formulation and when the patient, in response, provides an appropriate Type Two derivative. Optimally, this takes the form of a selected fact (Bion 1962) which organizes the known material in a new and unforeseen manner that reveals its latent meaning.

The same principles as apply to the supervisee's interventions to the patient apply as well to any additional formulations he might offer during supervision. This predictive, validating methodology is so essential to supervision that it must be applied without exception to every clinical formulation developed; further, it must be taught to the trainee in order to help him master the listening process and all its components—including the validating process (Langs 1978c).

As with interventions in the therapeutic situation (see Langs 1973, 1976a, 1978c), there is for supervisory interventions a definitive hierarchy of indications. Virtually without exception, and in marked contrast to the principles governing interventions in therapy, the supervisor should be prepared to intervene one or more times in any supervisory hour. Though the subject merits considerable empirical investigation, I propose the following order of precedence for problems calling for definitive supervisory interventions (with a full understanding that patience and tact should prevail, and that these interventions should be derived in specific fashion from the process notes at hand): first, indications in the direct supervisory interaction, or, more indirectly, in the therapeutic situation, of the presence of countertransference difficulties in the supervisor (defined here as any expression of his psychopathology)—including any crisis in supervision; second, any indication of countertransference difficulties in the supervisee, including any crisis in therapy; third, any major issue regarding the framework of the supervisory or therapeutic situations; fourth, any major accumulation of resistances within the patient, or any stalemate in the therapeutic interaction; and fifth, the appearance in the material from the patient of derivatives related to core pathological unconscious fantasies, memories, and introjects. This hierarchy should serve as a rough guide in respect to the order of importance of supervisory issues, and as a framework for the supervisor's decisions on intervening.

In general, the supervisor should, at the beginning of each supervisory hour, allow the description of the session at hand to unfold for a while. At a point when he is able to develop a pertinent formulation related to any of the issues just described (or any other important aspect of the material or interaction), he should voice his conceptualization in a form comparable to the silent hypotheses made by the therapist in the opening phase of each session. These formulations are then open to validation from the subsequent material.

The next major juncture for supervisory comments occurs when the supervisor spots an indication for intervention that the supervisee has missed. In order of precedence, this would occur in the presence of countertransference difficulties unconsciously introjected by the patient from the supervisee; the appearance of related interactional resistances; a major rupture in the therapeutic alliance; any basic alteration in the framework; or the presence of coalescing derivatives related to resistances and core fantasies, memories, and introjects. The supervisor's formulation and proposed intervention (the latter should be stated in the actual language that would have been used with the patient) are then open to subsequent Type Two validation in the material that follows. Implicit here is an assessment that the therapist's silence reflects a countertransference-based failure to intervene—a topic that can be introduced through the material that follows from the patient, who will, as a rule, respond to such errors with unconscious supervisory communications (see below).

A third point of supervisory intervention occurs whenever the supervisee has himself intervened. In principle, this is a vital moment for definitive supervisory work. It is crucial here first to define the formal nature of the intervention (beyond silences, this includes questions, clarifications, confrontations, interpretations, reconstructions, and managements of the framework; see Langs 1978b), and, second and more important, to delineate the unconscious communicative qualities of the intervention. It is these qualities that will be most crucial to the patient's responses, as they define the underlying nature of the adaptive context the patient will be working over—consciously and unconsciously, validly and with distortions—in the associations that follow an intervention. An appreciation of this material, which is best viewed as a *commentary* on, and *transversal communications* related to, the therapist's effort (see Langs 1978d), of this material, is feasible only if these unconscious elements have been identified and stated as a means of predicting the patient's response—a step then open to Type Two validation.

All supervisory interventions should, then, be as specific and clinically definitive as possible. Validation from the subsequent therapeutic interaction is vital and should be evaluated independently by both supervisor and supervisee. It is through his own application of the validating process (Langs 1976d, 1978c,i) that the supervisee should assess the quality of the supervisor's interventions—and of his silences or failures to comment, as well. In addition to this basic clinical foundation, the first priority in supervision, the supervisor should, as a second priority, feel free to allude to the pertinent literature, to suggest relevant readings, and to discuss briefly the broader issues raised by the material of the therapeutic interaction.

Last in order of precedence in supervisory teaching, though somewhat overlapping with the priorities already described, is attention to a basic teaching program, outlined for the one or two year period over which most supervisory experiences are extended. In general, with many exceptions based on the requisites of the therapeutic interaction under study and the immediate needs of the patient and the supervisee, teaching should begin with the listening and validating processes (Langs 1978c), since this is fundamental to the understanding of every transaction in both the therapeutic and the supervisory situations. In this respect, the application of what I have termed *listening exercises* (1978c) is a basic teaching vehicle well worth repetition in early supervisory sessions.

These exercises entail listening to a segment of material from the patient, identifying the central adaptive context, formulating the manifest content and Type One and Type Two derivatives, and monitoring them in terms of the ongoing therapeutic interaction, especially along the me/not-me interface, recognizing that every communication from the patient refers on some level to the therapeutic experience, and quite specifically to both patient and therapist. Each formulation so derived is then evaluated for its veridical and valid, and its fantasied and distorted, elements. Full use is made of the abstracting-particularizing process, as well as the self-knowledge of the therapist.

Perhaps most overlooked in this regard is the importance of applying the listening process to the patient's unconscious perceptions and introjections of the therapist's communications. Even more neglected are the patient's unconscious perceptions and introjections of the *supervisor's* interventions as they are consciously and unconsciously communicated to the patient through the supervisee. There has been a great tendency among therapists and analysts to focus on the "me" part of this interface—the patient's self-representations and projections onto the therapist (mainly transference and distortion) and to neglect the "not me" part—the usually valid, though sometimes distorted introjections of qualities of the supervisee and the supervisor, and the patient's object-representations and introjective experiences vis-à-vis the therapist. In the supervisory situation, it is this not-me dimension that proves most difficult and yet critical to formulate in regard to both the therapeutic and the supervisory interactions; it is of course the essential realm of countertransference-based influences, from both supervisor and supervisee, and the most likely arena for blind spots and other cognitive difficulties.

After the listening and validating processes, the nature, functions, and implications of the ground rules of therapy deserve emphasis, since the therapist's establishment and maintenance of the framework expresses his holding and containing capacities, and provides the essential conditions and medium for the interactional expression of the patient's neurosis (a term used here in its broadest sense to allude to all psychopathology) in a manner that is analyzable and open to shifts toward adaptive mastery. The therapist's explication of these basic tenets is rich in unconscious communication and determines, as well, the basic communicative properties both of the therapeutic situation and of supervision. Next, the supervisor should concentrate on the therapeutic relationship, especially the unconscious communicative interaction, and, finally, on a study of interventions (Langs 1978b). With this as the fundamental model of the supervisory situation and its transactions, let us now turn to a number of clinically relevant and relatively neglected problems that may arise in the course of supervision.

Some Communicative Properties of the Supervisory Bipersonal Field

Depending on a wide range of factors within the supervisor, the supervisee, and the patient under supervision, as well as in the structure and maintenance of the framework, the supervisory bipersonal field will acquire communicative characteristics which may, however, fluctuate. The ideal supervisor, of course, uses predominantly the Type A communicative mode, through which he formulates, abstracts and particularizes, uses language symbolically, and maintains the framework of supervision in a manner permitting full play to illusion and fantasy, while promoting understanding and learning.

Unfortunately, many supervisors are quite unaware of their usual communicative style; in addition, a particular supervisee or patient may prompt the supervisor to a shift to the Type B or Type C mode. It is, of course, the responsibility of each supervisor to be aware of his propensities toward these latter modes of communication and supervision, and to undertake the necessary self-analytic work that will enable him to become primarily a Type A communicator. In addition to self-awareness, a monitoring of the supervised therapeutic bipersonal field for its communicative qualities, which often mirror those within supervision, may provide clues that should then prompt the necessary investigation of the supervisory bipersonal field for Type B and Type C trends.

Almost always without his conscious awareness, the Type B supervisor uses the supervisory situation for unburdening himself of his own inner mental disturbances and for pathological projective identifications into the supervisee. He may tend to fragment the framework of the supervisory field and will intervene in a manner, despite his conscious intentions to the contrary, that satisfies his own pathological needs for action-discharge far more than the needs of the supervisee for understanding and guidance.

The Type C supervisor, by contrast, may just as likely maintain a rigid framework as one that is fragmented, but his supervisory work will be characterized by frequent failures to intervene, by the use of psychoanalytic clichés, and by relatively superficial formulations that are dynamically irrelevant or of only peripheral pertinence to the material being presented. His main efforts will be toward maintaining intrapsychic and interpersonal barriers designed to seal off any threat of inner disturbance or of the arousal of the psychotic part of his own personality, as well as that of the supervisee and the patient. While the Type A supervisor makes consistent and elaborate use of the listening and validating processes, and of the predictive methodology described here, neither the Type B nor the Type C supervisor will apply these processes with any sense of regularity, depth, or meaning. The Type B supervisor is likely to flit about, preferring to dump into the supervisee a variety of pressured formulations, while the Type C supervisor will hardly be concerned at all with validation or with the complexity of the material at hand; he will tend to oversimplify.

For his part, the supervisee capable of using the Type A mode of communication is able to present from process notes that are neither overly long nor too condensed. His formulations of the material from the patient is in the symbolic mode, and he has a strong capacity to understand the symbolic implications of the supervisor's communications. The Type B supervisee, by contrast, usually presents fragmented and disorganized notes, and becomes engaged in intense efforts to relieve himself of inner tension and to projectively identify pathological contents and mechanisms into the supervisor. In response, the supervisor must be capable of metabolizing these interactional pressures toward understanding, so that he may intervene in a manner that reflects a true capacity for reverie (Bion 1962). These supervisees often evoke crisis situations in therapy and supervision that will require direct discussion in addition to the usual supervisory efforts.

Finally, the Type C supervisee will tend to produce either extremely terse or overly lengthy notes, which serve primarily as a barrier to an affective, symbolic, meaningful understanding of the therapeutic interaction. His formulations will be abbreviated, clichéd, mechanical, and lacking in dynamic pertinence, and will as a rule tend to neglect the ongoing therapeutic interaction. Initial teaching efforts must therefore be directed toward the supervisee's pathological style of communication and presenting, in order to create the necessary conditions of the supervisory bipersonal field within which true learning and growth can occur. In general, then, the teaching approach of the supervisor should be greatly influenced by the communicative mode of the supervisee.

As part of the interaction between the supervisory and therapeutic bipersonal fields, the communicative style of the patient may have considerable influence on the supervisory dyad. The Type A patient opens both therapist and supervisor to regressive pressures and exposes both to the psychotic parts of each of the three principals. While this may foster a therapeutic regression and a very constructive supervisory learning situation, this generally will not occur without a strong measure of anxiety and threat, which entails a risk of the use of pathological defenses in either supervisor or supervisee.

The Type B patient may reinforce comparable communicative propensities, if present in both supervisor and supervisee. At times such a patient may even prompt the use of Type C barriers by either the therapist or his mentor, based largely on their inability to metabolize and understand the prevailing interactional pressures. The Type C patient may promote the use of a comparable communicative mode in the supervisor or supervisee, or may evoke provocative countertransference-based projective identifications. Patients of this type often contribute to very hollow and stalemated supervisory experiences.

As a fundamental component of the supervisory bipersonal field, the communicative styles of supervisor and supervisee, as well as of the patient, deserve first-order attention in the supervisory experience. Any trend toward the use of a pathological communicative mode in the supervisor must be identified, rectified, and subjected to self-analysis while such disturbances in the supervisee must be a matter of fundamental supervisory concern. Communicative mode is basic to the nature and function of the supervisee's presentation, and therefore to the material available from the therapeutic situation for teaching purposes. Since the supervisee's communicative style will be reflected in his work with both the patient and the supervisor (an aspect of the reflection process described in Searles 1955), it is, as a rule, feasible to use the presentation of process notes to confront and discuss disturbances in communicative style in the supervisee. Every effort should be made to carry out such discussions on this basis, though at times of crisis a more direct confrontation may be necessary. It is here, by the way, that some of the limitations of the supervisory situation become evident.

The Supervisor's Countertransferences

There has been a rather striking neglect in the literature of the supervisor's countertransferences, the expressions of his psychopathology as they are manifested in the supervisory interaction. Since they are, however, a first-order influence on the nature of the supervisory field, work, and experience, they deserve systematic consideration, especially with regard to how they are expressed and detected. In fact, the supervisee himself should be taught to make efforts to apply the listening and validating processes to the supervisor's interventions, and to be prepared to express his disagreement and, especially, to point out situations in which Type Two validation does not appear. All supervisory errors must be considered to contain significant elements of countertransference, as indeed every supervisory intervention, successful or not, inevitably includes some such ingredient (these principles are parallel to those that apply to the therapist's interventions; see Langs 1978b).

The supervisor must carefully though silently monitor all transactions in the supervisory and therapeutic bipersonal fields for expressions of his countertransferences. Evidence should be sought in all pertinent spheres: his own subjective reactions, the material from the patient (serving here as an unconscious supervisor for the supervisor), and the communications from the supervisee—both to his patient and in supervision. It is to be stressed, however, that the supervisor's countertransferences, while they should at times be directly acknowledged to the supervisee, should not be overstated or worked over in the supervisory bipersonal field. They are matters for the private self-analysis of the supervisor, or for his personal therapy, and should not become the direct burden of the supervisee.

In terms of the principles being established in this paper, any deviation from standard supervisory practices should be investigated for significant countertransference-based inputs. The supervisor, who can never be free of countertransference, has a responsibility to attempt to be aware of its presence and expressions, and especially of its influence on what would otherwise be unrecognized biases in his approach to the therapeutic material. These may take many forms, including a preference to work with certain types of derivatives and material, a need to focus almost exclusively in one communicative sphere, a tendency to shift to manifest content, a preference to work with one of the three macrostructures (id, ego, superego), and so on. The ultimate goal is, of course, to recognize these prejudices, to modify them through self-analysis and, especially, to exercise sufficient care in monitoring the transactions in both bipersonal fields, the therapeutic and the supervisory, to detect the unanticipated introduction of a countertransference-based difficulty into the supervisory work.

The Supervisory Introject

There has been some discussion of the literature of parallel and reflectional processes in supervisory and therapeutic bipersonal fields (see for example Arlow 1963, Searles 1955), much of it focused on the manner in which the supervisee plays a pivotal role in evoking comparable responses in both the patient and the supervisor. As a consequence, the latter may make special use of his subjective reactions to the supervisee and his presentation, accruing information (this information is, of course, open to validation in the presentation itself) regarding the therapeutic interaction that may not for the moment be imparted directly in the process notes.

In contrast, little has been written with respect to the influence of the supervisor on the therapeutic bipersonal field, and especially in regard to the development of what I shall term a *supervisory introject* within the supervisee. This introject, which is a precipitant of the supervisory interaction, includes the conscious and unconscious communications of the supervisor and its implications as they are selectively introjected by the supervisee on both a conscious and an unconscious level, and then processed in keeping with the latter's pathological and nonpathological needs. It is an important interactional amalgam with crucial kernels of truth and valid conscious and unconscious perceptiveness, intermixed as a rule with some degree of pathological elaboration, which then exerts a significant influence on the supervisee's work with his patient.

In brief, this introject may be primarily either pathological or nonpathological, a fairly complete representation of the supervisor's communication or a rather constricted selection. It may be adequately processed and metabolized by the supervisee, and then integrated into his self-representation and ego functioning, or it may remain a poorly metabolized, ego-alien introject identified with the supervisor and not experienced to any significant extent as part of the supervisee's self-representation and own capacities. The latter alternatives apply whether the introject, as derived from the supervisor's interventions, are primarily pathological and disruptive, or nonpathological and constructive.

Failure to metabolize and integrate essentially constructive supervisory interventions are related to learning blocks, to the supervisee's countertransference difficulties, and to problems in his functioning as a therapist. The overinclusion of pathological and countertransference-based interventions from the supervisor has similar implications, although one must take into account the enormous pressures toward conformity and even blind acceptance that are exerted upon some supervisees by certain supervisors. On the other hand, an adequate metabolization of a pathological supervisory introject would entail the conscious understanding of the supervisor's error and the decision on the part of the supervisee to largely dispute or disregard that particular intervention.

It is, of course, the supervisory introject that serves as the vehicle through which the supervisor influences the therapeutic bipersonal field and indirectly communicates with the patient. Because the patient is consciously and unconsciously exposed to this introject, his own communications are under the sway of the supervisor's efforts. In this regard, the patient too has the usually unconscious choice of refuting or containing these pathological and nonpathological introjects, and of metabolizing them in keeping with his own appropriate or inappropriate needs. Under most circumstances, positively toned introjects will be accepted and will have a therapeutic effect when communicated to the patient through the supervisee's largely valid interventions, whether interpretations or management of the framework.

Pathological supervisory introjects are communicated through the supervisee's erroneous interventions and are usually introjected by the patient and worked over in terms of his own inner needs. The most common response is the patient's initial exploitation of the introject for the maintenance of his own pathology, and then the undertaking of unconscious curative efforts directed first and foremost toward the supervisee as therapist, though clearly, when a pathological supervisory introject is involved, these efforts are ultimately directed toward the supervisor himself. It is this type of interactional sequence, occurring between the supervisory and therapeutic bipersonal fields, that renders useful the supervisor's monitoring of the presented process notes for unconscious commentaries—mixtures of valid and distorted perceptions and fantasies—on his supervisory work, as they are reflected in both the supervisee's interventions and the patient's behavioral responses and verbal associations. It is on this level that the patient serves in an important manner as supervisor to the supervisor.

Dealing with the Supervisee's Countertransferences: The Patient as Unconscious Supervisor

In addition to failures to establish a basic predictive, validating methodology, the single most unresolved problem in supervision may well be how to deal with indications or expressions of the supervisee's countertransferences as they emerge in the therapeutic situation and, at times, in the supervisory experience. Recommendations have ranged from using the supervisee's therapist or analyst as his supervisor, to ignoring these phenomena or treating them as learning difficulties to which the supervisor should respond with educational measures. My own resolution of this particular dilemma has followed from an understanding of the therapeutic interaction itself, through which it is discovered that the expressions of the supervisee's countertransferences lie mainly in essentially erroneous attitudes and interventions (inappropriate silences—which constitute failures to intervene—verbal misinterventions, and mismanagements of the frame). These errors entail unconscious communications that are, in a complex way, introjected by the patient in terms of their manifest and latent meanings and functions, and the resultant pathological *therapist introject* is then worked over in a variety of ways by the patient.

In the presence of a significant countertransference-based input into the therapeutic bipersonal field from the therapist, the interface of that field shifts toward the working over of the expressions of his pathology. As a rule, the patient unconsciously becomes preoccupied with this disturbance, and becomes involved in its exploitation and resolution. At such times the patient will embed or conceal his own usually related psychopathology within that of the therapist, so that it is not, for the moment, available for interpretation. Instead, the unconscious focus of the therapeutic work within the bipersonal field shifts momentarily to the identification, rectification, and understanding of the therapist's pathology and the patient's responses to it, to which the therapist himself must add self-analytic endeavors undertaken privately without burdening the patient.

Lest this description (derived from actual clinical observation) be misunderstood, let me repeat that the therapeutic bipersonal field is not designed for the therapy of the therapist, that it should be no more than minimally occupied with such endeavors, and that the therapeutic work in which these countertransference difficulties are resolved is in no way comparable to that undertaken on behalf of the patient. That such considerations arise is simply an inevitability which should, however, always be kept secondary, and which may, if properly understood and resolved, provide the therapist incidental gain. The patient in such situations is himself offered a special opportunity for unconscious and, ultimately, conscious insights and gains, based on his unconscious therapeutic functioning and on the analysis of his inappropriate responses.

During these countertransference-dominated interludes, the patient responds in part with unconscious interpretations and other corrective efforts directed toward the therapist himself and the introjected disturbance (Langs 1976a).

The recognition of these endeavors, however, depends on a correct evaluation of the unconscious communicative qualities of the technical error, and a recognition that that patient's responsive material is to be taken as Type Two derivatives—commentaries and transversal communications with both perceptive and inappropriate qualities—in response to that particular adaptive context. These corrective and therapeutic efforts, which tend to be expressed on a rather general level but which rather often are quite perceptive, constitute on one level the patient's unconscious efforts to supervise the therapist (and his supervisor). A sensitive therapist can therefore benefit from these communications as long as he truly understands their implications. Similarly, the supervisor needs only tune in on the patient's unconscious supervisory efforts and play them back to the supervisee in his own teaching idiom in order to initiate his own corrective efforts in supervision. Thus the patient truly functions as the key unconscious supervisor in both the therapeutic and the supervisory fields.

Often the supervisor will already have discussed a particular intervention with the supervisee, and will have identified its unconscious communicative qualities. It therefore becomes feasible to anticipate or predict the patient's unconscious responses; validation occurs when the patient, through Type Two derivatives, indirectly works over in his own idiom the erroneous intervention of the therapist in a manner that confirms and elaborates the supervisor's predictive assessment. Failure to obtain such validation should lead the supervisor to reassess and reformulate; it suggests that his own countertransferences may be active and may be influencing both his supervisory interventions and the therapy at hand.

Among the many implications of these findings and formulations, many of which are beyond the scope of this paper, this understanding of the therapeutic interaction gives considerable emphasis to nondistorted and introjective processes within the patient, while according projective and distorting processes their due. Since these observations indicate that in the presence of a countertransference-based intervention, the therapeutic work of the bipersonal field and the responses of the patient are momentarily preoccupied with those inputs, this view suggests that the supervisor must of necessity deal with these countertransferences and the patient's reactions to them; he has no choice but to focus his teaching here. In effect, it is not a question of whether he will comment on or ignore the supervisee's countertransferences; he must do his teaching in this area because it is what both patient and therapist are dealing with and need from him.

This approach also offers a definitive means of dealing with the supervisee's countertransferences in the supervisory situation. In principle, the supervisor makes use of his assessment of the unconscious communications in the therapist's interventions, and very specifically employs the patient's unconscious perceptions and fantasies (introjections) of these interventions as a means of identifying their presence and of stating, within the limits possible in the supervisory situation, their underlying basis. The identified unconscious elements, then, are discussed almost entirely in terms of the communicative qualities of the therapist's interventions and the patient's unconscious commentaries. In this way, the supervisor relies on the patient's unconscious supervisory and curative efforts, understands them to contain valid and perceptive elements in addition to whatever distortions are present, and translates these communications into conscious understanding. He uses the patient's unconscious perceptions, interpretations, and teaching efforts in response to the supervisee's countertransferences, while at the same time he carries out his supervisory work in the main area of concern for both patient and therapist. Because of the conditions of the supervisory bipersonal field, it is, by and large, inappropriate for the supervisor to add any significant remarks to the patient's unconscious formulations; he should maintain the principle of doing his teaching from the process notes of the therapy. On occasion, when there is evidence of a major countertransference problem, a brief extraneous comment may be in order, though it should not, as a rule, be an attempt at interpretation; rather, it should be confined to a gentle and tactful confrontation.

Common Supervisory Problems

It would be helpful if supervisors could develop a literature on the most common problems seen in supervisees and their therapeutic work, and in supervision itself. Preliminary efforts of this kind suggest the lack of a consensus, despite the likelihood that there are patterns of difficulties shared by therapists-in-training (for a different approach to this problem, see Langs 1976d). Evaluations in this area clearly relate to the supervisor's model of therapy and to his conceptions of the listening process, the therapeutic interaction, and interventions.

To offer some brief preliminary impressions, it seems to me that the single most overriding difficulty in supervisees (and the same applies, by and large, to more experienced therapists as well) is learning how to listen to derivatives, and how to organize them specifically as Type Two derivatives around a significant adaptive context. The tendency in therapists is overwhelmingly toward attention to manifest content and Type One derivatives, and this is largely derived from a related trend, namely, to divorce the patient's material from the ongoing therapeutic interaction. This second pitfall is prevalent because therapists-in-training fail to monitor the patient's associations for unconscious perceptions and fantasies related to the actualities of the therapeutic experience, constructive or destructive, as they evoke mixtures of transference-based and nontransference-based responses. Especially neglected are the principles that every communication from the patient refers on some level to the therapeutic interaction, and to both himself and the therapist (the *me/not-me interface;* Langs 1978c), and that every intervention must on some level be connected to the actualities of this interaction in terms of both the reality stimuli and their unconscious, communicative, and intrapsychic meanings.

Thus, supervisees tend to work manifestly and to avoid the therapeutic interaction except when the patient directly refers to it or in the face of an obvious and blatant countertransference-based input—and even then dealing with it only in terms of the surface of the material rather than through derivatives organized around the usually covered-over and defended-against countertransference-related adaptive context. Another common problem in supervisees is really just another dimension of these trends: the tendency to treat the patient's communications as largely distorted and transference-based, as primarily displaced from past pathogenic experiences, and as occurring largely in the projective mode. The patient's functioning is viewed almost entirely in terms of intrapsychic fantasies, memories, and introjects that are placed by him into the therapeutic situation or projected onto the therapist, thereby distorting his image and the patient's responses to him. In keeping with this, transference resistances and fantasies tend to be interpreted almost entirely in terms of their supposed genetic basis, in a manner that virtually denies any actual pathological contribution from the therapist despite the finding that an element of countertransference is present in every intervention (Langs 1978b). Genetic interpretations are therefore frequently used as a defense against the pathogenic actualities of the current therapeutic interaction, especially as a means of consciously and unconsciously denying the therapist's pathological contributions to the patient's experience and responses. Overemphasis on the projective aspects of the patient's communications is used to deny their very crucial introjective dimensions and the countertransferences which contribute to introjects. Instead, a balanced approach should be taught, one that recognizes cycles and intermixtures of introjective and projective processes in both patient and therapist, and that allows for a sensitive appreciation of the constructive and disturbed functioning of both.

In general, then, it has not been my experience that most supervisees tend to become involved in wild analysis or therapy, nor that they tend to prematurely shift to overly deep id interpretations. Quite to the contrary, they tend to remain rather superficial and, in addition, to offer a variety of unconscious interactional defenses and Type C barriers designed to seal off the more chaotic aspects of their linkage and interaction with the patient, and of their respective inner mental worlds.

Supervisory Crises

There are two major types of crises in supervision. The first arises when there is an emergency or critical period in the therapy situation, such as a threat by the patient to terminate, an uncontrolled regression, a danger of suicide, or the like. The second involves a major difficulty in supervision itself, such as the supervisee's conscious dissatisfaction with supervision and his wish to terminate it, or a feeling by the supervisor that his teaching efforts are falling on deaf ears. In the first type of crisis, there is no need to modify the basic supervisory field and methodology, since the understanding of a therapeutic crisis must derive from a study of the process notes of the session. Under these conditions it is quite crucial for the supervisor to identify the critical adaptive contexts that appear to be evoking the disruptive responses in the patient or therapist, and to think of the severe resistance or regression as an interactional syndrome with contributions from both participants. He should allow the material from both members of the therapeutic dyad—especially the derivative communications of the patient—to generate the necessary understanding of the critical interlude. The supervisor should not, under these conditions, succumb to the tendency in many therapists to forgo the complexities of the listening process, and to shift to manifest content-based interventions and modifications in the framework;

instead, he should recognize that such crises have important and pivotal unconscious foundations and that his task is to identify the unconscious contributions of both patient and therapist.

In virtually every crisis situation in therapy there are significant countertransference-based inputs; these will be revealed in the process notes through the therapist's interventions and the patient's associations and behaviors, and should not be neglected. A supervisor who, with relative calm, is able to contain, metabolize, and conceptualize the unconscious basis for a therapeutic crisis affords his supervisees both essential cognitive insights into the source of acute disturbances and the measures necessary for their resolution—whether these are rectifications of unneeded deviations or offers of necessary interpretations. He affords them also the opportunity to incorporate a supervisory introject that will provide them positive introjective identifications that embody a sense of control and understanding and an appreciation for the analytic approach.

Supervisory crises are also interactional amalgams, with inevitable contributions from both participants (although as a rule either the supervisor or supervisee will bear the brunt of the responsibility for the urgent situation). Undoubtedly, the major blind spot under these circumstances is the failure of the supervisor to fully recognize and comprehend his own contributions to the crisis at hand, and his likely tendency to blame the supervisee and to exonerate himself. In addition, the supervisory crisis is to be viewed in interaction with the therapeutic situation; whenever possible, the material from the process notes should be used as a guideline in determining the unconscious basis for the critical issues in supervision, and the role played by both the student and his mentor.

The supervisor's contribution to the crisis will vary depending on a wide range of factors, including his psychological liabilities and assets, his communicative style, his specific response to the supervisee and to the patient under study, and the like. A supervisor who uses a

Type A communicative mode is likely to threaten any poorly defended supervisee. His sensitive formulations and capacity to identify the patient's unconscious perceptions of, and interpretations to, the supervisee can generate intense anxiety and threats of regression in the latter. An especially fragile supervisee will respond with thoughts of interrupting or terminating the supervision; still, efforts to validate these factors as the main source of the problem are essential. A shadow of doubt should always cross the supervisor's mind; with fragile supervisees, he must attempt to slow down his teaching efforts and must offer considerable direct support. His own role in a crisis must never be denied.

On the other hand, the Type A supervisor may repeatedly offer the same incorrect formulations, and this can create a more valid wish on the part of a supervisee to end the supervision. Crucial to this general distinction between appropriate and inappropriate wishes in the supervisee to end supervision is the use of the validating process by both participants in assessing the material from the therapeutic interaction and the supervisor's formulations; this should serve as the basic means of determining the extent to which the student's complaints have some realistic, cognitive basis. Here too, the self-knowledge of the supervisor plays an important role.

The supervisor who uses the Type B mode will tend to projectively identify into the supervisee intensely pathological communications—both contents and mechanisms—that can generate an intense crisis and wishes to terminate supervision. A Type C supervisor can so stalemate the teaching situation that it becomes virtually useless to the supervisee, and at some point of urgent need a supervisee may decide to terminate. As a perspective on these possibilities, however, it is well to recognize that often supervisees do not allow themselves to be consciously aware of their valid dissatisfactions with supervision and, for a variety of countertransference-based defensive and inappropriately gratifying needs, continue in noninstructive supervisory situations. The supervisor himself should therefore monitor the quality of his teaching efforts and the progress or lack of progress of both the supervisee and his patient.

A supervisor may feel that a particular supervisory experience has reached crisis proportions when he finds his supervisee unable to learn and unable to modify intensely countertransference-based defenses and interventions. On the whole, it is the responsibility of the supervisor to explore the process note material and his own interventions for contributions to the supervisee's difficulties and, beyond that, to patiently continue with his teaching efforts, focusing on the supervisee's countertransferences and their expressions in his therapeutic work. Even when the situation reaches crisis proportions and the therapy is endangered, the supervisor must remember that he has made a basic and physicianly commitment to the supervisee; in general, the chronic pathology of the supervisee is not a sound basis for interrupting supervision. In fact, such a step generates a very destructive supervisory introject which would only further traumatize the supervisee and intensify his countertransferences. A period of months or even years of patient work is indicated under such circumstances, and from time to time, especially when material from the therapeutic interaction suggests it, the supervisor may point to the supervisee's need for personal therapy.

An acute supervisory crisis may call for brief comments from the supervisor that are divorced from the process notes of the psychotherapy under supervision. This may occur when the supervisee directly confronts the supervisor with complaints about his work, attitude, teaching method, or the like. The supervisor's response to such complaints should be offered with great restraint and tact, should be kept to an absolute minimum, and should always include an appreciation for the valid aspects of the supervisee's criticisms—no matter how inappropriate they may seem to be after intense evaluation and self-analysis by the supervisor. At such times, the supervisor should take care to avoid a sense of criticism and hostility toward the supervisee, and yet should feel free to patiently establish some of the inappropriate factors in the supervisee's dissatisfaction with supervision, as long as these can be documented in both the supervisory and therapeutic situations, and as long as the supervisor's own contributions are acknowledged. In general, a brief and direct discussion of this kind should end on a note of new resolve to work cooperatively.

Limitations to Supervision

As might be expected, the results of a supervisory experience have most definite limitations, established by the framework and nature of the supervisory bipersonal field, and by the assets and psychopathology of both supervisor and supervisee. Although the framework precludes an insightful therapeutic experience for the supervisee, it does not eliminate opportunities for isolated segments of conscious insight and growth which may at times extend into unconscious working over. Nonetheless, the supervisee's psychopathology will, in various ways, prove to be a major, definitive limiting factor to the outcome of a supervision, and much will depend upon his motivation for supplementary therapy and the actual treatment he obtains.

In this last respect, important complications and limitations develop for the supervisory situation when the supervisee's own therapist is using poor technique and has established a therapeutic situation with major drawbacks. The presence of such flaws in the work of the supervisee's therapist often has drastic consequences for the outcome of supervision; it may, in addition, contribute to supervisory crises, especially under two conditions: first, when the supervisor's work is far more valid than that of the supervisee's therapist, raising major questions regarding the latter situation which tend to generate extensive turmoil in all participants and in the three bipersonal fields involved; and second, when the supervisor's work is quite inadequate as compared to the therapist's abilities, leading to supervisory crises based on the actuality of poor supervision.

The literature has tended to neglect the interaction between the three bipersonal fields now under consideration: between the supervisee and his patient; between the supervisee and his therapist; and between the supervisee and his supervisor. To these a fourth may be added when the supervisor himself is in some form of psychotherapy or psychoanalysis. Clearly, there is an extensive interaction among these bipersonal fields in which both projective and introjective processes play a crucial role, and whereby a disturbance in any of the four can create a ripple effect that influences the other three.

Also to be considered here are disturbances and limitations to supervision that arise from the countertransferences not only of the supervisor, but also of the supervisor's therapist or analyst, whether past or present. Here once again, it is ultimately the application of self-analysis leading to in-depth self-knowledge, as well as the use of the listening and validating processes in respect to communications within each of these bipersonal fields, that provides the supervisor the necessary methodology for investigating these issues and for identifying the limits of the teaching experience.

The presence of limitations to supervisory outcome, however difficult they may be to define precisely, should not, however, be a source of discouragement for the supervisor. They must be accepted as inevitable restrictions on any teaching effort and especially to the teaching of psychotherapy, which so intensely impinges upon the personal assets and pathology of the participants. As the material from the process notes permits, the supervisor may point to specific sources of limitations in a given supervisory situation, in the hope that, when they apply mainly to the supervisee, such confrontations will motivate him toward personal therapy or self-analysis. Those restrictions that derive from problems within the supervisor himself may also be modified through self-analysis and personal therapy, though recognizing and accepting the residuals of one's limitations in this regard is also ultimately a necessity.

Supervision and Creativity

For quite some time I felt apologetic, even lacking in insight, because I realized that most of my ideas were developed in the course of supervisory work. While some new concepts arose, though in a primarily tangential way, in the course of my work with patients, and while it proved necessary to validate the concepts derived from supervision in my own therapeutic endeavors, I was nevertheless faced with that realization and the fact that my colleague seemed to devalue psychoanalytic understanding founded on the supervisory situation.

Yet in time my attitude changed. I began to realize that there is considerable validity to the use of supervision as an arena for creativity. The supervisor does not have, as does the primary therapist, the intense and overriding responsibility to think and respond to the greatest extent possible to the patient's therapeutic needs, and to set all other considerations aside. While responsible for teaching the supervisee and for safeguarding the therapy of the patient, the supervisor nevertheless enjoys a good deal of room in which to generate original insights and conceptualizations based on the material presented him. In fact, such use of the supervisory situation for discovery and innovation, as long as it is not the overriding purpose of supervision and does not detract from the teaching of the supervisee or the management of the therapy, finds support in the work of Freud. After all, Freud's basic discovery of transference was greatly facilitated by the fact that he in a sense served as supervisor to Breuer (Breuer and Freud 1893-1895). The very fact that the supervisor has some distance on the patient, and is functioning as an observer, facilitates the creative process in the supervisor, despite the obvious deficiencies that arise from the crucial absence of direct emotional contact and interaction with the patient.

Another benefit of supervision in this regard accrues to therapists and analysts who recognize the need for total confidentiality in their own therapeutic work and who, like myself (see Langs 1975b, 1976a,d), will make no use of material from patients—past or present—for any purpose other than the therapy of the patient within his sessions. For them, material from supervision offers a means of clinically documenting new psychoanalytic ideas. Since the clinical material of these therapy sessions has already been made "public," in the interests of the patient, whose therapy with an inexperienced practitioner must be monitored, and of the supervisee, who cannot learn to do therapy except through the detailed presentation of his own work, the use of such material, totally disguised, is a reasonable means of serving the needs of the therapeutic community at large, while safeguarding the rights of patients.

Self-Supervision

Ultimately, of course, responsibility for supervision, an attitude and a formal process essential to every therapeutic situation, must rest upon the therapist himself. With the assistance of the ever-present unconscious supervisory efforts of the patient, every therapist must, in the course of each session, maintain a silent and continuous level of self-supervisory work. Such an attitude is inherent in the conception of the therapeutic bipersonal field presented above, and is one way of characterizing the listening and validating processes—the predictive methodology—that is at the heart of this presentation and, I make bold to say, of valid psychotherapy. It is an aspect of the therapist's essential therapeutic attitude which calls for a continuous monitoring of countertransference-based influences, as well as for sound formulations and interventions. It implies continual efforts at self-understanding and self-analysis.

In keeping with the principles that the therapist

should enter each session without desire, memory, or understanding, and that each session should be its own creation, these self-supervisory undertakings, as a rule, should be confined to the session with the patient and should not spill over into sessions with other patients or into efforts at self-reflection after hours. However, when a therapist is faced with a stalemate or crisis in therapy, such after-hours efforts to review the material from the session, and to search for pathological contributions from the therapist himself and from the patient, may prove necessary. In extreme circumstances, direct consultation with a supervisor may be necessary, and such a step is preferable to referring the patient to another therapist for an evaluative consultation. The latter option shatters the framework of the original therapeutic bipersonal field and has disastrous unconscious implications and consequences. As a rule, if an impasse or crisis has proven unresolvable, referral to a new therapist (but never to one who has supervised the particular case, as this would be a major contamination of the second bipersonal field) is to be preferred.

A Clinical Vignette

I will present a brief vignette through which some of the issues and processes outlined in this paper can be illustrated.

Mr. A had been in therapy in a clinic with Dr. B, a woman therapist in the middle phase of her training. He sought treatment for depression and for feelings that he was getting nowhere in his life; he was in his twenties. The early sessions had been characterized by extensive activity on the part of the therapist, who asked many questions, made frequent noninterpretive interventions, including self-revelations, and who had failed to establish any semblance of a secure frame for the treatment. Just before the session excerpted here, Dr. B had changed both the hours of the patient's sessions and her office, because of her professional advancement. Much of this therapist's work could be characterized as a mixture of seductiveness and hostility: she tended to tease and chide this patient, who responded in kind.

In the session to be described here, the patient began by saying that he had recently become involved with two girls who worked in another department of the factory at which he worked. The girls had been quite seductive and teasing with him, and they had really stirred him up sexually; he had responded with a great deal of teasing of his own that they in turn seemed to find quite exciting. During his coffee breaks and lunch hours, he would go over to their department and banter with them. Their boss, who was quite seductive himself, seemed to object and spoke to Mr. A, implying that he was coming on too strong and didn't know his place. He seemed to want to get rid of Mr. A and was quite demeaning in his attitude. The patient said maybe this boss was right, that maybe he *was* overdoing it, but he was still furious with this fellow and imagined all sorts of ways of getting even. His favorite fantasy was of writing fake love letters to him, as if he were some girl who was arranging a date, coming on strong to him, and then standing him up.

At this point, evidently struck by the therapist's relative silence (in fact, under the influence of an initial supervisory session, this was the longest period of silence the therapist had yet maintained with Mr. A), the patient remarked that Dr. B seemed very quiet today. He began to tease her and to plead with her to ask him a question—to say something. He laughed nervously and thought about his wishes to take vengeance on the supervisor of the two girls he had recently met. It occurred to him that he himself tended to be very impulsive, and that it really took a lot of strength to control oneself—to let tension build inside of you without acting impulsively.

The therapist now intervened and said that the patient seemed to be talking a great deal about levels of relationships. Mr. A said that he was puzzled by what she meant, and he then went on to ruminate a great deal about how he likes to be in control of situations and how insecure he feels at times. He went on and on in this vein, and the therapist interrupted him, pointing out that he had been on a date the previous weekend and that he had not said anything about it. The patient said that the date had been fine, described some of the details, and tried to shrug off the subject. In response to another question, he thought of a terrible neighborhood he and his date had wandered into, and how dangerous the situation had seemed. In the balance of the session, the therapist asked a series of detailed questions, introduced a number of subjects that she wished the patient to discuss, and again became involved in a series of self-revelations. The patient's material became rather disorganized and bleak, and included a reference to how, when he gets depressed and feels isolated, he likes to flit about from one bar to another. He ended the session feeling rather discouraged with treatment.

The material described here was presented in a second supervisory session. The first hour of supervision had been devoted to supervisory efforts at identifying the details of the listening process and at showing the therapist the patient's unconscious perceptions and introjections of her seductive, hostile, and self-revealing interventions—all of which had generated frightening and critical, yet somewhat excitingly gratifying, introjects which the patient had been working over in derivative form—his own unconscious supervisory efforts. The supervisee had responded to these supervisory interventions with a sense of relief, since she had herself felt that the treatment situation was chaotic and that her interventions had been relatively uncontrolled and lacking in a much-needed neutrality.

The supervisor had been guided by the principle of initiating supervision with major attention to the listening process, though within that framework he responded to the acute needs of both the supervisee and the patient. These needs dictated a discussion of the meanings and functions of the framework and the need for its definition and rigorous maintenance, as well as a tactful and tentative effort to help this therapist to an awareness of the extent to which her interventions were countertransference-based and disruptive of the therapeutic interaction and work. Stress was therefore placed on slowing the supervisee down, so to speak, and helping her to sit back, listen to her patient, and appreciate the complexities of the therapeutic interaction. Some initial reading, all related to the listening process, was recommended, though it was mentioned that if the supervisee had additional time, a number of articles related to the ground rules and framework of psychotherapy would serve her well.

The opening segment of the session just described demonstrates the influence of a positive supervisory introject on a supervisee who was relatively amenable to its constructive qualities. The supervisor had been quite patient, had been able to contain, metabolize, and understand the unconscious implications of the communications from both the supervisee and her patient, and had imparted some of his insights, along with some direct support, to the supervisee; he had then validated them from the subsequent process note material. These capacities, along with his more direct teaching efforts, through which he encouraged the therapist to sit back and listen, had had a salutary effect. Due to limitations inherent in the early stages of supervision, however, these effects were maintained for only half the session. Still, this is an extremely positive response in a supervisee who had initially been so active and disorganized; it augured well for the future of this particular teaching situation.

In this second supervisory hour, the supervisor had been silent until the supervisee had made her first intervention. At that point, he undertook a series of *listening exercises* through which the therapist was encouraged to identify the adaptive contexts for the session, as well as the available first-order, general, and second-order themes (see Langs 1978c), which were then to be organized around the most significant adaptive contexts. All of this was then to be related to the ongoing therapeutic interaction, considered along the me/not-me interface, and assessed for elements of reality and fantasy. Listening exercises of this kind are basic to the teaching of psychotherapy and, if not spontaneously produced by the supervisee, should be introduced as an essential component in the evaluation and formulation of the process note material. It is on this basis that hypotheses can be generated, predictions made, and validation sought.

In this situation, the supervisee suggested that the main adaptive contexts for this session were the move of her office, the change in hours, and her hostile and demeaning interventions to the patient. She was then asked to review the material for indications of any additional qualities to the therapeutic interaction to which the patient might unconsciously be responding; at this point she recognized the derivative allusions to her seductiveness—especially since, she now added, the patient, in describing the seductive boss, had said directly to her: "You know the type."

It is not uncommon for supervisees (and therapists in general) to be far more readily aware of the derivatives of their unconscious aggressive fantasies toward their patients than they are of the derivatives of their unconscious sexual fantasies. Still, this therapist was able to organize this material as Type Two derivatives around the adaptive contexts now identified, and to recognize the patient's unconscious perceptions and introjections of her teasing, provocative, hostile, and seductive interventions. The supervisor was then able to extend these formulations by pointing out that the patient unconsciously viewed these interventions as efforts to get rid of him, especially in light of the recent changes in his hours and in her office, which seemed to make him feel that he was in her way. However, the supervisor did not voice his impression that these interventions, as unconsciously perceived and introjected by the patient, had qualities of disruptive and pathological projective identifications into the patient, and that these had created pressures toward a Type B communicative field. Nor did he suggest that there was a manic-like and unreal quality to all this excitement which the patient experienced as a lie and falsification that would lead ultimately only to hurt and disappointment (the fake letters and the jilting fantasy). Instead, because it was so early in supervision, the supervisor confined himself to some general comments on how disruptive, hurtful, and detrimental Dr. B's interventions had been; he stressed also how sensitive Mr. A had been to these effects.

Next, the supervisor introduced a more positive note and discussed the influence of the therapist's temporary rectification of the frame—the momentary creation, through Dr. B's initial silence, of a necessary sense of distance, modulation, neutrality, and anonymity. In this regard, the supervisor might well have commented earlier on this part of the session, doing so once it had become clear that the supervisee had changed her style of work. He could then have predicted the appearance of a positive introjective identification within the patient, and would have had his prediction validated through Type Two derivatives in the patient's reference to the value of controls and restraint when under pressure. This would have offered the supervisee a living model of the predictive-validating approach to psychotherapy and supervision that the supervisor was trying to develop with her. As the actual supervision unfolded, these aspects were discussed in retrospect and had a less powerful effect. While unfamiliarity with the supervisee's therapeutic style played a role in this oversight, the supervisor also looked to his countertransferences for possible influences; he felt that he might have been too focused on the patient's negative introjects of the therapist and on her countertransferences, and that this may have led him to fail to fully appreciate the change in Dr. B's style of work.

The therapist's initial silence, as I indicated, reflected a positive supervisory introject which was then unconsciously communicated to the patient, who rather sensitively incorporated some of its most helpful attributes. We see here the influence of the supervisory bipersonal field on that of therapy, and the effects and validation of the supervisor's constructive efforts, which had been derived primarily from the unconscious supervisory efforts of the patient (these were reported in the first supervisory hour and are not detailed here). In this therapeutic situation, the positive supervisor-therapist introject may well have been especially welcomed by this patient, who, in the initial part of the present situation was (1) intensely involved in unconscious supervision of his own (offering a series of derivative commentaries and transversal communications related to the inappropriate aspects of the therapist's work and its negative consequences—derivatives which also alluded to aspects of his own pathology which later could be analyzed once the pathological contributions from the therapist were analyzed and rectified) and (2) expressing his hope for supervisory interventions that could, in part to his regret, set some limits and establish some controls for both himself and the therapist (clinic patients implicitly or explicitly expect that their therapists will be supervised—note the reference to the modulating boss).

In the actual therapy and supervision, both supervisee and supervisor drew upon the patient's unconscious introjection of the supervisee's erroneous interventions and aspects of their underlying basis, and on his efforts at unconscious confrontation, interpretation, and supervision. These efforts were essential guiding factors in the supervisor's interventions, and had also helped the therapist remain silent in the opening part of this session. She stated rather directly that as she began to understand the material from the patient as derivative communications around the adaptive context of her recent interventions, she had experienced a considerable need to sit back, to control these inputs into the bipersonal field, and to understand both herself and the patient. She was also quite aware that when her initial intervention, which was an attempt to provide a bridge between the experiences at work and the therapeutic situation, evoked a ruminative response in the patient, she had become quite discouraged and confused, and no longer felt certain of the derivative meaning of the material. She then experienced a rather sudden urge to actively search for new associations and to ask questions. She was well aware of the loss of control involved and of some of the technical errors that these interventions reflected.

Relying on the patient's unconscious supervisory efforts, the supervisor was now able to show the therapist that the tone of the patient's derivatives had then changed from positive to negative, and that her nonneutral interventions had created a threatening and dangerous atmosphere once again—the reference to the bad neighborhood. At this point, the supervisor added, the patient himself became depressed, partly out of disappointment with the therapist and partly through an introjection of her own underlying depression, and he endeavored to join in with her manic defenses and to unconsciously suggest (interpret) that the therapist's need for activity was a defense against distance, separation, and depression. At this point, sensing a need for further clarification of the functions of the framework, and for the understanding of the nature of interventions, the supervisor briefly outlined some basics in these two areas and suggested some pertinent readings for the supervisee.

In the main, this vignette reflects a supervisory situation in which clear-cut ground rules had been established, including the need for sequential process notes. The supervisor was capable of utilizing the Type A communicative mode and of cognitively understanding the communications from the patient and the therapist; he also had the capacity to contain and metabolize the projective identifications from both of these parties as they were communicated in the initial supervisory hour. The supervisee communicated in a mixed fashion that had qualities of both the Type A and the Type B styles. She was clearly capable of symbolic communication and understanding, though there was in addition an overintensity and an overdetailed quality to her presentation that reflected a need to projectively identify into the supervisor her sense of disorganization, her manic defenses, and her manic-like fantasies. The supervisor's unconscious cognitive processing and understanding of these efforts—reflecting a type of supervisory reverie (Bion 1962)—had served this supervisee well, despite the subsequent setback. As early as this second supervisory session, there were indications that she was shifting toward a greater use of the Type A communicative mode with both her patient and her supervisor.

In the supervisory session described here, the supervisor attempted to ascertain whether his countertransferences had contributed in any way to the therapist's difficulty in maintaining her distance and neutrality once her initial intervention had failed—not unexpectedly—to evoke a confirmatory response. He had briefly reviewed the intervention with the supervisee, stressing its nonspecific and superficial qualities, the failure to use daydreaming (fantasy) language, and the need to wait for bridges to the therapeutic situation from the patient rather than trying to promote their expression. (At this point, he decided against a more extensive discussion in this area.) As for his own countertransferences, he considered the possibility of his having been stimulated or titillated by the supervisee's seductive style, taking his cue from the patient's allusion to flitting around from bar to bar; this was seen as a possible reference to a need in him to share the manic defenses of both patient and therapist as a defense against his own possible depressive trends. He wondered whether he should have been more definitive in recommending the use of silence and in suggesting a limit, except in an emergency, of but one or two interventions. It proved possible for him to subjectively validate the presence of a countertransference-based input, though it was clear that the major countertransferences lay within the supervisee. This recognition is comparable to the recent realization (Langs 1978b) that every intervention from the therapist contains at least some measure of countertransference-based input. The same principle applies to every supervisory intervention, and the supervisor has the responsibility for monitoring his work in order to detect its influence and to become engaged in subsequent self-analytic work designed with its rectification and resolution in mind. Such endeavors may be described as the self-supervision of the supervisor, another level of supervisory work that needs continuous attention.

Concluding Comments

The supervisory situation is filled with complexities and is the scene of a critical, and often moving, communicative interaction. In general, writers on the subject have failed to recognize many of the practical and difficult issues or the pitfalls that pertain to the supervisory experience, and, in addition, have neglected its creative potential.

My most recent observations of the unconscious communicative interaction between patient and therapist has led me to a more balanced view of both participants. Until now, the patient was viewed as primarily sick and the therapist as essentially healthy, and the constructive functioning of the patient as well as the pathological functioning of the therapist had been relatively neglected. In this connection, the realization that, unconsciously, the patient is capable of extensive, valid, and perceptive understandings of the therapist, and that in addition—still largely on the unconscious level—he is capable of significant therapeutic and supervisory efforts, has led to an image of the patient as someone who is significantly disturbed or dysfunctional on a behavioral and conscious level, while rather gifted and sound in certain sectors of his unconscious functioning. In addition, the patient's exquisite sensitivity to the therapist's errors, as well as his own use of a largely unconscious yet sound validating process (Langs 1976d, 1978f) and his unconscious capacities to understand his therapeutic needs and whether they are being met, suggests that every human being is, in some perhaps inherent as well as unconsciously developed way, a capable therapist and supervisor. This thesis is a variation on Searles's point (1975) regarding the newborn infant's almost innate therapeutic tendencies in his relationship with his mother.

This conception has meaning for the supervisory situation: it implies that each of us is, in a sense, a natural born (and subsequently developed) therapist, although many of these therapeutic qualities exist on an unconscious level and within the realm of our unconscious functioning. It is other, more disruptive sectors of our personalities, and the major obstacles that develop in trying to make these abilities conscious and directly available for expression, that make it necessary for us to formally learn how to do psychotherapy (or to undergo a personal therapeutic experience). Still, our conception of supervision and the nature of a supervisor's work takes on a particular valence when these actualities and potentials are recognized. The main problem in supervision, then, is not so much a matter of teaching and developing new techniques and ideas, as it is to find the ways of freeing up the supervisee's unconscious sensitivities and capabilities.

This line of thought also implies that there is hope for every supervisee, no matter how grossly disturbed or disruptive his therapeutic work may at first seem. It should foster a positive attitude in the supervisor as he approaches work with each of his supervisees. It also should prompt us to remember, as supervisors, that we too once were supervisees and that through the efforts of our own supervisors (and, as a rule, personal therapy or analysis) we have experienced many constructive, however painful, transformations and periods of growth. We too, then, once were neophytes, confused and disturbed; today, presumably, we are far more integrated and capable. It is now our responsibility to create the conditions and to offer the supervisory interventions through which such constructive growth may be afforded each and every supervisee who comes to us to learn and mature.

Chapter 6

A Strategy for Supervision

The goals of this paper are twofold: first, to present a format for the supervisory situation that can serve as a fundamental framework for all supervisory work; and, second, to offer perspectives on several supervisory issues that have not as yet received full clarification.

A Basic Format for Supervision

Because of its many dimensions, it has proven difficult to develop a basic and consistent approach to supervision that is sufficiently organized to safeguard the thoroughness of the supervisory work and yet open enough to allow for free and spontaneous discussion. In chapters 1-5 I have advocated a methodology that places the central focus of supervision on the ongoing therapeutic interaction, to which is appended the entire gamut of possible discussions, e.g., the patient's dynamics, genetic considerations, the influence of countertransferences, the nature of psychopathology, problems of technique, and the relevant literature. In an attempt to develop an even more systematic strategy, I suggested an overall sequence of teaching (which should be modified in keeping with the immediate needs of the therapist and the patient), undertaken in the order of listening-validating, the framework, the therapeutic relationship, and intervening. I also defined a hierarchy of indications for supervisory interventions which included, in order of precedence, indications of countertransference in the supervisor or of a crisis in supervision, signs of countertransference in the supervisee and of a crisis in the therapy, any major framework issue in either situation, and, last, the appearance of material in the therapeutic interaction that calls for teaching and discussion.

While these have proven helpful guides, they fall short of a definitive methodology. However, such a strategy has emerged from my most recent efforts at clarifying aspects of the therapeutic interaction, especially in regard to the interplay between the therapist's efforts at listening, formulating, and validating on the one hand, and intervening on the other. The outcome has been the crystallization of a basic format for supervision, a reticulum which functions both as a set of checkpoints for the supervisory work and as a specific means of developing all necessary supervisory comments. It also serves admirably as a basis for self-supervision (see chapter 7).

There are three focal points for this strategy of supervision: (1) the *indicators* in the material from the patient of a need for an intervention, the *therapeutic context* which provides a secondary focus for listening; (2) the *communicative network*, which includes the adaptive context, the manner in which that context is represented, the nature of the derivative complex, and the bridge to therapy; and (3) the type of *communicative field*, especially the patient's current prevailing communicative style.

To clarify, indicators are gross behavioral and symptomatic responses that express a need within the patient for an intervention from the therapist; whether it is given, however, will depend largely on the nature of the communicative network. Indicators fall into two groups: symptoms within the patient, and problems within the therapeutic interaction. The latter include (in order of importance) mismanagements of the framework and interpretive errors, efforts by the patient to modify the frame, and the presence of gross resistances such as silences and absences. In general, the communicative network, once understood, is organized secondarily around these indicators (which are best termed *therapeutic contexts* when the listening process is under consideration) as a means of comprehending their unconscious meanings and functions. These indicators are weighted so that major and serious symptoms call far more strongly for intervention than do minor symptomatic occurrences; alterations in the framework, major errors by the therapist, gross ruptures in the therapeutic alliance, and threats to the continuation of treatment constitute major causes for intervening as well.

The decision to intervene and the exact nature of the intervention is next influenced by the properties of the communicative network, and especially by the nature of the adaptive context and how it is represented. The adaptive context for the patient is virtually always the therapist's most recent and most meaningful intervention, which serves as the prime evocator of the patient's neurosis-related intrapsychic responses—unconscious perceptions and unconscious fantasies. At times, the adaptive context and therapeutic context may be identical, such as when the therapist has made a major interpretive error or has mismanaged the framework. At other moments, the adaptive context is quite distinct from the therapeutic context, such as when a patient is threatening to terminate (the therapeutic context) because of a major technical error by the therapist (the adaptive context).

At the core of every intervention must lie the adaptive, rather than the therapeutic, context; the latter is a second-level organizer. A valid interpretation is, however, ultimately related to the indicators, and in addition entails the identification of an adaptive context and the derivatives that represent the patient's responsive unconscious perceptions and fantasies. A valid management response will include such interpretations along with the rectification of the framework. Among the most significant *adaptive contexts* are the therapist's errors and his other, unavoidable hurts to the patient, such as his vacations and the like.

The single most critical factor in intervening is how the adaptive context is represented in the patient's material. There are four possibilities: it may be alluded to directly and manifestly; it may be represented in some derivative form through material related to the therapeutic relationship; it may be represented in derivative form through an allusion to an outside relationship; and it may be virtually entirely repressed and therefore not meaningfully represented at all. The first two include the critical *link* to the therapist which enables the material to be readily organized around the therapeutic interaction; this facilitates an interpretive response. In contrast, representations of the context through outside relationships and its total repression makes an interpretive intervention unlikely and quite difficult.

With the adaptive context identified, the derivative complex may then be evaluated. Critical here is the extent to which the patient has communicated derivatives which coalesce to illuminate various dimensions of the adaptive context: its unconscious meanings to the patient and to the therapist, its genetic implications to the patient, its dynamic functions within the therapeutic interaction, and the like. This complex may organize around a variety of unconscious perceptions and fantasies, or it may be fragmented, noncoalescing, scattered, flat, or empty. The more coalescent the network, the closer (less disguised) the derivatives, the more meaningful the therapist's intervention will be.

Finally, there is the determination of the presence of a bridge to therapy—some reference, even nonspecific, to the therapist or treatment situation that occurs toward the latter part of the session and justifies a general connection between the earlier material and the therapeutic interaction itself.

In general, when the adaptive context is represented with the link to the therapist, and the derivative network seems likely to coalesce, there will be a bridge to the therapy as well. The therapist will then be in a position to respond interpretively and with rectification of errors or the framework when needed. If the link to the therapist is lacking, there are two possibilities: when the indicators are relatively weak, the best intervention is continued silence, which permits the patient to work over his resistances and to eventually communicate more clearly; when the indicators are more powerful, the best intervention will be the playing back of specific derivatives organized around the adaptive context which lacks the link to the therapist (Langs 1978b). Such an effort can help the patient identify consciously the critical adaptive context, a step that then permits an interpretive intervention by the therapist.

Before this work can be undertaken, the communicative qualities of the bipersonal field must be determined, especially the communicative style of the patient. When the patient communicates in the Type A mode, the therapist can sit back and allow the derivatives to unfold. In general, when the Type B mode predominates, there is an experience of pressure and a need to intervene perhaps a bit sooner than one might with a Type A patient. With the Type C style, it is incumbent upon the therapist that he intervene whenever he has a meaningful communicative network, even if the derivatives are sparse. Failure to do so will lead the patient to intensify his use of Type C barriers, and the opportunity to intervene will have been lost.

In supervision, then, often at a point when the therapist has intervened but at other significant moments as well, it seems best to ask the supervisee to formulate the material of the session in terms of the three focal points outlined here. I would once again advocate a systematic approach, beginning with the identification and evaluation of the indicators, and moving next to a study of the communicative network in the sequence outlined above;

finally, a broad consideration of the communicative field and style of the patient can be undertaken. In the course of such work, as already noted, many issues arise, and each can be explored and discussed. The ultimate goal, of course, is to discuss first the factors within both patient and therapist that have led to the particular indicators and associational network at hand, and, second, to determine the best possible intervention under the prevailing conditions. The use of this particular framework as an approach to each supervisory hour creates the greatest likelihood that the critical issues in each therapy session will be identified and discussed. There is a comprehensive basis for specific discussions which will arise from the issues generated by each individual session. Among its most exciting and remarkable features is the finding that each hour, while it may fall under certain broad characterizations, is remarkably unique and presents some nuance or problem that is quite its own. Thus, this methodology permits the development of broad and general categories of supervisory and therapeutic problems and the means for their resolution, while also affording considerable room for individuality and freshness.

A Supervisory Hour

I have selected at random an hour recently presented to me in supervision in order to demonstrate this particular approach. In brief, the patient was a twenty-eight-year-old young woman who had been in twice-a-week therapy for about a year. Prior to the session to be presented, the therapist had changed an hour for a relatively frivolous reason, after having refused to change another hour when the patient needed a different time because of a commitment on her job. There had been a rather chaotic response by the patient, and the therapist's attempts to interpret her reactions to this chaos had been rather inadequate and confusing.

The patient was five minutes late to this session, and was

then silent for twenty minutes. She said that she had discovered that her boss was about to hire someone else for a job that she had expected to be given. She hadn't been hired for that particular job, which itself would represent an advancement, but she thought that she was in line for that promotion even though she had been on her new job for only a few months. It was evident that he didn't think that she could do it, and she should now think of leaving. Her present job was all too vague; her boss must have a bad impression of her. After another five-minute silence, the patient said that an odd thing had happened. She plays tennis with a young man who wanted a sexual relationship with a woman. The patient had fixed him up with her girlfriend, and they had hit it off. The other night the patient was out with the two of them, and two other couples, and she felt extremely depressed, as if she was excess baggage. The session ended; the therapist had not intervened.

No comment had been made in supervision until that point, primarily because no major issue had risen. The supervisee was now asked to analyze the session. Since he was familiar with the supervisory model being proposed here, he began by reviewing the indications for intervention: he identified the patient's depression, and her lateness and silences, and saw the latter two as modifications in the framework. Through questions, the supervisor brought out that the therapist had failed to mention the background of his own recent alterations of the framework, and his subsequent efforts to restore the frame. Inquiry was made as to an implied indicator for an intervention, and the supervisee pointed to the derivative communication about the patient's thoughts about leaving the job where she was no longer appreciated—a possible representation of thoughts of terminating her therapy. In response to another question, the supervisee thought that there was a moderately strong need for an intervention in this session, and he next turned to the communicative network.

Here, he began spontaneously by identifying, as a first adaptive context, his rather muddled intervention in the previous hour: he had defensively clarified certain criticisms and misperceptions that the patient had reported of an earlier intervention, rather than attempting to deal with the material in terms of the prevailing adaptive context of the recent change in the time of her session. He suggested that another context was his having maintained the frame when, two sessions earlier, the patient had conveyed her thoughts of taking a sudden vacation, and he had had an opportunity to indicate that she would be responsible for her sessions. In all, it was decided that there were three major adaptive contexts: an incorrect intervention, inconsistency with the ground rules, and recent efforts to secure the frame.

The supervisee spontaneously turned to the material to see how each of the contexts was represented in the patient's associations. Here he experienced some difficulty, and seemed uncertain as to how the muddled intervention was represented. He thought of the allusion to her boss's feeling that she couldn't do the job, and wondered if this implied an unconscious perception of him as incapable of doing the therapy. There was a sense of foul-up or uncertainty, which the therapist also linked to his intervention.

As for the inconsistency with the frame, the therapist had a problem in seeing how it was represented, and I suggested that it could be reflected once again in the allusions to being confused about the job and the reference to being hired for one thing, and wanting something else. Both the supervisee and I felt that these representations were rather poor and distant, and that the link to the therapist was not in evidence. This led to a supervisory discussion of how to identify derivative representations of the adaptive context, and the importance of the presence of a link to the therapist. I especially noted the finding that interventions are difficult without such a link. It was noted also that with a clear-cut representation of the adaptive context and its link to the therapist, interpretations of the patient's responsive unconscious fantasies and unconscious perceptions becomes feasible. In the absence of such a representation, the therapist is usually limited to the playing back of selected derivatives.

Next the supervisee was asked to define the derivative complex. Here, he described a considerable degree of difficulty and initially felt that he could not relate the material to any of the adaptive contexts. A discussion of the importance of generating Type Two derivatives around specific adaptive contexts ensued, and the supervisee was encouraged to identify some isolated Type Two derivatives. He then suggested again an unconscious perception of himself as unable to do the job, and felt that somehow the patient's depression must be connected to the problems that he was having in handling her therapy. Perhaps she somehow felt like excess baggage—though again the supervisee verbalized his difficulty in connecting this to the adaptive context.

After further efforts of this kind, I demonstrated ways in which this material could be viewed as Type Two derivatives around each of the specific adaptive contexts. I pointed out that the supervisee in general tended to overlook instinctual drive derivatives, such as the reference to the young man who wanted a sexual partner. This aspect of the material was therefore separated from the adaptive context of his errors with the ground rules and in intervening. To demonstrate how this could be linked up, I suggested that in derivative form the patient was suggesting that some type of unconscious sexual conflict was interfering with the therapist's adequate functioning. The supervisee responded with several manifest images, and it became clear that he tended to think of the material quite narrowly; as a result, I suggested that he shift to broad themes before attempting to fit specific and detailed themes into the context.

It also became clear that the supervisee lacked the general means of conceptualizing Type Two derivatives, and as a result I suggested that he think of the material as representations of himself, and as conveying unconscious perceptions and introjects, before he thought of the material in terms of the patient's fantasies and distortions.

Derivatives, I went on, can be thought of as representations and then as reactions to these representations; in this way I hoped to provide the supervisee with concepts that might better help him characterize a particular derivative complex.

Finally the supervisee sought to determine the presence of a bridge to therapy, and felt that none was present. With all of this considered, I asked him to identify the best possible intervention based on this evaluation, and to discuss whether he might now have intervened or not. In response, the supervisee said that he was having a problem maintaining a clear image of the adaptive contexts, and had not been able to generate an understanding of their derivative representation and of the related derivative complex. Because of this, he had decided not to intervene, and even in the face of this supervisory discussion, he did not feel that he would have been in a position to clearly identify the patient's unconscious responses to his recent errors. When asked to offer the best possible intervention that he could conceive of for the moment, the supervisee hesitated for a while, and then said that perhaps the patient could be told that somehow she felt that he couldn't do the job because he had intervened in a confusing way and had handled her appointments with a major degree of confusion as well.

I responded that I felt that an intervention of this kind would introduce too much that was not reflected in the material from the patient. I next asked the supervisee to identify the patient's prevailing communicative style, and the supervisee responded that there were fragments of the Type A mode present. However, I stated that I felt that the patient's communicative resistances had destroyed a meaningful representation of the adaptive context, and that because of this, the patient should be thought of as a Type C communicator. The supervisee confirmed this by stating that there were many sessions in which the patient associated without a clear-cut adaptive context.

Since the supervisory hour was drawing to a close, I suggested that because of the patient's Type C style and major block in associating, and in light of her sense of depression and apparent thoughts of terminating, that despite the poor communicative network it might have been valuable to intervene by playing back the best available derivatives in the hope of introducing a new sense of understanding that could be coupled with recent efforts to secure the framework. Such an intervention might also restore the patient's sense of faith in the therapist, which was clearly at low ebb. I suggested, therefore, that the supervisee could have begun his intervention by alluding to the patient's silence, which was a readily available indicator that could serve as a bridge to therapy. Thus, he might have said that the patient had been silent for long periods during this session. She was now talking about how she was disappointed that she would not be getting a promotion that she wanted, something that would have satisfied her needs. She was speaking of her boss's view of her as being unable to do the job, and this sense seems to pervade the therapy situation both in respect to the patient and himself, the therapist. She had also alluded to a sense of vagueness, to something sexual that created distance between herself and a young man, and of feeling unwanted or superfluous. She also felt disappointed and depressed, and, clearly, something within treatment of late must be evoking these images and her silences.

Having illustrated what I felt to be the best possible specific intervention, I acknowledged its thinness and weakness, and discussed again the reasons for offering it under the prevailing conditions. I stressed the transversal qualities of this effort, and the need to treat the material as a mixture of unconscious perception and response, with small qualities of possible unconscious fantasies.

The balance of the supervisory hour was spent in listening to the second session of the week, and in using it to further clarify the indications that the therapist should have intervened in the hour just presented (much of this because the patient was late again, silent for thirty minutes, and still considerably depressed; in addition, there were even fewer viable derivatives in the second hour than in the first). The remainder of the discussion centered around the principles of how to listen to derivative complexes, and how the therapist's problems in this area made it especially difficult for him to intervene in the session he had presented. It was also suggested that the therapist take other sessions in which the adaptive context was clear, and engage himself in listening exercises in which he attempted to identify the nature and function of the patient's various derivative representations of, and responses to, these contexts.

It is beyond the scope of this paper to discuss in detail the many complexities of this representative supervisory hour. It has been offered primarily to illustrate the proposed basic format for supervision, and to demonstrate how it can be used as a takeoff point for the discussion of various clinical issues relevant, first, to the patient's therapeutic needs, and, second, to the supervisee's requisites for learning.

This particular supervisee had been in supervision for some time, and had now reached the point where selected issues relating to listening and validating could be addressed, while much of the basic listening process had already been reviewed and relatively mastered. In addition, he had worked over a variety of problems related to the ground rules and framework, and for this reason I did not especially focus on the material in light of his recent inconsistency—this had been the subject of several recent supervisory hours. Because of the nature of the material, there was no extensive discussion of the therapeutic relationship, although his erotic countertransference problem, which tended to cover over the patient's erotic transference, was pointed out. Much of the recent efforts in supervision had been directed toward difficulties that this supervisee had been having in formulating clear-cut interventions. The part of the listening process most clearly related to intervening, and the formulation of specific interventions, was therefore the primary focus of this supervisory hour—an effort that was clearly in the common interests of both patient and supervisee.

Some Efforts at Clarification

As new discoveries are made about the psychotherapeutic and psychoanalytic processes, new techniques of supervision are bound to follow. Similarly, as new insights into the supervisory process are developed, improvement in our understanding of the therapeutic situation, and of our techniques, should occur. The practice of psychotherapy and its supervision must be characterized by a balance between open and loose creativity, and the use of discipline and validation. It seems more than evident that until now there has been too much openness and too little effort at validation and organization (see Langs 1976d), and that under such conditions our techniques will grow stale, remain overladen with countertransferences; far too many treatment situations will fail. By developing and clarifying a verifiable listening process, it is possible to bring some degree of order into this relative chaos for both the supervisory and therapeutic situations. In doing so, we must maintain a spirit of flexibility within appropriate limits, and must teach with all the necessary human qualities that characterize any type of sound treatment or educational effort.

Much of the furor over the discovery of new truths about the therapeutic and analytic situations—and their supervision—and about the two participants to what Bion (1965) has so aptly described as a dangerous undertaking, appears to relate ultimately to the most chaotic and psychotic parts of the personalities concerned. Such truths are bound to provoke anxiety and inner tumult. Their necessary delineation in the supervisory situation will of course entail periods of disturbance and disorganization, but clearly these are essential to learning and growth (Bion 1962). It is well, however, to bear in mind the nature of the underlying issues when doing supervisory work; this provides an important perspective and softening effect on the supervisor's efforts.

A supervisor and therapist learn quickly that truth is a burdensome commodity, to be dispensed with utmost caution, tact, and sensitivity. Still, it is crucial for the supervisee to have a model of a supervisor capable of identifying the most compelling truths of a given psychotherapeutic moment, and of developing the most constructive formulations and interventions through which sound symptomatic relief may be derived—primarily, of course, for the patient, but secondarily for the supervisee and even the supervisor himself. It is no easy task to approach these issues with a sense of humility, a capacity for necessary support and yet an ability to be forthright and definitive, so that one may offer specific formulations and take the necessary risk of open validation. Of course, there are frightening qualities to such undertakings for both supervisor and supervisee, but clearly, they provide a model to the supervisee that enables him to realize that there are precise aspects to the technique of psychoanalytic psychotherapy and psychoanalysis, even in the midst of continued uncertainty. The use of a predictive methodology in itself provides a strongly constructive model of treatment usually lacking in other types of supervision.

Many unique issues of pedagogy and methodology arise in connection with the supervision of psychotherapy. Too little attention has been paid to the need to delineate rules of teaching that take into account the more unusual aspects of supervision as an educational experience. The usual teaching ambience calls for the establishment of a situation of relative safety, openness of expression, and appropriate support, along with careful measures designed to gear the level and rate of instruction to the learning capacities of the student. Ideally, too, the teaching would begin on a relatively simple level and accrue complexities as it moved along.

These principles do, of course, have their place in the supervision of psychotherapy. However, there are at least four major qualifying factors that can be identified in this situation that would lead to alterations or addenda to the usual principles of teaching: (1) the supervisory situation is distinguished from the usual learning setting in that it is geared to the needs of not one, but two, specific individuals, the patient and the therapist; (2) both the teaching and the learning of psychotherapy occurs under the relatively intense influence of unconscious and highly personal factors, many of them related to countertransference, to a degree that is far greater than in other learning situations; (3) the supervision of psychotherapy often deals with very personal factors in the supervisee, along with his psychopathology and countertransferences; and (4) the process of learning to do psychotherapy differs from mastering most other types of material, in that it cannot unfold in a linear fashion that deals with materials of increasing complexity, but is such that a number of major interrelated areas require delineation, each to some degree requisite to the understanding of the others. The topics covered toward the end of such work enable the supervisee to go back to the earlier subjects studied, and to more fully comprehend their implications. The process is like reading a book that must be read in its entirety before the reader can return to the first chapter and fully understand its implications (see, for example, the remarks in Bion 1962).

These four aspects of the supervision of psychotherapy dictate the need to develop a unique theory and pedagogical model for the supervising experience, and throughout this volume I have attempted to indicate my thinking in this regard. In this connection, we must be reminded again that the supervisor must give prime consideration to the therapeutic needs of the patient, though he must in addition shape his teaching in terms of the requirements and capacities of the supervisee. After all, the supervisor must make every effort to teach in a manner that will enable the supervisee to constructively utilize the understanding imparted to him. Still, it must be expected that there will be times when the patient's material reflects a need for supervisory interventions that will evoke conflict and discomfort for the supervisee, no matter how tactfully the supervisor presents his comments. The immediacy and frequent urgency of the therapeutic situation therefore exerts a major influence on the supervisory experience, and this consideration will sometimes necessitate teaching communications that might otherwise have been kept for a moment more propitious for the student.

Similarly, the importance of unconscious and personal factors makes demands on the supervisor and supervisee that are seldom encountered in the usual teaching situation. This may occasion conflicting requirements for the supervisory situation, in which impingements upon both participants may be necessitated that would be extremely unusual in other types of learning experiences. The relevance and exposure of one's own personality in psychotherapeutic work thus lends a special charge to the supervisory experience.

Finally, the unusual degree to which the various dimensions of psychotherapeutic understanding and technique are fundamentally interrelated severely limits the degree to which they can be isolated for pedagogical purposes. The basic sequence I have suggested for the teaching of psychotherapy provides only a start toward the resolution of the teaching dilemmas arising from this particular characteristic of psychotherapy. The full solution still awaits us.

For the moment, I would like to stress the importance of establishing a proper holding environment and background of safety for the supervisee in the supervisory situation. This is accomplished implicitly and explicitly in countless ways: by assuring the supervisee of the total confidentiality of the supervisory work when possible, and by maintaining group confidentiality as well; by approaching supervision with a well-defined but somewhat loose set of ground rules, and maintaining them constructively in the face of stress; by conveying a basic attitude of understanding and support, a sense of sharing in the supervisee's frailties and even limitations, and yet conveying as well the supervisor's quietly expressed greater knowledge and competence, and his sense of patiently expecting slow but gradual maturation and growth in the supervisee; by developing virtually every supervisory intervention from the material of the therapeutic interaction, from the spiraling unconscious communicative unfolding of the treatment situation, and without bias, prejudice, and personal need or innuendo, though with a sense of compassion and forthrightness which must characterize both sound therapy and teaching; by being available as a directly supportive and helpful figure in times of crisis, and yet being able to maintain the essential model of supervision in the face of chaos, thereby demonstrating its serviceability; and through countless other nuances which convey the supervisor's appropriate belief in his therapeutic method and supervisory practices, and in himself, the supervisee, and especially the patient.

I have offered in this paper an illustration of the methods being developed here. It should be recognized, however, that this supervisory hour was developed with the idea of using it for this presentation; in that sense it is not truly representative of a basic approach to supervision designed entirely for the needs of the supervisee and his patient. In this context, it should be recognized that teaching methods must vary in keeping with the nature of the supervisory situation—individual, group, recorded for publication, or whatever. The ideal is the one-to-one experience; as a rule the needs of individuals other than the supervisee and his patient—and this includes the supervisor—will loom much larger as modifications in supervisory privacy are introduced. This will lead as well to shifts in teaching policies, most of which move away from the requirements of the two central figures to supervision.

These effects can be seen in my published supervisory seminars (1976a, 1978c), in which the teaching approach is actually rather different in important ways from that I adopt for individual supervision (for comparison see the vignettes in chapters 5 and 7, as well as in the present chapter). While the basic method of supervising should remain essentially comparable in all supervisory teaching situations—e.g., in each the format presented in this paper should be used—many other aspects of supervision may be modified. This can be seen, for example, in the need to focus in *The Listening Process* (Langs 1978c) almost exclusively on that one topic to the relative neglect of almost all else. As one approaches different supervisory situations, it is well to keep these factors in mind. A careful study of the pertinent variables and variations should prove illuminating.

Some confusion may also arise from the need to state aloud in supervision hypotheses that are developed and maintained as *silent hypotheses* in the therapy situation. This teaching device, which is so essential for a predictive approach to supervision, permits an assessment of the validity of supervisory hypotheses and the candid revision of formulations that are not supported. The open search for confirmation in supervision has its parallel in the *silent validation* of *silent formulations* by the therapist through the patient's continuing associations in the actual treatment situation. The supervisor must make it clear that these direct discussions in the learning situation have their counterpart in the *silent* work of the therapist during much of the therapy hour, especially the initial half or so. In this way methodology, discipline, and the value of patient listening are introduced into the supervisee's armamentarium. This fosters his use of speculation, while encouraging him to formulate specifically from time to time; overall, it promotes both listening and a more controlled approach to intervening.

Another issue that deserves fuller consideration relates to the expectations that a supervisor should have of his supervisee, and to the acceptance, as well, of limitations to supervisory work (see chapter 5). In this regard I would stress that it is—and should be—the *patient*, not the supervisor, who has expectations and makes demands on the supervisee—his therapist. It is the supervisor's function to identify the manifestations of these needs, to help the supervisee recognize their presence and implications, and to teach in accordance with their requirements. The patient's therapeutic needs are not only a burden to the supervisee and his supervisor, but are also an important, constructive stimulus to learning and growth.

It should be recognized, too, that despite limitations posed by the level of the supervisee's training and of his own personal therapy, it becomes possible as teaching methods improve to impart a great deal that can be absorbed by any supervisee. Much can be learned by a relative neophyte, even in the sphere of his own countertransferences and their influence on his work. While discussions of countertransference are especially difficult with such therapists, they can have salutary effect when undertaken at the conscious or unconscious prompting of the patient, and when based on the material of the therapeutic interaction. If nothing else, they may prompt a troubled therapist to seek treatment. It appears that most supervisors have tended to underestimate the capacities of supervisees, just as most therapists have minimized or neglected the positive potential in their patients.

Supervisory work is rendered both especially painful and enormously productive by the realization of the patient's exquisite unconscious sensitivity to the therapist's errors and countertransferences. There has been considerable use of denial in this regard, in therapists and supervisors alike. Systematic teaching in this area, done tactfully and restricted to material from the sessions, is undoubtedly among the most critical factors in the sound development of a therapist. It is also essential for the patient, who, during countertransference-dominated interludes, is unconsciously working over the therapist's psychopathology, which becomes for the moment the only truly meaningful link to the patient's own pathology. Such supervisory work is difficult for all concerned, but clearly it deals with the essential truths of the therapeutic situation at that point in time; it is therefore at that juncture the only vehicle for sound teaching. With these matters somewhat settled, then, let us now turn to the subject of self-supervision.

Chapter 7

Self-Supervision

With a broadening of one's understanding of the therapeutic process, neglected issues attract attention, many of them silently maintained as collective bastions of the field of psychotherapy and analysis. Yet, while I have identified and attempted to resolve many such collective blind spots, few have inspired as much resistance as those pertaining to supervision. The present volume includes repeated efforts to investigate a variety of neglected dimensions of supervision, but I turn only now—at the very moment that this book takes its final steps toward publication—to a study of what seems perhaps the single most disregarded aspect of this topic: self-supervision.

It is no coincidence that the final paper in this volume deals with the self-supervisory efforts of the practicing psychotherapist or analyst (the two will not be distinguished in this presentation). It is a subject that was added as an afterthought to the seminar on supervision, and as a final comment in my paper on this topic (chapter 5.) More broadly, I know of no paper which attempts a comprehensive investigation of this problem, despite several studies of the self-analytic process—itself, one aspect of self-supervision—during the postanalytic phase (see Kraemer 1959, and especially G. Ticho 1967).

There are evident reasons for this bastion. On the cognitive level, it tends to be assumed that everything learned by a given therapist will be used to scrutinize his therapeutic work. In the usual two-person supervisory situation, it is taken for granted that both consciously and unconsciously the supervisee will identify with and incorporate the supervisory attitudes and approach of his mentor. In the course of a personal analysis or therapy, it is implicitly expected that the accrued insights will be maintained on some level as part of a self-examining process related to each therapeutic experience. Perhaps too there is an attitude in many therapists and analysts—to my knowledge the matter is almost never discussed—that the format and considerations that he develops in his own capacity as supervisor to others will be applied to some extent in his own work. Still, the absence of explicit discussion and investigation strongly suggests that many of these assumptions are not translated into actual practice, and that the time has come for a more disciplined approach.

In my own work, especially in *The Bipersonal Field* (1976a) and *The Listening Process* (1978c), I attempted with some consistency to address matters of self-supervision, especially in terms of the therapist's responsibility for monitoring his own inner experiences and the communications of the patient for unconscious perceptions of, and commentaries on, his therapeutic endeavors. I also developed an extensive listening and validating process (1976a,d, 1978c,g,i) and considered the influence, detection, and rectification of countertransferences from a number of vantage points (Langs 1974, 1976a,d, 1978c, 1979). However, I too had essentially expected that my particular approach to supervision would influence the self-supervisory practices of my supervisees without requiring specific delineation or discussion—an assumption I now find only partly justified.

As my writings on the therapeutic interaction broadened and deepened, I translated much of my new understanding into supervisory practice and discussion. Quite unreflectingly at first, I did indeed make use of my basic model of supervision as a rough structure for self-supervision. Because of my special interest in the analytic and therapeutic processes, and in the subject of validation, I took particular pains to develop a systematic and sound approach to self-supervision. Refinements that emerged through my own personal work were then translated into supervisory practices and discussions, thereby completing the enriching circle between a supervisor's own therapeutic work and his efforts as a teacher.

Despite several years of improved self-supervisory practices and growing specificity, I did not actually focus on the subject of self-supervision until I had crystallized the format for the teaching situation described in chapter 6. I had quickly discovered that in my personal therapeutic and analytic work this particular format served admirably as a structured means of evaluating each session with a patient, and as a basis for establishing checkpoints through which key issues relevant to self-supervision could be identified and worked through. The earlier basic insights into the patient's unconscious supervisory efforts on the therapist's behalf could then be integrated with the growing understanding of the role of self-awareness and self-knowledge, generating a formal approach to self-supervision with a basic structure that nonetheless permits great flexibility and lends itself readily to the entire gamut of self-supervisory problems.

The realm of self-supervision is clearly broader than that of self-analysis. The former is the more inclusive term, and so complex as to include every aspect of therapeutic work and the influences upon it. It may be defined, then, as constituting all attempts to monitor and evaluate one's therapeutic endeavors, and to identify and learn more about the factors which impinge upon them. It entails not only the search for errors and countertransferences, but also the identification of the positive aspects of the therapist's work and its effects upon the patient. It entails a search for flaws in practice, understanding, and conceptualizing, and the development of corrective measures as needed—through self-analysis, reading, discussion with colleagues or teachers, and the like. Finally, it is a process that requires its own methodology—predictive and validating—and which must be put to consistent use by the therapist in the course of each therapy hour.

On the emotional side, the avoidance of self-supervision suggests first a general lack of systematization, methodology, and standards; and, second, self-protecting countertransference-based defenses directed against the awareness of what undoubtedly are significant limitations in the self-supervisory practices of most therapists and analysts. Viewed in the worst light, the lack of literature on the subject might be taken as evidence of a considerable degree of neglect, disinterest, and fear of self-supervision, not only in terms of formal investigations, but also in respect to actual practice.

The present paper, then, is designed to identify some fundamental dimensions of self-supervision, to present a basic format and methodology, and to discuss selected key issues. The goal is both to open the way for further definitive investigations and to offer a set of specific proposals and comments designed to enhance the actual practice of self-monitoring, self-educational, and self-analytic measures.

A Model and Format for Self-Supervision

The therapist begins each session without desire, memory, or understanding (Bion 1970, Langs 1978c). In this way, his attention and efforts are centered on the patient's therapeutic needs, and self-supervision is undertaken with that goal in mind. This approach, supplemented by the thesis that each session shall be its own creation, tends to favor a state of mind in the therapist in which the past—sessions, knowledge, attitudes, etc.—is relatively obliterated; where it is remembered, this occurs with relative effortlessness and passivity, at the prompting of material from the patient and the therapist's own subjective responses. Designed originally to foster the search for the unknown with the patient, it serves secondarily in a similar manner in respect to the therapist and his self-supervision. It helps create a state of mind in which old concepts can be discovered anew, and revised as needed, and new self-supervisory issues can best be detected, while old ones are remembered in a specific context during the session. In all, this approach fosters the setting aside of relatively fixed self- and general knowledge, in favor of the fresh discovery of truths about oneself, the patient, and the therapeutic process.

Self-supervision is one dimension and aspect of the therapist's silent activities during a session. It is a continual process which must exist in every session, and which will, as a rule, come to the fore only from time to time as part of the reflective, self-observing functions of the therapist—an aspect of his functioning which tends to alternate with less self-conscious, open and unencumbered listening, formulating and intervening. It entails reflection upon, and evaluation of, all aspects of the therapeutic interaction: the therapist's silent hypotheses and interventions, his efforts at validation, his actual interventions to the patient, his subjective thoughts, feelings, and fantasies, and the patient's associations, behaviors, and responses to interventions. Unlike the search for countertransferences, which is usually triggered by some type of dysphoric or unusual response within the therapist, self-supervisory efforts should continue even when matters seem to be moving along quite well.

The basic model of self-supervision calls for the presence of these efforts intermittently within each session, without extension into the sessions of other patients or the free time of the therapist. It is my belief that this process should be an inherent part of the ongoing, spiraling unconscious communicative interaction between therapist and patient. With sufficient self-knowledge and sophistication, it can and should be confined to the session at hand; further, it functions most optimally under such conditions. Unfinished issues will arise in subsequent sessions, enabling eventual resolution. In this way, self-supervision is an integral part of the therapeutic interaction and is not artificially separated from the ongoing relationship between therapist and patient. It is also undertaken without notes and is based largely on the rapid identification of key problems, evaluation, and resolution—supplemented, at times, by formal efforts at learning outside of sessions.

Certainly, in situations where the therapist is unable to resolve an important self-supervisory problem within these optimal limits, it will be necessary to extend himself beyond the immediate session. It hardly needs saying that this should not be done during another patient's session; such efforts must be restricted to free moments, preferably in the therapist's office and occasionally while at home (the quiet moments before falling asleep are often put to such use). In principle, it is best to carry out this work relatively spontaneously and without recorded material. If such efforts falter, further compromises will be needed. The first of these may well be the writing of notes *after* the session (never during the hour because of the detrimental consequences of such a modification in the framework; see Langs 1975b, 1976a,d, 1978c). These can then be scrutinized quite formally, in sequence and using a model of self-supervision quite close to direct supervisory practices. Beyond that measure, of course, lies the possibility of presenting such material to an outside supervisor, but this should be resorted to only when absolutely necessary. Ultimately, a major failure in self-supervision might require referral of the patient to another therapist or analyst.

The Format

The basic method and tools of self-supervision are

comparable to those used in the supervision of others. The format presented in chapter 6 serves extremely well as a reticulum for all types of self-supervisory endeavors, and as a means of identifying nodal points that should be accounted for in evaluating one's continuing therapeutic work. There are six steps involved, and from time to time the therapist turns to these as a means of checking out his evaluation of the hour and his efforts at self-supervision. Let us look briefly at each checkpoint in this light.

1. The first checkpoint may be identified in terms of several key questions: What are the indicators for intervening, and how heavily should each be weighed? Have any been missed? Here, self-supervision serves to direct the therapist toward blind spots and defenses that often can be modified on a conscious, cognitive level.

This checkpoint leads to additional self-directed questions. What is the basis for the indicators? To what extent has the therapist contributed to modifications in the frame, resistances, and the like? Here self-supervision is undertaken in an interactional framework, with a consistent effort to identify the contributions of both patient and therapist to the prevailing therapeutic contexts. These efforts prompt the therapist to seek out possible countertransference-based contributions, as should be done at every evaluatory juncture.

In all, then, the first step is to identify indications from the patient of a need for an intervention from the therapist, and to ascertain its basis in both participants. All formulations are then subjected to silent validation and they may, as well, lead to further self-searching, especially when difficulties, blocks, and errors are detected. Scrutiny of the intensity of the indicators and their sources serves to prepare the therapist for the extent to which he is likely to intervene—self-supervision serves many constructive functions.

2. The next checkpoint is identification of the major adaptive contexts for the patient in the particular hour at hand. Here, self-supervision calls for a gradual review of the therapist's most recent interventions, especially those

alluded to in the material from the patient. This effort requires an examination of the unconscious nature and functions of these contexts, a consideration of any repetitive or acute countertransference-based inputs, and a search for adaptive contexts not immediately identified by the therapist yet powerfully inherent in the patient's conscious and, more usually, unconscious communications.

It can be seen, then, that in the first step the focus is largely on the material from the patient and on surface indications of a need for intervention; only secondarily do the contributions from the therapist play a role—unless the therapeutic context takes the form of a technical error or deviation in the ground rules. It entails, primarily, a direct monitoring of the patient's associations and behaviors, and only minimally draws upon his unconscious communications or the subjective responses of the therapist. In contrast, the second step—that of identifying the adaptive context—requires a more rigorous examination of the patient's unconscious communications, which in their complexity include the patient's unconscious supervisory efforts and directives; in addition, this step requires an important degree of self-awareness and sensitivity to the implications of the therapist's interventions. In general, as self-supervisory efforts move toward the understanding of unconscious processes and contents, primarily within the patient and secondarily within the therapist, these two major resources—the patient's unconscious supervisory efforts and the therapist's self-awareness and its underlying implications—come more intensely into play.

3. Next the therapist seeks to determine how the adaptive context is represented in the material from the patient. Here the therapist experiences the ease or difficulty with which he is able to deal with matters of representability and derivative (indirect) communication. Further, since this is a critical factor in intervening, self-supervision at this point often deals with the development of silent hypotheses that lead to tentative interventions held in abeyance. At this juncture, the

therapist's cognitive functioning is open to extensive countertransference and noncountertransference influences, as well as to effects from the patient; self-supervision becomes more clearly an interactional product.

4. Next we have the evaluation of the derivative complex as it pertains to each specific adaptive context. It is here that most supervisees have their greatest degree of difficulty, and it seems likely that most cognitive and countertransference-based problems in self-supervision will take place in this area. There are no easy correctives. In principle, it is best to begin with the most important adaptive context, and to attempt to relate every communication and cluster of associations from the patient in some meaningful way to this precipitant. It is here that much of the therapist's general knowledge comes into play, since he is attempting to formulate unconscious perceptions, introjects, fantasies, and memories; genetics and dynamics; reactive and defensive responses; additional matters of representability and unconscious communication—and a host of other relevant factors. His capacity to understand derivative, unconscious communication is tested and evaluated. It may well be that the most important principles—among many—are to begin with perception before fantasy, therapist before patient, and valid unconscious communications before those that are distorted. It is, however, beyond the scope of this presentation to identify and discuss every possible learning difficulty in this area; such an effort would be tantamount to writing an extensive text on the psychoanalytic and psychotherapeutic interactions.

In regard to self-supervision, then, the therapist will strive to gain some sense of the viability of his formulation, and to identify specific problem areas. He will also be developing a central silent hypothesis, and attempting to silently validate its components through the patient's continuing associations and his own subsequent subjective reactions. Eventually, after developing a silent intervention, he will intervene directly to the patient and initiate efforts at comprehending the presence or absence of a validating response. In particular, the patient's reaction to his intervention will be heavily laden with unconscious supervisory activities and will address difficulties in any of the six basic components of the format being presented here. These communications should be used to further the therapist's own supervisory endeavors. Clearly, these are complex matters that need a sound foundation in clinical understanding and in the continual resolution of major countertransference difficulties; nonetheless, they are capable of a significant degree of relative mastery.

5. The next step entails the identification, toward the latter part of the session, of a direct bridge to the therapist or therapy. This is a manifest phenomenon that is readily recognized; often it signifies a sound juncture for intervening—the culmination of earlier preparatory work.

Throughout the session, the patient's ongoing material can be used consistently as a means of verifying self-supervisory efforts and coalescing formulations, and as a guide to modifying those hypotheses that do not gain ongoing support and must therefore be revised. Before the therapist has intervened, the patient's assistance through unconscious supervisory efforts is often implicit, and is usually based on either unconscious efforts to alert the therapist to a particular issue that he should deal with or responses to his extended silence, especially when it is inappropriate. As I have already indicated, once the therapist has intervened, he can expect the patient to condense into his response more intense unconscious supervisory efforts—along with such qualities as validation or its lack, the offer of additional dynamic and genetic material, unconscious curative efforts directed toward the errant therapist, and the like.

The use of these promptings toward self-supervision and of the resources in the patient is, of course, extensively supplemented by the therapist's own self-scrutiny, through which he identifies his ongoing thoughts, affects, fantasies, and the like, all in addition to his continuous efforts at listening, formulating, and validating. These are complex, interdigitating processes and must eventually culminate in actual corrective measures. Since I have written at length on this subject, especially in regard to the search for countertransference-based influences (1978c), I will add only this: it is critical here to apply the entire range of the listening and validating processes to the therapist's subjective experiences. It must be recognized that his *conscious* thoughts, fantasies, and affects are surface phenomena, and that they must be traced out through self-analysis and self-understanding to their roots in *unconscious* perceptions, fantasies, introjects, and memories. All too often, self-supervision is undertaken on an entirely conscious level and no effort is made to determine the relevant unconscious processes and contents critical to every aspect of the therapist's work, especially to repeated errors and learning blocks. The outcome of self-supervision will be markedly curtailed unless these deeper factors are tapped.

6. Finally, the therapist attempts to ascertain the patient's general communicative style, and his communicative mode in the session at hand. Here, he makes use of a variety of clues in the material from the patient which serve to define this dimension; in general, his self-supervisory efforts will be directed toward determining any countertransference-based contribution to any pathological aspect of the patient's communicative style, and toward recognizing problems in distinguishing among the three basic communicative modes.

To summarize these principles: There is a basic format for self-supervision, which establishes the following checkpoints: (1) indicators and therapeutic contexts; (2) the presence of major adaptive contexts, their unconscious implications, and the availability of a link to the therapist; (3) the manner in which the adaptive context is represented in the material from the patient; (4) the nature of the derivative complex; (5) the presence of a bridge to the therapist or therapy; and (6) the communicative style of the patient. Each checkpoint brings up critical self-supervisory issues which can be explored and resolved once brought into focus and analyzed in depth. In addition, this schema implies a rather general temporal sequence of self-supervisory activities.

This basic format can be readily integrated with other schemas for self-supervision. For example, it overlaps and interdigitates with a model of self-supervision that uses as its checkpoints the listening and validating processes, the generation of silent hypotheses and silent interventions, the silent validation of these formulations, the offer of an intervention to the patient, and the evaluation of the patient's response—in terms of validation and other implications. This model is also based on a general temporal sequence which integrates listening-validating sequentially with intervening and revalidating.

Still other self-supervisory agendas may be identified and integrated with this basic format. Another important set of checkpoints derives from the four major realms of supervision: listening-validating, the ground rules and framework, the therapeutic relationship and interaction, and intervening. Within each of these broad realms are found many self-supervisory issues. As a rule, these arise in no set temporal sequence, depending instead on the nature of the ongoing therapeutic interaction and the patient's associations. With the basic format as the reticulum, each of these spheres can be checked out in terms of the six fundamental nodal points. In all, then, any general self-supervisory concern can be studied quite carefully within the major framework proposed here.

Finally, it should be recognized that self-supervision is, in every sense, an interactional product—a dimension of the bipersonal field. It is under the constant influence of the patient, in addition to deriving its primary impetus from within the therapist. These efforts are not merely a matter of therapeutic conscience and responsibility, as influenced by many factors within the therapist; self-supervision is a process that can either be facilitated or interfered with by the patient.

To clarify, certain patients will enhance the therapist's self-supervisory efforts both directly and indirectly. There are many ways in which this is done: by producing relatively clear material that can be readily organized for self-supervisory scrutiny; by maintaining a level of work that in general implicitly encourages the therapist to maintain his self-supervisory attitudes in the best interests of the treatment experience; by communicating without pressure and turmoil, thereby leaving room for calm self-scrutiny by the therapist; and by engaging unconsciously in a variety of readily detectable unconscious supervisory endeavors, especially after the therapist has intervened. This list is by no means exhaustive, and the patient may facilitate self-supervision through particular qualities of every aspect of his contribution to the therapeutic relationship. By contrast, patients whose material is flat and dull, or overly complex, who are strikingly seductive and provocative, or in turmoil, who tend to attack and destroy the therapist's formulations and interventions on some level, and who engage in minimal unconscious supervisory activities will tend to hamper and disrupt the therapist's own efforts at self-supervision.

These observations also pertain to the important issue of the motivations for self-supervision. Clearly, the primary motivational system lies within the therapist (e.g., ego ideals, professional standards, and personal needs to be an effective therapist, to name but a few of the more surface aspects which, of course, extend into deeper unconscious motivational systems). However, additional motivating factors derive from the needs and communications of the patient. They are conveyed consciously and unconsciously to the therapist and strongly influence his self-supervisory work. Patients vary, for example, in the intensity of their unconscious wishes for insightful cure, and the related unconscious wishes to evoke in the therapist sound interventions and secure self-supervisory efforts. In many ways, then, while self-supervision is the primary responsibility of the therapist, it is greatly affected by the patient.

Some Major Issues

Two basic types of difficulty arise in self-supervision: first, problems related to engaging in and carrying out self-supervisory activities themselves; second, the wide range of problems that may have to be dealt with in the course of these efforts. Since, as I have already intimated, the latter group includes every conceivable problem pertinent to the therapeutic experience, I will focus here on selected problems related to the self-supervisory process itself.

Perhaps the most fundamental difficulty can be identified as the appearance of resistances, sometimes quite unconscious, within the therapist against undertaking self-supervision, or against carrying out certain essential steps in the self-supervisory process. Here we touch upon the critical subject of the manner in which the therapist's psychopathology—his countertransferences—detrimentally influence his approach to self-supervision. While the resolution of these underlying countertransferences must be a matter of personal or self-analysis, it is nonetheless possible to characterize attitudes that will facilitate this most important aspect of the therapist's work. It seems critical to recognize the importance of intermittent self-supervisory efforts in every session with a patient. We should also recognize that as therapists and analysts we have a relatively intense, basically healthy but sometimes pathological narcissistic investment in our interventions and their essential correctness. There are extensive indications that many therapists make little effort to validate their therapeutic work, and to make full use of the the validating process which must culminate in the emergence of Type Two derivative validation, the presence of a *selected fact* (Bion 1962, Langs 1976a, 1978c). There is a strong tendency among therapists to anticipate confirmation of their interventions, and to shape or even distort the patient's responses in ways that seem validating, even where a more neutral observer might entertain serious doubts.

These impressions suggest a need to advocate a relatively neutral, less self-invested self-supervisory attitude, and the use of checks and balances designed to minimize inevitable tendencies toward blind spots. This approach could take the following form: having offered a verbal intervention that the therapist believes at the moment of its expression to be valid and compelling, and to best express the truths related to the patient's neurosis at the moment, he might well shift to a somewhat different attitude in attending to and formulating the patient's responses. Thus, he might adopt a stance of skepticism regarding his intervention, and therefore actively reconsider its merits. He might also make special efforts to identify nonconfirmatory responses from the patient and should maintain stringent criteria for cognitive and interactional validation (see also Langs 1978i). Along different lines, he could approach all of the material from the patient in terms of a search for its valid core before attempting to identify the distortions and fantasies. After an intervention, he should, of course, accept the patient's material as an extensive *commentary* (Langs 1978c) on his intervention, with many essential truths, before searching for the patient's lies and falsifications—his distortions. Rather than being enamored of his own work, the therapist should adopt an attitude of uncertainty and wariness, a healthy means of dealing with the pathological narcissistic aspects of his work.

Another constructive self-supervisory attitude is implicit in the recognition that every experience within the patient is a product of the bipersonal field, with contributions from both participants. Even interludes in which the patient improves and does well require self-supervision to trace out the underlying basis for the improvement. In circumstances in which the patient becomes symptomatic, regresses, or acts out, the therapist should turn actively to self-supervisory efforts as a means of determining his contribution before considering its basis within the patient.

Another related problem involves the level at which self-supervision is undertaken. All too often therapists engage in such activities only when they have made a major and almost self-evident blunder, or have experienced a gross indication of blatant countertransference difficulty. For some, self-supervision may be restricted to very apparent cognitive errors, or even confined to the search for indications of countertransference—thereby neglecting a wide range of additional self-supervisory problems. Usually such work occurs on an entirely conscious level, with no pursuit of the underlying unconscious processes, fantasies, memories, and introjects. Failure to continually monitor the entire gamut of self-supervisory needs and problems, and to search out through brief periods of silent free associating the unconscious roots of technical difficulties, will leave the therapist vulnerable to repeating the same error over and over again.

Finally, it seems clear now that it is necessary for a supervisor to teach his supervisee the practice of self-supervision. This implies that selected presentations in supervision should include allusions to the supervisee's own self-supervisory efforts—both in the session with the patient and in the course of his presentation to the supervisor. In this way, specific problems in the practice of self-supervision by a given supervisee can be dealt with entirely in the context of the therapeutic interaction under consideration. In addition, I have found it useful to suggest to the supervisee that he engage in self-supervisory exercises comparable to, but more elaborate than, the listening exercises I have recently described (Langs 1978c). It proves especially helpful to work over a particular block in technique by engaging in self-supervisory exercises with a variety of patients. Some of this can be done as part of the valid therapeutic effort of each session, but where necessary the practice can be extended into endeavors undertaken during free hours.

For too long now we have taken self-supervision for granted, neglecting the development of a basic format and failing to attend to the very specific problems involved. As with every other dimension of the therapeutic experience, self-supervision can rely only minimally on the therapist's natural proclivities and basic understanding; much must be done to sharpen these assets and to bring them into full awareness so that they might serve as efficacious therapeutic tools.

Clinical Illustrations

I selected, at random and in advance, a particular supervisory hour with a supervisee of intermediate experience; in that hour he would report his self-supervisory efforts as part of the supervisory presentation. I will describe the transactions of that particular supervisory hour, and will add general comments pertinent to the main purpose of this paper.

The patient being presented was a young woman in twice-weekly psychotherapy who sought help for episodes of depression and difficulties in relating to men. She had been in therapy for over a year, and there had been many problems in the treatment process. Most recently this had taken the form of erratic management of the framework by the therapist in respect to changes in the time of the patient's sessions and several rather diffuse and poorly organized interventions offered as part of his efforts at rectifying and interpreting these deviations.

The supervisee began by reporting that the patient had been five minutes late; while waiting for her, it occurred to him that this was an indicator for intervening. Upon her arrival, he had handed her a business card on which his present office address was crossed out, and his new address written in (he was planning to change his office three weeks hence). At that point he told the patient that he had decided to move his office, and that the new location was written on the card. They would have their first session in that office three weeks from today. To himself, he thought that he was now modifying the framework and that he had an especially important indicator for the present session.

The patient looked at the card and asked the therapist:

What does A.C.S.W. mean? The therapist responded, Academy of Certified Social Workers. To himself, he had the thought: I shouldn't have handed her a card; I should simply have told her about the move, because once I gave her the card I had to answer her question in order to clarify what was on it.

To comment here, we can see that the supervisee, during the opening moments of the session, had identified certain possible implications of the patient's lateness and his own behavior, and had implicitly become involved in an aspect of self-supervision which, upon inquiry, he had not been consciously aware of and had not subjected to further self-reflection. His thought that he should not have handed the patient a card with his address on it reflected the supervisee's sense of difficulty in handling the consequences of this step; but on another level it reflects a partial self-supervisory effort which, had it been more conscious and explicated in terms of the therapist's likely conflicts and anxieties about moving his office, related countertransferences, and confusion about the nature and functions of the frame, might have proven quite helpful in understanding the balance of the session.

The patient's question about the A.C.S.W., in addition to its other implications, constitutes an unconscious supervisory effort. It is her way of saying that if the therapist gives her something of his, she will want more and more. The card unnecessarily extends the boundaries, she is implying, and the therapist should realize that this creates pressures for both of them. It leads the patient to want to know more about him personally, and is therefore essentially inappropriate.

Thus, based on this very brief communication from the patient, the therapist could have become engaged in rather extensive self-supervisory efforts which would have led to the tentative conclusion—the silent hypothesis—that handing the patient the card had been an unnecessary alteration in the framework and that it would need both rectification and interpretation in the session; based on the material from the patient, including her unconscious supervisory directives, the therapist could have taken back the card, read the address to the patient, who could then make note of it on her own, and interpreted the unconscious implications of the entire transaction.

Self-supervisory efforts must be validated, not only subjectively, but also—and especially—through Type Two derivatives from the patient. Self-supervision is not simply a matter of identifying a problem here or there based on intuition or sudden insight, but entails the formulation of silent hypotheses which are, in the main, pertinent to the material from the patient. The formulation just outlined has such qualities and it obtained initial validation when the patient lay down on the couch and was silent for ten minutes—the deviation apparently had interfered with the openness of the communicative field.

Returning now to the supervisory session, the supervisee stated that he had considered the ten-minute silence yet another indicator for intervening, and experienced the situation with a mixture of discomfort and relief. He though of the problems he had been having in processing the material from the patient and was not at all unhappy about having less material to integrate and understand. He recognized the evident manifestation of countertransference, but was unable to analyze it or do more than attempt to consciously struggle against his sense of inappropriate gratification and defense. He then experienced concern because he had felt that she had been more communicative in the prior hour and he had hoped she would continue. He began to think about his main intervention in the earlier hour and to feel that he had screwed things up; perhaps this had led her to withdraw. Still, the more immediate context was giving her the card. He felt that her question and silence made it clear that he should not have done so and he began to wonder why he had made the error.

The patient then spoke. She had just left her job; she had worked overtime with a group of co-workers. While leaving the office with them, she had realized from what they were saying that all of the craziness was not in herself—it pervaded the entire office. The therapist saw this material as reflecting a positive introject; in the past the patient would see herself as the only one who was crazy, while now she realized that others were crazy as well. He traced this supposed positive introject to his recent effort to secure the framework and to an intervention in the early part of the previous hour which had been validated by the patient. He sensed a mixture in the patient's current response in keeping with his constructive work and its subsequent deterioration in the form of the confusing final intervention.

To comment, the therapist's view of this material as reflecting a positive introject represents some confusion and misunderstanding in the therapist, since there appears to be little evidence of such a process in these initial associations. The basis for the therapist's thinking was his belief that there had been some change in the patient's self-image, but this formulation appears to ignore other possibilities which seem more meaningful and relevant for the moment.

Here, a major problem in self-supervision is reflected: how are erroneous formulations to be recognized? The therapist quickly departs from an attitude of seeking continued commentary on his last intervention—handing the patient a card. He now shifts to the previous session as a means of excluding the present adaptive context; this is a countertransference-based block. It can be rectified only by consistently monitoring the material in terms of sequences of adaptive contexts and responses, and by listening further to the material from the patient for validating material. In addition, she may become involved in unconscious supervisory efforts if she detects the difficulty within the therapist. In this regard, it becomes clearer why much of a patient's unconscious supervisory efforts take place in response to interventions by the therapist. Prior to such communications, the patient has little way of knowing what is going on in the therapist's mind—with the possible exception of those situations where the patient unconsciously experiences a need for an intervention and the therapist fails to respond. Under such circumstances, however, the patient has few clues as to the nature of the therapist's problem, even though she will experience its presence.

In the actual supervisory session, the therapist was allowed to present the entire hour without comment from myself. I then returned to these segments and was able to discuss specific difficulties apparent in his effort to develop a self-supervisory attitude; in addition, it was possible to point out the types of problems that were reflected in his actual work with the patient.

It was proposed as a silent hypothesis that this first cluster of associations, organized around the adaptive context of handing the card to the patient and viewed along the me/not-me interface, indicates that the patient experienced this measure as an attempt to drive her crazy and as a reflection of some type of craziness within the therapist. Any self-supervisory formulation that would have considered the business with the card a positive step would have to be rectified in light of this particular communication.

The growing recognition of the apparent implications of this deviation would further prepare the therapist to intervene: he now had confirmation that he was dealing with a powerful therapeutic context, an indicator that would make both rectification and interpretation essential; in addition, the adaptive context was quite apparent and directly represented in the opening exchange between therapist and patient. This latter would facilitate intervening, an anticipation further supported by the strikingly meaningful qualities of the first derivative communication —the derivative complex shows considerable promise. In addition, it now seemed likely that the prevailing communicative style would be in the Type A mode, another factor that would favor intervening.

In keeping with the principles advocated here, as part of his self-supervisory efforts, the therapist should have attempted first to apply the image of craziness to himself and his most recent intervention. Instead, he revealed a split in both self-image and self-understanding: on the one hand he had felt that the patient was unconsciously indicating that his handing her the card was an error, while on the other he proved refractory to applying the image of craziness to himself—a hint of countertransference, which, once detected, would require tracing out, self-analysis, rectification, and education.

The supervisee continued his presentation, indicating that the patient went on to state that her boss had offered her a position as head of her department, in lieu of the relatively minor promotion she had expected. She was bothered, however, by the way he did it, because he had been quite devious. He had a reason for doing it that way because there was this macho guy who was going to take the position, but he turned out to be a bozo and her boss just had to find some way of getting rid of him. Here the supervisee again saw mixed images: the boss had been devious and the macho man was a bozo, but on the other hand the patient had received an important promotion. He attempted to organize this material along the me/not-me interface, and wondered if the boss did not represent himself.

To comment, we see here efforts to organize the material, but an absence of a self-reflective, self-supervisory process. Attempts to formulate the material must be distinguished from supervisory efforts; while they will often overlap, they differ as well, largely because self-supervision is focused on an evaluation of the therapist's formulations and interventions, including efforts at their revision and validation, and, in addition, at self-analysis and learning.

In terms of self-supervision, the therapist might have turned to the basic format presented in this paper and quickly recognized that he was now formulating derivatives in isolation—Type One derivatives—instead of linking them to a specific adaptive context. The indicators were superficial and transparent, and had provided no special problems other than a need to maintain an awareness of their presence and of their unconscious implications (latent content and functions), and to eventually relate the implications of the communicative network to the therapeutic context. It is to be remembered that the unconscious meanings of a given indicator are determined by the communicative network, and by the implications of derivative communications—fantasies and perceptions—as organized around the specific prevailing adaptive contexts.

Lacking any such format, the supervisee began to lose the sense of definitive unconscious meaning, primarily because he had divorced the derivatives from the adaptive context of his having given the patient the card. Thus, the therapist might have viewed this next segment of the derivative complex as suggesting an unconscious hope in the patient that in his new office he would function positively and adequately for a change. The material could also be viewed as reflecting a positive unconscious perception of the anticipated move, but a negative perception of the manner in which the therapist decided to provide this information to the patient—the devious qualities of the altered framework, his handing the patient the card.

This last communication can also be seen as part of the patient's unconscious supervisory efforts: she is indicating to the therapist that the card intervention is devious, an attempt on his part to be macho as a defense against feeling like a bozo. It also is a reflection of a problem with separation—the reference to finding a way to get rid of someone—a derivative communication that approaches an unconscious interpretation. The therapist, recognizing these implications as unconscious supervisory efforts on the patient's part, might then translate them into self-supervision aimed at better understanding the decision to hand the patient the card. In general, self-supervisory efforts should center around the major adaptive context and its indicators—the main sources of disturbance for both patient and therapist—in a given session. Additional efforts may be made around secondary problems, but the most meaningful self-supervisory work will be focused in this way. In this therapeutic situation, both the therapist's subjective feelings and the patient's communications indicate quite clearly that handing the patient the card is the central issue for both of them. The most effective self-supervisory efforts would undoubtedly take place in this area.

The supervisee went on, stating that the patient described going to dinner with several people from her office, where she sat between a man and a woman. She felt that she had clicked with the guy, and that she could work with him when the macho fellow left. In talking, she and this fellow came up with a lot of good ideas for her section; the gal didn't have much to say. Here the therapist thought that the images continued to be quite mixed: on the one hand, she had clicked with the fellow and had worked creatively, but on the other, the girl did not have much to say. Somehow, he felt, these images must be related to himself and to treatment.

At this point, the supervisee's problems are similar to those identified in his response to the previous cluster of associations. Self-supervision might have taken the following form: Is the patient saying something about the therapist's gratifying himself through what he had done? There is still some positive hope within the patient, and yet also some need to withdraw. Does the reference to the girl who does not speak serve in part as an unconscious directive that the therapist intervene? The supervisee should be checking out the further implications of this set of derivatives around the adaptive context of handing the patient the card; he should explore in addition the material as a commentary on his present silence. Self-supervision entails consistent questioning of one's techniques in light of the material from the patient.

The patient went on: We took a cab here, the three of us, and they went on together. In my fantasy, they were involved with each other sexually and I resented it. Somehow, my priorities are always wrong. After some silence, she ruminated about how much work she has to do over the next few weeks, so much so that she cannot even think of this process (referring to therapy). Here the therapist recognized the bridge back to therapy, and decided to intervene. He pointed out to the patient that she puts herself on the spot, something that she expresses in her lateness and silence. She also works over her difficulties verbally. This must connect to her sense of chaos, both within and without. Immediately after this intervention, the therapist sensed that he had avoided the sexual reference—a recurrent problem with him. He didn't like the intervention, and quickly realized as well that he had failed to utilize an adaptive context and to present an integrated comment.

Clearly, the adaptive context of handing the patient the card was totally neglected in this intervention, including the implications that the patient perceived it as an unconscious sexual invitation against which she had a need to defend herself. It also imposed a great deal of work upon her, and prompted a type of avoidance—not wishing to think about treatment. A more valid intervention would have begun with the adaptive context of handing the patient the card and would have led the therapist to point out that the patient had seen this as a bit of craziness, as an attempt to be macho and seductive, and as a kind of incompetence that has to be gotten rid of—or corrected. Using the reference to the need to fire the incompetent worker, he could hint at the need to rectify the framework by taking back the card, in the expectation that the patient would then provide additional material on which to base a more definitive effort in this critical direction. In the meantime he might interpret the patient's unconscious perceptions of his behavior and, using a transversal intervention, hint at possible underlying unconscious fantasies.

In terms of self-supervision, we see little in the way of any effort by this therapist to define silent hypotheses or to check out their validity in light of the patient's unconscious commentaries. While the supervisee did make some effort to seek meaning in the patient's derivative communications, he did so in an extremely limited manner, often losing sight of the adaptive context, and failed to review the checkpoints in the format presented here. He did, however, evaluate his intervention once it had been made, and recognized certain deficiencies which, if he now remained open to the patient's unconscious supervisory activities, could be validated in her responsive material and eventually rectified.

In the session, the patient reacted by asking the therapist what he meant by the phrase "working it over verbally." The therapist answered directly: Now you are putting me on the spot with your question. Subjectively, he remembered such pressures from the patient a few weeks earlier and felt satisfied with the intervention. The patient asked the therapist if he meant that she did that instead of just thinking about things. To himself, the therapist felt that this was a validating response, since that was, indeed, exactly what he meant. He therefore added to his previous intervention by pointing out that her questions about the A.C.S.W. was another effort to put pressure on him. The patient responded by saying that if he thinks that that is putting pressure on him, he must really be insecure. Now the therapist felt quite chaotic and that he had used the A.C.S.W. comment incorrectly. He felt attacked, but sensed that the patient was essentially correct: he is insecure. He then felt terrible. On this note the session ended.

In brief, when a patient responds to an intervention with a question, self-supervision calls for a re-examination of the intervention in light of the possibility that it is not only unclear, but also essentially incorrect. Technically, it is best to respond with silence and to permit the patient to free associate in order to receive her unconscious and conscious commentaries. When the therapist subjectively feels pressured by the patient, he should treat this as an interactional product and immediately ask himself if this in any way implies that he has created pressure for the patient—here, through handing her the card and making an erroneous intervention. The feeling of pressure can also be taken as a clue that some technical error has been made, and might lead to a review of the session, including efforts at reformulation based in part on the patient's continued associations. With the therapist's failure to rectify the frame and interpret in this context, his intervention, the altered frame itself, and the patient's responses shifted to a Type B communicative mode.

Finally, when a session ends on a disquieting note, the communications from the patient should be taken as an effort to call to the attention of the therapist some type of failure in intervening. It should initiate an immediate self-supervisory effort to review the session, once over, to determine where the therapist went astray. This therapist had done just that, and had quickly realized that he had divorced the material from the prevailing adaptive context of handing her the card; from there he began to investigate his feelings about moving his office—his separation anxieties and the underlying specific unconscious fantasies and memories. He recognized too a countertransference-based trend which led him to blame the patient for his own confusion and for the pressures that he was creating on her, and he reviewed his own sense of confusion and disorganization during such interludes.

The supervisee went on to present the second hour of that week. The patient was on time, which was unusual for her, but she was then silent for fifteen minutes. Subjectively, the therapist felt furious because the patient had been on time and was now attacking him with her silence. He had fantasies of killing her and of her shoving something up his ass with her silence. He felt both pissed off and pleased. He thought of the adaptive context as the craziness of his interventions at the end of the last session: he had been half-assed himself.

We can see that here the supervisee expresses himself in a manner heavily laden with affective and instinctual drive qualities. Self-supervision would call for an awareness of the intensity of the therapist's feelings and impulses, and an effort on the one hand to trace out the interactional and intrapsychic sources and underlying meanings and functions of such a response; while on the other hand it would be well to keep an eye on the tentative proposed interventions that would unfold in the session in order to safeguard as much as possible their neutrality and relative freedom from the acting out of these strong fantasies and impulses. Such subjective experiences therefore call for a search not only for underlying countertransferences and stimuli from the patient, but also for cognitive self-supervisory efforts directed toward both understanding and management of the relatively tumultuous inner response within the therapist. An experience like this may also facilitate both recall of the disturbing factors in the previous session and further self-supervisory efforts in that area.

In the session, the patient began to speak about her trouble in establishing priorities, and how she feels unable to focus on the things she needs to do. She very much needs structure. To himself, the therapist felt that the material was organizing around his last intervention, which was relatively unfocused and which avoided the issue of sexuality.

Here the therapist made some use of the unconscious supervisory endeavors of the patient, though he failed to follow an important principle: that framework issues must take precedence over all else, and that the reference to the patient's need for structure should have directed him back to the previous session—specifically, to his modification of the framework by moving and especially by presenting the patient his card. In this way, the basic format discussed in this paper can be seen to integrate well with the four fundamental areas for self-supervision: listening-validating, the framework, the relationship, and intervening. A sense of priorities is, as the patient points out, quite necessary, and in general it should be: framework, relationship, listening-validating, and intervening.

In the session, the patient went on to state that if she focuses on her work she tries also to take care of herself physically. She will work and do exercises, and cook, and then have no time for anything else. The situation becomes unmanageable and she must establish priorities. At this moment she looked over her shoulder at the therapist and stated that because of her job she would have to leave the session ten minutes early. The therapist thought that this was an indicator for an intervention and therefore responded by pointing out that the patient had begun the hour by expressing her need for structure and priorities, and that she seemed upset about being unable to focus. It was interesting that she had come for her session on time, something that had been difficult for her in the past, but now she stated a need to leave the hour early. While there were realities in connection with her work, there was a need now to explore the additional implications of her request.

To himself, immediately upon making this intervention, the therapist recognized that he had failed to include an adaptive context in his intervention. He realized that he was somehow excluding himself from his interventions and, especially, that he was omitting any reference to his recent errors—which he still conceptualized mainly in terms of his last verbal intervention.

More adequate self-supervision would call for a specific examination of the nature of the framework when the patient proposes her own deviation, no matter how realistic the surface need. On one level, this communication from the patient serves to validate the self-supervisory effort presented here in terms of a working over of the implications of the therapist's alteration in the framework. For the moment, the derivatives point more to the therapist's decision to move his office—to leave—than to his giving the patient his card. In situations where the therapist has not self-analytically explored such issues, an announcement of this kind should serve to redirect his self-supervisory efforts, a shift that might well lead to a better understanding of the prevailing focus of the unconscious and spiraling communicative interaction.

In the hour, the patient explained that she had an appointment with her boss and could not be late. She had to make that a priority over therapy, and if she had to make a list, it would be her job and physical state first, and if necessary she would let go of this process. Here the therapist experienced a fear that the patient might leave therapy. The patient went on to remind the therapist that he had once said that her weight problem—she suffered from extreme thinness alternating with some degree of obesity—was caused by her emotional problems, and the therapist silently recalled many noninterpretive interventions he had made early in this patient's treatment, and even more recently. The patient went on to say that that might be so, and maybe giving up therapy would not be good for her, but still, those are the kind of priorities she has. At that point she fell silent and then said that she had to leave—and left. The therapist felt quite anxious that the patient might not return.

In a way, the patient had provided the therapist ten minutes for self-supervision, and with a sense of anxiety that might well stimulate such endeavors. The theme of priorities is reiterated, and could have led the therapist to review the priorities of therapeutic work, and hopefully to recognize that his own alteration in the framework has had a considerable impact on the patient—and on himself—and that it must be considered first. The patient also hints that unconsciously she views the therapist as self-serving—having his own selfish priorities that disregard her and her therapy (the move and the erroneous, self-serving interventions). She implies that because of this she might indeed attempt to find another form of help. There is a sense in the therapist of having failed to intervene adequately, an experience that should prompt a definitive reconsideration of at least the last two sessions—an undertaking that should be as structured as possible, in keeping with the principles expounded here.

Finally, it can be stated that the relatively chaotic and uncertain ending of this particular hour can be taken as a reflection of the therapist's failure at self-supervision. On another level, the same material served, as it must, as a signal for self-supervisory efforts in respect to my role as supervisor of this therapeutic experience. Clearly, as I have indicated elsewhere in this volume, a supervisor must himself engage in self-supervision in order to avoid succumbing to blind spots and learning blocks of his own. Self-supervision is a necessary adjunct to all therapeutic and supervisory work.

Self-Supervisory Crises

Self-supervisory crises may take many forms. Examples are acute symptomatic responses in the therapist during a particular session; repetitive symptoms or blocks in comprehension and intervening with a particular patient or on a particular workday; and any acute therapeutic crisis with a given patient, including acute symptomatic regressions, major resistances and ruptures in the therapeutic alliance, and sudden and premature termination. These more acute and circumscribed crises clearly call for major self-supervisory efforts, and therapists are as a rule strongly motivated to undertake such work in an effort to resolve their own symptoms, to restore their equilibrium and that of the therapy, and to be sufficiently free of disturbance to be of help to the patient. In addition to these conscious motives for self-supervisory work, many intense pathological and nonpathological needs are mobilized in such situations; as a result, these episodes provide special opportunities for important new cognitive and emotional insights into techniques, countertransferences, and the therapeutic process.

Under these conditions the therapist may be inclined to extend his self-supervisory efforts beyond a particular session with a patient, and may even resort to note-writing after the hour and to supervision with another therapist or analyst. Self-supervision at such times often provides soothing, meaningful, and constructive compensation for the many painful and guilt-provoking qualities in the therapist's awareness of his inappropriate contribution to the troublesome situation. Self-supervision is therefore among the most adaptive responses to the recognition of major errors on the part of the therapist. A brief vignette will serve to illustrate some of the problems and techniques of self-supervision in such situations.

Mrs. E was in intensive psychotherapy with Dr. W because of problems in her relationship with her husband and difficulties in getting along with her mother. A second problem was occasional episodes of asthma. Over a period of two years, she had shown considerable improvement in all spheres, though she had had a rare episode of asthma about three months prior to the sessions to be described here. For his part, the therapist had distinctly mixed feelings about this patient and her therapy: on the one hand, he was satisfied with her progress, although he felt that he had not dealt with or helped the patient work through her conflicts as they related to her asthma, especially the link to her father's death when she was three years old; on the other hand, this patient was most frustrating for him to work with, since she was a Type C communicator who spend many sessions ruminating and providing him little material for interpretation. There were therefore many flat and empty periods during this treatment, and lately almost all of the sessions had had this quality.

The therapist was also aware of distinct countertransference problems with this patient that he had been unable to resolve despite efforts in personal therapy, supervisory presentations, and attempts at self-analysis. He knew that the relevant issues were separation and death, and he was aware of angry feelings toward the patient for her chronic resistances. He also recognized other, more fleeting difficulties, though of late he mainly experienced the patient as an enormous burden he would gladly shed. Frustrated, he continued his efforts to resolve the underlying countertransferences, as well as the occasional blocks in comprehension and intervening that they created for him. While not glaring, the problems remained: all too often, he misconceptualized the material from the patient and either failed to intervene when he should have, or intervened erroneously. At other times, however, he was able to offer more accurate interpretations or was appropriately silent.

I will now turn to two sessions from this treatment. I will leave aside any discussion of the material and the initial efforts at self-supervision, and will instead present these two sessions, define the crisis facing the therapist, and indicate the nature of the initial supervisory presentation and discussion of this material; only then will I detail the type of self-supervision in which the therapist became engaged. This will provide us the opportunity to observe the interplay between self-supervision and a supervisory experience with a consulting therapist, and to review the important subject of self-supervision under crisis conditions.

The patient began this particular session, which occurred after the Christmas holiday, by describing a complicated family situation that took place in the context of the holiday dinner. She had been unhappy because she felt superior to most of the people at the dinner, and she had also felt some resentment toward one of her married sons, who now spent more time with his in-laws than with her. She thought of one of her two daughters, who had visited her separately with her husband, and she had felt much closer to them. She didn't like herself for feeling superior, but she could accept that image. She thought of her mother, who sat alone during much of the family gathering, and identified with one of her daughters-in-law, who seemed to feel excluded. At her job as a legal assistant she had discussed with one of her bosses a recent wave of suicide attempts among teenagers that had been reported in the news; some of them had used gas from ovens and this had reminded her of concentration camps. Her boss had brought up a recent assassination of an African leader, and kept avoiding the references to suicide. She wanted to talk to him about it again. In all, she had been feeling well even though she sometimes felt excluded. As she left the hour, she told the therapist that she would have his check next time; she meant to write it, but kept forgetting.

She began the next hour by saying she had been thinking

about it a lot and that she wanted to stop treatment. She didn't want to wait until the end of the session to say this. She reviewed her reasons for having come into treatment: hurts from her husband, conflicts with her mother, and the rest, and she stated that she felt she had worked these out. She now saw certain problems in separating from her children, but recognized that this is what has to be done. Some things still bothered her, but she felt they wouldn't change; she might still feel hurt that her husband doesn't help her around the house, but she no longer wants him to do that. She had become more assertive in her relationships, and wanted to try it on her own. She said she knew that she could come back to therapy if necessary, and that that was comforting because some things still disturbed her. A cousin had made a joke when his mother threatened to turn on the gas. He said wait until the grandchildren have left after the weekend. The patient didn't see any humor in the remark and thought a great deal about what happens when people get old, and how that disturbs her. It no longer seems so far away. She wished that the therapist would say something, realized that he probably wouldn't since that's his style, and said that that was all right with her because his approach had been helpful.

The therapist intervened and pointed out that the patient had been referring to gains she had made in the course of her treatment, and he mentioned several of these. She had also, he added, spoken of things that are disturbing to her, such as gas and death, but that she seemed to be saying that she didn't want to deal with these problems now. The patient responded that she had been at a party with an uncle who was dying. They had talked a lot about a man who had committed suicide and this had made her think of fears that she has about her husband becoming ill. Still, she was managing things well, felt good, and even though some things still disturbed her, such as feeling excluded and deprived, she thought mainly now of how much she had changed since beginning treatment. She had become more direct with her husband and others. Also, she could no longer stand people who are superficial; she now found herself quite critical of superficial chitchat. Sometimes she became jealous and possessive, but she was looking forward to a trip to Africa she would soon be taking with her husband, and she knew she could return to treatment if necessary. She was afraid of stopping, but knew that she must. She thanked the therapist, said she'd miss him, and added that she hoped she would see him around.

The therapist had mixed feelings about this experience. After weeks of relatively flat and empty, Type C communicative sessions, the patient had recently begun to talk about how well she was doing in her work, with her husband, and in her feelings about herself. In the supervisory hour prior to these sessions, I had suggested that despite the evidence that the unconscious basis for her asthma had not been analyzed and worked through, it might be necessary to think of the possibility of terminating this patient if she maintained her symptom-free state and improved functioning. I therefore suggested that the therapist be on the alert for any possible communications from the patient about termination. I added that in all likelihood any indication from him that he would accept eventual termination with the patient would usher in a final phase of treatment in which the patient's separation anxieties, residual conflicts and pathological fantasies and introjects based on the death of her father, as well as the factors underlying her asthma, might well emerge in analyzable form. Certain moderate indicators of underlying countertransference difficulties were also identified, and while there were evident links to issues related to separation, loss, and death, the patient's material permitted little understanding of her unconscious perceptions of the therapist's problems. As a result, I was confined largely to pointing to the indicators of countertransference and leaving the rest to the therapist. Not only was there a sense of stalemate in the therapy, but a similar quality also pervaded the supervisory situation and the therapist's work with this patient.

Before presenting these two sessions in supervision, the

supervisee had had a mixed reaction to the termination. On the one hand, he felt pleased that the patient had ended her therapy on a positive note, and that she had now left treatment. He had also become more aware in retrospect of how intensely he felt tortured by the patient's frustrating Type C communicative style, whatever his own contribution to this might have been. He felt that he had intervened in the final session as best he could, in a way that supported her decision, and that perhaps this was all that could have been done under the circumstances.

On the other hand, he had had a disquieting feeling that the termination had been a bit too abrupt, and that he might have missed something in the material from the patient that could have been interpreted. He felt too that he had been suddenly abandoned, and he experienced a sense of depression that had led him to wonder about the basis for the particular manner in which the patient had ended her treatment. He was also somewhat disappointed in no longer having her as a patient, and had an ill-defined feeling that something was amiss. Nonetheless, efforts on his part to formulate underlying factors within himself that might have contributed to this sudden ending bore no fruit, nor did a rather cursory review of the material of the last two hours.

We can see then that the therapist had distinctly mixed feelings about this termination, and that he was motivated toward efforts at self-supervision, which met with some degree of resistance—undoubtedly on an unconscious countertransference basis—and which provided no sense of clarification or resolution. The therapist essentially had failed in his attempt to comprehend and resolve his countertransferences, or to understand the unconscious factors in the termination experience.

By the time the supervisee arrived for his supervisory session, he felt additional concern about the manner in which this treatment had ended. It seemed clear that the approach of actual supervision had mobilized the doubts he had had concerning his management of the final hour, but his thinking on the matter remained relatively unclear.

In supervision he discovered, in reporting the first session, that he had completely forgotten the allusions to suicide and assassination, derivatives of anxieties, fantasies, and self-destructive impulses that seemed to contradict on some level the patient's sense of well-being and which foreshadowed the appearance of several critical derivatives in the final hour. Nonetheless, in presenting that last session, the therapist was still unable to identify an appropriate intervention that might reasonably have raised questions about the patient's abrupt termination—a type of comment that he felt was strongly indicated in this hour. Failing that, he had elected to support the patient's decision to terminate, and to allude to certain surface communications that hinted at underlying anxieties—though he recognized that here too he indirectly supported the patient's wish to avoid dealing with them.

In the supervisory discussion I asked the therapist to formulate the session using the format presented in chapter 6. We agreed that there was a major and overriding indicator in the form of the patient's plans for an abrupt termination, which clearly included major resistance elements. There was strong evidence that the patient was attempting a framework deviation cure, supported by Type C barriers in the form of unconscious lies and falsifications and reinforced by an effort to break the link with the therapist. The therapist was faced with a type of situation, rather rare, in which it was his responsibility to offer the patient the best possible interpretive intervention under the conditions, and to maintain as much of the frame as possible. In the face of a Type C communicative style, this was bound to be difficult. In general, a major rupture in the therapeutic alliance in the presence of a poor communicative network carries with it a poor prognosis.

As for the communicative network, the adaptive context was difficult to identify. Outside the therapeutic situation, there was the existence of the holiday period and the family-oriented experiences which seemed likely to evoke memories and conflicts related to the patient's loss of her father. Within treatment, there had been the therapist's silence, which had repeatedly been linked to the death of her father; in addition, the patient was planning to miss both a single session within the ensuing two weeks and a group of sessions some months hence. Finally—and this context is supported by the latent material in earlier hours—the patient had been speaking of late of her sense of improvement and benefit from therapy, suggesting that another likely precipitant might be her anticipation of termination.

The therapist's silence is represented directly in the material from the patient, though the derivatives are filled with denial and would not lend themselves to intervening. The relevant derivative complex could be formulated in terms of the patient's sense of loss and of her rageful suicidal and homicidal responses.

The more central adaptive context of the termination of her treatment is also represented manifestly in the material, though once more it is infused with denial and presented in a form that makes it difficult to relate the context to the derivative complex. Nonetheless, it is feasible to suggest that in this particular adaptive context the patient's associations indicate a view of termination as a form of death and even suicide (i.e., her own wish to terminate is viewed as a self-destructive act), designed, in part, to projectively identify and evoke comparable fantasies and impulses in the therapist. There is evidence too that the patient feared she would not survive the termination process, and that she had powerful needs to deny these anxieties and possibilities by becoming superficial. The threat to take gas links these anxieties and unconscious fantasies to the patient's asthma and hints too at a fear within the patient that a more gradual termination would prompt not only an asthmatic attack, but a major depressive syndrome.

The patient does provide a bridge back to therapy by asking the therapist to speak, and while I would have preferred to wait for some additional derivatives—in the hope of obtaining clearer indirect material—an initial effort at intervening could have been undertaken based on this analysis of the material at this point. (I have attempted to integrate all of the derivatives in this hour around the issue of abrupt termination. I have set aside the fact that the patient reponded to the additional adaptive context of the therapist's intervention, which was infused with his own denial and superficiality, and his dread of the termination experience—as perceived by the patient, his own fears of depression, self-destructive impulses, and loss.)

It was suggested that the therapist could have pointed out that the patient was now considering termination, and that she wished to effect it at the end of this hour. However, her thoughts suggested an underlying dread of the termination experience and a fear that it might prompt suicidal fantasies or even as asthmatic attack—here, making note of the allusion to the gas—and that in addition it seemed to conjure up images of growing old and dying. Apparently, rather than tolerating the meaningful emergence of such feelings and fantasies, the patient wished to end her treatment abruptly in order to laugh off these threats—a type of effort of which she herself was critical. Though the therapist had initially failed to take an interpretive approach (his own response addressed the manifest content, was implicitly supportive of the patient's defenses, and made no use of Type Two derivatives), he still had an opportunity to intervene more definitively toward the end of the hour. While it cannot be known how the patient would have responded to such an intervention, the therapist could have pointed out, based on the material after his intervention, that the patient came back again to themes of dying and suicide, and to her own wish not to be superficial. While these thoughts undoubtedly alluded to her perception of the therapist's intervention as somewhat superficial, they must also refer to the anxieties and responses the patient saw as attendant on a more extended termination. (The connections to death and loss are quite evident and it seems clear that the patient is attempting to shut them out by being superficial—despite her own criticism of such efforts. Clearly, the attempt to terminate in a single session was designed to maintain a level of superficiality that could serve as a barrier to the underlying anxieties and thoughts connected with suicide and death.)

It is of course not possible to validate these proposed interventions, since the patient did in fact terminate. Their importance for this discussion lies in the fact that the following week the therapist came to his supervisory hour prepared to present another patient. He wished, however, to make some final comments about the present patient. In doing so, he reported that he had carried out, quite spontaneously and much of it while jogging, an extensive self-supervisory effort that had now proved extremely successful. While he felt quite upset over having failed to intervene interpretively in the last hour, he had experienced an extensive number of insights into the interfering countertransferences and the actual implications of the material from the patient in the final session.

His understanding extended in many directions. For example, he realized that he had been suffering with this patient because she presented major separation anxieties and problems, but then tended to cover them over with Type C barriers which frustrated their interpretation and resolution. At the same time, however, they thwarted the therapist's desire to analyze not only the patient's separation problems, but comparable problems of his own. He realized too that he felt hurt by the patient's sudden abandonment, and experienced it as a projective identification of her separation anxieties and the underlying separation trauma of the loss of her father; he was now the victim, while she could survive and leave him as well. This insight led him to realize that there had been a great deal to interpret to this patient, and that her sudden flight carried with it extensive indications of unresolved psychopathology and resistances, as well as transference and nontransference responses.

Next he had recognized that the patient's announcement of termination had activated in an acute form the unresolved aspects of his countertransferences as they pertain to issues of object loss. He felt at sea as to how to deal with this threat from the patient, as he did with his own unresolved problems. He recognized too that the same unresolved issues led him to be relatively insensitive to the allusions to murder and suicide, and to fail to identify the evidently intense underlying anxieties within this patient.

He thought too of a recent experience in his own therapy, where his efforts of termination were being thwarted by his therapist, leading to considerable resentment and stalemate. He realized now that he had quite unconsciously behaved in a directly opposite manner. On another level, he recognized some relief in terminating quickly with the patient as a means of avoiding a more chaotic termination experience, and that this sense of relief was supported by the patient's positive feelings toward treatment—responses that he feared disrupting had the therapy been extended.

Then too he thought of the possible influences of supervision on his response to the patient. He was mindful of the fact that I had mentioned the possibility of termination, and he wondered now if I had presented this as a reflection of my having given up on the patient, thereby reinforcing his own feelings along those lines. He had found that presenting this patient to me had been especially unrewarding, and indeed somewhat disturbing insofar as he had experienced repeated difficulties in intervening in any meaningful and valid manner. It would be a relief presenting another patient.

In all, the therapist was able to formulate a number of aspects of his block in understanding and interpreting to this patient, and to trace it out to factors in supervision, in his relationship with the patient, and within himself. He was able to connect these difficulties to a constellation of unconscious countertransference fantasies and memories that had not been clearly accessible to him prior to this self-supervisory effort. These realizations also lead to extensive self-analytic endeavors, and to a number of insights of which he had previously been unaware. While painful, the outcome had nevertheless afforded him considerable gratification.

We can see, then, that many factors influence the nature of self-supervision. These may stem from any area of the therapist's professional and personal life, and transactions related to supervision and the actual treatment situation with a given patient are among the most important. We have seen too the expression of major countertransference-based resistances to self-supervisory work, many of them quite beyond the therapist, who simply experienced great difficulty in understanding what had happened with this particular patient. Despite his conscious efforts at self-supervision, it was not until he presented the material to me and heard my own formulations that he was able to modify these massive resistances and to engage in fruitful self-supervisory work. It seems evident, then, that this particular line of action may sometimes be necessary in the face of self-supervisory blockage. The supervisory work was not directed toward an analysis of the supervisee's countertransferences—as they related both to the patient and to self-supervision—though it was possible to delineate the implications of the material the therapist had failed to interpret. This provided the supervisee a major clue as to the nature of his underlying countertransferences, and seems to have been a key factor in resolving the self-supervisory resistances. The material illustrates the comprehension that follows sound self-supervisory work; it leads both to further self-analysis and to additional educational efforts.

Concluding Comments

Self-supervision is clearly an arduous task, vulnerable to countertransference-based influences and blocks, and yet potentially meaningful and rewarding to the therapist who makes consistent efforts in this direction. There are two main responses to a disturbing therapeutic experience and the likelihood of unconscious contributions from the therapist: the insightful and open pursuit of self-supervision or the development of major resistances to that process. Thus, while the first step must be that of recognizing the need for self-supervision, the second must be that of resolving resistances, both to self-supervision itself and to cognitive and personal comprehension generally. This is by no means an easy task, and clearly those therapists who have experienced a relatively successful therapeutic or analytic treatment of their own will be in a far more favorable position in this regard. The effects of countertransferences are legion, and self-supervision must include a search for them in all areas of therapeutic and self-supervisory work, including even the very effort to insightfully detect and resolve them. Once the relevant major resistances have been sufficiently modified, self-supervision can proceed more easily—though never entirely without resistance—in all necessary directions.

I might mention in closing that I was somewhat chagrined to realize that I had neglected the critical topic of self-supervision in my initial investigations of the supervisory experience and the development of this very book. And yet, perhaps in illustration of the rewards that accrue to those who can modify countertransference-based resistances, I feel I have been able to conclude this work with a relatively satisfactory discussion of the subject. If in these pages I have been true to the spirit of psychoanalytic investigation and progress, and have thereby helped resolve a major psychoanalytic bastion, no author could ask for a more fitting ending to his labors.

Glossary

Abstracting-Particularizing Process, the. That aspect of the listening process in which first-order, manifest themes are used to derive more general or abstract themes, from which second-order specific themes are generated. The latter are often monitored in terms of the therapeutic relationship and the me/not-me interface.

Adaptational-Interactional Viewpoint, the. A clinical-metapsychological approach to the patient and therapeutic interaction which takes into account both intrapsychic and interactional processes, conscious and unconscious in both spheres.

Adaptive Context, the. The specific reality stimulus that evokes an intrapsychic response. *Direct* or *nonneurotic* adaptive contexts are those stimuli which evoke linear intrapsychic reactions and nonneurotic communicative responses; in essence, they are unrelated to psychopathological reactions and mechanisms. *Indirect* or *neurotic* adaptive contexts are those precipitants that evoke convoluted, derivative intrapsychic responses that contain pathological unconscious fantasies, memories, and introjects; they are related to psychopathology and to neurosis. Often an adaptive context outside of the therapeutic relationship will have a direct context within its manifest content, and an indirect context in its latent content. The latter is, as a rule, a derivative of a significant adaptive context within the therapeutic situation itself, communicated in disguised form. On the whole, the major indirect and neurotic adaptive contexts derive from the therapeutic interaction. The term *primary adaptive task* is a synonym for adaptive context.

Adaptive Context, Form of Representation. The manner in which the patient portrays the manifest and latent contents of the adaptive context, and its links to the therapist, in the course of his behaviors and associations. A key factor in determining the possibility of interpretive and reconstructive interventions by the therapist, it is comparable to the mode of representation through which the manifest dream portrays latent dream contents and meanings.

Associational Matrix. See *Communicative Network*.

Bastion. A term first used by Baranger and Baranger (1966) to allude to a split-off part of the bipersonal field which is under interactional repression and denial, so that the contents involved are avoided by both patient and therapist or analyst.

Bipersonal Field, the. A term first used by Baranger and Baranger (1966) as a metaphor for the therapeutic situation. It stresses the interactional qualities of the field, and postulates that every experience and communication within the field receives vectors from both patient and therapist or analyst. The metaphor requires the concept of an *interface* along which communication occurs between the two members of the therapeutic dyad, and points to the need to conceptualize the presence, role, and function of a framework for the field.

Bridge, to the Therapist. A manifest allusion to the therapist or therapy occurring in the patient's associations toward the latter part of a session. Its importance lies in facilitating both interpretive interventions and the playing back of selected derivatives that pertain to an unmentioned adaptive context related to the treatment situation.

Commentary. A term used to describe the patient's responses to an intervention from the therapist (management of the framework or verbal). These associations and behaviors contain validating and nonvalidating communications, and they are to be viewed as a mixture of fantasy and reality, accurate perceptiveness and distortion. Often, commentaries take the form of *transversal communications;* unconsciously, they convey the patient's evaluation of the intervention.

Communication, Convoluted. An image used to describe the presence of derivatives and the indirect expression of pathological unconscious fantasies, memories, introjects, and interactional contents and mechanisms. It is one of the hallmarks of neurotic communication. See *Neurotic Communication.*

Communication, Linear. A sequence evoked by an adaptive context in which the intrapsychic response is relatively logical, readily apparent or easily inferred, directly responsive, and relatively undisguised. It is a form of reaction that characterizes the direct adaptive context and nonneurotic communication. See *Nonneurotic Communication.*

Communicative Field. The amalgam from patient and therapist that characterizes the dominant mode of communicative interaction in a given bipersonal field. See *Bipersonal Field, Type A Field, Type B Field, Type C Field.*

Communicative Interaction, Unconscious and Conscious, Spiraling. A term used to describe the central transactions between patient and therapist within the bipersonal field. It alludes to the conscious but, more especially, the unconscious exchanges between the two participants to therapy, as these exchanges take place as part of a to and fro interactional process.

Communicative Network. That aspect of the material from the patient which contains conscious and especially unconscious meaning. It comprises the adaptive context, the derivative complex, and the bridge back to the therapist or analyst. As a rule, analysis of the unconscious implications of the communicative network will reveal the implications of the therapeutic context or indicator. The term is synonymous with *associational matrix.*

Communicative Space. A metaphor for the interior of the bipersonal field and for the realm in which communication occurs between patient and therapist or analyst. The image suggests that there are a number of possible communicative spaces, each with a set of defining attributes. It allows, too, for the recognition that patient and therapist may be in separate communicative spaces, rather than sharing the same mode.

Communicative Style or Mode. The form of communicative expression that characterizes the interactional thrusts and form of relatedness of the patient and therapist or analyst. See *Type A Field and Mode, Type B Field and Mode, Type C Field and Mode.*

Conception. A term first used by Bion (1962, 1977) to describe the outcome when a preconception mates with appropriate sense impressions. More broadly, the term may be used to describe the saturation of a preconception through a realization that satisfies its inherent expectations.

Confirmation, Primary. A term used to describe the

patient's initial response to an intervention, often in the form of direct affirmation or negation. In general, direct agreement has little bearing on the validity of the intervention, while negation often suggests nonvalidation, though, in exceptional circumstances, it will constitute a defensive response that emerges prior to secondary confirmation.

Confirmation, Secondary. The extended response to the therapist's interventions (management of the frame and verbal) which contain selected facts, uniquely original and previously unknown communications from the patient that extend the intervention, especially in the form of Type Two derivatives. Psychoanalytic confirmation of an intervention requires the presence of truly unexpected Type Two derivatives. In general, their absence constitutes nonconfirmation. A synonym is Type Two derivative validation.

Contained, the. A metaphor first used by Bion (1962, 1977) to allude to the contents and psychic mechanisms that are projectively identified by an infant into his mother, and by a patient into his analyst. More broadly, they allude to the contents and functions of a projective identification emanating from a subject toward an object.

Container, the. A metaphor first used by Bion (1962, 1977) for the recipient of a projective identification. The container may be open to containing such projective identifications, or may be refractory. The metaphor also implies the processing or metabolizing of the introjected contents and functions. An adequate container is seen as being in a state of *reverie.*

Containing and **Containing Function.** A metaphor used to describe the taking in and processing of projective identifications. An adequate containing function has been described by Bion (1962, 1977) as a state of *reverie* in the mother or analyst, and may also apply to the therapist or patient. Containing function alludes to the receptiveness to projective identifications, and to an ability to metabolize and detoxify pathological *interactional projections,* returning them to the subject in appropriately modified form. For the therapist or analyst, this process implies the metabolizing of a projective identification to conscious insight, imparted to the patient through a valid interpretation and through the maintenance of a secure framework and hold.

Countertransference. A term used in this volume to allude to all inappropriate and pathological responses of the therapist to his patient. These reactions are founded on pathological unconscious fantasies, memories, introjects, and interactional mechanisms (see Langs 1976d).

Day Residue. A term first used by Freud (1900) to allude to the reality stimulus for the dream. More broadly, it may be seen as the external stimulus, filled with latent and unconscious meaning, that evokes any intrapsychic response. In that sense, it is virtually synonymous with the *adaptive context.*

Denudation. A term used by Bion (1962, 1977) to metaphorically represent one type of effect that the contained may have on the container, and the reverse: the generation of a disruptive and destructive experience and set of affects, leading to some form of inner disturbance that often is characterized by the destruction of function and meaning.

Derivative Complex. A term used for the material from the patient as it is organized around a specific adaptive context in order to reveal unconscious implications, Type Two derivative meaning. This is one of the four elements involved in the basic formulation of each session.

Derivative Complex, Convoluted. See *Derivatives, Coalescing.*

Derivative Complex, Linear. A simplistic group of derivatives, related to a particular adaptive context, which tend to flatly repeat a single theme or function, without complexity or depth. See also *Communication, Linear.*

Derivatives. Manifest communications, verbal and nonverbal, which contain in some disguised form expressions of unconscious fantasies, memories, introjects, and perceptions. These are, then, the communicative expressions of neuroses, and the basis on which they are maintained. See *Type One Derivatives, Type Two Derivatives.*

Derivatives, Coalescing. A derivative complex which, when organized around a specific adaptive context, indirectly and quite unconsciously reveals a wide range of divergent, underlying meanings and functions in relationship to that context. Such a group of derivatives may include unconscious fantasies and unconscious perceptions, and reflect as well a variety of unconscious dynamics and genetics. They may also include the patient's unconscious interpretations and other speculations pertaining to both the therapist and himself. Together, they form a divergent but organizable entity which reveals a multiplicity of meanings pertaining to the relevant adaptive context. The term is a variation on the concept of convoluted communication. See also *Communication, Convoluted.*

Derivatives, Close. Associations from the patient which contain disguised representations of unconscious processes and contents in a form that is readily detectable, minimally defensive, and easily understood as a manifestation of the underlying qualities.

Derivatives, Distant. Those aspects of the patient's associations which represent unconscious processes and contents with considerable disguise, barely detectable meaning, and great defensiveness and resistance.

Derivatives, Embedded. A representation of an unconscious fantasy, memory, introject, or perception that is communicated as a seemingly irrelevant component of a sequence of manifest contents, in a form that seems peripheral to the main conscious intention and to the major first-order and general themes.

Derivatives, Playing Back. An intervention offered in the presence of a strong indicator and a meaningful derivative complex, but in the absence of any clear representation of the adaptive context with an evident link to the therapist. It is designed to create a state of tension and need—a preconception—which can be transformed into a condition of fulfillment—a conception—only through the direct recall and clear representation of the adaptive context—a step that is essential to further interpretive work.

Detoxification. A term used to describe the metabolism of a projective identification so that its relatively primitive and destructive qualities are altered through some appropriate means, usually through cognitive understanding directed toward insight. This process is an essential quality of *reverie*.

Empathy. A form of emotional knowing and noncognitive sharing in, and comprehending, the psychological and affective state of another person. Empathy involves both affect and cognition, and is based on a relatively nonconflicted interplay of introjective and projective mechanisms, and a variety of forms of unconscious sharing. It is a temporary form of immediate engagement and understanding, which must then be processed and validated along the lines designated for any subjective experience by the therapist or analyst—or patient.

Faith. A term used by Bion (1962) to describe a form of passive listening or intuiting by the therapist or analyst that is founded upon entering each session without desire, memory, or understanding. It implies a fundamental belief that the patient will put into the therapist or analyst in derivative form all that he needs for his own cure, and all that the latter requires for his interventions. It also implies an appreciation of the principle that each session should be its own creation, and that, unconsciously, the patient will provide the therapeutic situation with all that is necessary for his cure, except for the therapist's or analyst's interpretive interventions and management of the framework, which are themselves based on the ingredients provided by the patient.

First-Order Themes. See *Themes, First-Order.*

Frame. A metaphor for the implicit and explicit ground rules of psychotherapy or psychoanalysis. The image implies that the ground rules create a basic hold for the therapeutic interaction, and for both patient and therapist, and that they create a distinctive set of conditions within the frame that differentiate it in actuality and functionally from the conditions outside the frame. The metaphor requires, however, an appreciation of the human qualities of the frame and should not be used to develop an inanimate or overly rigid conception.

Framework. A term used synonymously with *frame,* usually as a means of referring to the ground rules of the bipersonal field.

Framework Cures. The maladaptive alleviation of symptoms through an inappropriate modification in the frame.

Framework Deviation Cure. Previously termed *framework cure,* this concept covers the maladaptive alleviation of symptoms through inappropriate modification of the framwork by either patient or therapist.

Framework Rectification Cure. The usually adaptive symptom alleviation that occurs through the establishment, securing, and maintenance of the ground rules of psychotherapy or psychoanalysis. Though unaccompanied by cognitive insight, such relief does derive from unconscious positive introjects of the therapist, in terms of his constructive management of the framework, and from the inherently supportive holding and containing functions that are expressed when the framework is maintained in a stable manner.

Functional Meaning. Synonymous with *Functional Capacity*. A term used to indicate that associations never exist as isolated mental products, and that among their most essential dynamic implications are the unconscious communications contained within the material as they pertain to the therapeutic relationship and interaction. In essence, it is a concept that stresses that all associations have some dynamic relevance to the therapeutic interaction.

Ground Rules. The implicit and explicit components of the analytic or therapeutic situation which establish the conditions for treatment and the means through which it shall be undertaken (for details, see Langs 1975b, 1976a,d).

Holding. A term used to describe the therapist's or analyst's establishment and maintenance of a secure and safe therapeutic situation. The result is a holding environment that is created through the implicit and explicit delineation of the ground rules, explicated through their maintenance, and significantly elaborated through valid interpretive efforts. The holding capacity of the therapist or analyst may be likened to his containing capacity, although the former is a more general concept, while the latter specifically refers to the taking in of interactional projections.

Identification. An intrapsychic process through which the self-representations and other aspects of the subject's internal mental world and defenses are unconsciously modified in keeping with a model derived from an external object.

Indicators. A clinical term that refers to all communications from the patient which point toward a need on his part for an intervention from the therapist. See *Therapeutic Context.*

Interactional Defenses. Intrapsychic protective mechanisms which are formed through vectors from both patient and therapist. This type of defense may exist in either participant to the therapeutic dyad, and has both intrapsychic and interactional (external) sources.

Interactional Projection. A synonym for projective identification (Langs 1976a).

Interactional Resistances. Any impediment to the progress of therapy that receives vectors, usually on an unconscious level, from both patient and therapist.

Interactional Symptoms. An emotional disturbance in either participant to the therapeutic dyad with significant sources from both participants (Langs 1976d).

Interactional Syndrome. Clusters of interactional symptoms (Langs 1976d).

Interface, Me/Not-Me. See *Me/Not-Me Interface.*

Interface of the Bipersonal Field. A metaphor used to describe a hypothetical line along which the communications between patient and therapist take place within the bipersonal field. It implies that vectors which determine this interface are derived from both patient and therapist, and that these may be contained in relatively fixed intermixtures or may vary considerably. Among the determinants of the qualities and location of the interface, pathological inputs from both patient and therapist are especially significant.

Interpretation. An attempt through verbal communication by the therapist to render unconscious meanings and functions conscious for the patient. Properly executed, this intervention alludes to an adaptive context, and to the relevant derivative complex in terms of unconscious perceptions and fantasies to which genetic implications are appended. Proper execution requires also that the intervention be stated in terms of the prevailing unconscious communicative interaction between the patient and the therapist, and its extension into the present and past from that nodal point, and that it illuminate the prevailing therapeutic contexts.

Intervention, Manifest. An intervention, usually verbal, offered by the therapist to the patient, designed to meet the therapeutic needs of the latter. The major interventions include silence, establishment and management of the framework, and comments designed to impart cognitive understanding, either through interpretation or reconstruction, or through the playing back of selected derivatives around an unmentioned adaptive context.

Intervention, Silent. A tentatively formulated intervention constructed as the therapist listens to the patient and subjected to silent validation before being presented.

Introject. An intrapsychic precipitate which stems from the process of introjective identification. Among its qualities is the extent to which it is transient or becomes structuralized, the degree to which it is incorporated into the self-image and self-representations or maintained as separate from them, the extent to which it is pathological or nonpathological, and the degree to which it is constructive or benign rather than destructive or malignant. In addition, these internal representations of conscious and unconscious traits and interactions have a variety of specific qualities in keeping with the nature of the object, the subject, their relationship, and the qualities of their separate and shared experiences. See *Unconscious Introject.*

Introjective Identification. The interactional process

through which introjects are formed. As a rule, it is invoked by a projective identification from the object, although it may also entail active incorporative efforts by the subject. The process is influenced both by the nature of the object, the contents and processes that are being taken in, and the inner state of the subject.

Intuition. An immediate form of knowing, understanding, or learning developed without the conscious use of reasoning and knowledge.

Latent Content. The hidden dimension of the patient's associations contained in disguised form within the surface of that material. The term is usually used to refer to readily available inferences from the manifest content—disguised specific unconscious fantasies, memories, introjects, and perceptions.

Listening Process, the. A term used in the broadest possible psychoanalytic sense to refer to all conscious and unconscious intaking and organizing processes within both patient and therapist. For the therapist, the term includes all available cognitive and interactional sources of information about the patient, verbal and nonverbal, and his own use of sensory and nonsensory, conscious and unconscious, sensitivities. Included too are efforts at synthesizing and formulating cognitive material, the experience of role pressures and image evocations, and the metabolism of projective identifications. The process culminates in conscious understanding or insight, in proper holding and containing, and in the formulation of a valid intervention. Similar processes take place within the patient, although, as a rule, much of it on an unconscious level.

Manifest Content. The surface of the patient's associations and the therapist's interventions. The term refers to the direct and explicit meanings so contained.

Me/Not-Me Interface. An imaginary interface of the

patient's communications so designed that every aspect refers on one level to the patient himself, while on another level to the therapist or analyst. The me/not-me is stated from the patient's vantage point and indicates that every communication contains allusions to both himself and the therapist or analyst.

Metabolism, or **the Metabolism of Projective Identifications.** A term first used by R. Fliess (1942) to describe the processing by the analyst of temporary trial identifications with the patient. The concept is used more broadly to refer to all efforts to work over sensory and nonsensory inputs from the patient, and in another specific sense to refer to the introjective identification and containing of a projective identification from the patient, ultimately processed toward cognitive understanding and insight. This last sense of the term may also be applied to the patient's efforts to introjectively identify and contain projective identifications from the therapist, so long as efforts are made toward understanding.

Misalliance. A quality of the basic relationship between patient and therapist, or of a sector of that relationship, which is consciously or unconsciously designed to bypass adaptive insight in favor of either some other maladaptive form of symptom alleviation or the destruction of effective therapeutic work (Langs 1975a).

Negative Projective Identification. A term used to describe an empty or voidlike interactional projection designed to destroy meanings within the bipersonal field and to disrupt the mental capacities of the object or recipient of the interactional projection.

Neuroses. A term used in a special sense to allude to all forms of psychopathology, ranging from symptomatic disturbances to character disorders, from neurotic disturbances to borderline syndromes and narcissistic disorders to psychoses, and from psychosomatic disorders to addictions, perversions, and other emotionally founded syndromes. In essence, then, the term refers to all types of syndromes based on intrapsychic and interactional emotional disturbances and dysfunctions.

Neurotic Communication. That form of behaving and conveying meanings that is related to the neuroses, and which is characterized by the use of derivative and convoluted sequences, related ultimately to pathological unconscious fantasies, memories, introjects, and perceptions.

Nonconfirmation. See *Nonvalidation.*

Noncountertransference. The essentially nonconflicted sphere of the therapist's or analyst's functioning expressed in his appropriate capacity to relate to the patient, listen, intervene, manage the framework, and the like.

Nonneurotic Communication. A means of conveying conscious and unconscious meaning that is essentially unrelated to neuroses. It is characterized by manifest messages, readily available inferences, and linear causal sequences.

Nontransference. The essentially nonconflicted areas of the patient's valid functioning within the therapeutic relationship. It is exemplified by validatable conscious and unconscious perceptions and reactions to the therapist, and by other spheres of adequate functioning and interacting.

Nonvalidation. A response to an intervention by the therapist or analyst (management of the framework or verbal) that is flat, lacking in unique contents or a selected fact, repetitious, linear, and without surprise. It is an indication that the intervention has been erroneous, and is largely in the sphere of secondary confirmation—here constituting secondary nonconfirmation.

Preconception. A term first used by Bion (1962, 1977) to represent a state of expectation and more broadly a state of need, a quality in need of fulfillment or closure, and unsaturated state, which, once saturated, would generate a *conception.*

Precipitant or **Reality Precipitant.** A synonym for *day residue,* and a term synonymous with *adaptive context* when used to refer to the evocation of an intrapsychic response.

Predictive Clinical Methodology. A mode of psychoanalytically oriented therapy founded on the validating process, and especially on efforts at prediction so designed that validation takes the form of Type Two derivatives.

Primary Adaptive Task. A synonym for *adaptive context* (Langs 1973).

Projective Counteridentification. A term coined by Grinberg (1962) to allude to all countertransference-based responses within the analyst to the patient's projective identifications. The term implies a failure to metabolize the relevant interactional projections and the reprojection into the patient of nondetoxified contents and mechanisms.

Projective Identification. An interactional effort by a subject to place into the object aspects of his own inner mental state, inner contents, and unconscious defenses. The term *identification* is used here in the sense of remaining identified with the externalized contents and wishing to evoke in the object an identification with the subject.

Proxy, Evocation of a. A form of projective identification described by Wangh (1962) which stresses an interactional effort to place into the object areas of malfunctioning and disturbance, largely as a means of evoking adequate responses which can then be introjected.

Psychoanalytically Oriented Psychotherapy, or **Insight Psychotherapy.** A form of psychotherapy which takes place within a well-defined bipersonal field and which is designed to provide the patient symptom relief based on cognitive insights and the inevitable positive introjective identifications that derive from the therapist's capacity to hold the patient, contain and metabolize his projective identifications, establish and manage the framework, and interpret the neurotic communications and expressions from the patient.

Psychoanalytic Cliché. An intervention based on psychoanalytic theory and on the material from the patient at a point at which it is communicated in a nonneurotic form. It is a statement of apparent psychoanalytic meaning or truth which is essentially and functionally false in light of the prevailing sources of inner anxiety and turmoil, conflict and disturbance within the patient and/or the therapist. It is therefore unconsciously designed to serve as a barrier to the underlying catastrophic truths and as a means of disrupting the meaningful relationship links between patient and therapist.

Reconstruction. An attempt by the therapist, through a verbal intervention, to indicate to the patient important events and fantasies from the past, most often in his childhood, of which he has no conscious recall. Such an intervention would begin with the adaptive context and the derivative complex, would be linked to a therapeutic context, and would on this basis derive implications in regard to past actualities; it would always be rooted in the current communicative interaction, and would extend into the past from there.

Regression, Nontherapeutic. A shift toward more primitive communication and expression of derivatives of unconscious fantasies, memories, introjects, and perceptions that takes place under conditions of unneeded modifications in the framework and in response to other errors in technique by the therapist or analyst. The impairments in the framework render such regressions difficult to analyze and resolve, and the restoration of the frame is essential to a shift from a nontherapeutic to a *therapeutic regression.*

Regression, Therapeutic. An adaptive form of re-regression that takes place within a secure bipersonal field and is a means of describing the constructive emergence of unconscious fantasies, memories, introjects, and perceptions related to the patient's neurosis as mobilized by the therapeutic interaction and based on earlier genetic experiences and traumas. This emergence of relatively primitive material occurs in a form and under conditions that render the neurotic components analyzable and modifiable through insight (Langs 1976a).

Resistance. A term used to describe any impediment within the patient to the work of therapy or analysis. It is a conception that is based on a subjective evaluation by the therapist or analyst. In its narrow clinical sense, these obstacles are founded on defenses against intrapsychic conflicts and anxieties, as they are expressed within the therapeutic relationship. See *Interactional Resistances.*

Resistance, Communicative. A term used to describe the appearance of defenses directed at some aspect of the communicative network. These defenses may be directed at one or all of the three major components of this network—the representations of the adaptive context, the derivative complex, or the bridge back to the therapist—and constitute efforts, more subtle than *gross behavioral resistances*, to disrupt the work and goals of therapy or analysis.

Resistance, Gross Behavioral. A term used to describe manifest expressions from the patient that reflect defenses within the context of the therapeutic relationship and interaction. It refers, then, to open efforts to disrupt the therapeutic work and to other evident attempts to oppose the work and goals of therapy or analysis. Their unconscious meanings are revealed by the communicative network, and their analysis is an especially important aspect of treatment.

Reverie. A term used by Bion (1962, 1977) to describe the state of the mother, therapist, or analyst who is capable of receiving the projective identifications from the infant or patient, appropriately metabolizing them, and returning them to the subject in a relatively detoxified form. In a psychotherapeutic situation, this implies a correct interpretation and appropriate management of the framework.

Second-Order Themes. See *Themes, Second-Order.*

Selected Fact, the. A term used by Bion (1962), borrowed from Poincaré, to describe a newly discovered formulation, finding, or fact that introduces order and new meaning into, and unites into a whole, previously disparate elements. It is the realization, then, that links together elements not previously seen to be connected.

Silent Hypothesis. A formulation derived from the various avenues of the intaking aspect of the listening process, developed, as a rule, around a specific adaptive context. Its development relies too on the abstracting-particularizing process, monitoring material around the therapeutic interaction, and utilizing the me/not-me interface, as well as all other means available to the therapist or analyst for generating dynamic, adaptive conceptions of the most pertinent unconscious meanings of the patient's material. In its most complete form, it will entail the identification of the most active unconscious fantasies, memories, introjects, and perceptions within the patient, and to his psychopathology. While these hypotheses may be developed at any point in a session, they are especially common in the opening segments of each hour, and are maintained by the therapist without intervening. In principle, they should be subjected to *silent validation* before the therapist or analyst intervenes, doing so most often at a point when there is a relevant bridge between the silent hypothesis itself and the communications from the patient.

Silent Question. An issue that arises within the mind of the therapist as he listens to the patient, leading him to raise it subjectively while not directing it to the patient. When pertinent, such queries will, as a rule, be answered in some derivative form by the patient's ongoing associations. In principle, silent questions are to be preferred to direct queries of the patient, which tend to serve a variety of defensive and countertransference needs within the therapist or analyst, and to impair the patient's use of indirect, derivative communication.

Silent Validation. An aspect of the evaluation of the material from the patient that follows the development of a silent hypothesis. When subsequent material further coalesces with the initial hypothesis, and supports it through the communication of Type Two derivatives, the silent hypothesis is seen as confirmed. See also *Validation*.

Supervisory Introject. A partly conscious, but primarily unconscious, incorporative percipitate within the supervisee based on his work with his supervisor. This introject derives from the conscious and unconscious communications of the supervisor, and may be positive or negative, constructive or destructive, in various intermixtures. The term *supervisory introject* implies the incorporation of mental processes within the supervisor and his transactions with the supervisee, while the related term *supervisor introject* would stress incorporation of dimensions of the supervisor himself—attitudes, mental contents, and the like.

Themes, First-Order. The general contents and specific subject matter that can be derived from an examination of the manifest content of the patient's material.

Themes, Second-Order. Derivative contents developed through the use of the abstracting-particularizing process. First-order manifest themes are identified and general thematic trends are then formulated; inferences derived on that basis are considered second-order themes. As a rule, such themes are developed in terms of the ongoing therapeutic relationship and interaction, and take on specific form and meaning when related to pertinent adaptive contexts within that relationship.

Therapeutic Context. A term synonymous with *indicator*, and a component of the listening process. It refers to any communication from the patient that suggests a need for understanding, resolution, and intervention from the therapist. Such communications serve as important second-order organizers of the patient's material. His associations and behaviors are first organized in terms of the communicative network—the adaptive context, its representation, the derivative complex, and the bridge back to the therapist—to provide Type Two derivative meaning in terms of unconscious processes, fantasies, perceptions, and introjects. Once these unconscious meanings and functions are identified, the material is then reorganized around the therapeutic context and the revealed derivative meanings pertain to the unconscious implications of the indicator. Therapeutic contexts may be divided into those involving symptoms within the patient (e.g., homicidal and suicidal concerns and impulses, acute regressions, acting out) and those involving disturbed aspects of the therapeutic interaction (e.g., alterations in the framework by therapist or patient, errors by the therapist, ruptures in the therapeutic alliance, and major and minor resistances).

Therapeutic Interaction. A term used to describe the

conscious and unconscious communicative interplays between the patient and therapist or analyst.

Therapeutic Misalliance. An attempt to achieve symptom alleviation through some means other than insight and the related positive introjective identifications with the therapist. See *Misalliance,* an essentially synonymous term.

Therapeutic Relationship. A term that embraces all components, conscious and unconscious, pathological and nonpathological, of the interaction between patient and therapist. For the patient, the therapeutic relationship involves both transference and nontransference components, while for the therapist it involves countertransference and noncountertransference elements. The term is strongly preferred to "transference" when describing the patient's relationship with the therapist, and equally preferred to "countertransference" when describing the therapist's or analyst's relationship to the patient. See *Transference, Nontransference, Countertransference,* and *Noncountertransference.*

Therapy, Lie. Any form of, or interlude in, psychotherapy or psychoanalysis in which the actual unconscious basis for the patient's symptoms, resistances, and the like are either not sought after or are sealed off. It entails both efforts at avoidance and attention to levels of meaning that in the therapeutic interaction serve primarily to create barriers and falsifications, to destroy more pertinent meaning, and thereby to seal off underlying chaotic truths.

Therapy, Truth. A form of psychotherapy or psychoanalysis designed to foster the emergence and discovery of the unconscious processes, fantasies, memories, introjects, and transactions which constitute the basis for the patient's neurosis.

Transference. The pathological component of the patient's relationship to the therapist. Based on pathological unconscious fantasies, memories, and introjects, transference includes all distorted and inappropriate responses and perceptions of the therapist derived from these disruptive inner mental contents and the related mechanisms and defenses. These distortions may be based on displacements from past genetic figures, as well as on pathological interactional mechanisms. Unconscious transference fantasies and mechanisms are always communicated in some derivative form, while the manifest communication may allude to either the therapeutic relationship itself (disguised, however, in regard to the latent content) or to outside relationships. Transference responses are always maladaptive and can only be understood in terms of specific, indirect adaptive contexts (see Langs 1976d).

Transversal Communication. Associations from the patient that bridge, and therefore simultaneously express, both fantasy and reality, transference and nontransference, unconscious perception and distortion, truth and falsehood, self and object. Such communications are, on one level, entirely valid, while on another level, essentially distorted.

Transversal Intervention. A particular type of communication from the therapist or analyst to the patient which is shaped in keeping with the presence of a transversal communication. In essence, such interventions, usually in the form of interpretations, although sometimes developed through the playback of derivatives related to an unidentified adaptive context, take into account the dual qualities of transversal communications, and are stated in a manner that is open to the contradictory elements contained in the patient's associations.

Trial Identification. An aspect of the listening process especially developed by Fliess (1942) as an important means of empathizing with and cognitively understanding the communications from the patient. It entails a temporary merger with, or incorporation of, the patient and his material in the presence of distinct self-object boundaries in most other respects. It is a temporary form of being and feeling with the patient, and the cognitive-affective yield from such experiences must then be processed toward insightful understanding and subjected to the validating process.

Type A Field, the, and **Type A Communicative Mode, the.** A bipersonal field and communicative style in which symbolism and illusion play a central role. Such a field is characterized by the development of a play space or transitional space within which the patient communicates analyzable derivatives of his unconscious fantasies, memories, introjects, and perceptions, ultimately in the form of Type Two derivatives. Such a field requires a secure framework, and a therapist or analyst who is capable of processing the material from the patient toward cognitive insights which are then imparted through valid interpretations. Such endeavors represent the therapist's capacity for symbolic communication. The Type A communicative mode is essentially symbolic, transitional, illusory, and geared toward insight.

Type B Field, the, and **Type B Communicative Mode, the.** A bipersonal field characterized by major efforts at projective identification and action-discharge. The field is not essentially designed for insight, but instead facilitates the riddance of accretions of disturbing internal stimuli. The Type B communicative mode is one in which efforts at projective identification and action-discharge prevail.

Type C Field, the, and **Type C Communicative Mode, the.** A field in which the essential links between patient and therapist are broken and ruptured, and in which verbalization and apparent efforts at communication are actually designed to destroy meaning, generate falsifications, and to create impenetrable barriers to underlying catastrophic truths. The Type C communicative mode is designed for falsification, the destruction of links between subject and object, and for the erection of barriers designed to seal off inner and interactional chaos.

Type C Narrator, the. A patient who utilizes the Type C communicative mode through the report of extensive dream material or the detailed description of events and experiences within his life or in regard to the therapeutic interaction. Such material is characterized by the absence of a meaningful adaptive context, the lack of analyzable derivatives, and the use of these communications essentially for the generation of nonmeaning and the breaking of relationship links. It is not uncommon for the Type C narrator to interact with a therapist or analyst who makes extensive use of psychoanalytic cliches, generating a therapeutic interaction falsely identified as viable analytic work, while its primary dynamic function falls within the Type C communicative mode.

Type One Derivatives. Readily available inferences derived from the manifest content of the patient's associations, without the use of an adaptive context. These inferences constitute one level of the latent content, arrived at in isolation and without reference to the dynamic state of the therapeutic interaction and to the adaptive-dynamic function of the material at hand.

Type Two Derivatives. Inferences from the manifest content of the patient's material that are arrived at through the abstracting-particularizing process when it is organized around a specific adaptive context. These disguised contents accrue specific dynamic-adaptive meaning when so organized, and are the main medium for the therapist's or analyst's interpretations, primarily in terms of the therapeutic interaction.

Unconscious Fantasy. The working over in displaced form of a particular adaptive context. The relevant contents are outside the patient's awareness and are expressed in derivative form in the manifest content of his associations. This is a type of daydreaming without direct awareness of the essential theme, and may be either pathological or nonpathological. The derivatives of unconscious fantasies are an essential medium of interpretive work and have important genetic antecedents. Among the most crucial unconscious fantasies are those related to the therapist, and when they are distorted they fall into the realm of transference, while those that are nondistorted belong to nontransference. These daydreams include representations from the id, ego, superego, self, and from every aspect of the patient's inner mental world, life, and psychic mechanisms.

Unconscious Interpretation. A communication from the patient to the therapist, expressed in disguised and derivative form, and unconsciously designed to help the therapist understand the underlying basis for a countertransference-based intervention. These interpretations can be recognized by taking the therapist's intervention as the adaptive context for the material from the patient that follows; hypothesizing the nature of the therapist's errors; and accepting the patient's material as reflecting an introjection of the error, and an effort to heal the disturbing aspects of that introject. Put in other terms, the patient's responses are viewed as a commentary on the therapist's intervention, and are found to contain unconscious efforts to assist the therapist in gaining insight in regard to the sources of his errors.

Unconscious Introject. A network of intrapsychic precipitants derived from interactions between the subject and object, in the past and present. They are derived from the process of introjective identification, and depend on the nature of the contents and mechanisms involved, as well as qualities within both subject and object. Introjects may be short-lived or relatively stable, pathological and nonpathological, incorporated into the self-image and self-representations or isolated from them, and may involve any of the structures of the mind, id, ego, and superego. In psychotherapy, an especially important form of introjection occurs in response to the therapist's projective identifications, either helpful or traumatic, nonpathological or pathological, which generate alterations in the inner mental world of the patient. Such a process is continuous with the therapeutic interaction and may, in addition, occur within the therapist as a result of projective identifications from the patient. See also *Introjects.*

Unconscious Memory. Derivative precipitates of past experiences—mixtures of actuality and distortion—expressed through indirect communication and inner representations of which the subject is unaware. Such reminiscences without awareness may be pathological or nonpathological, and the former are an important aspect of the genetic basis of the patient's psychopathology.

Unconscious Perception. A term used to describe evidence of valid perceptiveness of another person's (an object's) communications and cues of which the subject is unaware. These may be identified through a correct appraisal of the nature of an adaptive context, including an accurate understanding of the object's unconscious communications. While outside the subject's awareness, his derivative communications demonstrate an essentially veridical perception in terms of the prevailing underlying realities. When the adaptive context is known, unconscious perceptions are reflected in Type Two derivatives. They are the basis for nondistorted introjects.

Validated Hypothesis. A silent hypothesis that has been

confirmed via Type Two derivatives, and especially an interpretation or management of the frame that has been communicated to the patient and which is affirmed through the development of Type Two derivatives and the appearance of a selected fact.

Validation, Indirect. See *Validation via Type Two Derivatives,* with which it is essentially synonymous.

Validation, via Type Two Derivatives. A form of confirmation that is synonymous with the development of a selected fact, and with the modification of repressive barriers. This type of indirect, derivative validation is the essential proof of the truth of a psychoanalytic clinical formulation and intervention. Every clinical psychoanalytic hypothesis can be accepted as a general truth only if it has been subjected to this type of validation.

Validating Process, the. A term used to describe conscious and unconscious efforts within either patient or therapist to affirm, support, and substantiate conscious or unconscious formulations and hypotheses. It is a crucial component of the listening process, receives its ultimate test in the patient's responses to the therapist's interpertations and management of the framework, and must take the form of confirmation via Type Two derivatives and the development of a selected fact (see Langs 1976d, 1978i).

References

Arlow, J. (1963). The supervisory situation. *Journal of the American Psychoanalytic Association* 11:576-594.

Baranger, M., and Baranger, W. (1966). Insight in the analytic situation. In *Psychoanalysis in the Americas*, ed. R. Litman, pp. 56-72. New York: International Universities Press.

Bibring, E. (1954). Psychoanalysis and the dynamic psychotherapies. *Journal of the American Psychoanalytic Association* 2:745-770.

Bion, W. (1962). *Learning from Experience*. In Bion 1977.

———(1965). *Transformations*. In Bion 1977.

———(1970). *Attention and Interpretation*. In Bion 1977.

———(1977). *Seven Servants*. New York: Jason Aronson.

Brenner, C. (1976). *Psychoanalytic Technique and Psychic Conflict*. New York: International Universities Press.

Breuer, J., and Freud, S. (1893-1895). Studies on hysteria. *Standard Edition* 2.

Chertok, L. (1968). The discovery of the transference: toward an epistemological interpretation. *International Journal of Psycho-Analysis* 49:560-576.

Eissler, K. (1974). On some theoretical and technical problems regarding the payment of fees for psychoanalytic treatment. *International Review of Psycho-Analysis* 1:73-101.

Ekstein, R., and Wallerstein, R. (1958). *The Teaching and Learning of Psychotherapy*. New York: Basic Books.

Fliess, R. (1942). The metapsychology of the analyst. *Psychoanalytic Quarterly* 11:211-227.

Freud, S. (1900). The interpretation of dreams. *Standard Edition* 4/5.

———(1905). Fragment of an analysis of a case of hysteria. *Stanard Edition* 7:7-122.

———(1913). On beginning the treatment (further recommendations on the technique of psycho-analysis, I). *Standard Edition* 12:121-144.

———(1918). From the history of an infantile neurosis. *Standard Edition* 17:7-122.

———(1925a). Negation. *Standard Edition* 19:235-242.

———(1925b) An autobiographical study. *Standard Edition* 20:3-74.

———(1937). Constructions in analysis. *Standard Edition* 23:255-269.

———(1940). An outline of psycho-analysis. *Standard Edition* 23:144-207.

Green, A. (1975). The analyst, symbolization and absence in the analytic setting (on changes in analytic practice and analytic experience). *International Journal of Psycho-Analysis* 56:1-22.

Greenson, R. (1967). *The Technique and Practice of Psychoanalysis Vol 1*. New York: International Universities Press.

———(1971). The "real" relationship between the patient and the psychoanalyst. In *The Unconscious Today*, ed. M. Kanzer, pp. 213-232. New York: International Universities Press.

Grinberg, L. (1962). On a specific aspect of counter-transference due to the patient's projective identification. *International Journal of Psycho-Analysis* 43:436-440.

Klein, M. (1952). The origins of transference. *International Journal of Psycho-Analysis* 33:433-438.

Kraemer, M. (1959). On continuation of the analytic process after psychoanalysis (a self-observation). *International Journal of Psycho-Analysis* 40:17-25.

Langs, R. (1972). A psychoanalytic study of material from patients in psychotherapy. In Langs, 1978h, pp. 71-111.

———(1973). *The Technique of Psychoanalytic Psychotherapy.* Volume I. New York: Jason Aronson.

———(1974). *The Technique of Psychoanalytic Psychotherapy.* Volume II. New York, Jason Aronson.

———(1975a). Therapeutic misalliances. In Langs 1978h, *International Journal of Psychoanalytic Psychotherapy* 4:77-105.

———(1975b). The therapeutic relationship and deviations in technique. In Langs 1978h, pp. 189-230.

———(1976a). *The Bipersonal Field.* New York: Jason Aronson.

———(1976b). Misalliance and framework in the case of Dora. In Langs 1978h, pp. 231-251.

———(1976c). On becoming a psychiatrist. In Langs 1978h, pp. 325-355.

———(1976d). *The Therapeutic Interaction.* 2 vols. New York: Jason Aronson.

———(1978a). Dreams in the bipersonal field. In Langs 1978h, pp. 537-586.

———(1978b). Intervention in the bipersonal field. In Langs 1978h, pp. 627-678.

———(1978c). *The Listening Process.* New York: Jason Aronson.

———(1978d). Misalliance and framework in the case of the Rat Man. In Langs 1978h, pp. 253-273.

———(1978e). Misalliance and framework in the case of the Wolf Man. In Langs 1978h, pp. 275-293. *Technique in Transition.* New York: Jason Aronson, 1978.

———(1978f). Reactions to creativity in psychoanalysts. In Langs 1978h, pp. 473-499.

———(1978g). Some communicative properties of the bipersonal field. In Langs 1978h, pp. 413-472.

———(1978h). *Technique in Transition.* New York: Jason Aronson.

———(1978i). Validation and the framework of the therapeutic situation. In Langs 1978h, pp. 381-411.

———(1979). Some interactional communicative aspects of

resistance. Submitted for publication.

Lewin, B. (1955). Dream psychology and the analytic situation. *Psychoanalytic Quarterly* 24:169-199.

Little, M. (1951). Counter-transference and the patient's response to it. *International Journal of Psycho-Analysis* 32:32-40.

Olinick, S. (1969). On empathy, and regression in service of the other. *British Journal of Medical Psychology* 42:41-49.

de Racker, G. (1961). On the formulation of the interpretation. *International Journal of Psycho-Analysis* 42:49-54.

Racker, H. (1957). The meaning and uses of countertransference. *Psychoanalytic Quarterly* 26:303-357.

Rangell, L. (1968). The psychoanalytic process. *International Journal of Psycho-Analysis* 49:19-26.

Reich, A. (1960). Further remarks on counter-transference.*International Journal of Psycho-Analysis* 41:389-395.

Sandler, J. (1976). Countertransference and role-responsiveness. *International Review of Psycho-Analysis* 3:43-47.

Sandler, J., Dare, C., and Holder, A. (1973). *The Patient and the Analyst: The Basis of the Psychoanalytic Process.* New York: International Universities Press.

Schuster, D., Sandt, J., and Thaler, O. (1972). *Clinic Supervision of the Psychiatric Resident.* New York: Brunner-Mazel.

Searles, H. (1955). The informational value of the supervisor's emotional experiences. *Psychiatry* 18:135-146.

———(1958). The schizophrenic's vulnerability to the therapist's unconscious processes. *Journal of Nervous and Mental Disease* 127:247-262.

———(1959). The effort to drive the other person crazy—an element in the aetiology and psychotherapy of schizophrenia. *British Journal of Medical Psychology* 32:1-18.

———(1962). Problems of psycho-analytic supervision. In H. Searles, *Collected Papers on Schizophrenia and Related Subjects,* pp. 584-604. New York: International Universities Press, 1965.

———(1965). *Collected Papers on Schizophrenia and Related Subjects.* New York: International Universities Press.

———(1970). Autism and the phase of transition to therapeutic symbiosis. *Contemporary Psychoanalysis* 7:1-20.

———(1971). Pathological symbiosis and autism. In *In the Name of the Life*, ed. B. Landis and E. Tauber, pp. 69-83. New York: Holt, Rinehart and Winston.

———(1973). Concerning therapeutic symbiosis. *Annual of Psycho-Analysis* 1:247-262.

———(1975). The patient as therapist to his analyst. In *Tactics and Techniques in Psychoanalytic Therapy, Vol. II: Countertransference*, ed. P. Giovacchini, pp. 95-151. New York: Jason Aronson.

Szasz, T. S. (1963). The concept of transference. *International Journal of Psycho-Analysis* 44:432-443.

Ticho, G. (1967). On self-analysis. *International Journal of Psycho-Analysis* 48:308-318.

Viderman, S. (1974). Interpretation in the analytic space. *International Review of Psycho-Analysis* 1:467-480.

Wangh, M. (1962). The "evocation of a proxy": a psychological maneuver, its use as a defense, its purpose and genesis. *Psychoanalytic Study of the Child* 17:451-469.

Winnicott, D. (1958). *Collected Papers*. London: Tavistock Publications.

———(1965). *The Maturational Processes and the Facilitating Environment*. New York: International Universities Press.

———(1971). *Playing and Reality*. New York: Basic Books.

Index